BEYOND THE SYMBIOTIC ORBIT

Advances in Separation–Individuation Theory

Essays in Honor of
Selma Kramer, M.D.

BEYOND THE SYMBIOTIC ORBIT

Advances in Separation–Individuation Theory

Essays in Honor of Selma Kramer, M.D.

Edited by Salman Akhtar and Henri Parens

THE ANALYTIC PRESS

1991   Hillsdale, NJ   London

Published by The Analytic Press, Inc.
365 Broadway, Hillsdale, NJ 07642

Library of Congress Cataloging-in-Publication Data

Beyond the symbiotic orbit : advances in separation–individuation
   theory : essays in honor of Selma Kramer, M.D. / edited by Salman
   Akhtar and Henri Parens.
        p.   cm.
   Includes bibliographical references and index.
   ISBN 0-88163-109-4
   1. Separation–individuation.   I. Kramer, Selma.   II. Akhtar,
   Salman, 1946 July 31–   III. Parens, Henri, 1928–
   RC489.S45B49   1991
   155.4'18--dc20   91-28939
                                                                    CIP

Printed in United States of America
10 9 8 7 6 5 4 3 2 1

Contents

I

Separation–Individuation Theory: Contrast, Comparison and Update

II

Psychopathology as Understood in the Light of Separation–Individuation Theory

III

Treatment Implications

Contributors

Salman Akhtar, M.D., Professor of Psychiatry, Jefferson Medical College; Faculty Member, Philadelphia Psychoanalytic Institute.

Harold P. Blum, M.D., Clinical Professor of Psychiatry, New York University Medical College; Training and Supervising Analyst, The Psychoanalytic Institute, New York University Medical Center.

J. Alexis Burland, M.D., Training and Supervising Analyst, Philadelphia Psychoanalytic Institute; Clinical Professor of Psychiatry, Jefferson Medical College

LeRoy J. Byerly, M.D., Training and Supervising Analyst, Philadelphia Psychoanalytic Institute.

Philip J. Escoll, M.D., Training and Supervising Analyst, Philadelphia Psychoanalytic Institute; Clinical Professor of Psychiatry, University of Pennsylvania School of Medicine.

Newell Fischer, M.D., Executive Director, Philadelphia Psychoanalytic Institute; Training and Supervising Analyst, Philadelphia Psychoanalytic Institute; Clinical Professor of Psychiatry, University of Pennsylvania School of Medicine.

Ruth M. S. Fischer, M.D., President, Philadelphia Psychoanalytic Society; Training and Supervising Analyst, Philadelphia Psychoanalytic Institute; Faculty, University of Pennsylvania School of Medicine.

Alvin Frank, M.D., Training and Supervising Analyst, St. Louis Psychoanalytic Institute; Chairman of the Committee on Scientific Activities
of the American Psychoanalytic Association; Professor of Clinical
Psychiatry, St. Louis, University.

Eleanor Galenson, M.D., Clinical Professor of Psychiatry, Mount Sinai
School of Medicine; Member, New York Psychoanalytic Society.

Jules Glenn, M.D., Clinical Professor of Psychiatry, New York University
Medical Center; Training and Supervising Analyst, The Psychoanalytic Institute, New York University Medical Center.

Stanley I. Greenspan, M.D., Clinical Professor of Psychiatry, Behavioral
Sciences, and Pediatrics, George Washington University Medical
School; Supervising Child Analyst, Washington Psychoanalytic Insti-
tute.

Otto F. Kernberg, M.D., Associate Chairman and Medical Director,
Department of Psychiatry, The New York Hospital-Cornell Medical
Center (Westchester Division); Training and Supervising Analyst,
Columbia University Center for Psychoanalytic Training and Re-
search.

Louis A. Leaff, M.D., Clinical Professor of Psychiatry, Medical College
of Pennsylvania; Training and Supervising Analyst, Philadelphia
Psychoanalytic Institute.

Leo Madow, M.D., Professor and Chairman of the Department of
Psychiatry (Emeritus), Medical College of Pennsylvania; Training and
Supervising Analyst, Philadelphia Psychoanalytic Institute.

John B. McDevitt, M.D., Training and Supervising Analyst, New York
University Psychoanalytic Institute; Director of Research, Margaret S.
Mahler Psychiatric Research Foundation.

Patricia A. Nachman, Ph.D., Director, Margaret S. Mahler Observa-
tional Research Nursery and Faculty Member, Graduate Psychology,
The New School for Social Research, New York; Clinical Instructor,
New York University Medical College.

Henri Parens, M.D., Professor of Psychiatry, Jefferson Medical College;
Training and Supervising Analyst, Philadelphia Psychoanalytic Institute.

Sydney E. Pulver, M.D., Training and Supervising Analyst, Philadelphia
Psychoanalytic Institute; Clinical Professor, Department of Psychiatry, University of Pennsylvania Medical School.

Joseph Rudolph, M.D., Clinical Associate Professor of Psychiatry,
Medical College of Pennsylvania; Training and Supervising Analyst,
Philadelphia Psychoanalytic Institute.

Calvin F. Settlage, M.D., Clinical Professor of Psychiatry, University of
California at San Francisco; Training and Supervising Analyst, San
Francisco Psychoanalytic Institute.

Estelle Shane, Ph.D., Founding President, Center for Early Education and College of Developmental Studies, Los Angeles; Assistant Clinical Professor, Department of Psychiatry, UCLA.

Morton Shane, M.D., Former Director of Education, Training and Supervising Analyst in Adult and Child, Los Angeles Psychoanalytic Society and Institute; Clinical Professor, Department of Psychiatry, UCLA.

Charles W. Socarides, M.D., Clinical Professor of Psychiatry, Albert Einstein College of Medicine/Montefiore Medical Center, New York City.

Troy L. Thompson II, M.D., The Daniel Lieberman Professor and Chair, Department of Psychiatry and Human Behavior, Jefferson Medical College; Faculty by Invitation, Philadelphia Psychoanalytic Institute.

Thomas Wolman, M.D., Clinical Assistant Professor, Jefferson Medical College; Faculty by Invitation, Philadelphia Psychoanalytic Institute.

Acknowledgments

We wish to thank the distinguished colleagues who contributed to this volume. We deeply appreciate their efforts, their sacrifice of time, and, above all, their patience with our requirements, reminders, and requests for revisions. As we acknowledge our debt to them, we are also reminded of some other colleagues who, owing either to space limitations or their prior commitments, were unable to participate in this venture. They too, we are certain, join us in celebrating the publication of this *Festschrift* for Selma Kramer.

We are also grateful to Troy L. Thompson II, M.D., who, as the Chairman of the Department of Psychiatry and Human Behavior at Jefferson Medical College, gave unwavering support and encouragement to our work. Paul Stepansky, Ph.D. and Eleanor Starke Kobrin of The Analytic Press offered us sound advice at each step on the way, and we thank them most sincerely. Finally, we wish to thank Gloria Schwartz, whose pleasant and skillful secretarial assistance was invaluable in this book's preparation. She made our work easier.

Introduction

Salman Akhtar
Henri Parens

This book is a tribute to Selma Kramer by her friends, colleagues, and students. The essays contained in it are original, having been written specifically for this volume. At the risk of using a cliché, this effort by so many distinguished individuals can only be described as a labor of love. It is an acknowledgment not only of their profound respect for Selma Kramer's accomplishments as a psychoanalytic clinician, theoretician, and administrator, but also of their deep fondness of her as an enthusiastic colleague, an outstanding teacher, and, above all, a good friend. The focus of this *Festschrift* on separation-individuation theory is also in keeping with Selma Kramer's own contributions and her long-standing involvement with the late Margaret Mahler (see "The Prelude," the biographical sketch of Dr. Kramer by Joseph Rudolph, Leo Madow and Leroy Byerly).

The book is divided into three main sections. The first section pertains to theory and consists of essays that compare and contrast the separation-individuation theory with other theoretical frameworks in psychoanalysis, for instance, the psychosexual theory, self psychology, and the views of Winnicott. An attempt is also made in this section to scrutinize Mahler's theory of symbiosis and separation-individuation in the light of contemporary infant-observation research. The second section of the book focuses on psychopathology. It highlights the many subtle ways in which the theory of separation-individuation facilitates the understanding of various forms of psychopathological disorders in children and adults. Included here are chapters on disorders in prelatency, latency, and adolescence as well as on adult neuroses, psychosomatic illnesses, eating disorders, character pathology, and sexual perversions. The discussions of theory and psychopathology in the first and second sections of the book naturally lead to its third section, which addresses aspects of psychoanalytic technique. This section includes essays on the treatment of prelatency children, psychoanalysis of predominantly preoedipal psychopathology, specific issues in the treatment of young adults, and termination. A more detailed description of each major section of the book follows.

Section I comprises six chapters. The first, by Henri Parens, addresses the relationship between psychosexual theory and separation-individuation theory. Parens critically examines the capabilities and limitations of these theories. With the help of wide-ranging theoretical arguments and convincing clinical data, he argues for their complementarity in psychoanalytic work. Besides providing meaningful insights in this realm, Parens's chapter has something special for the young professional—a condensed overview of various psychoanalytic models of early development.

Parens's contribution is followed by Thomas Wolman's essay, which fills a striking lacuna in psychoanalytic literature by providing a detailed comparison of Winnicott and Mahler. Not only does Wolman draw some interesting parallels in the personal lives of these two eminent developmental theorists, he also sets up an imaginary dialogue between them and, in this innovative fashion, compares various aspects of their work. Among these are the mother–child dyad, the origin of psychic defense and ego distortion, illusion–disillusion, the visual modality, verbalization and symbolization, and psychoanalytic technique.

Next is the chapter by Estelle and Morton Shane, proponents of the need in psychoanalysis for the complementary use of multiple models of psychic experience and functioning. On several earlier occasions, they have quite successfully compared the work of Mahler and Kohut. Here they continue that work and draw from it an integrated view of early development. They demonstrate the application of their developmental point of view to the clinical situation.

Stanley Greenspan's essay outlines, step-by-step, the author's recently developed model of ego development. Greenspan's approach is comprehensive and takes into account inborn factors, maturational unfolding, cognition, drives, affects, objects, and environmental facilitation in the development of ego. He proposes both normal and pathological outcomes at various stages and his description of the latter is not restricted to childhood but hints at the potential implications for adult psychopathology as well.

Chapter 5 by Otto Kernberg, contains a thorough exposition of his views of early psychic development and their correlation with those of other theorists, including Margaret Mahler. His discussion of the complex interplay of pregenital and genital developments, and of the important links between affect, memory, learning, and structure formation during early infancy, is particularly stimulating.

This section of the book concludes with the chapter by Patricia Nachman, in which she comparatively explores major aspects of separation–individuation theory and findings from developmental psychology. Nachman is soundly knowledgeable in both domains. In a highly scholarly chapter, she draws attention to the two research methods, to their differing domains of exploration, their differing questions and objectives, and their resultant differing findings. She points out that while the research methods thus differ, they inform and complement each other richly. This is a unique contribution, invaluable for our field.

Section II pertains to psychopathology as understood in the light of separation–individuation theory. It contains nine chapters, the first by John McDevitt. McDevitt stands out as one of the few psychoanalysts who have studied individuals psychoanalytically both as prelatency-age children and subsequently as adults. Using data arising from these subjects, whom he studied from differing approaches—clinical analyses, direct observation in childhood, and follow-up in latency and adulthood—McDevitt attempts to cross-test the inferences made from the data gathered from these subjects by each method. Scrupulously observant and cautious in his inferences, McDevitt documents (with case material) and reaffirms the view that "disturbances in separation-individuation may play a significant role in determining . . . the conflicts typical of the phallic-oedipal phase." And he asserts that "it is no longer helpful to think in terms of preoedipal versus oedipal determinants of prelatency psychopathology."

Next is Jules Glenn's chapter, which constitutes yet another step toward the much-needed interdigitation of separation-individuation theory with Oedipus complex theory. Its outstanding contribution is the concept of psychic "transformation" of separation-individuation in latency. This idea is elucidated through the changing functions of children's games. The description of how games that seek mastery of separation-related issues come to acquire specific drive-related, oedipal connotations is superb. Also informative is the discussion of the factors that might govern a patient's recall of rapprochement-like conflicts as occurring during latency and not earlier.

Glenn's delightful piece is followed by Louis Leaff's discussion of the vicissitudes of separation-individuation during adolescence. Leaff underscores the significance of Mahler's developmental concepts to understanding adolescent turmoil while pointing out the conceptual difficulties that result from using similar terminology for both separation-individuation and adolescence. He distinguishes the "noisy" and the "nonnoisy" times of psychic development and their relative impact on character formation. His pointing out the former's disorganizing and the latter's slow and cumulative organizing potential is a thought-provoking contribution.

Next, Newell and Ruth Fischer provide detailed illustrations from the analyses of two adolescents, one male, the other female. By highlighting their patients' similarities and differences, the authors raise significant questions regarding gender-related differences in psychic development, character organization, neurosogenesis, and transference propensities. The authors are mindful of the complexity of the factors involved here, and it is this complexity that gives their contribution its provocative (in the best sense of the word) quality.

In chapter 11, Alex Burland suggests ways by which separation-individuation influences the eventual development of the infantile neurosis and clinical neuroses. He illustrates his thesis with poignant clinical vignettes revealing problematic rapprochement subphase experiencing that invariably influences and gives shape to the Oedipus complex. Burland's chapter is especially important because it addresses an area of psychopathology regarding which the vicissitudes of separation-individuation are often not well appreciated.

The same can be said of Troy Thompson's essay on psychosomatic phenomena. Thompson brings together much of the classic and contemporary psychoanalytic literature on psychosomatic illness. He also includes a succinct review of contemporary psychophysiologic research. Thompson underscores that psychosomatic phenomena may represent a number of psychological conflicts and defenses, including those involving unresolved separation-individuation.

In the next chapter, Salman Akhtar adds to his earlier work on severe personality disorders by presenting the reader with a not-so-well recognized aspect of character pathology pertaining to certain unconscious fantasies that metaphorically express unresolved separation-individuation processes. Akhtar's detailing of the dynamic significance of his patients' "someday," "tether," and "a long embrace" fantasies is convincing and once again demonstrates the powerful organizing function of fantasies as well as their remarkable explanatory capability.

Following Akhtar's contribution is that of Harold Blum. In it, Blum reports on the analysis of a woman who suffered from anorexia while growing up and in the course of her analysis revealed how her own problems contributed to the emergence of feeding difficulties in her young child. As a result of her analysis, the mother improved and was able to change her parenting behavior, leading to the amelioration of her child's problems. Since many adults with children do not specifically address their parental roles during their analyses, Blum's report provides a unique piece of analytic material. His chapter meaningfully illuminates the understudied area of cross-generational transmission of psychopathology.

The last chapter in this section is by Charles Socarides. His is a comprehensive consideration of the multitude of factors involved in the "choice" of perversion. Socarides takes into account drives, ego structure, superego, object relations, fantasy, traumatic events, transformations in latency, and adolescence. His chapter contains ample clinical illustrations and, despite the complex nature of the matters involved, is engaging and highly readable.

Section III comprises five chapters pertaining to treatment-related issues. In chapter 16, Eleanor Galenson describes a tripartite therapeutic approach to the psychological problems encountered in very young children. This method consists of two to three joint weekly sessions with the young child, the mother or father, and one of the two therapists, and a weekly session between the parent(s) and the second therapist. Galenson highlights the merits of this approach by a detailed account of the conjoint treatment of a severely disturbed 21-month-old child and her equally disturbed mother. Galenson's excellent exposition is a valuable contribution to the elucidation of this recently emerging therapy.

Her chapter is followed by Alvin Frank's contribution. In his characteristically elegant literary style, Frank registers concern about the unclear uses of the terms "construction" and "reconstruction." Construction, he proposes, is the dynamic constellation an individual conceptualizes postoedipally to explain his or her childhood experience. The correction of this constellation by analytic work results in a reformulation, that is, a reconstruction. Though Frank acknowledges uncertainty whether his definitions will be widely accepted, his ideas remain clear, cogent, interesting, and provocative.

Next, Calvin Settlage nicely summarizes the developmental significance of self- and object constancy and the consequences of pathological outcomes pertaining to these structures. He provides a lively and evocative account of the analysis of a three-year-old girl and through it demonstrates the interdigitation of separation-individuation themes with phallic-oedipal fantasies. He also highlights the transformations that various symptoms, ego functions, childhood games, and coping strategies undergo both with developmental thrust and the influence of psychoanalytic treatment. Settlage also reports on the interpretive technique with affective reenactments in the analysis of a young woman with depression and phobic avoidances.

In chapter 19 Philip Escoll skillfully discusses the implications of separation-individuation theory for the analytic treatment of young adults. Escoll points out that the life situation of young adults entails a series of expectable separations and characteristically causes a revival of separation-individuation conflicts. He presents in detail two cases in which the reconstruction of childhood perceptions of maternal unavailability during the rapprochement subphase seemed crucial to the progress of the analytic process. In doing so, he alerts the reader to the myriad ways in which separation-individuation problems become intertwined with conflicts during later stages of development and to the technical consequences of such conceptualization in working with young adults.

The last chapter of the book, by Sydney Pulver, is, fittingly, about termination. Pulver notes that the assertion of autonomy and independence, while a developmentally appropriate way of separating from the analyst during the termination phase, may stir up conflicts related to issues of the separation-individuation phase of development. Understanding these manifestations, he feels, may have specific effects on technique, including a greater need for activity and a focus on some of the real aspects of the analyst's experience, especially in the treatment of patients with early pathology.

This brief summary of the book's contents cannot do justice to their depth and richness. Its purpose is simply to whet the reader's appetite. By offering a condensed overview of the text that follows, this summary may also make the task of the reader a bit easier. In addition, recounting the various contributions to the book emphasizes its essentially collaborative nature. Significantly, all three purposes of this summary—whetting the appetite, making learning easier, and acknowledging the shared nature of an enterprise—are also attributes of a good analyst and a good teacher. Selma Kramer is both, and this book aspires to be a fitting tribute to her.

The Prelude, or Growth of an Analyst's Mind

Joseph Rudolph
Leo Madow
LeRoy J. Byerly

We could not resist borrowing from Wordsworth's autobiographical poem, because the title so appropriately describes Dr. Selma Kramer and her evolvement as a psychoanalyst. Dr. Kramer has a multifaceted personality. In her professional life she is an interested colleague, a scholar, an author, a clinician, an educator, and an initiator. In her private life she is a loving wife, mother, and grandmother. In both areas she creates a warm and supportive environment. With her soft, easygoing manner she has influenced many of us. Where and when did her journey toward becoming a psychoanalyst begin?

Dr. Kramer was born to Jennie and Morris Kramer in 1920, the second of three children. Her sister Carolyn is three years older and brother Morton is five years younger. Her father had a pharmacy in the Northern Liberties section of Philadelphia, and her mother worked right along with her husband, "the Doc." The neighborhood was a bustling melting pot of diverse nationalities and ethnic groups with one thing in common: "the American dream" and the awareness that the royal road to success was through education.

Dr. Kramer began her education in this milieu by teaching herself to read by the age of four. At five she was enrolled in a neighborhood public school but was soon transferred to the Thaddeus Stevens School, a demonstration school for selected children. She continued to be an outstanding student throughout junior high and Girls' High School of Philadelphia; she graduated during the Great Depression. Money was scarce, so although she was accepted at the University of Pennsylvania, she elected to enroll at Temple University because she was offered a scholarship. She graduated from Temple at age 20 and then matriculated at the Woman's Medical College (now called the Medical College of Pennsylvania).

Dr. Kramer's fascination with medicine began with several childhood experiences: one was her maternal grandmother's death, caused by pneumonia; another was her brother's bout with meningitis, which left him deaf. During this same period Dr. Kramer's father decided to become a physician. He graduated from medical school after years of hard work (with the help of his wife, he had continued operating the pharmacy while in medical school). Dr. Kramer identified with her father's physician role, but equally important, she identified with the compassion and hard work exemplified by both her parents. One of us, Dr. Joseph Rudolph, a childhood friend of Dr. Kramer's, can personally attest to the influence these sacrificing and goal-oriented parents had on her.

While she was in medical school, two members of the psychiatric staff stimulated Dr. Kramer's interest in their discipline. The seeds thus planted in her mind fell on fertile ground, the preparation for which had begun as far back as childhood. At that time she was not only typically curious but was already a good listener. While helping her mother in the pharmacy's luncheonette, she became aware that behind the conversations of the customers was a myriad of unspoken thoughts and feelings. She was privy to them because she remained a silent listener.

After graduating from medical school in 1944, Dr. Kramer interned at St. Luke's and Children's Medical Center of Philadelphia, and there she became the first woman intern in the history of that hospital. Her fund of knowledge, diligence, sense of responsibility, and especially her pleasant imperturbable self made her a cherished member of the medical staff.

During this internship period, Ernest Witkin, who later became her husband, was very supportive. At this hectic time of her life, it was he who offered her love and stability. They married in 1945. They have two children: Karen, who has a doctorate in psychology from Bryn Mawr College, and James, who has a law degree from Harvard University. In addition, they have two outstanding grandchildren, Joshua and Jeremy (the adjective was supplied by the unbiased grandmother).

While she was at St. Luke's Hospital, one of the senior staff members, Dr. Harold Lefkoe, recommended that Dr. Kramer consider child psychiatry as her specialty. She spoke to Dr. Fred Allen, then director of the

Philadelphia Child Guidance Clinic, who told her that she would be welcome but that a prerequisite was training in adult psychiatry.

Dr. Kramer took Dr. Allen's advice and became a psychiatric resident at Norristown State Hospital, where she stayed from 1947 to 1949. It was there that she was first exposed to psychoanalytic concepts. Several analysts on the staff—and one in particular, Dr. Herbert Herskovitz—encouraged Dr. Kramer to consider psychoanalytic training. Although not an analyst, Dr. Arthur Noyes, the superintendent of the hospital, was warmly disposed toward psychoanalysis. It was his policy to regard analytic training and the personal analysis as part of the psychiatric resident's training, for which he allowed compensatory time.

The gentle proddings of the analysts at the hospital, her attendance at Dr. Gerald Pearson's child analytic clinic, plus her own natural inclination made it inevitable that Dr. Kramer would become a child analyst. In preparation for this she took her child psychiatric training at the Child Study Center at the Institute of the Pennsylvania Hospital from 1951 to 1953.

During her first year of didactic courses in the adult analytic training program at the Philadelphia Psychoanalytic Institute, Dr. Leroy Maeder suggested to Dr. Kramer that she also apply for child analytic training. She completed both adult and child work in six years (1949 to 1955). Concurrent with her analytic training, Dr. Kramer also worked as a volunteer, first at Lankenau Hospital and later at St. Christopher's Hospital for Children. Her primary effort at both institutions was to establish better communication between pediatricians and psychiatrists.

Shortly before Dr. Kramer began her child analytic training, Dr. Margaret Mahler, a former pediatrician and world-renowned psychoanalyst, accepted an invitation to organize a child psychoanalytic training program for the Philadelphia Psychoanalytic Institute. Dr. Kramer was fortunate to be one of the candidates selected to be part of this nascent program.

Dr. Mahler's vast knowledge and experience were put at the disposal of the candidates. Mahler, an outstanding educator, inspired the candidates— her protégés, "her children"—of which Dr. Kramer was one of the stars. However, to be so selected was not without its difficulties. The demands that Mahler placed on such candidates were exacting and fraught with uncertainty and apprehension. Under Dr. Mahler's tutelage, there was a solidification of those qualities that endear Dr. Kramer to us. She became the arbitrator, indeed the peacemaker, tactfully avoiding confrontations, resolving conflicts, always acting with compassion toward the members of the child analysis group. It was during those years that Dr. Kramer established her long-standing relationship with Dr. Mahler, first as a student, then as a valued colleague and friend, and finally as a daughter surrogate. In this long relationship, she recognized that Margaret Mahler was as strict a taskmistress on herself as she was on those she trained. Her child analysis candidates came to realize that Mahler was most demanding and stern with those whose work she valued most.

In the beginning of the child analysis training program, Dr. Mahler came to Philadelphia every other weekend to conduct continuous case seminars and to supervise and teach a course on the technique of child analysis. On alternate weekends, the candidates traveled to New York for the same purpose. The child analysis candidates, Dr. Kramer among them, soon formed a cohesive and vibrant unit. The original group included Stuart Finch, Catherine Buckner, George Russell, E.S.C. Ford, and Earl Loomis. Some time later, others joined the group of candidates: Robert Prall, Kenneth Gordon, Calvin Settlage, Jules Abrams, George Kochis, Saul Harrison, James Delano, Victor Satinsky, Norma Wohl, Herman Staples, Robert Gaukler, LeRoy Byerly, Marilyn Curran, Paula Elkisch, and Herbert Schiele. Mahler taught these candidates not only the principles and technique of child analysis; she taught them to become future teachers and leaders in the field.

After five years, in order to reduce Dr. Mahler's travel time, the group traveled to New York, initially once a month, and then twice a month for all their classes, supervision, and continuous case seminars. After several members graduated, Dr. Kramer among them, the locus of the teaching shifted back to Philadelphia, except for three weekends a year in New York, at which times Dr. Mahler gave advanced technique conferences. (For more detail, read Kramer and Prall's paper describing the history, function, and operation of the program in *Separation Individuation: Essays in Honor of Margaret S. Mahler* [1971].)

Each spring Dr. Mahler continued to come to Philadelphia for a long weekend conference. At Dr. Kramer's suggestion, this conference became the Margaret S. Mahler Symposium. Mahler, Kramer, and Prall planned the first symposium as we know it today. It was supported by the chairman of the Department of Psychiatry at the Medical College of Pennsylvania, Dr. Leo Madow, who made the facilities of that department available. Grants were obtained from pharmaceutical companies. Under the able guidance of Dr. Kramer (and much hard work), the symposium quickly gained national recognition as a scientific forum, distinguished by its excellent speakers and discussants. Each symposium addressed specific problems and/or advances in child development from a psychoanalytic point of view. Drs. Kramer and Mahler chose the topics and selected the speakers most familiar with the themes. Dr. Kramer has been the organizer and chairperson of the twenty yearly Symposia that have occurred since its inception. In addition to their contribution to psychoanalysis, the Symposia have been an opportunity to renew old friendships, both locally and nationwide. Dr. Kramer and her husband host a buffet dinner the night before the event in honor of the speakers and discussants; this "gemütlichkeit" has enhanced the proceedings, as will be confirmed by those who have attended these gatherings.

In 1964 Dr. Madow, then chairman of the psychiatry department at the Medical College of Pennsylvania, asked Dr. Kramer to organize and become the chairperson of the section of child psychiatry. Dr. Kramer agreed but wisely suggested she combine her efforts with her longtime friend Dr. Robert C. Prall, who already headed a child psychiatry residency program at Eastern Pennsylvania Psychiatric Institute (now part of the Medical College of Pennsylvania).

In her usual diligent manner Dr. Kramer developed one of the most highly regarded child psychiatry programs in the East. Her deep appreciation of and commitment to child analysis led her to advocate vigorously the principles of analysis. She had the ability to stimulate the child psychiatry residents to reach their potential and created within them the desire to learn more about children and especially to enlarge their knowledge of the various psychotherapeutic approaches to treating children. A gifted teacher, she served as a role model for the residents, many of whom went on to become child analysts. She remained professor of child psychiatry at the Medical College of Pennsylvania until 1988, when she left to become professor of child psychiatry at Jefferson Medical College.

Both locally and nationally Dr. Kramer is recognized for her impressive accomplishments and for her dedication to psychoanalysis. Locally, in addition to her academic positions in medical schools, she is very active in the Philadelphia Psychoanalytic Institute and Society. Dr. Kramer became a supervisor in child analysis in 1955 and a supervising and training analyst in 1962. In the latter capacity she and Calvin Settlage, who graduated from psychoanalytic training soon after she did, convinced the members of the Education Committee of the Institute of the importance of understanding child development, normal and pathological, for candidates in both child and adult psychoanalysis. As a result, child analysts now teach normal and psychopathological development as part of the adult curriculum. In addition, candidates are required to attend at least one year of child and adolescent continuous case seminars.

The child analysis program started by Dr. Mahler flourished under Dr. Kramer's direction. Before long, more child supervisors and faculty members were appointed. Dr. Kramer forged a Child Analysis Committee within the Philadelphia Psychoanalytic Institute that is responsible for all child analytic programs and training. She served as chairperson of the Child Analysis Committee from 1969 to 1974. Her additional accomplishments within the Philadelphia Psychoanalytic Institute and Society include the following: President of the Philadelphia Psychoanalytic Institute, 1979 to 1982, and Chairman of the Executive Committee of the Institute, 1979 to 1982.

On a national level Dr. Kramer has held the following positions: supervising analyst in the Columbia Institute, 1976; member of the editorial board of the *Journal of the American Psychoanalytic Association,* 1972–1975; assistant editor, 1975–1979, and associate editor, 1979–1983, of this same journal; book review editor of the *Journal of the American Academy of Child Psychiatry,* 1962–1965; and chairperson of the Committee on Child Analysis of the American Psychoanalytic Association, 1974–1981. More recently, in 1988, she became president of the Margaret S. Mahler Psychiatric Research Foundation, an organization that she helped found along with Dr. Mahler, Dr. Prall, and Mr. Ernest Witkin.

At the time of this writing, Dr. Kramer has just received the Commonwealth Award of the Medical College of Pennsylvania for the outstanding woman in medicine in the state of Pennsylvania.

We asked Dr. Kramer for her curriculum vitae and were not surprised to find it was eleven pages long, single spaced, just for the list of her publications. That list will appear in the appendix of this book.

This chapter cannot end without describing Dr. Kramer's most dominant trait, her humanity. In preparation for this chapter, we asked ourselves what Selma Kramer means most to us. We were unanimous on one word—*friend.* Dr. Kramer once mentioned that her husband called her "the friend of the little people." He meant children, of course, but we feel it should be more inclusive, that it refers also to the students and candidates, past and present, whom she has taught. Like Mahler, she perceives the child analysts she has trained as her protégés. She has the knack of making each one of them feel special, and she in turn has become special to them.

We have attempted to present Dr. Kramer's life in terms of her early background, her education and training, her accomplishments, and her work. She has become a powerful voice in psychoanalysis. We have also tried to describe the meaning she has given to the lives of so many, both professionally and personally. Our hope is that we have conveyed in some way the respect and regard we have for her. And our sincere gratitude.

Publications by
Selma Kramer, M.D.

(1961)

Review of *Psychoanalytic Treatment of Children* by Anna Freud. *Psychoanalytic Quarterly,*
30:271–275.

(1962)

On the concepts and techniques of child analysis. *Journal of the American Academy Child
Psychiatry,* 1:509–535.

(1968)

Review of *Child in Collectives* by Peter Neubauer. *Journal of the American Academy of Child
Psychiatry,* 8:553–556.

(1971)

The adolescent recapitulation of a childhood psychosis. In: *Separation and Individuation:
Essays in Honor of Margaret S. Mahler,* ed. J. B. McDevitt and C. F. Settlage. New
York: International Universities Press, pp. 487–498.
A child psychoanalysis training program. In: *Separation and Individuation: Essays in Honor of
Margaret S. Mahler, M.D.,* ed. J. B. McDevitt & C. F. Settlage New York: Interna-
tional Universities Press, pp. 486–498. (With R. Prall).

(1974)

Episodes of severe ego regression in the course of an adolescent analysis. In: *The Adolescent
and the Analyst at Work,* ed. M Harley. New York: Quadrangle Press, pp. 190–231.

Panel: Vicissitudes of infantile omnipotence. *Journal of the American Psychoanalytic Association*, 22:588–602.
Review of *Therapeutic Consultation in Child Psychiatry* by D. W. Winnicott. *Psychoanalytic Quarterly*, 43:315–318.
Review of *Playing and Reality* by D. W. Winnicott. *Psychoanalytic Quarterly*, 43:318–319.
Discussion of paper by John A. Sours. *International Journal of Psycho-Analysis*, 55:577–579.

(1976)

On the girl's entry into the Oedipus complex. *Journal of the American Psychoanalytic Association*, 21:79–107. (With H. Parens, L. Pollack and J. Stern).

(1977)

Psychoanalysis of the latency child. *International Encyclopedia of Psychiatry, Psychology, Psychoanalysis and Neurology*, ed. B. Wolman. New York: Human Sciences Press. Vol. 3, pp. 136–143. (With L. Byerly).

(1978)

Technique of psychoanalysis of the latency child. In: *Child Analysis and Therapy*, ed. J. Glenn. New York: Aronson, pp. 205–233. (With L. Byerly).

(1979)

On child analysis training programs. *American Psychoanalytic Association Newsletter*, 13(1):2,4.

(1980)

Thirtieth anniversary of the institute's child analysis program. In: *Philadelphia Psychoanalytic Institute and Society Newsletter*, 8:1–3.
The technical significance and application of Mahler's separation-individuation theory. In: *Psychoanalytic Explorations of Technique: Discourses of the Theory of Therapy*, ed. H. Blum. New York: International Universities Press, pp. 240–262.
Residues of split-object and split-self dichotomies in adolescence. In: *Rapprochement: The Critical Subphase of Separation-Individuation*, ed. R. Lax, S. Bach, and J. A. Burland. New York: Aronson, pp. 417–437.
Sylvan Keisser's *Superior Intelligence: Its Contribution to Neurosogenesis: A Neglected Classic. Journal of Philadelphia Association for Psychoanalysis*, 7:88–91.
The latency stage. In: *The Course of Life, Vol. II, Latency, Adolescent and Youth*, ed. S. Greenspan and G. Pollock. Washington, DC: U.S. Department of Health and Human Services, 109–119. (With J. Rudolph).

(1981)

Pathological doubting as it relates to maternal incest. *Bulletin of the Menninger Clinic*, 45:557–560.

(1982)

A biographic note on Henri Parens. *Psychoanalytic Inquiry*, 2:177–180.

(1985)

Object-coercive doubting: A pathological response to maternal incest. In: *Defense and Resistance*, ed. H. Blum. New York: International Universities Press, pp. 325–351.

(1986)

Identification and its vicissitudes as observed in children: A developmental approach. *International Journal of Psycho-Analysis*, 67:167–172.

(1987)

A contribution to the concept "The Exception" as a developmental phenomenon. *Child Abuse & Neglect*, 11:367–370.

(1988)

The developmental context of internalized preoedipal object relations: Clinical applications of Mahler's theory of symbiosis and separation-individuation. *Psychoanalytic Quarterly*, 47:547–576 (with S. Akhtar).

(1990)

Residues of incest. In: *Adult Analysis and Childhood Sexual Abuse*, ed. H. B. Levine. Hillsdale, NJ: The Analytic Press, pp. 149–170.

(1991)

The latency stage. In: *The Course of Life: Psychoanalytic Contributions Toward Understanding Personality Development*, (2nd ed.), ed. S. Greenspan and G. Pollock. New York: International Universities Press, pp. 319–331. (With J. Rudolph).
The Trauma of Transgression: Psychotherapy of Incest Victims. Northvale, NJ: Aronson. (Edited with S. Akhtar).
Psychopathological effects of incest, In: *The Trauma of Transgression: Psychotherapy of Incest Victims*, ed. S. Kramer and S. Akhtar. Northvale, NJ: Aronson, pp. 1–12.
The technical handling of incest-related material, In: *The Trauma of Transgression: Psychotherapy of Incest Victims*, ed. S. Kramer and S. Akhtar. Northvale, NJ: Aronson, pp. 168–180.

(In Press)

When The Body Speaks: The Search for Psychological Meaning in Kinetic Clues. Northvale, NJ: Aronson. (Edited with S Akhtar).
Non-verbal manifestations of unresolved separation-individuation in adult psychopathology. In: *When The Body Speaks: The Search for Psychological Meanings in Kinetic Clues*, ed. S. Kramer and S. Akhtar. Northvale, NJ: Aronson.

BEYOND THE SYMBIOTIC ORBIT

Advances in Separation– Individuation Theory

Essays in Honor of
Selma Kramer, M.D.

I Separation–Individuation Theory: Contrast, Comparison, and Update

1

Separation-Individuation Theory and Psychosexual Theory

Henri Parens

Margaret Mahler's research-derived separation–individuation theory has added an invaluable tool to our increasing understanding of human experience, behavior, development, disturbance, and the clinical situation. With her collaborators (a number of whom were her former students) Mahler forged separation–individuation theory with the tools of ego psychology, structural theory, drive (sexual and aggression) theory, and, what some of us consider to be classical object relations theory (major pieces of which Freud formulated in his theories of the Oedipus complex (1900, 1923, 1925), ego and superego formation (1913, 1923), identification (1917, 1921, 1923), mourning (1917), his danger-situation series (1926), and more (see Parens and Saul, 1971, on Freud's contributions to the theory of dependence/self-reliance).

Among Mahler's former students and collaborators, Selma Kramer stands out as a contributor to the teaching, clarification, and demonstration of the clinical usefulness of separation–individuation theory and as foremost promulgator of it as a model powerfully capable of furthering classical psychoanalytic explication. Like Mahler, Kramer sees separation–individuation theory as one to be added to, not as a replacement of any of, the long-standing complement of classical theories.

The search for *the* best model, whatever the inquiry, seems to be compelling. How much this search reflects the thinker's bias depends much on our individual dynamics. Where domains of inquiry are simple enough, a best model may be possible. However, with regard to human development and dynamics, I have long felt this search to be flawed, just as I think it a flaw to extol parsimony in theorizing and to value brevity—only too often at the expense of clarity—in psychoanalytic interpretation (Parens, 1980, 1989a). The greatest problem with searching for the best model is that psychic functioning and development are so complex that their totality and details cannot be apprehended by any one model.

I think it is not regrettable that we cannot produce an all-inclusive model and that in order to understand our tasks as psychoanalysts well enough we must accommodate to a cluster of models of varying levels of conceptualization (Freud, 1923; Waelder, 1962), topical concerns, and explanatory limitations. There are advantages to having such a cluster of models to help us find our way clinically and in research. Having varying levels of conceptualization gives us unidimensional frameworks for detail, such as lines of development and multidimensional frameworks for complexity and interdigitation of constituent lines or sectors of experience and development. Structural theory, drive theory, object relations theory, and theories of the self give us critical details about development and personality. Both Oedipus complex theory and separation–individuation theory richly weave a set of unidimensional theories in their multidimensional construction. Waelder detailed how levels of theorizing can be conceptualized in terms of their distance from observable clinical phenomena, those closest to clinical data being most trustworthy and those most removed being most abstract and, as many psychoanalysts have argued, most at risk for falsification.

In this chapter I want to briefly discuss some conceptual aspects of separation–individuation theory and psychosexual theory, address some of their capabilities and limitations, and endorse their complementary implementation in psychoanalytic work, both clinical and research. First, though, I want to note the remarkable proliferation of models made available to us over time by psychoanalytic child developmentalists, compelled by their specific and various research interests and findings.

PSYCHOANALYTIC MODELS OF DEVELOPMENT

In this chapter I briefly describe several models of early development that I find compelling and integral to psychoanalytic work. There are others that I do not include because I am not well enough acquainted with their details; I have, however, found them useful too. These latter include some of Melanie Klein's views of psychic development, Piaget's detailing of epistemologic development, and some of Kohut's ideas about the development of self and narcissism.

Psychosexual Theory

The oldest, psychosexual theory, dates back to Freud's (1905) "Three Essays on the Theory of Sexuality." As is well known, Freud proposed this theory to explain psychic aspects of sexual development, conceptualized as occurring in the following sequential phases: the oral phase, corresponding to the first 18 months of life (Abraham, 1924, suggested that the period from about 6 months on be called the oral sadistic phase); the sadistic-anal phase, from 18 to 30 months, relating to the expelling and retentive aspects of anal experience; and the phallic-oedipal phase, from about two and a half to five or six years, with the Oedipus complex evolving out of the phallic phase. The infantile resolution of the Oedipus complex leads to the latency phase, which runs its course during the next six to ten or so years. Then comes the true genital phase, adolescence, during which there is a resurgence of unresolved oedipal wishes and conflict and a further and fuller resolution.

The Danger-Situation Series

Not as frequently considered in its totality is the danger-situation series, which Freud proposed in 1926 in an effort to state the epigenesis of anxiety-producing experiences. Although Freud addressed this issue in response to and in rejection of Rank's ascribing the paradigmatic condition for anxiety to the birth experience, his conceptualizing led to a new developmental model that was meant to parallel the phases of psychosexual development. The first psychically perceivable anxiety-producing situation that occurs during the oral phase is that of fear of loss of the object. During the sadistic-anal phase, with the (proposed) emergence of ambivalence, the foremost danger is fear of loss of love from the object. During the phallic-oedipal phase, it is the dread of loss of the highly invested genital, the penis, according to Freud's 1925 formulation of sexual development, in which he stated this fear to be operative in both boys and girls. The last danger Freud proposed in this series is that which coincides with the psychosexual latency phase—namely, fear of loss of love from the superego, which is now established as an intrapsychic agency. Freud's preeminent observation of separation anxiety (1920, 1926) played a key part in the need for this model, of a series in which each activator of anxiety is the perceived threat of a loss.

THE STRUCTURING OF THE LIBIDINAL OBJECT

Spitz's structuring of the libidinal object (1946a, 1946b), fully described in his 1965 book, is a remarkable and, I believe, insufficiently recognized model, which gave rise to Bowlby's more widely known attachment theory as well as to a number of animal attachment studies (e.g., Liddell, 1958; Harlow and Zimmerman, 1959; Harlow, 1960). As I reconstruct it, Spitz's 1930–1940 studies on the effects of humans' first-year object loss experiences (1945, 1946a, 1946b) parallel in importance and in time the findings of Lorenz (1935, 1953) and his formulations of *imprinting*, findings which themselves spurred many animal studies (e.g., Hess, 1959; Schneirla and Rosenblatt, 1961; Scott, 1963).

Crucial as well (and acknowledged recently, though insufficiently, by Stern, 1985) is the fact that Spitz was among the first pioneer psychoanalytic clinician–researchers (along with Anna Freud, in collaboration with Burlingham and with Dann and later with J. Sandler and a group of clinical child researchers; E. Kris, who worked with Senn and a group of brilliant collaborators and students, including Solnit, Ritvo, and Provence; and Bowlby, Winnicott, and others) to look directly, with the eye of the psychoanalytically trained clinician, at children in structured naturalistic settings as well as in clinical settings.

Furthermore, Spitz was the first to conceptualize a psychoanalytic development model that did not grow out of psychosexual theory. Rather, Spitz pieced together a cluster of notable behavioral findings: the "social smiling" response (1946b), "eight month anxiety" (1965)—wherein the child gives evidence of beginning to "know" his or her mother at this point in the first year of life—and the dramatic finding that loss of the libidinal object during the second half of the first year of life led, in some children, to anaclitic depression (1946a). Ascribing depth-psychological sign-function (A. Freud, 1965) to these, Spitz (1965) conceptualized the three steps by which the infant "constructs" his or her first libidinal object. First, during the first 6 weeks to 3 months of life, is the objectless stage, in which the infant is governed by "nondifferentiation" of id and ego, self and object, and inner and outer reality. The second stage begins from about 3 months with the emergence of the social smiling response and continues to about the emergence of "eighth month anxiety," which is elicited by separation from the mother and by the appearance of a stranger and is the precursor of the object stage. By virtue of the infant's differentiating ego capabilities, the object is becoming a libidinal object. This capacity and intrapsychic structuring are first achieved during the third stage, the establishment of the libidinal object stage, from about the middle of the first year on. Spitz's theorizing was confirmed by Mahler (and others) and, I believe, strongly influenced her, and was incorporated within separation–individuation theory.

Psychosocial Theory

Erikson's psychosocial theory (1950, 1959) was conceptually based on the psychosexual model but was extended to address the entire life span. Erikson sought to describe and detail that aspect of psychic experiencing, structure formation, and development he identified as "ego identity". Ego identity is the growing sense of an adaptive self, of the inner capability that organizes the self's experiencing in relation to its inner and outer environment. Erikson's epigenetic model grows out of psychoanalytic conceptualizing wherein the self is intrapsychically experienced as a social organism.

Erikson's concern was to state a theory of the child's development that addressed issues not explicated by psychosexual theory. He formulated the following psychosocial stages of development: first, during year one the infant achieves a sense of Basic Trust versus (a sense of) Basic Mistrust; during the second year the child attains a sense of Autonomy versus (a sense of) Shame; from 2 to about 6 years is a sense of Initiative versus Guilt; from 6 to 12 years is a sense of Industry versus Inferiority; from 13 to 20 years is a sense of Identity versus Identity-diffusion. Adulthood is then differentiated into the stages of Young Adulthood, Adulthood, and Mature Age. During Young Adulthood the self-identity achievement is one of Intimacy versus Isolation; in Adulthood it is a sense of Generativity versus Self-Absorption; and in Mature Age it is a sense of Integrity versus Disgust, Despair. Erikson's conceptualization of development using an epigenetic model (borrowed from embryology) makes a number of substantial contributions to the question of psychic development (which time and space do not permit me to elaborate on here).

Separation–Individuation Theory

Mahler's separation–individuation theory, first spelled out in summary form in 1965, was elaborated extensively in 1968, 1975, and lastly in 1980 (with McDevitt) and in many papers in between. When she first formulated her theory, Mahler proposed that for the first 6 or so weeks of life the infant experiences a Normal Autistic Phase. During this phase the infant perceives little beyond his or her own body and is governed by the need to achieve homeostatic equilibrium and by a hypercathexis of his or her inner state. This conceptualization was challenged even by Mahler's closest collaborators, who cited the capacity of the infant of less than one month to attend to the outside world during states of alert wakefulness (Wolff, 1966) and to the mother's face during feeding (Parens, 1979a). Mahler identified the period from about 6 weeks to about 8 or 9 months as the Normal Symbiotic Phase. This intrapsychic progressively organizing experiencing of the primitively perceived self and mother as one entity contained within a "symbiotic membrane" was heralded by the infant's perception that help comes from outside the self (Mahler, 1952). During this period the child's nonspecific attachment to the mother becomes specific (Mahler agreed with Spitz's theory on the structuring of the libidinal object), and the ego becomes organized as an agency. The inner sensations organize into the core self and the sensoriperceptual system becomes "the peripheral rind of the ego" (Mahler, 1968).

Mahler proposed that this self-experiencing of a "dual unity," the symbiotic self-experiencing, differentiates within the child's experiencing and perception by means of the separation–individuation *process*. This process proceeds along two intertwining tracks: *individuation*, that is, the evolving of intrapsychic autonomy and self structure, and *separation*, the intrapsychic process of disengagement and effecting separateness of self from the symbiotic partner. At about 5 to 6 months of age, at the peak of the symbiosis, the separation–individuation phase is set into motion; it achieves its end point at about 30 to 36 months of age with the establishment of a sufficiently well organized and stable sense of self-identity and object constancy (Mahler and McDevitt, 1980; McDevitt and Mahler, 1980). The Separation-Individuation Phase organizes into four distinguishable, evolving subphases. First, the Differentiation Subphase, extending from about 5 to 9 months, is defined by Mahler as the period of psychological (emotionally experienced) "hatching" from the symbiotically enveloped dual unity. The infant scans the world outside of mother, beginning to physically pull away from her even when on her lap or in her arms. The infant then also begins to explore and compare the inner world with mother and the non-mother outer world. From about 9 months to 16 or 18 months, the Practicing Subphase continues the process begun during differentiation. During its early part, the infant crawls away from mother, climbs, rights himself or herself. The Practicing Subphase proper is initiated by upright locomotion, a crucial achievement that orients and makes possible the child's remarkable explorations of his or her world.

Mahler emphasized the child's mood of excitement and exhilaration as part and parcel of this period; it is as if the world is his oyster, she liked to say.

With the emerging cognitive, affective, emotionally-organizing and representational capacities of the ego (Spitz, 1957, cited the child's ability to say no, that powerful sign of early efforts at individuation), and a newly evolving reality-testing capability, the child gives evidence of actively effecting separateness and individuation from mother. During the Rapprochement Subphase, which extends from about 16 to 24 months, the child experiences the polar inner pressures to, on one hand, separate and individuate from mother and, on the other, to remain one with her. In some children, this intrapsychic polarization is intense and is experienced as an intrapsychic conflict, which Mahler labeled the "rapprochement crisis" (Mahler, Pine, and Bergman, 1975). The resolution of this rapprochement crisis is the task of the last subphase of separation–individuation, that of On the Way to Object Constancy and the Consolidation of Self-Identity (self-constancy). This subphase extends from about 24 to 36 months and is a developmental period a bit akin to the process of working through in the clinical psychoanalytic process. This subphase, and even the rapprochement subphase, according to Mahler and associates (1975) overlaps with the beginning of the phallic-oedipal phase of psychosexual development.

Lines of Development

Anna Freud's concept of lines of development, published in preliminary form in 1963 and superbly elaborated in 1965, was principally proposed as a means of evaluating development in the clinical context. This model recognizes lines or component parts of development of central concern to the psychoanalytic clinician, which are stated in terms of specific developmental task achievements. For instance, a child can be evaluated in terms of her or his *age-adequate* progression from Dependency to Emotional Self-Reliance and Adult Object Relationships, from Egocentricity to Companionship, from Irresponsibility to Responsibility in Body Management, and along other such lines of development.

With the concept of lines of development Anna Freud introduced a strictly clinical model, one several levels away from metapsychological models (Waelder, 1962) and from the ego psychology model. Anna Freud's model is compatible with the latter but is much closer to clinical data than are more abstract models like structural, drive, and even object relations theory.

Adaptive Child–Mother Interaction

Louis Sander, following his studies of very early life mother–child inter-action (1962, 1964; Sander, Stechler, and Burns, 1979), pushed outside the strictly psychoanalytic domain of intrapsychic experiencing. A number of factors probably contributed to his move to the interactional domain. Psychoanalytic clinician–researchers who directly observe infants (i.e., children under three years of age), including Winnicott (who said, "There is no such thing as an infant, there is only an infant–mother"), Fraiberg (1980), Greenspan and Lieberman (1980), Settlage et al. (1985), and Parens et al. (1987), are poignantly cognizant of the need to examine psychoanalytically pertinent parent–child interpersonal factors, which not only contribute to but, in fact, codetermine the child's intrapsychic experience. In the 1960s Sander proposed an attractive and simple model of adaptative child–mother interaction (1962, 1964). The first period, from birth to two and a half months of age, is one of Primary Modulation, during which child and mother adapt to one another interactionally, behaviorally, and physically. Although the observation is of a dyad, the goal is to explicate the child's experience. The period from two and a half to five months marks the beginning of reciprocal emotional exchange and regulation; it is a period of Social Affective Modulation. From five to nine months, the infant begins to direct activity with intentionality in interac-tion with the mother (Hartmann, 1950a); Sander called the period one of Initiative (defined differently from Erickson's 1959 model). From 9 to 15 months is the period of Focalization on Mother, and from 12 to 18 months, the period of Self-Assertion. Although there is some disagree-ment between observer–theorists in the use of terms—for example, "initiative," or the "focalization on mother" (Sander) at a time when Mahler speaks of the child's beginning to "differentiate from" mother and "practice" ego functions that serve autonomy—their models are defining and elucidating. Disagreements do not necessarily make for incompati-bility for hypothesis-testing, research, and clinical usefulness. More re-cently, Sander's (1983) views have been shaped by a systems theory conceptualization.

Dependence in Humans

Using a confluence of models, especially those of psychosexual theory, separation–individuation theory, lines of development, and psychosocial theory, Saul and I outlined a developmental model of dependence in humans (1971), in which we propose an epigenesis of normal dependence versus self-reliance in humans covering the life span. The phases of this developmental model are organized for the first 3 years along the framework of the separation–individuation model; then the period from 3 to 6 years is presented in terms of the Oedipus complex framework, which is followed by the latency and adolescent phases. This epigenesis continues with the model proposed by psychosocial theory, namely, early adulthood, adulthood, and late adulthood. We organize dependence along two coordinates: Dependence on Whom and Dependence for What. Dependence on Whom addresses our reliance on others (or substitutes for others) in the fulfilling of our needs. We organize human needs, Dependence for What, in three interrelating groups: the physiological needs, such as the need for food, shelter, and whatever is needed for physical survival; the emotional, especially libidinal, needs, including affectional and sensual needs; and the ego-developmental needs, such as the need for adaptation, the need to develop skills, and the need for training and education. In this model we emphasize the normality of our needs for others and the variability of these needs during the life span. Interestingly, this formulation bears on the theory of narcissism elaborated in Kohut's self psychology (1977).

More recently, several additional psychoanalytic models of development have been proposed. These include my model of the epigenesis of aggression in early childhood (1979a, 1989b); Greenspan (1981), following on his integrative study of psychoanalysis and Piaget's (1979) developmental epistemology, proposed a developmental structuralist model of early development (1981) which he states in terms of ego development this volume; and Stern's model of the development of self in earliest childhood (1985).

Epigenesis of Aggression in Early Childhood

My model of the epigenesis of aggression in early childhood (1979a, 1989b) is an attempt to trace the development of aggression during the first five years of life. My assertion that I cannot describe the development of aggression in well-structured phases like, for example, the phases of psychosexual development, is critical. This is because the development of aggression seems codetermined by other component psychic developments and especially because experience profoundly affects the generation, vicissitudes, and ultimate stabilization of aggression in the psyche. Basic to this model is a formulation of a theory of aggression, which holds that aggression is constituted of three major trends that are ultimately linked: nondestructive aggression, nonaffective destructiveness, and hostile destructiveness (Parens, 1979a, 1984, 1989a). Of most concern here are nondestructive aggression and hostile destructiveness. Because the evolving of the latter is codetermined by experiences of excessive unpleasure (EU), the role of experience in its development is relatively predictable and explains the notable range of variation of hostility found during early childhood and later.

Briefly, I propose that all forms (trends) of aggression are evident at birth or soon thereafter. A biologically determined upsurge of aggression appears at about eight months of age, consonant with other psychic developments that occur at this time, which significantly heightens the level of aggression experienced. I (1979a, 1989b) also detail the role played by the structuring of the libidinal object at this time, a second determiner of the vicissitudes of aggression. During the last two or so months of the first year of life, this structuring of the libidinal object is crucial to the *beginnings* of internalization and of superego precursor formations. These are especially the product of the powerful thrust to autonomy that is fueled by nondestructive aggression. This thrust to autonomy and normal narcissism combine to create battles of wills with the libidinal object from near the end of the first year on which lead to ambivalence, intrapsychic conflict, and internalization of superego precursors and will later, at about 18 months, influence the character of the anal conflict (psychosexual theory), to which stubbornness has heretofore been ascribed.

During the second year of life, side by side with the battles of wills, the vicissitudes of both nondestructive aggression and hostile destructiveness are significantly influenced by the character and quality of the child's rapprochement crisis (Mahler et al., 1975). During the 2½ to 6 years period, differences in aggression in boys and girls now first become manifest, especially under the influence of phallic aggression. I believe phallic aggression to be the result of an inherent differentiation of both libido and aggression. Its appearance was much more pronounced in the boys we observed than in the girls. Furthermore, I believe the conflict of ambivalence inherent in the Oedipus complex has a powerful influence on the vicissitudes of hostile destructiveness in the child. Linking the development of hostile destructiveness (and consequently of nondestructive aggression as well) with the development of ambivalence, I propose the normal development of two basic conflicts of ambivalence—the first, dyadic object–related (bound to separation–individuation); the second, triadic object–related (Oedipus complex)—and propose from it a reformulation of superego formation in the girl (Parens, 1979b, 1990a).

Ego Development in the Early Years

Greenspan (1989, this volume) has conceptualized stages of ego development. He emphasizes that in viewing the infant psychoanalytically in
terms of ego functioning, "one must not simply look at the infant's
capacities, but at how he organizes around age-specific critical psychological tasks" (p. 89). Furthermore, the "pattern of in-depth psychological
growth is different from [the] pattern of cognitive growth . . . and [we
must] not 'assume' or 'generalize' from [cognitive] functioning in other
domains" (p. 89). First, Greenspan suggests, in keeping with Hartmann's (1939) ideas about primary autonomous apparatuses, that ego
development in its earliest stage (birth to 3 months) corresponds to the
infant's efforts at achieving homeostasis (self-regulation and interest in the
world). This is a somatic, preintentional world self-object, with a lack of
differentiation between the physical, self, and object worlds. This is
followed by the stage of Attachment (at 2 to 7 months), which is
characterized by intentionality and part self-object, or undifferentiated
self-object, organization. "There is no evidence of the infant's ability to
abstract . . . an organization of the whole-object" (p. 91). Then comes
the stage (at three to ten months) of Somatopsychic Differentiation
(purposeful communication); note the wide overlap with the Attachment
stage. This stage is "characterized by a differentiation of aspects (parts) of
self and object in terms of drive-affect patterns and behavior" (p. 91).
Cause and effect interactions emerge, as well as intentionality of action and
influence of "self" on an "other" (p. 93).

Fourth is the stage of Behavioral Organization, Initiative, and Internalization (9 to 18 months). There is now a complex sense of self. Ego
organization is "characterized by an integration of drive–affect behavioral
patterns into relatively 'whole' functional self-objects . . . [with] integration of drive affect polarities (e.g., shift from splitting to greater integration)" (p. 95). The fifth stage is that of Representational Capacity (9 to 18
months). "Ego organization, differentiation, and integration are characterized by an elevation of functional behavioral self-object patterns to
multisensory drive–affect invested symbols of intrapersonal and interactive
experience (mental representations) . . . (p. 96), that is, they are characterized by the capacity for psychic representation. Awareness, in a
symbolic sense, is expanding rapidly as in pretend play and the functional
use of language (p. 96). The last stage Greenspan details is that of
Representational Differentiation (about 24 to 48 months). "Ego organization, differentiation, and integration are characterized by [a] . . . higher
level representational organization differentiated along dimensions of
self–other, time, and space." Ego functions include representational

differentiation, characterized by genetic, dynamic, and "microstructural" (i.e., affect, impulse, and thought) integrations, structure formation, and self and object identity formation (pp. 98–99).

The Development of the Self

In 1985 Stern proposed a model of the development of self quite apart from the propositions of Kohut and self psychology. A trained psychiatrist and psychoanalyst, Stern is a full-time researcher, well trained in developmental psychology method and engaged in a different kind of observational research and theorizing than that of psychoanalytic clinician–researchers of the Anna Freud, Kris, Spitz, Mahler genre. Much influenced by developmental psychology, Stern asserts that the development of self is not phasic but rather consists of component self structures that emerge in sequence and continue to develop through the course of life. Stern proposes that first to be experienced is a Sense of an Emergent Self. As I see it, Stern invokes the classical concept of primary narcissism, which is modified to include a primitive sense of awareness of internal events and of objects. During the middle of the third month, the Sense of a Core Self begins to emerge, a sense of being a different—to a degree an integrated—whole. Self-agency, self-coherence, self-affectivity, and self-history all begin, these capabilities constituting the emerging sense of a core self. From about 8 months on, the Sense of a Subjective Self begins. Now the infant begins to recognize that he or she has feelings and a mind and that others do too. These feelings can be shared and are experienced as occurring in others as well. Here begins that critical experience of intersubjectivity and emotional interrelatedness. And from about 15 months, the child begins to develop a Sense of a Verbal Self. Now the self can relate to others, expressing his or her experiencing through symbols, through words. A new way of experiencing the self with others is added, multiplying the capacity for self-experience and the experiencing of others.

My effort here is not to do justice to these various models but simply to give a view of them, especially for the young professional, and to whet the reader's appetite in the hope that he or she will consult the original writings.

This proliferation of psychoanalytic models of early development, not surprisingly, is the product of child psychoanalytic researchers whose interest in development is bound to their work. Given the enrichment provided by these many expansions of our view, we can no longer be oriented by just one model or the other; nor—if we have clinically tested and judged them to have merit—are we wise to make one more or less important than the rest. There is much to be gained by the co-implementation of several or even all of the perspectives these models provide in informing our clinical work and research.

Differing Characteristics of the Models

Of much interest is the fact that if the clinician and researcher cautiously discern the level of conceptualization and the limitations of each model, most of the models proposed can be used compatibly with each other. Unlike the difficulties encountered in attempts to integrate or even just interrelate models from different disciplines, for example, classical psycho-analytic theories of development with Piaget's development of intelligence (Anthony 1956, 1957; Wolff, 1960; Greenspan, 1979), fewer difficulties exist among those described in this chapter—except for Sander's model. The latter is an interpersonal model, rather than an intrapsychic one, and interrelating attempts create difficulty by virtue of the different domains addressed.

While these are all psychoanalytically conceptualized models—some may reject Sander's model; I, however, do not—they do differ in some often disregarded ways, which makes their interrelations and integration uneven or constituted of unmatched parameters. There are at least two parameters that characterize them: (1) the span of development the model addresses and (2) the degree of complexity or level of conceptualization at which each is defined. For instance, in terms of developmental span, Spitz's structuring of the libidinal object model is the shortest, addressing only the first eight or so months of life whereas Erikson's psychosocial theory and Saul's and my dependence theory are lifelong models. With regard to their degree of complexity or level of conceptualization, some models are predominantly unidimensional (consisting of a single theory) while others are multidimensional (woven of several theories). For instance, Freud's and Abraham's psychosexual theory (I will cast doubt on at least one aspect of this theory being unidimensional shortly), my aggression theory and Spitz's structuring of the libidinal object theory are all uni-theoretical; each essentially emphasizes one major component of psychic develop-ment—the sexual drive, the aggressive drive, and object relations, respec-tively. On the other hand, psychosocial, separation–individuation, and Oedipus complex theories are multitheoretical; they are constituted of several defined theoretical models—drive theory, structural theory (ego development especially but that of the superego as well), self theory, and object relations theory. It can, of course, be argued that none of these models of development encompasses the entire psychic experiencing of the person and that each addresses only a component of that entirety and exists in relationship to all the other component theories; in that sense, none is a purely uni-theoretical model. Even the simplest of these models, Spitz's structuring of the libidinal object, is—while dominantly an object relations theory—is also heavily indebted to drive and ego concepts for its existance. Nonetheless, these distinguishing levels of conceptualization are pertinent to this effort to examine and support the complementary use of psychosexual theory and separation–individuation theory.

THE THEORY OF PSYCHOSEXUAL DEVELOPMENT

Given the familiarity of clinicians and theorists with this superb and productive model, and due to space limitations, I shall not review its vast literature. As the reader knows, a number of contributions have been made to this model over time, the majority coming from clinical confirmations and amplifications. Recently, several studies coming from depth-psychological direct early childhood observation, both clinical and empirical, have amplified the model and raised questions about some basic hypotheses contained in the theory. For example, Roiphe and Galenson, in several papers and culminating in a book (Roiphe and Galenson, 1981), have proposed that a prephallic genital phase emerges during the second half of the second year of life, a phase that is dyadic in character and antecedent to the emergence of the triadic genital phase that gives rise to the Oedipus complex. Blum, in addition to making individual contributions to superego formation (1976a, 1985), edited a volume containing updating and innovative contributions (1976b). Stoller has emphasized the existence of primary femininity and has contributed substantially to our understanding of sexual development and the emergence of gender formation (1968, 1976). My collaborators and I have reported observational studies that lead us to propose that the girl may not enter her oedipal stage by means of the castration complex (Parens et al., 1976). We have also addressed the question of the child's wish to have a baby and have concluded that the wish is not solely a reaction to the girl's castration complex (Parens and Pollock, 1979); and I have proposed a revised conceptualization of superego formation in the girl (1990a). Contributions such as these and many others need not concern us here, however, since the thesis I develop does not impinge on the questions and proposed modifications and elaborations psychosexual theory has undergone since 1905.

Fundamentally, psychosexual theory is the detailing of the libidinal drive as it differentiates within and impacts upon the person from infancy to adulthood—or, as I have suggested elsewhere, to parenthood (Panel, 1975). Perhaps a thorough study of Freud's letters would elucidate exactly how psychosexual theory first emerged in his thoughts. Three elements of it stand out: (1) it is about sexual life, (2) it is about the Oedipus complex, and (3) it is about the development of sexuality, including its preoedipal differentiations. Which element came first and led to the others? My construction of it is that Freud first reported identifying sexuality as the source of neurotic symptoms (Breuer and Freud, 1895). Then came his conceptualization of the Oedipus complex, well developed in the dream book (1900), and then, by 1905 in "Three Essays on the Theory of Sexuality," the conceptualization of the three major phases of infantile psychosexual development, namely, the oral, anal, and (infantile) genital phases; these were followed by a latency period and, finally, adolescence, the true genital phase. It is not surprising that after proposing the centrality of sexuality to neurosis and of the Oedipus complex as its critical determinant, Freud (1923) would extend the latter momentous conceptualization back to the child's "prehistoric" development, that is, to the preoedipal period. We are all well acquainted with Freud's felicitous grasp of the centrality of sexuality to neurosis, even if this centrality was at the expense of less specific conceptualizations of the part also played by aggression (hostility) in neurosis (Freud, 1913, 1926) as well as object relations, without which explication of the Oedipus complex is impossible.

What I am trying to say is this: although the Oedipus complex was uncovered in the context of Freud's efforts to explain the dynamics and interrelations of sexuality and neurosis, the Oedipus complex as an entity is constituted of a set of component theories—namely, instinctual drive theory (sexual and aggressive drives), structural theory (including all agencies), and object relations theory (about which Freud had much to say, as I noted in the Introduction of this chapter). Freud uncovered the importance of sexuality to psychic life and the oedipal conflict; this discovery led to his conceptualizing the sexual drive differentiations in detail, but he placed secondary (until 1915 and 1920) to sexuality the theory of aggression, which is critical to the central conflict in the Oedipus complex, and he did not conceptualize as such what others have insisted is crucial for psychoanalysis, namely, object relations theory. The resulting problem is that preoedipal development, Freud said in 1923, is the "prehistory" of the child, underscoring the overarching centrality, in his view, of the Oedipus complex. We bear in mind that it was not until 1926, in reaction to Rank's birth trauma theory, that Freud recognized and wrote what this prehistory might be— although he did touch on it in 1921 when he spoke of the child's preoedipal identifications, a topic he explored following his attempts to explain mourning and uncovering identification as part of its solution (Freud 1917, 1921, 1923).

The issue for our present concern is that although Freud's formulation of preoedipal sexual development has served us well for decades, it has also met with major problems. In his formulation of preoedipal development the component theories operative in the supraordinate Oedipus complex conceptualization are not all extended back through the earliest period of life: that is, drive theory is, but structural theory is not, and object relations theory is only partly, indeed insufficiently, expanded. It seems to me that prior to Spitz's conceptualization of the structuring of the libidinal object and Erikson's formulations of basic trust versus basic mistrust and autonomy versus shame, the concepts of the oral phase and anal phase were stretched and strained to accommodate issues they could not accommodate satisfactorily.

For instance, questions pertaining to the relation of the object during the oral phase were for decades conceptualized in terms of the object as the breast. Melanie Klein (1939) was among the first to reasonably propose concepts of the internalized bad object and the good object. Unavoidably, the concepts of the "bad breast" and the "good breast" could not suffice the child analyst who recognized that the object invested with the earliest derivatives of libido and aggression during earliest childhood cannot be sufficiently represented only as "the breast." Spitz's observational studies, which led him to conceptualize the structuring of the libidinal object, revealed that the infant's attention during breast- or bottle-feeding is divided between sensory input from the mouth and from the eyes; through the mouth the infant perceives and registers intrapsychically the gratifying or frustrating breast (or bottle), and through the eyes the infant perceives and registers intrapsychically part of the mother's face (the area around and including the mother's eyes and forehead). In fact, Spitz (1965) suggested that the perception of this part of the mother's face, which elicits the social smiling response, may represent an innate releasing mechanism (IRM; see Lorenz, 1953) that triggers attachment to the mother; therefore, at the very least, internalization and structuring of the libidinal object are not via the breast alone. Spitz thus brought to his psychoanalytic conceptualization imprinting theory, which holds that attachment is activated by an IRM specific for each species (for humans, the "mask" area of the face), thus ensuring attachment to objects of the infant's own species (Lorenz, 1935, 1953; Hess, 1959).

Although the oral experience is an important determinant of several experiential parameters of earliest life, it cannot account for other parameters of experience critical to our understanding of the infant's total experience. For instance, when 10-day-old Bernie stared at his mother's face for minutes on end while feeding at the bottle, the composite experience consisted of such oral factors as gratifying feeding, the gratification of oral libidinal (object-attaching) needs, and gratification of oral erotic needs. But it also contained major elements of self–object relatedness, such as *object-dependent* libidinal gratification, steps toward libidinal object structuring with the earliest internalizations (even if only beginning image representations) of mother's face, the earliest primary narcissistic emotional perception of gratifying nondifferentiated self–mother experiencing, and the laying down of precursor experiencing that will lead to "confident expectation" (Benedek, 1949) and eventually basic trust (Erikson, 1959).

Furthermore, perhaps as critical as the oral mode of organizing experience is the drive-derivative/affective experience of good feelings and bad feelings, precursor feelings of love and hate (Parens, 1979b, 1990b). I find Erikson's (1950) emphasis on orality *as a mode* of perceiving and organizing experience very helpful. It is important to us throughout life, bringing much pleasure and/or frustration. But even in earliest childhood orality cannot sufficiently explain or account for the drive-derivative/affective experience of rage (determined by excessive unpleasure) versus a feeling of well-being (Parens, 1979a, 1990b; Emde, 1983, 1989) nor the experience, however primitive, of feeling a sense of self (primary narcissism) that is one with the object (Mahler, 1965, 1968; Mahler et al., 1975; Kohut, 1977; Stern, 1985), nor the experience of basic trust (Benedek, 1949; Erikson, 1959). In fact, I at times consider, in questioning which experience of the infant has preeminent priority, that what is a greater determinant of early experience than orality or self–object experiencing is the balance of well-being and positive affective experiencing versus excessive pain and negatively valenced affective experiencing—a balance that critically influences the qualitative experiencing of orality, self–object experience, and basic trust/mistrust. Of course, the importance to the child of the affective-emotional experiencing in object relations has been duly emphasized by psychoanalysts (e.g., Klein, 1939; Kernberg, 1966, 1976; Mahler, 1968).

Consider also the distortions to which the anal phase concept has been subjected. For instance, to begin with, I question Freud's and Abraham's implication that the conflict, which they described for this psychosexual phase as "*the* anal conflict," first appears during the anal phase. Elements ascribed to the anal phase as typical of this phase we now know emerge well before the anal phase appears; in the course of observational studies on the development of aggression in early childhood, we found much evidence of obstinacy and stubbornness from the last quarter of the first year on in the child's battles of wills with the mother. This is associated with the child's powerful thrust to autonomy, a thrust fueled by nondestructive aggression, especially evident during the practicing subphase of separation–individuation. This autonomy thrust—which was also elaborated by Erikson (1959) and explored by Peller (1965) and which puzzled Hendrick (1942, 1943), Winnicott (1955), and Greenacre (1960), among others—leads the practicing subphase child into many a risky exploratory situation that draws limit-setting responses from the responsibly caring libidinal object and will, in many a well-endowed child, trigger a battle of wills (see Parens, 1979a, for a literature review and discussion of nondestructive aggression, mastery, and autonomy—the practicing subphase conflict). The more the child is endowed with healthy nondestructive aggression and the more sufficiently determined the mother is to protect her child against harm to self or others, the more likely the battle of wills will ensue. Obstinacy and stubbornness are well known to parents of such children even before anal or toilet training issues have surfaced.

These studies, furthermore, showed us that the emergence of ambivalence, which has also classically been linked to anal phase developments, occurs earlier than generally assumed. I have reported observational data and proposed from these that ambivalence seems to emerge from the turn into the second year of life in accord with Abraham, 1924, who specified its emergence with *oral* sadism, well before evidence of anality or the anal conflict surfaces (Parens 1979a, 1979b, 1989b).

Prior to these findings and conceptualizations, battles of wills and their resultant ambivalence were ascribed to the anal phase, thus masking their origin in the powerful thrust to autonomy and the need to preserve the emerging sense of self-identity and integrity to which aggression makes a major contribution. The uniqueness of anality has, as a result, become biased and diluted. Its hallmark, the *erotization* of anal function—the letting go, the delaying and retaining, the bursting and exploding, the smearing on a wall or canvas and on the self—is only too often associated with the battles of wills, ambivalence, and sadism. To be sure, Freud labeled this period the *sadistic*-anal phase. But Abraham, also limited to only psychosexual theory, was right to also press for an *oral-sadistic* subphase, and, indeed, observation amply shows the emergence of hostile destructiveness well before the onset of the anal phase. Sadism predates anality, and the negative bias toward anality, the predominant view of anality as sadistic, years ago softened by Andreas-Salome (1916) and recently elucidated by Shengold (1988), may well result from ascribing its origin to the battles of wills (with mother) and linking it predominantly with the hostile destructive trend of the aggressive drive.

The phallic-oedipal phase—except for the major problem arising from

Freud's (1925) duly criticized and challenged masculinized view of the girl's development—has served our clinical and theoretical understanding of development better. This is so because the oedipal component of this phase is much more capable of explicating the child's complex and integrative development than is the phallic component. The oedipal component addresses issues of drives, psychic structure, and triadic object relatedness, a complex and remarkably interwoven fabric. The phallic component, like the oral and anal phases, is conceptually limited to sexual drive development. To be sure, the role of the phallus in psychic life is large in both male and female, but it is nonetheless unitheoretical and more limited in explanatory capability than is the multitheoretical Oedipus complex. More on this later.

SEPARATION–INDIVIDUATION THEORY

As I suggested in my description of separation–individuation theory (Mahler 1952, 1965, 1968; Mahler, Pine, and Bergman, 1975; Mahler and McDevitt, 1980; McDevitt and Mahler, 1980), its basic propositions provide a model of the child's inferred intrapsychic experience of self in relation to his or her mother during the first three years of life. The model holds that during the first weeks of life the infant's experience is governed by primary narcissism—regrettably labeled by Mahler as the normal autistic phase to emphasize the inwardness she inferred of the newborn's experience—and an absence of boundaries between self and object, internal and external reality not yet being experienced. At about six weeks, perception that "help comes from the outside" (Mahler, 1952) heralds the normal symbiotic phase. During this phase the child's inferred experience is of feeling as if one with the symbiotic partner, usually the mother, as if enveloped with her in a "symbiotic membrane" (Mahler, 1968). The self is then experienced as a composite self–object, which may come closest to Kohut's (1971, 1977) selfobject concept.

From the middle of the first year, at the peak of the child's intrapsychically experienced symbiosis, the intrapsychic separation–individuation process begins; Mahler proposed that it spans the next two and a half years, thus overlapping with the earliest part of the oedipal period. Mahler identified this period as the separation–individuation *phase* but held that the *process* probably continues to evolve and further stabilize throughout life (see also Jacobson, 1964), with regressions at times of stress, especially in late adulthood.

The first half of the separation–individuation phase, from 5 to 6 months to about 18 months, consisting of the differentiation and practicing subphases, seems initiated within the child by sharply increasing (and fueled by aggression) autonomy strivings (Mahler and McDevitt, 1980; McDevitt and Mahler, 1980; Parens, 1980), exercised and growing adaptive ego functions, and heightened narcissism and omnipotence. Mahler proposed that at about 16 to 18 months, evolving as if compelled within the child by a new, the third, level of psychic organization since birth[1] (Spitz, 1965; Emde, 1980; Zeanah et al., 1989; Parens, 1990b), the child's now newly differentiating reality testing and cognitive ego functions (e.g., the capacity for object permanence [Piaget, 1937]) make the child aware that self and mother are not one, are not a self–object. Within the child, this new functional capacity triggers the process of resolving the symbiotic oneness with mother and contributes to the creation of a self as an entity more or less deeply emotionally related to an object entity, a self that is individuated and separated from that now sufficiently stable internalized love-object. Contrary to Kohut's inference that selfobjects remain constituents of normal psychic life, Mahler's proposal is that, except in times of sufficient stress and regression, this second part of the critical process of separation–individuation resolves and stabilizes during the subphase toward self and object constancy, resulting in a sufficiently organized self and object that are entities bound by a powerful, internally stable emotional (drive-bound) relationship.

It is evident throughout Mahler's writings, and the concept is a distinguished contribution to our psychoanalytic theories and clinical work, that this model of the child's earliest inner self-experiencing in the context of the relationship to his or her mother is forged out of the depth-psychological concepts of ego development and functioning, the concepts of drive-derived inner forces (libidinal and aggressive) and her own innovative contribution to object relations theory. Mahler's focus is the child's inner experience, the child as entity, and the child's ego, drives, and internalized object relations. Striking in her work is the contribution this model makes to a powerfully more meaningful explication of the child's experience than we were able to achieve by means of the more limited concept of *preoedipal* psychosexual development. It is not my intention to lessen the enormously important part psychosexual theory has played and continues to play in our theoretical work, and in the clinical situation. Nor do I believe it will decrease in importance to us. My point simply is that we have overburdened the concepts of the oral phase, the

---

[1]The first shift in organizational level in the psyche occurs at about six weeks of age (Mahler, 1952; Benjamin, 1963; Emde, 1980), the second at about 6 to 8 months (Spitz, 1946b, 1965; Parens, 1979a, 1990b; Emde, 1980).

anal phase, and even the phallic phase by stretching them to cover object relations concepts such as the bad breast or the breast as part object or that we have secondarily appended aggressive drive theory to it such as in the concepts of the oral-sadistic and sadistic-anal phases.

THEORETICAL LEVELS OF CONCEPTUALIZATION AND SOME IMPLICATIONS

The thrust of this chapter is that the theories of the Oedipus complex and of separation–individuation are at the same holistic theoretical level whereas psychosexual theory is not. Let me underscore that although the theory of the Oedipus complex is historically and conceptually imbedded in psychosexual theory, in the phallic phase, psychosexual theory per se is unitheoretical. As I stated earlier, separation–individuation theory is conceptualized implementing multiple psychoanalytic theories and elaborates further on differentiations of and contributions by libido theory (e.g., libidinal investment in self and object), aggressive drive theory (e.g., practicing subphase, ambitendency–ambivalence, and the thrust to autonomy), structural theory (e.g., development of ego functions, especially cognitive and defenses, the "practicing" of new ego skills, and the formation of superego precursors), and object relations theory (symbiosis, separation–individuation process, object and self constancy); separation–individuation theory even introduces a normal intrapsychic conflict occurring during the rapprochement subphase, the rapprochement crisis, thereby contributing further to psychoanalytic conflict theory. Similarly, Oedipus complex theory is conceptualized implementing several psychoanalytic theories. This theory details dramatically the differentiations of libido theory (it is, in fact, the apex of psychosexual theory), of aggressive drive theory (castration complex, hostile destructiveness toward the loved parent of the same sex, ambivalence), and of structural theory (ego differentiations—secondary identification, sublimation, "neutralization" of aggression, and so forth—and superego formation); and it has introduced the dramatically organizing but also neurosogenic intrapsychic conflict within the Oedipus complex, thereby contributing centrally to psychoanalytic conflict theory. These stand in sharp contrast to the more restricted capability of psychosexual theory.

I do not underestimate the valuable mass of information psychosexual theory opened to us. First of all, it gave us a model that first organized psychoanalytic thoughts on human development. Then, following the recommendations of Kris (1950), Hartmann (1950b, 1958) and A. Freud

(1958), direct observations of infants by depth psychologists enhanced the further probing of the framework first outlined by the oral and anal phases of psychosexual development. These recommendations came out of the recognition that Kris (with Senn), Spitz (1946a, 1946b), Benjamin (1961, 1963), A. Freud (with Burlingham, 1944, and with Dann, 1951), and Mahler (1952; with Gosliner, 1955) were finding in their own work this avenue of exploration feasible and fruitful. While A. Freud did not formally directly explore preoedipal life in the early days of these studies, Spitz, Benjamin and Mahler did, and made eye-opening discoveries. These too, of course, have since become springboards for even newer elaborations of what we know to date.

My point here is that because preoedipal psychosexual theory is not conceptualized at the same holistic level as is oedipal theory, it cannot of itself broadly enough complement Oedipus complex theory in theoretical and clinical work. Complementing preoedipal psychosexual theory, however, with separation–individuation theory makes for a dual model that is more powerfully explanatory of what happens intrapsychically to the preoedipal child and this, indeed, brings our understanding of the child's entry into the Oedipus complex on track, all wheels adhering firmly to the ground.

The concept of separation–individuation complementing the concept of oral stage places the oral experience in the context of the child's experiencing of the self–mother relationship. Orality as a mode of experiencing (Erikson, 1950) at times clearly influences relating; the feeding infant internalizes (incorporates) the quality of this relating. Although orality codetermines this feeding experience, it does not represent all modes of experiencing of the infant less than 18 months old. For instance, orality does not account for the cardinal experiencing, quality, and progression of attachment; orality per se does not explain attachment. Nor does it explain satisfactorily what the following crucial experiences mean and why they occur: social smiling responsiveness, separation anxiety, stranger anxiety, reunion reactions—all organizing experiences of the first 1½ years of life. To explain these in terms of orality is procrustean. Freud himself was compelled to develop another model to accommodate separation anxiety. For this he conceptualized the danger situation series to answer the question, What causes anxiety, what is the prototypic anxiety, and what is its epigenesis, if it has one? To assume that the danger of losing the object is preeminently due to the dread of not being gratified orally misses the major point we all know from clinical experience, especially with children, which is manifested by separation and stranger anxiety, that is, the structuring of self and libidinal object.

CLINICAL ILLUSTRATIONS

Glenn was brought to psychoanalysis at 3 years 9 months of age because of intense anxiety on separation from his mother, a persisting and oppressive need to control virtually everything his parents did, whether in the course of his care or not, and much repetition and routinization of whatever he did, be it in getting dressed, in eating, in separating, or in play. Glenn's history of feeding, sleep difficulty, and difficulty to soothe and calm from birth on suggested the clinical picture of CNS immaturity and minimal brain dysfunction (MBD) with difficulty in organizing physiologic and adaptive experiencing. Nonetheless, Glenn was bright and affectionately and deeply related to objects. At moments of intense anxiety he seemed to withdraw and evidenced some echolalia.

Early in psychoanalysis Glenn's more regressive symptomatology ceased quite readily. I soon found in fantasy much triangular conflict relatedness and fantasy enactment of a specific oedipal theme with a number of variations and much castration anxiety. During his analysis preponderant sources of anxiety came from the threat of castration and the threat of separation. On several occasions in the course of his analysis, separation experiences produced anxiety that seemed more intense and more poorly mediated by him than that produced by experiences in which I saw evidence of castration anxiety; that is, separation anxiety appeared more disorganizing than castration anxiety.

Over time, it seemed to me that Glenn may have been made more vulnerable to separation by his immature neonatal psychobiological equipment and an ego that was not age-adequately organized. As a result of this immaturity, during separation–individuation, during the peak of the symbiosis, and during rapprochement Glenn experienced anxiety as more than usually disorganizing—in fact, as traumatizing to him. When the threat of castration emerged, he was initially severely burdened, had difficulty holding an age-adequate level of functioning (despite hefty obsessive–compulsive defenses), and regressed intermittently into worrisome pathologic formations. However, with engagement in our analytic work his strengths came to the fore, his ego became better organized and his defenses better able to mediate anxiety than before. Much working through addressed especially the rage he experienced at separations and at his parents' reasonable resistances to his coercive control of them; the dread he experienced of his own suppressed and inhibited rage; the powerful, oppressive erotic feelings he had toward his mother; his oedipal rivalry; and his castration anxiety. Glenn gradually adapted better, and as his anxiety decreased and was better contained and mediated, he seemed to grow in adaptive capabilities, catching up to his age level quite well.

Interestingly, when termination of analysis was in process at 6½ years of age, Glenn made meaningful efforts to terminate his analysis and elaborated several themes on separating from me and on how to survive without my intervening in his behalf. The last two sessions were noteworthy. The next to last session took me a bit by surprise; it consisted of an entire 45 minutes of intense manifest anxiety and episodic rage states with pleading, commanding, and coercion of me and his mother (he had moved the session into the waiting room when in progress) to reset the termination date (which we had already done once) to the following week. I found it also remarkable that although I had worried that the last session might be a painful repetition of this intense anxiety and rage state—I had explored my countertransference reaction and had also wondered if I had misjudged the work done—Glenn came into the consultation room for the last session self-contained and sad but smiling softly; on his own initiative and preplanning he took a series of photographs of the office, of me, of the highly cathected puppets he had used well, of his drawer, and—turning the camera on himself—of himself in this transference setting. And he took all of his drawer's contents with him.

I understood 3½-year-old Glenn's anxiety to have been more than usually disorganizing and reconstructed that he had experienced separation during separation–individuation as more traumatizing than many children do for at least two interacting reasons: (1) his ego was not organized age-adequately when this developmental task was in progress in large part because of his organic diathesis (MBD), and (2) the intense hostile destructiveness generated in him by his excessively painful anxiety states circularly further intensified his anxiety and further burdened his ego. When I saw Glenn at 3½ years, the added burden of emerging castration anxiety led him to intensify obsessive-compulsive defenses, rigorous strategies (mediated by narcissistic demandingness and coercive pleading) aimed at controlling the environment and objects, and transient withdrawal and echolalia associated with a high anxiety state. When the threat of castration emerged in age-adequate sequence, the anxiety it generated was taxing to the point of leading to a regression too pathologic, a defense too controlling and restrictive. Because of this vulnerability to anxiety I recommended analysis for him in order to reduce the helplessness of the ego and to then make anxiety more manageable and therefore less likely to interfere with his potential structural and overall development by eliciting less of the rigid, global obsessive–compulsive defenses he was then using to mitigate it.

It is pertinent to the thesis of this chapter that I viewed Glenn's separation anxiety as a response to the threat of intolerable separateness for reasons more global than the threat of lack of oral gratification. His solution to his last separation crisis, the termination of his analysis, was to acquire a photo record of his transference constellation, of himself in my office, of me, and of his puppet-objects; this behavior was only a piece of a cluster of data suggestive of the loss of the object leading to the dread of loss of a cohesive, integrated self related to a highly valued object, indeed, a self–object. I found much data suggestive of his not having resolved, in a stable, age-adequate manner, the overall task of experiencing himself as a cohesively integrated entity in the absence of the libidinal object, the major task begun during the rapprochement subphase and resolved during the subphase "on the way to self and object constancy." In contrast, I found the analysis (exploration of wishes, of the conflict, and of his inability to accept nongratification) of his infantile neurosis much easier to manage quite effectively even though it made enormous demands on his overburdened ego. Although some residual, organic cognitive-processing problems remained, the intense anxiety that led this child to overly control himself, his love-objects, and his environment with a proliferation of obsessive–compulsive defenses had abated greatly and his emotional development caught up substantially and was proceeding quite satisfactorily.

Here, more briefly, is a further illustration of the progression from the task of separation–individuation, not of oral or anal phase mastery, to Oedipus complex experiencing. Five-year-old Valerie had much difficulty going to sleep. Ritualistic preparations for bedtime mitigated but did not contain her intense anxiety sufficiently. Valerie was otherwise a well-developing and well-adapting child. Much evidence pointed to separation anxiety presenting as a continuation of moderate difficulty in nighttime separation that dated back to the end of her first year of life. This then became associated with much oedipal conflict–generated anxiety, quite apparent to me; for example, she was most agitated in the evening when mother and father were alone together without her. She then did all she could (unconsciously motivated) to interfere with this situation. We found in this case that Valerie's father's loss of his own father at a young age, which had made him at the time and for some time thereafter neurotically symptomatic, made him (in his own words) "fear the loss of this beloved child." The father and I both assumed this to be contributory to Valerie's own dread of separation and loss. Although Valerie's symptomatic difficulty in falling asleep was predominantly a separation fear of separation–individuation origin, it became heightened by Valerie's oedipal conflict. Again, this separation anxiety just could not be satisfactorily explained by addressing issues of orality or of anality (i.e., issues of psychosexuality per se).

Much clinical and direct observational experience led Spitz, Bowlby, and Mahler, among others, to propose that the earliest and most long-lasting danger of earliest childhood is that of intrapsychically losing that "other" part of the self, earlier conceptualized by Spitz as the intrapsychically experienced "auxiliary ego" and the libidinal object who helps the infant organize experience, who protects the infant from danger and anxiety, *and* who gratifies oral needs.

Similarly, separation–individuation concepts complement and add to anal stage conceptualization. Already prior to toilet training, much practicing subphase activity leads to battles of wills that in turn lead to the earliest feelings of ambivalence in the child (Parens 1979a, 1979b). Then, as Mahler et al. (1975) and McDevitt (1983) proposed, ambivalence is further organized during the rapprochement crisis. This crisis now parallels the emergence of anality, and thus the earliest pre-anal conflict of ambivalence is further organized by anality and especially by anal erotization. The autonomy conflict (practicing subphase conflict) precedes the anal phase conflict, giving the latter its shape. The thrust of and the integrity of autonomy, then, the need to protect the emerging sense of self, represents the genesis of this conflict, which, when anality heightens, can then include the child's erotization of anal functions and the need to possess feces (and objects) and exercise control over their discharge.

There is no inherent antagonism or contradiction between separation–individuation theory and psychosexual theory. Each contributes to our growing understanding of psychic experience.

SUMMARY

There is much value in the complementary use of soundly developed psychoanalytic models in clinical, observational, and theoretical psycho-analytic work. Our collective years of observation in the clinical situation and in longitudinal direct observational research with infants have made this necessary. I can not address an anaclitic depression in terms of oral deprivation, given—as Spitz (1946a) proposed—that it is primarily deter-mined by a profound libidinal object loss or deprivation experience. Nor can I (or my patients, I believe) adequately understand an oedipal conflict without due emphasis, in addition to the transgressive sexual wishes, on the wish to destroy (aggression) the beloved mother or father. The combined use of psychosexual theory with aggression theory, separation–individuation theory, and structural theory richly details the multiple factors at play in this crucial conflict.

REFERENCES

Abraham, K. (1924), A short study of the development of the libido. In: *Selected Papers of Karl Abraham.* New York: Basic Books, 1953, pp. 418–501.
Andreas-Salome, L. (1916), Anality and sexuality. *Imago,* 4:249–273.
Anthony, J. (1956), Six applications de la theorie génétique de Piaget a' la th'eorie et la pratique psychodynamique. *Schweitzerische Zeitschrift fur Psychologie und ihre Anwendungen,* 15:269–277.
———— (1957), The system makers: Piaget and Freud. *Br. J. Med. Psychol.,* 30:255–269.
Benedek, T. (1949), The psychosomatic implications of the primary unit: Mother–child. *Amer. J. Orthopsychiat.,* 19:642–654.
Benjamin, J. (1961), Some developmental observations relating to the theory of anxiety. *J. Amer. Psychoanal. Assn.,* 9:652–668.
———— (1963), Further comments on some developmental aspects of anxiety. In: *Counterpoint: Lididinal Object and Subject,* ed. H. S. Jaskill. New York: International Universities Press, pp. 121–153.
Blum, H. (1976a), Masochism, the ego ideal and the psychology of women. *J. Amer. Psychoanal. Assn.,* 24(5):157–192.
————, ed. (1976b), Female psychology. *J. Amer. Psychoanal. Assn.,* 24(5):1–350.
———— (1985), Superego formation, adolescent transformation, and the adult neurosis. *J. Amer. Psychoanal. Assn.,* 33:887–910.
Breuer, J. & Freud, S. (1895), Studies on hysteria. *Standard Edition,* 2:1–305. London: Hogarth Press, 1955.
Emde, R. N. (1980), Toward a psychoanalytic theory of affect: I. The organizational model and its propositions. In: *The Course of Life: Vol. I. Infancy and Early Childhood,* ed. S. I. Greenspan & G. H. Pollock. Washington, DC: Government Printing Office, pp. 63–83.
———— (1983), The pre-representational self and its affective core. *The Psychoanalytic Study of the Child,* 38:165–192. New Haven, CT: Yale University Press.
———— (1989), The infant's relationship experience: Developmental and affective aspects. In: *Relationship Disturbances in Early Childhood,* ed. A. J. Sameroff & R. N. Emde. New York: Basic Books, pp. 33–51.
Erikson, E. H. (1950), *Childhood and Society.* New York: Norton.
———— (1959), *Identity and the Life Cycle Psychological Issues,* Monogr. 1. New York: International Universities Press.
Fraiberg, S. (1980), *Clinical Studies in Infant Mental Health.* New York: Basic Books.

Freud, A. (1958), Child observation and prediction of development: A memorial lecture in honor of Ernst Kris. *The Psychoanalytic Study of the Child*, 13:92–124. New York: International Universities Press.

———— (1963), The concept of developmental lines. *The Psychoanalytic Study of the Child*, 18:245–265. New York: International Universities Press.

———— (1965), *Normality and Pathology in Childhood*. New York: International Universities Press.

———— & Burlingham, D. (1944), *Infants Without Families*. New York: International Universities Press.

———— & Dann, S. (1951), An experiment in group upbringing. *The Psychoanalytic Study of the Child*, 6:127–168. New York: International Universities Press.

Freud, S. (1900), The interpretation of dreams. *Standard Edition*, 3 & 4. London: Hogarth Press, 1953.

———— (1905), Three essays and the theory of sexuality. *Standard Edition* 7:123–243. London: Hogarth Press, 1953.

———— (1913), Totem and taboo. *Standard Edition*. 13:1–161. London: Hogarth Press, 1955.

———— (1915), Instincts and their vicissitudes. *Standard Edition*, 14:111–140. London: Hogarth Press, 1957.

———— (1917), Mourning and melancholia. *Standard Edition*, 14:239–258. London: Hogarth Press, 1957.

———— (1920), Beyond the pleasure principle. *Standard Edition*, 18:1–64. London: Hogarth Press, 1955.

———— (1921), Group psychology and the analysis of the ego. *Standard Edition*, 18:67–143. London: Hogarth Press, 1955.

———— (1923), The ego and the id. *Standard Edition*, 19:3–66. London: Hogarth Press, 1961.

———— (1925), Some psychical consequences of the anatomical distinction between the sexes. *Standard Edition*, 19:243–260. London: Hogarth Press, 1961.

———— (1926), Inhibitions, symptoms and anxiety. *Standard Edition*, 20:77–174. London: Hogarth Press, 1959.

Greenacre, P. (1960), Consideration regarding the parent–infant relationship. *Internat. J. Psycho-Anal.*, 41:571–584.

Greenspan, S. I. (1979), *Intelligence and Adaptation*. New York: International Universities Press.

———— (1981), *Psychopathology and Adaptation in Infancy and Early Childhood*. New York: International Universities Press.

———— (1989), *The Development of the Ego*. New York: International Universities Press.

———— & Lieberman, A. F. (1980), Infants, mothers and their interaction: A quantitative clinical approach to developmental assessment. In: *The Course of Life: Vol. 1. Infancy and Early Childhood*, ed. S. I. Greenspan & G. H. Pollock. Bethesda, MD: National Institute of Mental Health, pp. 217–312.

Harlow, H. F. (1960), Primary affectional patterns in primates. *Amer. J. Orthopsychiat.*, 30:676–684.

        & Zimmerman, R. R. (1959), Affectional responses in the infant monkey. *Science,* 130:421–432.

Hartmann, H. (1939), *Ego Psychology and the Problem of Adaptation.* New York: International Universities Press, 1958.

        (1950a), Comments on the psychoanalytic theory of the ego. In: *Essays on Ego Psychology.* New York: International Universities Press, 1964, pp. 113–141.

        (1950b), Psychoanalysis and developmental psychology. *The Psychoanalytic Study of the Child,* 5:7–17. New York: International Universities Press.

        (1958), Comments on the scientific aspects of psychoanalysis. *The Psychoanalytic Study of the Child,* 13:127–146. New York: International Universities Press.

Hendrick, I. (1942), Instinct on the scientific aspects of psychoanalysis. *Psychoanal. Quart.,* 11:33–58.

        (1943), The discussion of the "Instinct to Master." *Psychoanal. Quart.,* 12:561–565.

Hess, E. H. (1959), Imprinting. *Science,* 130:133–141.

Jacobson, E. (1964), *The Self and the Object World.* New York: International Universities Press.

Kernberg, O. (1966), Structural derivatives of object relationships. *Internat. J. Psycho-Anal.,* 47:236–253.

        (1976), *Object Relations Theory and Clinical Psychoanalysis.* New York: Aronson.

Klein, M. (1939), *The Psychoanalysis of Children.* New York: Grove Press, 1960.

Kohut, H. (1971), *The Analysis of the Self.* New York: International Universities Press.

        (1977), *The Restoration of the Self.* New York: International Universities Press.

Kris, E. (1950), Notes on the development and on some current problems of psychoanalytic child psychology. *The Psychoanalytic Study of the Child,* 5:24–46. New York: International Universities Press.

Liddell, H. S. (1958), A biological basis for psychopathology. In: *Problems of Addiction and Habituation,* ed. P. H. Hoch & J. Zubin. New York: Grune & Stratton, pp. 94–109.

Lorenz, K. (1935), Companionship in bird life. In: *Instinctive Behavior,* ed. C. H. Schiller. New York: International Universities Press, pp. 83–175, 1957.

        (1953), Comparative behaviorology. In: *Discussion on Child Development,* ed. J. M. Tanner & B. Inhelder. New York: International Universities Press, pp. 108–117.

Mahler, M. S. (1952), On child psychosis and schizophrenia: Autistic and symbiotic infantile psychoses. *The Psychoanalytic Study of the Child,* 7:286–305. New York: International Universities Press.

        (1965), On the significance of the normal separation–individuation phase. In: *Drives, Affects Behavior, Vol. 2,* ed. M. Schur. New York: International Universities Press, pp. 161–169.

        (1968), *On Human Symbiosis and the Vicissitudes of Individuation.* New York: International Universities Press.

_____ & Gosliner, B. J. (1955), On symbiotic child psychosis: Genetic, dynamic and restitutive aspects. *The Psychoanalytic Study of the Child*, 10:195–212. New York: International Universities Press.

_____ & McDevitt, J. B. (1980), The separation–individuation process and identity formation. In: *The Course of Life*, ed. S. I. Greenspan & G. H. Pollack. Bethesda, MD: National Institute of Mental Health, pp. 395–406.

_____ , Pine, F. & Bergman, A. (1975), *The Psychological Birth of the Human Infant*. New York: Basic Books.

McDevitt, J. B. (1983), The emergence of a hostile aggression and its defensive and adaptive modifications during the separation–individuation process. *J. Amer. Psychoanal. Assn.*, 31:273–300.

_____ & Mahler, M. S. (1980), Object constancy, individuality, and internalization. In: *The Course of Life: Vol. 1. Infancy and Early Childhood*, ed. S. I. Greenspan & G. H. Pollack. Bethesda, MD: National Institute of Mental Health, pp. 407–423.

Panel on Parenthood as a Developmental Phase (1975), H. Parens, reporter *J. Amer. Psychoanal. Assn.*, 23:154–165.

Parens, H. (1979a), *The Development of Aggression in Early Childhood*. New York: Aronson.

_____ (1979b), Developmental considerations of ambivalence. *The Psychoanalytic Study of the Child*, 34:385–420. New Haven, CT: Yale University Press.

_____ (1980), An exploration of the relations of instinctual drives and the symbiosis-separation-individuation process: Part 1. Drive motivation and psychic development with special reference to aggression and beginning separation–individuation. *J. Amer. Psychoanal. Assn.*, 28:89–114.

_____ (1984), Toward a reformulation of the theory of aggression and its implications for primary prevention. In: *Psychoanalysis: The Vital Issues*, ed. J. Gedo & G. Pollock. New York: International Universities Press, pp. 87–114.

_____ (1989a), Toward a reformulation of the psychoanalytic theory of aggression. In: *The Course of Life: Vol. 2. Early Childhood*, ed. S. I. Greenspan & G. H. Pollock. New York: International Universities Press, pp. 643–687.

_____ (1989b), Toward an epigenesis of aggression in early childhood. In: *The Course of Life: Vol. 2. Early Childhood* (2nd ed.), ed. S. I. Greenspan & G. H. Pollock. New York: International Universities Press, pp. 689–721.

_____ (1990a), On the girl's psychosexual development: Reconsiderations suggested from direct observation. *J. Amer. Psychoanal. Assn.*, 38:743–772.

_____ (in press), A view of the development of hostility in early life. *J. Amer. Psychoanal. Assn.*

_____ & Pollock, L. (1979), *The Child's Wish To Have a Baby, Parts I and II*. Audiovisual media section, Film #4 (a & b). Eastern Pennsylvania Psychiatric Institute (MCP), Philadelphia.

_____ , Pollock, L., Stern, J. & Kramer, S. (1976), On the girl's entry into the Oedipus complex. *J. Amer. Psychoanal. Assn.*, 24(5):79–107.

_____ & Saul, L. J. (1971), *Dependence in Man*. New York: International Universities Press.

———— , Scattergood, E., Singletary, W. & Duff, A. (1987), *Aggression in Our Children: Coping With It Constructively.* New York: Aronson.

Peller, L. (1965), Comments on libidinal organization and child development. *J. Amer. Psychoanal. Assn.,* 13:732–747.

Piaget, J. (1937), *La Construction due Reel chex L'Enfant.* Neuchatel: Delachaux et Niestle, 1963.

Roiphe, H. & Galenson, E. (1981), *Infantile Origins of the Sexual Identity.* New York: International Universities Press.

Sander, L. W. (1962), Issues in early mother–child interaction. *J. Amer. Acad. Child Adolesc. Psychiat.,* 1:141–166.

———— (1964), Adaptive Relationships in Early Mother-Child Interaction. *J. Amer. Acad. Child Adolesc. Psychiat.,* 3:231–264.

———— (1983), Polarity, paradox and the organizing process in development. In: *From Tears of Infant Psychiatry, Vol. 2,* ed. J. D. Call, E. Galenson & R. L. Tyson. New York: Basic Books, pp. 333–346.

———— , Stechler, G. & Burns, P. (1979), Change in infant and caregiver variables over the first two months of life. In: *Origins of the Infant's Social Responsiveness,* ed. E. Thomas. Hillsdale, NJ: Lawrence Erlbaum, pp. 349–407.

Schneirla, T. C. & Rosenblatt, J. S. (1961), Behavioral organization and genesis of the social bond in insects and mammals. *Amer. J. Orthopsychiat.,* 31:223–253.

Scott, J. P. (1963), The process of primary socialization in canine and human infants. Monographs of the Society for Research in Child Development, 28, No. 1.

Settlage, C., Afterman, J., Bemesderfer, S., Gassner, S., Hart, K. B., Larsen, C. S., Morrison, C., Rosenthal, J. & Spielman, P. M. (1985), The appeal cycle phenomenon in early mother–child interaction. Presented at the winter meeting of the American Psychoanalytic Association, New York City.

Shengold, L. (1988), *Halo in the Sky.* New York: Guilford Press.

Spitz, R. A. (1945), Hospitalism. An inquiry into the genesis of psychiatric conditions in early childhood. *The Psychoanalytic Study of the Child,* 1:53–74. New York: International Universities Press.

———— (1946a), Anaclitic depression: An inquiry into the genesis of psychiatric conditions in early childhood. *The Psychoanalytic Study of the Child,* 2:313–342. New York: International Universities Press.

———— (1946b), The smiling response: A contribution to the ontogenesis of social relations. *Genetic Psychol. Monogr.,* 34:57–125.

———— (1965), *The First Year of Life.* New York: International Universities Press.

Stern, D. (1985), *The Interpersonal World of the Infant.* New York: Basic Books.

Stoller, R. J. (1968), *Sex and Gender.* New York: Science House.

———— (1976), Primary femininity. *J. Amer. Psychoanal. Assn.,* 24(5):39–79.

Waelder, R. (1962), Review of *Psychoanalysis, Scientific Method, and Philosophy,* ed. S. Hook. *J. Amer. Psychoanal. Assn.,* 10:617–637.

Winnicott, D. W. (1950), Aggression in relation to emotional development. In: *Collected Papers.* New York: Basic Books, 1975, pp. 204–218.

Wolff, P. (1960), The development psychologies of Jean Piaget and psychoanalysis. *Psychological Issues,* Monogr. 5. New York: International Universities Press.

———— (1966), The causes, controls, and organization of behavior in the neonate. *Psychological Issues,* Monogr. 17. New York: International Universities Press.

Zeanah, C. H., Anders, T. F., Seifer, R. & Stern, D. (1989), Implications of research on infant development for psychodynamic theory and practice. *J. Amer. Acad. Child Adolesc. Psychiat., 28:657–668.*

2

Mahler and Winnicott
Some Parallels
in Their Lives and Work

Thomas Wolman

At first glance, Margaret Mahler and Donald Winnicott seem unlikely subjects of comparative study, given their obvious differences of sex, language, culture, and ethnicity. However, two recent biographical sources (Stepansky, 1988; Phillips, 1988) reveal a number of striking coincidences in their life histories: They were born within a year of each other, 1896 to 1897, and grew up in provincial towns. Their early lives were much influenced by their fathers, who held the local public offices of health official and mayor, respectively. With their fathers' backing, they both decided to enter medicine, then a rather nonconformist vocation. Subsequently, they went on to specialize in the pioneering field of pediatrics, capitalizing on their gift for working with children and their passionate interest in the early mother–child relationship, despite being childless themselves. It was this interest, in part, that motivated them to seek out psychoanalysis and the unique opportunity to correlate its new findings with child observation. This fateful conjunction set them on parallel paths toward major contributions in the areas of preoedipal development, maternal psychology, and psychosis.

The parallels also extend to certain aspects of their unconscious dynamics. By their own admission, they were driven by the psychology of the exception (Freud, 1916) and possibly by the fantasy of being an only child. In her memoirs Mahler writes, "I arrived in Vienna convinced of my own specialness and, at my initial interview, I fantasized that I would also have a 'favorite child' relationship with my analyst, Mrs. Deutsch [Helene Deutsch] (p. 59) (Stepansky, 1988, p. 59). She goes on to say, "I came to Mrs. Deutsch convinced that I was, and ought to be, an 'exception' " (p. 59). Winnicott (1945) states his claim for exceptional status in the following revealing quotation:

> I shall not first give an historical survey and show the development of my ideas from the theories of others, because my mind does not work that way. What happens is that I gather this and that, here and there, settle down to clinical experience, form my own theories, and then, last of all, interest myself to see where I stole what. Perhaps this is as good a method as any [p. 145].

In part, Mahler's and Winnicott's special status arose from their membership in the very small club of pediatricians trained in psychoanalysis at that time (which also included René Spitz). The analytic community relied on these special people to confirm psychoanalytic hypotheses about child development and to provide a referral base of patients for child psychoanalysis (Stepansky, 1988). Their earliest observations of sick children confirmed the onset of psychopathology in infancy and the importance of the mother in the first year of life (Winnicott, 1962a).

Perhaps it was this connection between disturbances in infancy and severe psychopathology that led Mahler and Winnicott to an interest in the psychoses. Such an interest, of course, furthered their special status, since psychosis was then at the frontier of the "widening scope of psychoanalysis" (Stone, 1954). Mahler did pioneering work with psychotic children; Winnicott devoted himself to the treatment of borderline and psychotic adults. These experiences helped to focus their attention on the problem of human identity, a theme that was to become central to their work. As Mahler put it, "For me, rather, the general problem of identity, and especially the way in which one arrives at a sense of self, has always been primary" (Stepansky, 1988, p. 36).

I believe this interest in the problem of identity derives, in part, from anxiety over their own status as exceptions. Mahler and Winnicott were always struggling to assert their independence. Winnicott's biographers (Davis and Wallbridge, 1981) note that Winnicott could not abide any sort of compliance because of the "trace of defiance in his own nature which led his colleagues to think of him at times as an 'enfant terrible' " (p. 6). Mahler also must have thought of herself at times as an enfant terrible through identification with her first analyst, August Aichorn, a notorious maverick. One of her early papers is, in fact, entitled "The 'Enfants Terribles' " (Mahler, 1949). Neither she nor Winnicott could play the role of a follower, and they both kept their distance from the titans of psychoanalysis, Anna Freud and Melanie Klein.

In her memoirs Mahler (Stepansky, 1988) describes the tension of being an insider and an outsider simultaneously. This precarious posture is best exemplified by Mahler's and Winnicott's positions within the psychoanalytic movement. As early as her gymnasium years Mahler was introduced to Michael and Enid Balint. Her sense of belonging to the Budapest circle contrasted with her feeling of estrangement from the Vienna circle, which included Anna Freud and Helene Deutsch. (Michael Balint later became a member of the British Middle group, to which Winnicott belonged.) A biographer (Rodman, 1987) notes that "as a member of the British Middle group, he [Winnicott] stood apart from the clusters around Melanie Klein and Anna Freud, lending heart to those of a similarly independent bent and, at the same time, forming a tenuous bridge between the two rival factions" (p. xiii).

To keep this bridge in good repair, Mahler and Winnicott felt the need to periodically reassert their allegiance to psychoanalytic tradition. Thus, Mahler felt obliged to state, "Indeed the intrapsychic is the main thing, but as I have undertaken to show over a lifetime of research and writing, the intrapsychic only evolves out of the differentiation from the initially undifferentiated matrix of mother and child" (Stepansky, 1988, p. 16). Similarly, Winnicott (Rodman, 1987) "shuddered lest [his] work should be taken as a weighing on the environmental side on the scales of the argument" although he held the view that "psychoanalysis can afford now to give full importance to external factors . . ." (p. xxx). Out of the same need periodically to reassert their allegiance to psychoanalytic tradition, Mahler and Winnicott sometimes sought to distance themselves from the work of Melanie Klein, despite the compatibility of several of her ideas with their own.

I wonder how these two highly creative individuals would react to being lumped together? Might they have actually met?[1] I imagine such a

---

[1]From the existing evidence I must conclude that Mahler and Winnicott never met. I have found no references to a meeting in their published papers and letters. And neither Selma Kramer, who was intimately acquainted with Dr. Mahler, nor Kenneth H. Gordon, who knew both Mahler and Winnicott, remember any reference to a meeting. I believe that a meeting, if confirmed by future historians, would be more than coincidental. There were, after all, many mutual friends and colleagues (Benjamin Spock and Phyllis Greenacre come to mind) who could easily have made introductions. It is almost as though Mahler and Winnicott were content to keep missing each other. Perhaps this was their "optimal distance" from each other.

hypothetical encounter as bristly and contentious, each theorist tending to focus on differences rather than on similarities. At best, they might acknowledge the parallelism in their lives and work but never the equivalence. Consider, for example, the two root metaphors that guided their work and defined their separate positions: symbiosis and the holding environment.

Winnicott (1956) had trouble with the word *symbiosis*. In the first place, he felt it was too heavily associated with the biological notion of physical interdependence. And in the second place, he thought that symbiosis implied a too great reciprocity in the early mother–child relationship. For example, he said it is wrong to equate the mother's identification with her infant and the infant's dependence on the mother (p. 300–301).

Almost as if she were responding to this criticism, Mahler (1975) stated, "The infant's need for the mother is absolute; the mother's need for the infant is relative" (p. 44). She initially intended symbiosis as a metaphor for the *child's* imagined fusion with the mother. However, in her later writings, Mahler (1975) tended to stress the interactional aspects of symbiosis, almost as if she found something unconsciously congenial in its imagery. In Mahler's words:

> This depends on a certain matching of the discharge patterns of the mother and the young infant, and later on their interactional patterns, behaviorally discernible in mutual cueing, as well as in the infant's earliest adaptive patterning and in his receptive capacities with the "good enough" holding behavior of his symbiotic mother (Winnicott, 1956). [p. 49].

In essence, Mahler is describing a kind of dialogue. She is saying that mutuality is present from the start, first in the "matching" between mother and baby and later in their "mutual cueing." She implies that mother and infant are actively influencing each other almost from the beginning.

Winnicott (1958) would no doubt acknowledge this aspect of the "good enough" holding behavior of the symbiotic mother. However, the word *holding*, as he uses it, is more akin to the function of a jar that holds water. The mother "holds" the child so that "impingements" that interfere with his "continuity of being" are kept to a minimum. She performs this function silently, unobtrusively, and without the child's knowledge. Even when the child is old enough to "contribute-in" to the relationship, the mother continues to act as silent partner in ways the child can not appreciate or know about. Her presence, for example, "even if represented for the moment by a cot or a pram or the general atmosphere of the immediate environment," facilitates the toddler's ability to be alone

(p. 30). Yet if she draws attention to herself in what is tantamount to a demand for communication, she will upset the delicate balance that enables "the infant . . . to become unintegrated, to flounder, to be in a state in which there is no orientation, to be able to exist for a time without being either a reactor to an external impingement or an active person with a direction of interest or movement" (p. 34).

Reading Mahler and Winnicott in parallel, it almost seems as though they are carrying on a lively conversation, each one vigorously defending a point of view. Note that the root meaning of the word *rapprochement* (derived from the French *rapprocher*) suggests a drawing together from a distance. I suspect that Mahler and Winnicott might feel their work is strengthened by the unexpected areas of confluence as well as by the sharp contrasts that help set them apart. In the balance of this chapter I try to continue this imaginary dialogue between Mahler and Winnicott. Specifically, I explore five areas of rapprochement between them under the following headings: Starting Point, Psychic Defense, Illusion–Disillusion, Visual Modality, and Symbolization. (I omit discussion of those areas of their work that are not overlapping.) In closing, I summarize the main points of contact and draw some conclusions about their developmental schemata as a whole; the chapter ends with a brief note on technique.

THE STARTING POINT: THE MOTHER–CHILD DYAD

Mahler and Winnicott treat the mother and her infant as a twosome from the start. For Mahler, this initial state is a necessary extension of intrauterine life. She affirms the primacy of the mother–child dyad, dubbing it "a kind of social symbiosis" in which "the rudimentary ego in the newborn baby and the young infant has to be complemented by the emotional rapport of the mother's nursing care . . ." (1975, p. 45). Or as Winnicott (1960a) put it, "The infant and the maternal care together form a unit" (p. 39).

Mahler and Winnicott take pains to always view the infant as part of a system. This is especially necessary at the beginning of life. Each posits, given the provision of adequate maternal care, an "inherited potential that includes a tendency towards growth and development" (Winnicott, 1960a, b). (Winnicott, 1960). And each postulates that the infant is initially unaware of the existence of the mother. In Mahler's (1975) autistic phase the infant is preoccupied with bodily experience derived from the proprioceptive–enteroceptive core. Winnicott (1960) uses the term "unintegration" in a similar vein, namely, to cover the related states of primary process, primary identification, autoerotism, and primary narcissism. In his view, "cohesion of the various sensori-motor elements belongs to the fact that the mother holds the infant, sometimes physically, and all the time figuratively" (p. 145).

The earliest stage of life presupposes a condition of psychosomatic unity. This means that at the beginning of human life there is no distinction between psychological and physiological processes. Mahler (1975) calls the earliest processes "somatopsychic," a term that implies that "physiological rather than psychological processes are dominant", and says that "the function of this period is best seen in physiological terms" (p. 41). Winnicott (1949) describes the initial continuity between psyche and soma as a partnership. The later psyche will evolve from the "imaginative elaboration of somatic parts, feelings, and functions, that is, of physical aliveness" (p. 244). Yet Winnicott sees the drives as potential disrupters of psychosomatic unity (Winnicott, 1960b), placing him at variance with Mahler as well as with Freud, who located them at the border between psyche and soma.[2] To the infant, however, they are, according to Winnicott, as external as a "clap of thunder" and can only be ego-strengthening when "gathered into the service of the ego by good enough mothering" (p. 41).

At this stage the physical factor in mothering is preeminent: babies have to be held physically before they can be held "figuratively." Mahler (1975) was deeply impressed with the importance of "contact perceptual experience of the total body surface" (p. 45). She reminds us "what an important longing many fairly normal adults preserve for holding and for being held, for hugging and for being hugged" (p. 45). Holding allows the mother to manage the infant's physical environment. The mother protects her infant "against extremes of stimulation" (Mahler, Pine, and Bergman, 1975, p. 41) and from "physiological insult" (Winnicott, 1960a) "by taking account of the infant's skin sensitivity, sensitivity to falling (action of gravity) and of the infant's lack of knowledge of the existence of anything other than the self" (Winnicott, 1960a, p. 48). These maternal activities, in effect, create a stimulus barrier around the child.

Holding also gathers all these details of care into a routine that does not waver. It creates a climate of consistency and predictability between mother and infant. The "good enough" mother is reliable, predictable, and physically present (Winnicott, 1962a) but not mechanically so. According to Winnicott (1960b), she must be emotionally available and, hence, guided by "an interplay of mutual cues and of empathy" (p. 48). She holds the infant not just in her arms but also in her sight and with her

---

[2]For a related perspective on drive theory, see Kohut (1971, 1977).

voice (Mahler, 1975) and in her mind. Mahler (1975) concurs with Winnicott that "the mothering partner's 'holding behavior,' her 'primary maternal preoccupation' in Winnicott's sense (1958), is the symbiotic organizer—the midwife of individuation, of psychological birth" (p. 47). And, we could add, "the midwife of object constancy." Of this Mahler (1975) wrote that "the establishment of affective (emotional) object constancy (Hartmann, 1952) depends upon the gradual internalization of a constant, positively cathected, inner image of the mother" (p. 109).

Winnicott (1960a) refers to the mother's holding behavior as the environmental provision prior to the concept of "living-with" or, in short hand, the environmental mother. At the stage of relative dependence, when "living-with" is a reality, the environmental mother survives as a particular use of the object. She continues to stage-manage the emotional climate around her child without his knowing much about it. At later stages of development, Winnicott (1958) writes, the child still needs the environmental mother to be "alive and available (available physically and in the sense of not being preoccupied with something else), to be herself, to remain empathic, to be there to receive the spontaneous gesture, and to be pleased" (p. 75).

Mahler's work confirms the importance of the mother's physical and emotional availability throughout the separation–individuation period. The mother must constantly readapt her involvement to her child's new level of development. Thus, in the early practicing subphase (1975) her task changes from that of physical holding to that of anchor or "home base" for "emotional refueling" (Mahler, 1975, p. 69). Mahler describes this shift as follows: "She [the mother] has to be availably present when the infant turns towards her. She must be there just when the child needs her to be there, even if there are periods when the child is unaware of her" (p. 69). This statement exactly captures the unobtrusive presence of Winnicott's "environmental mother." The mother's quiet availability is also crucial during the rapprochement subphase, when it aids identificatory processes and ego capacities like thinking and reality testing (Mahler et al., 1975).

During the rapprochement crisis the mother is called upon to bear the strain of being pushed away by her child, just when he is demanding all her attention. The oscillation between "shadowing" and "darting away" can be maddening (Mahler et al., 1975). One of the mothers Mahler studied verbalized her annoyance toward her child as follows: "A moment ago, you did not want to be with me. Well now I don't want to be with you" (Mahler et al., 1975, p. 96). Winnicott defines the mother's task as learning how to survive her child's attacks. She survives by maintaining her consistency and by not retaliating against her child's aggressive behavior.

To accomplish this, she must acknowledge and work through her own hate so she can continue to love her child. Success in this task will enhance her child's reality testing (Winnicott, 1971).

Mahler and Winnicott were both well aware of the demands of this task on the mother. Winnicott (1951) was amazed at the energy, selflessness, and tenacity of the ordinary devoted mother. He saw that "success in infant care depends on the fact of devotion, not on cleverness or intellectual enlightenment" (p. 238). Nor did it depend on perfect adaptation to need, since that "is tantamount to magic, and inhibits the capacity to separate" (p. 238). Yet Winnicott's "good enough mother" did need a strong capacity to absorb her infant's assaults without deviating, withdrawing, or retaliating. In Mahler's (1966) words, the mother had to "tolerate his [her child's] protest over her withholding of her omnipotence, his increased coercion and shadowing, hostile dependency and ambivalence, increased wooing, grief and sadness" (p. 70). Quite a tall order. Mahler (1971) added that in many families the father intervenes in the separation–individuation struggle as a "protector from the by then, in so many cases, contaminated (Kris, 1954) potentially overwhelming "mother of separation" (p. 182).

But if Mahler and Winnicott are united on the importance of the mother's presence, they differ in the stronger accent Mahler places on the word *presence*. For Mahler the word implies more than mere background, especially in the later subphases of the separation–individuation period. In early rapprochement, for instance, the role of the mother changes from that of "home base" to one of active participation, of sharing in the child's adventures (Mahler et al., 1975). And at a pivotal moment, "it is necessary that she (the mother) show her willingness to let go, by giving her child a 'gentle push'—an encouragement toward independence" (p. 79).

In Mahler's view, therefore, the mother plays an active role in determining her child's self that goes well beyond her role as facilitator. Even in the earliest phases of development, Mahler (Mahler et al., 1975) saw her shaping and molding her child's preferred body posture and activity level, creating, in effect, the child who "reflects her own unique and individual needs" (p. 60).

Mahler found that mothers vary considerably in their ability to facilitate different phases of their child's development. Her work underscored the psychopathology of everyday mothering. In the earliest phases a chief cause of disturbed symbiosis is the mother's unpredictability. During rapprochement some mothers "are not able to let go, and so become literally the shadowers of their child. Others are not emotionally available, so that the child is forced to woo them, a process that absorbs all his emotional energy needed for development" (Mahler et al., 1975, p. 80).

In general, Mahler found the mother's behavior determined by three variables: "1. The mother's personality structure. 2. The developmental process of her parental function (Benedek, 1959). 3. The mother's conscious, but partly unconscious fantasy regarding the individual child" (p. 202). In short, the mother appeared as much a "variable" as she was a "constant" in her child's development.

These findings led Mahler (1975) to question the constancy of Winnicott's "good enough mother" as to both her function and actual personality. Winnicott tended to assume that the ordinary mother's resources were usually adequate to her task. Mahler might have been addressing Winnicott directly when she wrote the following:

> We learned how much we had to expand and broaden the category of Winnicott's "ordinary devoted mother" (1957). We experienced also how unspecifiable—in terms of cause and effect—the influence of middle range variations of "ordinary devoted mothering" is in creating minor pathology in the child. In other words, the concept of "good enough" mothering (Winnicott, 1962) came under scrutiny [p. 202].

THE ORIGIN OF PSYCHIC DEFENSE AND EGO DISTORTION

Mahler and Winnicott observed signs of mental illness in very young children. Winnicott (1960b) ascribed these disturbances to a failure of the holding environment and of the "good enough mother" in particular: "The mother who is not good enough is not able to implement the infant's omnipotence, and so she repeatedly fails to meet the infant's gesture; instead she substitutes her own gesture which is to be given sense by the compliance of the infant" (p. 145). The key phrase "substitutes her own gesture" refers to a pattern of intrusive action. In Winnicott's language such an action constitutes an "impingement" or break in the child's continuity of being. By forcing the child to become aware of the mother's needs, impingements may precipitate a premature differentiation.

The mother's intrusive action leaves the child no alternative but to react; he may either comply with or reject the mother's action. His freedom of action, his nascent spontaneity, is severely restricted. Winnicott (1962a) says that "if reacting that is disruptive of going-on-being recurs persistently, it sets going a pattern of fragmentation of being" (p. 60). At the extreme, "disintegration is a sophisticated defense. It produces chaos, thus turning a passive experience into an active one, and one within the area of the baby's omnipotence" (p. 61).

Winnicott understood these early reactions as the prototypes of psychological defense. In a way they are like primitive reaction formations to the unthinkable anxieties of going to pieces, falling forever, having no relationship to the body, or having no orientation (Winnicott, 1962a, p. 38). Thinking, for example, is a reaction to the "unthinkable" and hence "a kind of organized defense against the break" (Winnicott, 1949, p. 246). Taken to its logical limit, this theory implies that the premature precipitation of a "mind," synonymous with mental structure, is defensive and potentially pathological. Such a mind imposes an artificial predictability that interferes with natural spontaneity, covering over a "gap" in the psyche. This premature mental activity forms the root of what Winnicott (1962a) calls the False Self. It is defined as a "specific defense of self-holding, or the development of a caretaker self and the organization of an aspect of the personality that is false (false in that what is showing is a derivative not of the individual but of the mothering aspect of the infant–mother coupling" (p. 58). The term *False Self* gathers together a collection of specific distortions of the ego, a collection that includes reaction formation, defense, disavowal, intellectualization, dissociation, prematurity, exaggeration, and self-holding. Martin James (1960), a colleague of Winnicott's, helped to place the concept within a more conventional psychoanalytic framework. James (1960) defines premature ego development as the taking over of the mother's function, in whole or in part, during the phase of primary narcissism.

Mahler (1967) accepted the idea of prematurity. She assumed that "the symbiotic partner—the auxiliary ego—is called upon to save the infant from the pressure of having to develop his own resources prematurely" (p. 85). At the extremes of her sample Mahler et al. (1975) found confirmation of Winnicott's original hypothesis in her own observations:

> With regularity, there was a tendency for infants to react to excessive intrusiveness on the mother's part with abnormal differentiation, including precocity. An active process of distancing would begin, with the literal pushing of the mother away (but the precocious maintenance of visual contact) [p. 60].

Mahler catalogued various types of pathological reaction assumed to be associated with the overburdened mother's unrecognized intrusiveness. One of the mothers studied seemed to require her child to stand erect on her lap, producing premature libidinization of this posture and creating an interference in development, that is, in the mastery of crawling. Another mother withdrew attention from her little girl because she was a late walker, causing her to play peekaboo with herself. Still another remained unaware of rocking her little girl in a tense, unrelated, mechanical way. This little girl "was forced to play mother to herself, because she could not rely on her partner to do the job" (Mahler et al., 1975, p. 59). The latter two children later developed the beginning of a False Self.

Interestingly, Mahler did not look on early defensive activity as necessarily abnormal. She found, for example, that most children tend to take over the mother's technique of management to a greater or lesser degree. And some children were able to transform the mother's direction into a creative "compromise formation." Mahler (Mahler et al., 1975) recounts a striking illustration of this in her example of the little boy who incorporated the mother's bouncing up-and-down pattern, which she had adapted to help wean him, into a peekaboo game used in socialization.

Mahler believed that "adaptation and defense have common roots" (Mahler and McDevitt, 1968, p. 102). The earliest behaviors can thus be viewed either from the perspective of adaptation or from that of defense. The phenomenon of "low-keyedness," for example, designates the child who is "struggling to maintain the inner condition that exists when mother is in the room with him" and who "must shut out affective and perceptual claims from other sources during her physical absence" (p. 107). From the side of defense, Mahler and McDevitt described this same phenomenon as a "narcissistic regressive phenomenon in the service of the development of the ego" (p. 107). During rapprochment, splitting between the bad mother of separation and the good mother of symbiosis as well as identification with the omnipotent mother, have both adaptive and defensive aims (Mahler et al., 1975).

A "crisis" in development (a term not found in Winnicott) signifies for Mahler an intensification of the defensive struggle that may result in either a healthy or a pathological outcome. The latter is likely for children when a "too sudden and too painful realization of their helplessness has resulted in a too sudden deflation of their previous sense of their own omnipotence, as well as of the shared magical omnipotence of the parents" (Mahler et al., 1975, p. 117). The pathological consequences include (1) a bad introject, with forces tending to eject it; (2) overwhelming aggression inundating the good-object representation, destabilizing it; (3) exaggerated ambivalence causing more permanent splitting of the object world; and (4) problems in the area of idealization and self-esteem regulation.

Winnicott (1960b) describes a third outcome in which a healthy resolution coexists with a dissociated area of psychopathology. In this case, a facade of normality hides an underlying withdrawal. Hence, the False Self is far more ubiquitous than one might think on the basis of superficial observation. Because it tends to be invisible, it often goes unnoticed, with serious consequences for the analysis of such patients.

ILLUSION–DISILLUSION

Mahler and Winnicott independently trace the normal developmental line of illusion–disillusion. On this point their theories describe a roughly equivalent sequence of events. Initially, "omnipotence is nearly a fact of experience" (Winnicott, 1951, p. 238). Later, the transitional object appears, when the mother is in transition from being "merged with the infant to that of being perceived rather than conceived of" (Winnicott, 1971, p. 115). This moment corresponds to Mahler's "hatching" or "differentiation," when the child is standing on the threshold, poised for the first step on the road to separation–individuation.

That step inevitably leads to the experience of disillusionment. For Mahler, the working through of disillusionment is a major task of the rapprochement subphase. In early rapprochement the child realizes that his wishes and those of the mother do not always coincide. Later, Mahler notes, "the child can no longer maintain his delusion of parental omnipotence" (Mahler et al., 1975, p. 79). Already able to differentiate self from object and realizing that his parents are separate objects with their own lives, "he must gradually and painfully give up the delusion of his own grandeur" (p. 79).

But if Mahler and Winnicott agree on the basic shape of the process, they disagree on its content. Winnicott (1951) views the experience of illusion–disillusion as normal and universal, and he would certainly object to Mahler's tendency to describe it in quasi-pathological terms. He views the initial omnipotence as a phase of normal illusion. "The mother's adaptation to the infant's needs," he writes, "when good enough, gives the infant the *illusion* that there is an external reality that corresponds to the infant's own capacity to create. In other words, there is an overlap between what the mother supplies and what the child might conceive of" (p. 239). According to Winnicott (1971), such an experience is necessary for the development of normal spontaneity, play, and creativity.

Winnicott uses the word *illusion* in contradistinction to Mahler's frequent use of the word *delusion*. In an important footnote (1951) to his original paper on the transitional object he writes the following:

I would prefer to retain the word fetish to describe the object that is employed on account of a delusion of a maternal phallus. I would then go further and say that we must keep a place for the illusion of a maternal phallus, that is to say, an idea that is universal and not pathological [p. 241].

Winnicott believed that the normal experience of illusion is paradoxical. In a classic statement (1951) he wrote that "of the transitional object it can be said that it is a matter of agreement between us and the baby that we will never ask the question 'Did you conceive of this or was it presented to you from without?' The important point is that no decision on this point is expected. The question is not to be formulated" (p. 239–240). In fact, Winnicott goes on to say, a premature decision on the question of reality or fantasy—in effect reducing the paradox to an either/or decision—is in itself pathological. It is this sort of "thinking" that culminates in a False Self.

Mahler's concept of rapprochement implies the paradox of coming together and separating at the same time. Mahler occasionally addresses this paradoxical quality, particularly in her exposition of the practicing subphase. She refers to Anthony (1971, p. 263), who writes of this phase that the child "can and cannot do without his mother" (Mahler et al., 1975, p. 72) and that the mother "can and cannot let him walk" (p. 72). Mahler was apparently very struck by Anthony's reference to a quotation by Kierkegaard describing the paradoxical quality of the child's first steps (Mahler et al, 1975, p. 72).

But frequently, in Winnicott's view, Mahler reduces the transitional phenomenon to a simple conflict between two wishes. For example, she says that "standing on the threshold would seem to be the perfect symbolization of conflicting wishes—the wish to enter the toddler world away from the mother and the pull to remain with mother in the infant room" (Mahler et al., 1975, p. 96). In one of her papers (Mahler and McDevitt, 1968), she states that "the precious transitional object and especially the fetishlike adherence to the night time bottle are indications that displacement of libido onto the transitional object are important both as a defense against reengulfment in symbiosis and as a facilitation toward individuation and therefore structuralization and adaptation." This prosaic definition of the transitional object is very "un-Winnicottian." Winnicott might have objected to the words *fetishlike adherence, defense,* and *displacement of libido*—all taken from the sphere of psychopathology.

But Mahler would point out that Winnicott's concept of illusion underestimates the role of primitive narcissism in normal development. During the practicing subphase, for example, "narcissism is at its peak" (Mahler et al, 1975, p. 71). There is little difference between the child's ego and his Ideal-ego. As Mahler et al. (1975) note, "It is as if the walking toddler has proved by his attainment of independent locomotion that he has already graduated into the world of independent human beings" (p. 74). Although not stated in so many words, Mahler is talking about a miniature manic episode that corresponds to her "low-keyedness," which she calls a "miniature anaclitic depression" (p. 74). These two expressions imply a rocky transition from illusion to disillusion that strains the boundaries of the "normal."

The laborious effort to preserve the internal image of the mother, characteristic of low-keyedness, implies the imminent possibility of object loss. "Low-keyedness may be an early precurser of mourning. In this case Mahler (1966) argues that object loss is usually not literal loss of the object but, rather, intrapsychic object loss. All children, to a greater or lesser degree, must mourn their illusion of symbiotic omnipotence. But they do not accomplish this without a struggle.

In a sense, the rapprochement crisis is the high water mark of this struggle against disillusionment (Mahler et al., 1975). At this stage children want "to have mother magically fulfill their wishes, without their having to recognize that help was actually coming from the outside" (p. 95). Some will even try to coerce the mother back into symbiosis with provocative gestures. Yet despite the passionate yearning to maintain the dual unity, the affects of sadness and anger begin to break through the facade of defensive restlessness and hyperactivity. Children will often use transitional objects specifically to deal with mother's absence in a fashion similar to the "linking objects" of adult mourning (Volkan, 1971). In girls, the discovery of anatomical sexual differences adds to their disillusionment, eliciting anger, sadness, and envy as well as attempts to deny the sexual difference (Mahler et al., 1975).

These struggles are almost entirely absent from Winnicott's conception of disillusionment. He portrays disillusionment as a gradual process that corresponds to the mother's graduated de-adaptation and that has no definitive end point. The process is essential, however, because "a too perfect adaptation to need, continued too long is tantamount to magic, and inhibits the capacity to separate" (Winnicott, 1951, p. 238). In this model the mother's graduated de-adaptation exactly matches the child's growing ability to deal with the mother's "failure."

Winnicott (1951) concedes a role for aggression in the process: "A measure of maternal frustration can actually aid the process of separation, since one has to be able to hate an object for it to be real" (p. 238). But note that a constructive aim underlies even this forthright statement on aggression. Throughout his references to guilt and mourning Winnicott tends to emphasize the "reparative" aspect. Thus, the rage of rapprochement is countered by the mother's "survival" of the attack and the child's "growing confidence that there will be opportunity for contributing-in" (Winnicott, 1963, p. 77).

According to Winnicott (1951), "It is assumed here that the task of reality-acceptance is never completed, that no human being is free from the strain of relating inner and outer reality, and that relief from this strain is provided by an intermediate area of experience which is not challenged (arts, religion, etc.)" (p. 240–241). But, again, he concludes on a positive note, leaving unresolved the question of what has been lost. Is there not a hint of paradise regained in his assertion that the transitional object is not mourned or forgotten but, rather, is diffused over the entire cultural field?

Indeed, this divergence on the relative importance of mourning affects the relationship of illusion to disillusion. Winnicott views the process as a complex development of illusion, Mahler of disillusion. Winnicott sees a gradual evolution of a capacity, Mahler a tumultuous and protracted struggle. Winnicott sees a lifelong continuum, Mahler a more self-limited process, culminating in a "crisis." Yet despite these differences, it is remarkable how close Winnicott and Mahler come on the issues of the transitional object, the paradoxical aspects of illusion, and the role of aggression in disillusionment.

THE VISUAL MODALITY

According to Mahler (Mahler et al., 1975), the early subphases of separation–individuation rely heavily on the visual modality. Differentiation is not possible until after the first libidinal shift from the enterosplanchnic to the peripheral receptors. This largely physical maturation lays the groundwork for the smiling response and later the focus on the mother's face. Mahler and her colleagues found that "the sight of the mother's face is necessary for the proper function of symbiosis" (p. 45). In the infant of six to seven months she observed a "peak of visual and tactile exploration of the face and body of the mother. This includes a fascination with objects associated with the mother like a brooch, pendant or pair of eyeglasses" (p. 54).

At about the same time, the child begins "a process of comparative scanning, of comparing mother's face with that of 'others', feature by feature. The same thing will be applied to her body and associated objects" (p. 55–56). Mahler summarizes this scanning mechanism the child uses as follows:

He then turns with more or less wonderment and apprehension to a
prolonged visual and tactile exploration and study of the faces and the gestalts
of others. He studies them from afar or at close range. He appears to be
comparing and checking the features of the stranger's face with his mother's
face, as well as with whatever inner image he may have of his mother (not
necessarily and not even predominantly visual). He also seems to check back
to his mother's gestalt, particularly to her face, in relation to other interesting
new experiences [p. 57].

As early as seven to eight months of age the visual pattern of "checking
back to mother" enables the child to maintain visual contact at a distance
(Mahler et al., 1975, p. 55). He soon learns how to gauge the distance
from his mother by keeping her in sight and also by "taking a sounding"
with his voice. Indeed, some children tolerate rather large distances from
their mothers because of their precocious visual recognition (Mahler et al.,
1975). However, with most children it is a question of finding the
"optimal distance" between forays into the world and returns to "home
base." With the onset of upright locomotion there is a dramatic change in
the plane of vision, enhancing visual orientation and permitting greater
distance from the mother (Mahler et al., 1975, p. 71). The "optimal
distance" must again be renegotiated during the wide oscillations of
rapprochement.

These changes reveal the capacity of mother and child to communicate
by signal. According to Winnicott (1960a), the mother "realizes that she
must allow him to give a signal, rather than have her divine his needs
through empathy" (p. 50). Doing so allows the child his first opportunity
of "contributing-in" to the dyad and hence of "gaining control of all the
good things that are going on" (p. 50). This change may be hard on the
mother, "because the shift from understanding based on empathy to that
based on understanding of cues and signals is subtle, and also because
children vacillate between one state and the other" (p. 51). There is
always the danger of continuing to do "all the right things at the right
moments," cutting off the "creative gesture, the cry, the protest, etc."
(p. 50).

Winnicott (1971) writes that "in individual emotional development the
precursor of the mirror is the mother's face" (p. 130). In other words,
"the mother is looking at the baby and what she looks like is related to
what she sees there" (p. 131). So "when the baby looks at the mother, he
sees himself" (p. 131). Mahler (1975) recognized the importance of these
mirror reactions in the establishment of the cohesive self and the body
schema. She saw them as the primary method of identity formation during

the symbiotic phase. The constant and mutual exchange of facial signals magnifies and reduplicates the self, amplifying normal narcissism (Mahler, 1967).[3]

Mahler also studied children's reactions to actual mirrors (Mahler et al., 1975). Her subjects learned to recognize themselves in the mirror at different ages, the average being about 16 months. The range of behaviors included excitement, a thoughtful relating of the body movements to those in the mirror, and deliberate movements aimed at sorting out the relationship between self and image. Mahler believed that early rapprochement children acted out these mirroring reactions in their social interactions through games of imitation, revealing a desire to have or do what other children had or did and anger when this goal was thwarted.

Mahler and Winnicott both observed pathological distortions of the mirroring relationship. In the extreme case the baby looks at the mother and sees nothing of himself; the mother's face is then not a mirror (Winnicott, 1971, p. 132). The result is that "perception takes the place of apperception" (p. 132); in short, the symbiotic dialogue simply does not develop. In less extreme cases "the baby will study the object intensively in the hope he may find something there" (p. 132). Some of these children become expert at reading the mother's mood in her face. Mahler might see in this phenomenon a variant of "customs inspection" (Mahler et al., 1975). She too confirmed the existence of children who are completely perplexed by the function of a mirror and who fail to react motorically to their own reflection (Mahler, 1975).[4]

The baby's relationship to the mother's face becomes an exchange of cues, gestures, and signals that constitute a spontaneous emotional dialogue. These gestures are meaningful in the sense that dance is meaningful; they help to "inhabit" the body and to personalize the sense of reality. Winnicott (1971) describes this dialogue as "a significant exchange with the world, a two way process in which self-enrichment alternates with the discovery of meaning in the world of seen things" (p. 132). Such dialogue, in effect, puts a "face" on the world, permitting contact with reality through what Winnicott calls "creative apperception" (p. 132).

---

[3]Here Winnicott and Mahler seem to have anticipated the work of Kohut (1971, 1977) on the mirroring transference.

[4]Greenacre (1953) may have been the first to draw attention to the connection between the visual modality and psychopathology. In a recent paper Mahony (1989) gives a nice review of the literature on this topic, citing Almansi's helpful contribution (1979).

VERBALIZATION AND SYMBOLIZATION AS A SEPARATE DEVELOPMENTAL LINE

Mahler and Winnicott draw a distinction between nonverbal interchange with the mother and later verbal communication. Winnicott (1960a) holds to the strict meaning of the word *infant* as one "who does not speak" (p. 40). "This implies," he says, "that communication at this stage operates by means of maternal empathy, and not through verbalization" (p. 40). The child's ability to say "Look, Mommy," "Hi," and "cookie" marks a significant turning point in Mahler's account of separation–individuation (Mahler et al., 1975, p. 94). Verbalization supplants the earlier gestural, mimetic communication in a relatively short time, according to Mahler. Henceforth, "further structuralization of the ego and the establishment of a cohesive self depend on the ability to find words for one's wishes" and "the ability to call the mother and command her attention" (p. 94).

Winnicott understood symbolic activity as a sophisticated derivative of the transitional object. Of the root of symbolism in time he wrote: "The use of an object symbolizes the union of two now separate things, baby and mother, *at the point in time and space of the initiation of their state of separateness.*" (Winnicott, 1971, p. 114). Subsequently, the transitional object evolves into symbolic play and later into religion, the arts, and other aspects of the cultural life of the adult (Winnicott, 1951).

Elsewhere Winnicott (1949) sees the origin of symbolic activity in the child's capacity for thought. During infancy "the mother tries not to introduce complications beyond which the infant can understand and allow for; in particular she tries to insulate her baby from coincidences and from other phenomena that must be beyond the infant's ability to comprehend. In a general way she keeps the world of the infant as simple as possible" (p. 245). However, the gradual emergence of the child's capacity to think allows him to "convert the mother's deficiencies and de-adaptations into growth through his understanding" (p. 245). By "understanding" Winnicott (1951) means to include all of the child's developing mental activity: "nascent time sense, auto-erotic activity, remembering, reliving, fantasying, dreaming, and integration of past, present, and future" (p. 238). The gradual rise of these symbolic activities matches the gradual decline in preverbal relational modes.

The two modalities come into sharpest relief in Mahler's (Mahler et al., 1975) vivid description of the rapprochement crisis. At that point, Mahler notes, the mother is "summoned by some magical gesture alone, rather than with words" (p. 95). She is used as "an extension of the self—a process in which the children somehow denied the painful awareness of separateness" (p. 95). Winnicott's (1960c) case example of a boy's use of string illustrates this same conflict. He interprets a boy's obsession with string as an attempt "to deny separation . . . as one would deny separation from a friend by using the telephone" (p. 126). At issue is the same resistance to verbalizing, of allowing oneself to be separated from the partner by a "string" of words.

Unlike the previous subphases of separation–individuation, the rapprochement crisis is resolved largely through verbal symbolic means. Mahler et al.'s (1975) analysis of this resolution recognizes three interrelated processes: (1) the development of language, especially the naming of objects, the capacity to put wishes into words, and the use of the pronoun "I"; (2) internalization of both the object and of verbal rules; (3) progress in the ability to use symbolic play to work through wishes, fantasy, and for mastery, etc." (p. 101).

In Mahler's view such activity lays the groundwork for the future development and resolution of the castration and oedipal complexes. Mahler and her colleagues (1975) proposed that inadequate resolution of the rapprochement crisis may contribute to the premature onset of the castration and oedipus complexes in little girls (p. 107). Moreover, these little girls exhibited a striking distortion in the use of words, which is symptomatic of a breakdown in symbolic activity (p. 107). In health, the verbal/symbolic channel advances to a new level with the oedipal crisis. Mahler and Kaplan (1977) call the oedipal crisis the "fourth psychological organizer." The oedipal complex represents for her "the acme not only of infantile psychosexual development, but also of object relations. It transforms the previous mainly external regulation of narcissism into internal self-esteem regulation by the superego" (p. 195). Most important, "its shape, resolution, and mode of dissolution can restructure earlier developmental events" (p. 195), a position with which Winnicott would probably agree.

Thus, the oedipal crisis alters irrevocably the future course of separation–individuation. Compare the distance created by a string of words with the earlier physical distance between mother and child. And compare symbolic play as a method of dealing with brief separation with the earlier more precarious focusing on the mother's image in "low-keyedness." These different mechanisms may imply the existence of two separate developmental lines. The overlap of both modalities during the rapprochement subphase would appear to support the idea that the verbal/symbolic line parallels the nonverbal line for a brief period before succeeding it.

DISCUSSION: CONTRASTING PERSPECTIVES

Mahler and Winnicott concur on the main areas of rapprochement, on the importance of the earliest environmental provision, on psychosomatic partnership, on the ongoing presence and involvement of the mother, and on the relationship of gross disturbances in "holding" to early distortions of the ego. Within a shared focus on the mother–child dyad, they diverge slightly on the quality of the mother's participation and on the universality of the child's adaptation to the mother's defenses. Each attributes a special quality to the child's experience in the dyad, describing it in words like "illusion", "delusion", and "omnipotence". Both envision a period of disillusionment on the way to independence, which is facilitated by the child's burgeoning symbolic activity.

The main issue over which we find them at odds is the legitimacy of working backward from psychopathology to normal phenomena. This conflict resembles a similar disagreement between Winnicott and Melanie Klein. Winnicott (1962c) championed Klein's work in the 1930s as a major contribution but gradually grew dismayed with what he perceived as an ideological rigidity in the Kleinian approach. In particular, he could not accept the wholesale equating of early developmental phases to adult psychopathological states. Thus, while accepting the validity of Klein's "depressive position," he tended to stress its status as an "achievement" implying a good deal of ego integration and ability to take responsibility for one's destructive drives (p. 176). This was not possible, according to Winnicott, until about eight months of age "or possibly much later still" (p. 176).

Melanie Klein's views must also have been a source of considerable conflict for Mahler. She rarely, if ever, refers to Klein's writings—an odd omission for one so versed in the psychoanalytic literature. In her memoirs Mahler acknowledges having met Klein but gives no opinion of her work or personality (Stepansky, 1988). Again, a strange omission when measured against her frankness concerning other analysts. Perhaps she was avoiding any suggestion of an identification with Melanie Klein. If so, she must have closed her eyes to the Kleinian cast of her own exposition of the rapprochement subphase, with its depressive affect, conflicts over aggressive drives, tendency toward "splitting," profound mourning for omnipotence, integration of the good and the bad object, and resolution through symbolic activities.

Nevertheless, Mahler's ambivalence toward Melanie Klein prompts her to stake out exactly the same middle ground Winnicott occupies:

At one extreme stand those who believe in innate complex oedipal fantasies—those who, like Melanie Klein and her followers, impute to earliest extrauterine human mental life a quasi-phylogenetic memory, an inborn symbolic process (Mahler, 1969; Furer, quoted by Glenn, 1966). At the other end of the spectrum stand those Freudian analysts who look with favor on stringent verbal and reconstructive evidence—organized on the basis of Freud's metapsychological constructs—yet who seem to accord preverbal material little right to serve as the basis for even the most cautious and tentative extension of our main body of hypotheses. . . . We believe that there is a broad middle ground among analysts who, with caution, are ready to explore the contributions to theory that can come from inferences regarding the preverbal period [Mahler et al., 1975, p. 14].

Basically, Mahler and Winnicott remain divided less on specific issues than on matters of accent, style, and perspective. Even where they agree in substance, I can imagine each of them reacting to the very different "feel" of the other's thinking; each covers the middle ground in a highly individualized way. Winnicott, as noted, is an intuitive, nonsystematic thinker who reinvents everything in his own language. Mahler, on the other hand, is a methodical, integrative thinker who incorporates much of the relevant psychoanalytic literature into her conceptual framework.

Implicit in their work are two very different versions of the "exceptional child." Winnicott's "exceptional child" is always in the process of becoming; it is a child in embryo, so to speak. This idea is suggested in a letter to Melanie Klein dated 17 November 1952: "One felt that if he were growing a daffodil he would think that he was making the daffodil out of a bulb instead of enabling the bulb to develop into a daffodil by good enough nurture" (Rodman, 1987, p. 35). The motto here is "Do not tamper with a natural process."

In contrast to Winnicott's child in embryo, Mahler's "exceptional child" is, I believe, a child *in statu nascendi*, struggling to be born. Birth is more than a natural unfolding, since it involves a wrenching labor for both mother and child. Likewise, psychological separation requires some pushing and pulling, as well as "good enough" nurture. Far from being inevitable, separation–individuation is the result of dynamic forces in vigorous conflict—even when the emotional climate is optimal.

Winnicott's child-as-embryo concept involves the matching of environmental provision with an emerging ego capacity. For example, the mother's unobtrusive presence matches the child's capacity to be alone; the mother's willingness to meet the child's gesture matches the child's capacity for "contributing-in"; and the mother's survival of the child's aggressive attacks matches the child's capacity to use an object. Statements like "Integration matches holding," "Personalization matches with handling," and "Object-relating matches with object-presenting" indicate an even more global matching (Winnicott, 1962a, p. 60).

The importance Winnicott attributes to capacities has been noted by many colleagues. A recent biographer of Winnicott (Phillips, 1988) has written that "he tends, throughout his work, to write of capacities rather than positions or stages. The emphasis on capacity in his work allows for individual differences. 'Capacity', with its implication of stored possibility, and its combination of the receptive and the generative, blurs the boundary between activity and passivity" (p. 58).

In contrast to Winnicott's concept of matching, Mahler's developmental model stresses the mutual molding of mother and child in the act of giving birth. Mahler et al. (1975) observed a "molding pattern" in the earliest months of life that tended to be specific for the mother–child dyad. These patterns were given desriptive names based on what they felt like in the arms of the observers: "molding well," "melting," "boardlike-stiff," "sack of potatoes" (p. 61). In Mahler's view, mother and child continue to influence each other throughout the separation–individuation period. Hence, Mahler would regard the achievement of walking, for example, as a product of interaction: a "gentle push" and the first step away from mother. Winnicott, on the other hand, conceives of walking as a natural unfolding (Rodman, 1987): "We cannot even teach them to walk, but their innate tendency to walk at a certain age needs us as supporting figures" (p. 186).

The matching and molding metaphors tend to capture somewhat different nuances of development. The matching metaphor stresses processes of de-adaptation, such as the mother's properly timed failure to respond assisting the child's intellectual development and his ability to view the object as external to self. The molding metaphor stresses a continual readaptation throughout the separation–individuation process. The molding viewpoint is more apt to distinguish synergy and noncoordination in the dyad. Mahler (1966) notes in this regard that "in some toddlers, a lag between their spurt in locomotor and autonomous ego functions and their emotional readiness to accept separation from the mother produces 'organismic panic' " (p. 61). She observed both delay and precocity in the onset of differentiation, the delay in some cases allowing time for the dyad to catch up (Mahler et al., 1975, p. 58–59).

I believe we should consider such a time lag when comparing the work of Mahler and Winnicott. Mahler must have been familiar with Winnicott's terminology in the early stages of her work whereas Winnicott learned of Mahler's views only after his were already formed. Terms like *unit-self, integration, differentiation,* and *separation* are obviously forerunners of *separation–individuation*. Hence, Winnicott's ideas (along with those of René Spitz) formed a conceptual baseline for Mahler's work. In retrospect, his oft quoted aphorisms sound like an introduction to her work. The relationship between Winnicott's earlier, "embryonic" theory and Mahler's later, more differentiated body of work suggests that Mahler gave birth to the baby that Winnicott helped to conceive. Such a fantasy grows out of the impression that Mahler and Winnicott were linked by a powerful transference, which in Mahler's case facilitated the creative flowering of her mature productivity.

A NOTE ON TECHNIQUE

It is hard to compare Mahler's and Winnicott's views on technique for the simple reason that Winnicott wrote a great deal on the subject whereas Mahler wrote comparatively little. I will therefore restrict myself to a few comments on the technical interface between them. Both writers took pains to correlate the course of adult analysis with the vicissitudes of early development and to show the persistence of archaic patterns. They were entirely agreed that separation–individuation problems are at the root of borderline and narcissistic psychopathology in adulthood. Mahler (1971) referred such conditions back to heightened body narcissism and "diffuse erogeneity of the body image" (p. 182). She stated that "in adulthood such patients will act out the role of an idealized body part of the parent" (p. 182). Mahler explained the "as-if" quality of her patient Charles in terms of compulsive narcissistic mirroring; Charles also needed to preserve an "inflexible optimal distance," since "he was incapable of being alone, yet was equally incapable of being 'a deux' " (p. 96).

Charles is a good example of what Winnicott (1960b) calls a "false personality." Winnicott felt that patients like Charles are not initially accessible to standard analytic technique:

> The analyst can only talk to the False Self of the patient about the true self. It is as if a nurse brings a child, and at first the analyst discusses the child's problem, and the child is not directly contacted. Analysis does not start until the nurse has left the child with the analyst, and the child has become able to remain alone with the analyst and has started to play [Winnicott, 1960b, p. 151].

Mahler appears to have treated her patient Charles with very few modifications of standard technique. Probably her only concession in this regard was a heightened sensitivity to the "optimal distance" in the transference (Bouvet, 1958). She was probably alerted to rapprochement conflicts in the transference by vacillations between intense intimacy and emotional distance (Mahler, 1975). The full analysis of the transference involved, in addition to oedipal material, the working through of rapprochement issues, along with the associated pathological defenses and narcissistic fantasies. Indeed, a pattern of imminent "rapprochement" between patient and analyst followed by withdrawal characterizes one type of negative therapeutic reaction. At these moments, Mahler may have experienced the same sort of countertransference she described so well in mothers of rapprochement-age children.

Mahler does tend to rediscover archaic material in her adult patients. She and Winnicott tend to emphasize separation–individuation issues in psychotherapy and psychoanalysis. Winnicott, especially, tends to define therapy and analysis as a sophisticated version of the early mother–child dyad. His whole technical theory, merely touched upon in this chapter, is based on this assumption. Thus, he will say that psychotherapy is "a complex derivative of the face" (Winnicott, 1971, p. 137) or of the child's play or of the environmental mother.

Yet, as if in reaction to this temptation, both Mahler and Winnicott go out of their way to reemphasize the verbal, reconstructive aspect of analysis. Winnicott (1960a), for example, distinguishes between traumas that can be "gathered within the sphere of omnipotence and ego control, achieving representations as projections of the psyche" (p. 37–38) and those that are "unrecoverable in the transference because the infant knew nothing about it, either in its good or in its ill effects" (p. 50). Thus, a healthy individual can respond to a stimulus without trauma "because the stimulus has a counterpart in the individual's psychic reality" (Winnicott, 1960b, p. 149).

In truth, neither Mahler nor Winnicott was able to fully integrate their discoveries with standard analytic technique. The unanswered technical questions raised by their work, concerning the limits of reconstruction, the role of acting out, the necessity of parameters, the special forms of countertransference, the possibility of compensation for environmental failure, have been taken up by their successors and will continue to challenge future generations of analysts.

REFERENCES

Almansi, R. (1979), Scopophilia and object loss. *Psychoanal. Quart., 48:601–619.*
Benedek, T. (1959), Parenthood as a developmental phase: A contribution to the libido theory. *J. Amer. Psychoanal. Assn., 7:389–417.*
Bouvet, M. (1958), Technical variations and the concept of distance. *Internat. J. Psycho-Anal., 39:211–221.*

Davis, M. & Wallbridge, D. (1981), *Boundary and Space: An Introduction to the Work of D. W. Winnicott.* New York: Brunner/Mazel.

Freud, S. (1916), Some Character types met with in psychoanalytic work. *Standard Edition*, 14:309–333. London: Hogarth Press, 1957.

———— (1926), Inhibitions, symptoms and anxiety. *Standard Edition*, 20:87–172. London: Hogarth Press, 1959.

Glenn, J. (1966), reporter, Panel on Melanie Klein. Meeting of the New York Psychoanalytic Society, May 25, 1965. *Psychoanal. Quart.*, 35:320–325.

Greenacre, P. (1953), Certain relationships between fetishism and the faulty development of the body image. *The Psychoanalytic Study of the Child*, 8:79–97. New York: International Universities Press.

Hartmann, H. (1952), The mutual influences in the development of the ego and id. *The Psychoanalytic Study of the Child*, 7:9–30. New York: International Universities Press.

James, M. (1960), Premature ego development: some observations on disturbances in the first three months of life. *Internat. J. Psychoanal.*, 41:288–294.

Kohut, H. (1971), *The Analysis of the Self.* New York: International Universities Press.

———— (1977), *The Restoration of the Self.* New York: International Universities Press.

Kris, E. (1954), reporter. Symposium on the widening scope of the indications for psychoanalysis. *The Psychoanalytic Study of the Child*, 9:16–71. New York: International Universities Press.

Mahler, M. (1949), Les "enfants terribles." In: *Searchlights on Delinquency*, ed. K. R. Eissler. New York: International Universities Press, pp. 77–90.

———— (1966), Notes on the development of basic moods: The depressive affect. In: *The Selected Papers of Margaret S. Mahler, Vol. 2.* New York: Aronson, 1979, pp. 59–77.

———— (1967), On human symbiosis and the vicissitudes of individuation. In: *The Selected Papers of Margaret S. Mahler, Vol. 2.* New York: Aronson, 1979, pp. 77–99.

———— & McDevitt, J. (1968), Observations on adaptation and defense in statu nascendi. In: *The Selected Papers of Margaret S. Mahler, Vol. 2.* New York: Aronson, 1979, pp. 99–119.

———— (1971), A study of the separation–individuation process and its possible application to borderline phenomena in the psychoanalytic situation. In: *The Selected Papers of Margaret S. Mahler, Vol. 2.* New York: Aronson, 1979, pp. 169–189.

———— (1975), On the current status of the infantile neurosis. In: *The Selected Papers of Margaret S. Mahler, Vol. 2.* New York: Aronson, 1979, pp. 189–195.

———— , Pine, F. & Bergman, A. (1975), *The Psychological Birth of the Human Infant.* New York: Basic Books.

———— & Kaplan, L. (1977), Developmental aspects in the assessment of narcissistic and so-called borderline personalities. In: *The Selected Papers of Margaret S. Mahler, Vol. 2.* New York: Aronson, 1979, pp. 195–211.

Mahony, P. J. (1989), Aspects of nonperverse scopophilia within an analysis. *J. Amer. Psychoanal. Assn.*, 37:365–401.

Phillips, A. (1988), *Winnicott*. Cambridge, MA: Harvard University Press.

Rodman, F. R., ed. (1987), *The Spontaneous Gesture: Selected Letters of D. W. Winnicott*. Cambridge, MA: Harvard University Press.

Stepansky, P., ed. (1988), *The Memoirs of Margaret S. Mahler*. New York: Free Press.

Stone, L. (1954), The widening scope of indications for psycho-analysis. *J. Amer. Psychoanal. Assn.*, 2:567–594.

Volkan, V. (1972), The linking objects of pathological mourning. *Arch. Gen. Psychiat.*, 27:215–221.

Winnicott, D. W. (1945), Primitive emotional development. In: *Through Paediatrics to Psycho-Analysis*. London: Hogarth Press, 1978, pp. 145–156.

———— (1949), Mind and its relation to the psycho-soma. In: *Through Paediatrics to Psycho-Analysis*. London: Hogarth Press, 1978, pp. 243–255.

———— (1951), Transitional objects and transitional phenomena. In: *Through Paediatrics to Psycho-Analysis*. London: Hogarth Press, 1978, pp. 229–243.

———— (1956), Primary maternal preoccupation In: *Through Paediatrics to Psycho-Analysis*. London: Hogarth Press, 1978, pp. 300–305.

———— (1958), The capacity to be alone. In: *The Maturational Processes and the Facilitating Environment*. New York: International Universities Press, 1965, pp. 29–37.

———— (1960a), The theory of the parent–infant relationship. In: *The Maturational Processes and the Facilitating Environment*. New York: International Universities Press, 1965, pp. 37–56.

———— (1960b), Ego distortion in terms of true and false self. In: *The Maturational Processes and the Facilitating Environment*. New York: International Universities Press, 1965, pp. 140–153.

———— (1960c), String: A technique of communication. In: *The Maturational Processes and the Facilitating Environment*. New York: International Universities Press, 1965, pp. 153–158.

———— (1962a), Ego integration in child development. In: *The Maturational Processes and the Facilitating Environment*. New York: International Universities Press, 1965, pp. 56–64.

———— (1962b). Providing for the child in health and crisis. In: *The Maturational Processes and the Facilitating Environment*. New York: International Universities Press, 1965, pp. 64–73.

———— (1962c), A personal view of the Kleinian contribution. In: *The Maturational Processes and the Facilitating Environment*. New York: International Universities Press, 1965, pp. 171–179.

———— (1963), The development of the capacity for concern. In: *The Maturational Processes and the Facilitating Environment*. New York: International Universities Press (1965), pp. 73–83.

———— (1971), *Playing and Reality*. New York: Penguin Books.

———— (1978), *Through Paediatrics to Psychoanalysis*. London: Hogarth Press.

3

Mahler, Kohut, and Classical Analysts
Theoretical and Clinical Considerations

Estelle Shane
Morton Shane

THE DEVELOPMENTAL ORIENTATION AND APPROACH

In this chapter we provide our own perspective on a developmental orientation as it is utilized in the clinical situation.

The developmental orientation had been formulated over a number of years (1971–1984) through the medium of COPER (Committee on Psychoanalytic Education and Research of the American Psychoanalytic Association) and post-COPER workshops under the personal influence and inspiration of Margaret Mahler. While we have modified and expanded our own version of this perspective, using self-psychological, object relations, and current infant observational formulations, we have never lost the essential spirit of the original vision. We believe that the heart of the developmental orientation has been and still remains, first, an abundant appreciation for the continuing, lifelong influence of the individual's experiences in infancy and early childhood in interaction with the caretaking surround, an appreciation informed not just by clinical reconstruction but by findings derived from the most subtle and sophisticated methods of direct observation and, second, a conviction that this focus on early childhood is balanced by the concept of development as a lifelong process. Thus, the developmental perspective that we present

61

here, despite its modifications of and expansions beyond the original developmental orientation and approach (Goodman, 1977), remains committed to this same twofold vision.

THEORY: A COMPARISON
OF MAHLER AND KOHUT

As we have stated elsewhere (Shane and Shane, 1989a), it is inevitable that psychoanalysts interested in developmental theory would seek correspondences between the work of Margaret Mahler and that of Heinz Kohut, the two authors many recognize as having most significantly influenced American psychoanalysis in this current, postclassical era of object relations and self-development. Their methodologies, of course, were significantly different: Mahler based her theory on systematic observation and careful documentation of the psychologically relevant behavior of infants and toddlers in interaction with their parents, while Kohut drew his from psychoanalytically derived reconstructions. Yet despite this difference in vantage point, congruencies in their investigative findings, as well as in their conceptual innovations, are to be expected, because both Kohut and Mahler began their respective inquiries with the same general frame of reference—that is, psychoanalytic—and because both stress the significance of the infant–caregiver unit in the earliest period of life. In fact, it seems that both Mahler and Kohut, at the beginning at least, had an expectation of these congruencies. Kohut, in response to a letter from Mahler asking about his view of how their respective works differed, responded that he saw himself and Mahler as "digging tunnels from different directions in the same area of the mountain" (Kohut, 1980, p. 477). It appears that Kohut had assumed earlier that the approaches of the observer of children and the reconstructor of childhood would generate findings that could meet or be integrated. But Kohut later changed his mind about the possibility of integration between them, not because of the differences in his and Mahler's methods of data gathering but because of differences that evolved in their respective schools of thought.

In this chapter we examine selected aspects of Mahler's developmental framework from the viewpoint of Kohut's conceptualizations, noting where the views overlap and where they part company.

For her conception of the autistic phase Mahler incorporates Freud's (1900) postulate of the extremely young infant living initially in solipsistic isolation and employing hallucinatory wish fulfillment to satisfy need. To remain consistent with this Freudian idea, Mahler introduces the concept of the delusion of fusion, a defense initiated by the infant as young as one to two months to protect against a state of unbearable separateness, thus inferring a capacity for defensive fantasy in the neonate (Mahler, Pine, and Bergman, 1975, p. 45). This would seem to conflict with the view emerging from current infant research that holds that this capacity only originates at the age of 18 months, when the child has achieved symbolic thought.

In contrast, Kohut did not posit a phase in which there is no psychological connection whatsoever to the outside world or to important others; rather, he postulated reconstructively, early in his articulation of self psychology, a primitive self–selfobject bond in the normal infant wherein the nuclear self experiences the other as a part of its self in an egocentric fashion, an idea closer to Mahler's concept of the symbiotic phase. However, by 1977 Kohut had departed entirely from such speculation regarding the presymbolic stage of development. He was only willing to postulate a "virtual self" in the young infant—that is, the self of the infant as envisioned in the mind of the parent—so that the congruence in his and Mahler's theories was weakened.

Current infant research strongly supports the importance to normal development of the close connectedness between the child and the primary caregiver from birth on, a belief consistent with both Mahler's concept of symbiosis and Kohut's concept of a selfobject merger; however, infant researchers criticize the view, implicit in both Mahler's and Kohut's theories, that the infant is perceptually unable to distinguish self from other. Rather, Stern (1985) considers the human being to be equipped at birth with predesigned emergent structures that prepare him to develop very early totally separate cognitive schemas of self and other. Lichtenberg (1983) adds that the theory of symbiosis is contested by the active role of the infant as behavioral initiator of interaction. And Emde (1988b) contends that the infant from the start of life is an active, affective, self-regulating social being.

Mahler points to a gradually increasing independence from the primary caregiver as a central goal for the normally developing child; she identifies an intrapsychic separation from the mother out of a symbiotic unity and the attainment of autonomy from the caretaking surround as the most important tasks of the first three years of life. Kohut conceptualizes the caregiver from the point of view of the self as supplying primitive selfobject functions, which, as maturation proceeds, are maintained increasingly by the self through the development of self-structure by means of transmuting internalization. There is a decreasing requirement for physical proximity to the primary selfobject caregiver as self-structure is consolidated and selfobject need becomes less peremptory. But the main function of this structure building is to permit a developmental progression from primitive to more mature selfobject need and need fulfillment, rather than the relinquishment of selfobject function, as the requirement for selfobjects remains throughout life.

Thus, while there is an apparent similarity between Kohut's concept of improved and consolidated self-structure by means of transmuting internalization and Mahler's concept of increasing autonomy from caregivers through ego development, there remains a difference between them. Kohut views the goal of autonomy from supporting caregivers, so significant to Mahler, as carrying with it a hidden moralistic stance, which self psychology, with its emphasis on the need for selfobject experiences throughout life, assiduously avoids. For Kohut, the issue of autonomy from supporting objects, recognized by mainstream analysis as the goal of normal development, is opposed by his own conception of the normality of lifelong dependence on selfobjects, thus resulting in an irreconcilable difference between his framework and that of classical analysis in general and between his and Mahler's viewpoints in particular, making integration between their developmental schemas, in Kohut's view, an impossibility. However, we believe that Kohut, by presenting an either/or alternative on this issue, exaggerated his own framework's distinction from Mahler's.

To begin with, for Mahler autonomy serves as an ideal that is never fully achieved, with the individual remaining forever in the open-ended subphase of separation–individuation termed "on the way to object constancy." Mahler describes the attainment of individuality, or self-constancy, as a lifelong task; autonomy, while of overriding importance in Mahler's developmental progression, is always seen to require support from the surround. This is not quite the same as Kohut's contention that the self requires selfobject functions throughout life: Mahler would postulate that while dependence on the environment remains throughout life, that dependency diminishes with age; Kohut would postulate that the dependency itself does not diminish but, rather, that the quality of the required selfobject tie and selfobject sustenance achieves a greater maturity. Yet the difference seems to us to be less significant than Kohut had assumed. Moreover, the either/or position itself is not supported by infant research, which suggests that the goal of normal development is most accurately described as the achievement of both autonomy and interdependence, not one or the other. As Emde (1988b) describes it, a developmental systems theory, such as Bowlby's, for example, speaks to the complementarity of the emergence over time of autonomy as well as connectedness. According to Emde, "An infant's emerging self reflects both, since security of attachment enables exploration and autonomy, while anxious attachment results in a sense of restriction and less autonomy" (p. 286).

We turn now to specific concepts arising out of particular subphases in the separation–individuation process in order to contrast them first with Kohut's formulations and then with current data from infant observation. During the subphases of differentiation and practicing, Mahler focuses on the "checking-back-to-mother" pattern, referring to this as a most important pattern in normal cognitive and emotional development. "Checking-back" is postulated by Mahler to be a defense against separation anxiety. Kohut, apparently using Mahler's observations to support his own thinking, views "checking-back" in the context of his own concepts of the mirroring selfobject and the grandiose self. He sees the pattern as the infant's attempt to achieve reassuring affirmation from the mother. The infant's developing capacity to become increasingly physically distant from the caregiver is viewed by Kohut not as the result of a diminution of anxiety because of increasing autonomy, as in Mahler's framework but, rather, as an indication of the progression from a primitive to a more mature selfobject tie. Hence, excessive stranger anxiety, seen by Mahler as a failure to acquire basic trust, becomes for Kohut (1984) an indication of self-fragility requiring "checking-back-to-mother" for a mirroring reaffirmation of the selfobject bond. This is a subtle difference. The greatest emphasis in self psychology is on the state of the self; in separation–individuation theory, however, the greatest emphasis is on trust in the new object relationship on the way to achievement of object constancy, with only a secondary focus on the integrity of the self. Yet, "refueling" and "perking up"—Mahler's phrases for the practicing subphase child's ability to use the mother as a means of reconstituting when the child feels threatened by new exploration—are quite similar to Kohut's concept of restoring the self through mirroring. Thus, in our view, self-cohesiveness and self-constancy, while based on different theoretical formulations, are nevertheless closely related concepts, indicating similarity between Kohut and Mahler.

Mahler's rapprochement subphase, characterized by the child's ambivalent and uneasy return to mother following a period characterized by confidence in turning away from her toward the larger environment, is widely accepted by clinicians, along with her description of rapprochement subphase resolution. Contained in these constructs are theoretical assumptions about an aggressive drive that create significant divergence between her views and Kohut's theoretical framework. While Mahler herself does not emphasize the innate aspect of the aggressive drive, Kohut chooses to distinguish himself from Mahler in particular and from classical analysis in general on this basis. Kohut points to the fact that the mainstream view of aggression as innately destructive does not fit with data derived from the clinical situation, thus committing himself instead to a view of aggression as reactive to frustration.

In conclusion, we would contend that the greatest difference between

Kohut and Mahler lies in their underlying theoretical frameworks, not in the particulars of their observations on the developing individual. We have followed closely the creative elaboration of these two psychoanalytic innovators; each has influenced as well as antagonized the other, and both have enriched the psychoanalytic world.

CASE ILLUSTRATION: THEORETICAL DISSONANCE AND A POSSIBLE DEVELOPMENTAL SOLUTION

We proceed by offering a clinical example serving not only to illustrate our own perspective incorporating modified separation–individuation and self psychology frameworks but also to convey our sense of the shortcomings of a too stringently conceptualized classical model that minimizes such frameworks. The experience with this patient suggests that a dimension of understanding of preoedipal development is necessary for individuals whose pathology is not centered on oedipal conflicts per se. Preoedipal processes must be understood as experiences of importance in their own right, over and above what influences they have on later development. We seek insights from modern infant observation, self psychology, and object relations theory, as well as from separation–individuation theory, in order to approach an understanding of early development gone awry, as illustrated in the following case material.

Two years ago a patient was referred to one of us (E. S.) by a colleague from the east coast, Dr. C. The patient, who was moving to Los Angeles, had been in analysis with Dr. C for five years and was quite close to termination. Nevertheless, Dr. C felt there would be some further work to do both in relation to separation from him and in relation to the termination process itself.

During the first several sessions with E. S., the patient, a 32-year-old defense attorney we will call Holly Stone, easily and with strong affect revealed both her life story and the essence of her previous analytic experience with Dr. C. Significant in her past were memories of her father abusing her both verbally and physically. In addition, she had suffered overhearing her parents in their loud sexual activities throughout her childhood and knew of her father's affairs with other women. Her mother was distant and passive, unable or unwilling to protect either herself or her daughter from the father's violent temper, and rebuffed her daughter on the one occasion that Holly could remember questioning her mother regarding the noise from within their bedroom. Ms. Stone grew up feeling that she was unloved and unlovable. She had difficulty enjoying sexuality and tended to select partners who were either inconsiderate or inconstant. In analysis she had come to understand her own contributions to the disturbing events she remembered from her childhood. She was impressed with Dr. C's interpretation that she had sought out her father's abusive attacks as a result of her sexual excitement, exacerbated by the reported primal scene experience and further by her sadomasochistic vision of her parents' lovemaking. She remembered masturbating as a child, and it was interpreted by Dr. C that she had done so to the accompaniment of fantasies of being sadistically attacked, although Ms. Stone could not herself recall this fantasy content; the only masturbation fantasy she *could* recall was a repeated and immensely disturbing one of falling into oblivion, a fantasy that continued throughout her adolescence and, despite her work with Dr. C, into the present. Though the fantasy was interpreted by Dr. C as defensive avoidance, it provided the first hint to her new analyst (E. S.) of a possibly different view of the patient's pathology; it seemed to represent more profound experiences of separation anxiety and annihilation anxiety. Ms. Stone told E. S. that she had found it reassuring but somehow not quite convincing to be told by Dr. C that her father, though seemingly brutal, had really loved her and was himself a helpless victim of her insistent provocation. While discussing with E. S. this masochistic-provocative-sadistic attack cycle postulated by Dr. C, Ms. Stone recalled a memory, which she had learned in her analysis to term a screen memory, wherein her father had accused her of not turning off the light switch and had slapped her across the face as a punishment for her oversight. In the subsequent interaction between father and daughter, Ms. Stone had stubbornly refused to admit to leaving the lights on, because she absolutely knew she had not done so, rebelling even despite her certain knowledge that her father would not stop punishing her until she confessed and asked for his forgiveness. Dr. C had shown Ms. Stone that she had gotten pleasure from this focused, albeit negative, attention from her father and had connected it to her unconscious oedipal fantasies. This core conflict uncovered in her analysis had been worked through in what had been understood to be an oedipal sadomasochistic transference characterized by conscious experiences of intense rage, aggression, and longings for physical closeness, worked through, that is, to the satisfaction of her analyst, and presumably herself, and were it not for the fact that she had opted to leave town to join another law firm, Ms. Stone maintained, she would have terminated with Dr. C in the near future, thus ending a successful analysis. When asked by E. S. how she was feeling at present, Ms. Stone said, somewhat ruefully, that she was still depressed, still had feelings of worthlessness and intense rage toward men, and in fact still—more often than she liked to acknowledge—had fantasies of committing suicide. When

E. S. expressed some surprise at these feelings and at the continuing suicidal ideation in conjunction with her plan to terminate and wondered how Dr. C had understood this situation, it was Ms. Stone's turn to be surprised. She recognized that she had not told these things to Dr. C because it was not what she imagined he wanted to hear—it would cause him unhappiness and he would like her less and become more distant. As it was, Ms. Stone knew Dr. C was proud of her for the psychological gains she had made, and she treasured that response, as well as the closeness that it engendered between them.

Thus it was that Ms. Stone, rather than winding down her previous analysis, found it necessary to embark on a new one, this time an analysis informed by and expanded through a developmental orientation (and this analysis is still in process). Now one might question whether it was the analyst's theory that had stood in the way of Ms. Stone's more fully resolving her difficulties. There are, as always, so many variables; after all, analysts differ in skill, in gender, in their match with a given patient, and in their countertransference proclivities and vulnerabilities, not to mention the fact that a patient may be at a different point in his or her psychological development when a second analysis is begun. Yet with all of that in mind, we remain convinced that Dr. C had difficulty with this patient at least partially because the reach of his theory did not adequately encompass the particular pathology that was troubling Ms. Stone. We believe that Dr. C fits into the category of analyst Lawrence Friedman (1988) describes as "reflectivist," a category that includes, he says, analysts like Schafer, Gray, and Brenner, for example. A reflectivist, according to Friedman, is an analyst who expects patients to *reflect* on their demands rather than to *insist* on them, to view their lives as of their own choosing, and, further, to see the life choices they made, right from the beginning, as informed by unconscious purposes. But, asks Friedman, in considering possible reasons for the attraction and popularity today of object relations theories, what if the transference neurosis does not follow the single script of the oedipal infantile neurosis? Furthermore, what if the patient does not view herself as the author of her own drama but as only a character in it, without the power to alter its lines? Moreover, what if the patient does not want to enter the *analyst's* world but demands instead that her *own* world be shared? In Ms. Stone's analysis with Dr. C, she was able, at least consciously, to enter into her analyst's world and accept his view that she was the author of her own early childhood experiences and that her neurotic conflicts were infused with her own unconscious purposes. She did this, it seems to us, because she needed at all costs to hang onto whatever her analyst was able to provide in the way of closeness, mirroring, holding, containment, affirmation, and approval, and she did it at the cost of not being free to express her authentic self in the analysis or to achieve a more stable individuation. She was willing unconsciously, and even to some degree consciously, to stifle and repress her dissatisfaction, despair, and (reactive) aggression in order to maintain the experience of having her analyst proud of her, a transference longing from childhood. This can be said now with some conviction; Ms. Stone has worked on these issues in her second analysis over the past two years.

It seems clear that Dr. C was informed by an overly restrictive classical theory, one not significantly expanded, broadened, or altered, at least insofar as Ms. Stone's report of his work with her is concerned, by any aspect of a developmental orientation such as we are describing here. Apparently Ms. Stone was viewed by Dr. C as having struggled in childhood exclusively with both sexual and aggressive drive derivatives, experienced as wishes toward her father, and with concomitant guilt over wresting her father's attention from her mother. The possibility that Ms. Stone's father was *really* brutally unresponsive to her childhood needs for understanding and protection and that her mother was *really* coldly distant and unresponsive to her developmental requirements, as well as unable to shelter her from the excessive and overstimulating intrusions she experienced from her parents' sexual activities and from her father's angry physical and emotional attacks, was apparently not given sufficient credence by Dr. C. From Ms. Stone's report at least, Dr. C seemed much more intent on showing her her own contributions, conscious and unconscious, to the intrapsychic representations of her parents that she had constructed over her lifetime and much less intent on her subjective perspective of the reality situation encountered in her childhood. In effect, then, when it came to Ms. Stone's reports of childhood memories of her parents, Dr. C accorded greater weight to her primary process thinking and its attendant reality distortions than to her secondary process thinking and its more or less veridical reflection of events.

At the beginning of this first analysis Ms. Stone did not readily accept Dr. C's version of her reality and, instead, raged against her analyst as unfeeling and as forcing his view upon her. But, Dr. C had a theory and, unfortunately, all theories tend to confirm themselves. That is, theories have built into them ways of either ignoring, dismissing, or explaining away responses that challenge their basic axioms; they therefore cannot be disproven in the clinical setting. This situation was certainly illustrated in Ms. Stone's first analysis (and, no doubt, could be illustrated in her second with E. S. as well). For example, Ms. Stone remembered the following dialogue between herself and Dr. C. She had told Dr. C about a memory that had made her feel proud of herself. She had on the occasion she remembered dared to protect her younger sister from her father's anger (just as, most likely, she had always wanted her mother to protect her). Her father responded by turning his anger onto Ms. Stone instead, striking her in his usual out-of-control fashion. Dr. C's response to Ms. Stone's vignette, which Ms. Stone had recounted to him with a conscious hope that her bravery and altruism would be recognized and admired by him, had been instead to point out that she had evidently *wanted* to provoke her father's attack and that her unconscious motive had been to satisfy her own masochistic wish. When Ms. Stone reacted with rage against Dr. C, feeling totally misunderstood and demeaned by him, Dr. C calmly pointed to her rage as a wish to provoke *him* into battle with her, which, he told her, she could then experience as a similarly satisfying sadistic attack. In effect, then, Dr. C was telling Ms. Stone that she was mad at him not because she thought him wrong but because she enjoyed the excitement of an aggressive exchange and the sense of being injured by the father in the transference. Ms. Stone remembered feeling intellectually pleased by the interpretive fit, seeing how the transference could come alive, and sharing her intellectual pleasure with Dr. C, which created in them both, apparently, a sense of comforting closeness, conviction (a confidence born of theory confirmed), and mutual admiration. And so it often went; and yet, in the background, as she came to discover in her second analysis with E. S., Ms. Stone was left with a nagging sense of having been betrayed by Dr. C, and by herself, for having so willingly capitulated in order to gain and maintain a sense of closeness to him and a sense of his approval.

In the second analysis, as we have indicated, a developmental orientation and approach were used. Of course, there was great benefit in knowing wherein Dr. C's work with Ms. Stone had been derailed and what her characterological response to such derailment was, namely, an almost unreflecting compliance with the analyst that was disguised as an intellectual engagement in the analytic venture. At first, then, Ms. Stone was listened to closely by E. S., with little interpretation offered, in order to avoid a premature imposition of some inference that the patient would most likely simply and compliantly agree to. Kohut, in the process of his discovery of what he had originally termed narcissistic transferences (1966, 1968, 1971) and later called selfobject transferences (1977, 1984), described such a method of psychoanalytic listening as a sustained empathic immersion in the subjective world of the patient, proclaiming this to be the most effective stance (a stance that Schwaber, 1981, 1984, has subsequently elaborated and extended). This is in contrast to the then more familiar classical stance expressed well by Greenson (1965, 1966) as listening with a naive, benevolent curiosity tempered by skepticism, a listening position we hypothesize had been used by Dr. C with this patient, with, perhaps, a greater emphasis on the skepticism. This latter perspective, employing a skeptical stance, is designed to pick up the unconscious latent meanings connected to all of the patient's productions whereas a focus on the naive and believing aspect of the benevolent curiosity instead of the skepticism, as accentuated by Kohut, is more likely to position the analyst within the patient's conscious subjective experience, closely attuned to the patient's fluctuating affect states (Socarides and Stolorow, 1984; Stolorow, Brandchaft, and Atwood, 1987). We certainly do not mean to pit one analytic stance against the other; both stances still have their important, and indeed indispensable, place in the spectrum of psychoanalytic listening, though we do think the analyst is more likely to get further, faster, with the majority of patients by tilting toward the naive believing, empathic immersion side of the spectrum.

The position the analyst most often chooses, whether to be skeptical or naive vis-à-vis the patient's reported experience, is no doubt informed at least in part by his or her philosophical vision of reality or view of man. This has been written about by Strenger (1989), who, following T. E. Hulme, has described a dichotomy in this philosophical perspective by arraying on one side those who hold a classical world view, that is, seeing man as intrinsically limited and requiring discipline and order to arrive at something fairly decent, as represented in the psychoanalysis field by Freud and Klein, and by arraying on the other side those who hold a romantic world view, seeing man as intrinsically good but spoiled by circumstance, as represented by Kohut and Winnicott. Strenger concludes that psychoanalysis is characterized by the tension to be found between these two viewpoints. The classic view of man distrusts the subjective and stresses the need to be objective and rational, a view that is reflected, he says, in an attitude of "benevolent suspicion." The romantic view sees man as "essentially striving for full selfhood" but thwarted in that pursuit by the environment. The difference between these points of view affects the clinical situation, including how one listens to and hears one's patient. Strenger warns that though embracing just one of these views may be an easier option for the analyst, "such a choice blinds us to the richness of the interplay between them" (pp. 608–609). Thus, Strenger too recommends a balanced view.

Let us continue our discussion of the analysis of Ms. Stone. Early in the analysis E. S. mainly confined herself to listening closely to her patient and making few interpretations. Ms. Stone responded by feeling protected, respected, and believed and came to view the analyst as wise, perspicacious and even as approaching an omnipotent perfection. For example, when she once heard E. S. discussed by a friend in the mental health field and described as "arrogant," Ms. Stone spent what seemed to be an inordinate amount of time in analysis defending her own view of the analyst. She apparently needed to experience E. S. unambivalently, as all-good and omniscient, and shunned the analyst's interpretation that she was defending herself against an opposite view. She held to this idealized vision of her analyst tenaciously, for it seemed to serve a necessary developmental function. She felt that her current analyst, in contrast to her parents and her former analyst, was in tune with her and was willing to see the world from her point of view. For the first time in her memory the patient felt safe, secure, and protectively enveloped, a state that Mahler (Mahler et al., 1975) has described as symbiotic closeness. In the ambience of this dyadic idealized maternal transference, Ms. Stone was able to give up the intermittent use of alcohol and tranquilizers, which had kept her contained in her first analysis and which was surreptitiously hidden from Dr. C, and to refrain from impulsive, promiscuous sexual engagements, which had been designed to avoid the anxiety she was suffering from being alone. Just recently she has been able to enter into a stable love relationship for the first time.

We can understand Ms. Stone's improvement in the analysis as at least in part the result of a development-enhancing new object experience (Shane and Shane, 1989b), for indeed it was a new experience for Ms. Stone to feel so closely listened to within a nonjudgmental analytic ambiance. Her mother had not acknowledged but instead had minimized the sense of danger the patient had felt from her father, as well as the threat she felt from the allergic reaction that had hospitalized her first at age six months and that continued to plague her throughout childhood, during which she repeatedly experienced abandonment and neglect. Ms. Stone had always been told that she was making things up, an experience that was apparently repeated in her first analysis through an actualization in the countertransference (Sandler, 1976). In contrast, she experienced E. S. as attending to and respectfully acknowledging her conscious and subjective perceptions of her mother and father. The suspicious and dismissive attitudes of her parents were interpreted by E. S. as constituting the beginnings of Ms. Stone's chronic self-doubt and as interferences with the unfolding of the process of individuation and selfhood.

Thus, in the main, the life narrative Ms. Stone arrived at in her first analysis was considerably altered by her work in her second analysis in the direction of seeing herself as having been traumatized by an insensitive and abusive father and by an ineffectual, distant, and inconsistent mother. It is interesting to note, in terms of the transference, that the strong idealization that began the analysis slowly evolved into a rapprochement-like ambivalence. This change resulted from the successful interpretation of the strong current of rage and disappointment stemming from the expectable disillusionments with her analyst, and from the strengthening of the patient's self and her ego functions, which enabled her to view her analyst in other ways and allowed her to move in other directions. In this context, Ms. Stone's tendency to split her ambivalence toward object representations into an all-good analyst (E. S.) and an all-bad analyst (Dr. C) was also interpreted to the patient (Mahler, 1971; Kernberg, 1984). Thus, Ms. Stone's earlier view of Dr. C as the attacking father, symbolically actualized in the transference (Modell, 1988), has been attenuated in the analysis with E. S. into a more balanced appreciation of the complexity inherent in this relationship too.

At present Ms. Stone, in the context of her own stable sexual love relationship, is contending with sexual urges toward her analyst and a new interest in her analyst's husband, with full bisexual oedipal ramifications. However, it is also apparent that the oedipal conflicts are heavily influenced by the effects of preoedipal events, including the effects of subphase inadequacies in the separation–individuation process. For example, Ms. Stone imagines that her analyst will abandon her abruptly and heartlessly should she reveal her sexual wishes toward her analyst's husband, a fantasy reminiscent of earlier fears of object loss. At the same time, Ms. Stone fears that her analyst's husband is jealous of his wife's closeness to her and that he will pull the analyst away from her precipitously, a fear that illustrates the same early separation anxieties. Ms. Stone's primal scene memories are now experienced by her in the transference on an oedipal level; nevertheless, the particularly agonizing form they take is conceptualized by the analyst and appreciated by the patient as the inevitable consequence of parental failure and abandonment during the oedipal phase and, especially, earlier. These oedipal level memories of primal scene dysphorias and conflicts are now understood, in contrast to the interpretations in the first analysis, less as masochistic maneuverings to encourage and provoke sexualized sadistic attacks that would gratify sexual and aggressive drive derivatives and more as the result of the parents' relative insensitivity to their child's phase-appropriate needs, fears, and vulnerabilities.

DISCUSSION

Our perspective as illustrated here is, in fact, an amalgam of several theoretical approaches to clinical psychoanalysis that we have adopted to form what we consider to be a coherent, internally consistent whole. We have developed this perspective in a series of papers outlining our own evolving and changing version of the bipolar/tripartite self (1980, 1982, 1985, 1986, 1988, 1989a, 1989b, 1990), a perspective designed to illustrate our continuing conviction that only by integrating Freud's Guilty Man with Kohut's Tragic Man can we "come to a closer approximation of reality, namely Protean Man" (Shane and Shane, 1988; see also, in another context, Lifton, 1971).

Crucial to these efforts has been the attempt to integrate Kohut and Mahler by reformulating their contributions in the light of infant observational research, as described earlier in this chapter. The previously presented clinical example serves to illustrate our developmental approach; in the discussion that follows we extend and elaborate the ramifications of the infant research we have already referred to (as well as additional infant research) in terms of its impact on our understanding of the clinical situation.

To begin with, infant research infers that the infant begins life not as an autistic being but firmly grounded in reality. The capacity to distort that reality for defensive and imaginative purposes becomes available to the child only with the advent of symbolic thinking, at age 18 months (see Stern, 1985, p. 255; 1989, pp. 53–54; see also Piaget, 1951, 1954).

In our view this contention has subtle but important clinical ramifications, standing on its head classical analytic thinking about cognitive development in infancy. Freud, once he had eschewed naive, veridical reality perception, along with the seduction theory, speculated that the infant gained a reality-based secondary process thinking and a capacity to be governed by reality only as a developmental achievement and only when the inherent capacity for fantasy failed to achieve the gratification of a persistent and sustaining perceptual identity sought by the infant in a state of need (Freud, 1900, 1911, 1915). This theoretical position has established a pervasive psychoanalytic stance that remains central to clinical practice to the present day; it creates a subtle (or not so subtle) diminishment of the importance or correctness of an approximately veridical secondary process memory while at the same time elevating the importance of primary process defensive distortion. Patients' conscious and preconscious memories thus become suspect, serving in psychoanalytic discourse mainly as manifest secondary process screens for the psychologically more important latent primary process content (as, for example, in Dr. C's ascribing screen quality to Ms. Stone's memory of the light switch episode or in his attribution of a repressed masturbation fantasy with specific content though the patient remembered none). As Kris (1956b) has written in his trend-setting paper "The Personal Myth":

> In a number of cases . . . individuals use their autobiographical memories—a term which I borrow from Freud's early (1899) writings—as a protective screen. In some cases this screen as a whole is carefully constructed and built

as some isolated screen memories tend to be . . . the firm outline and the richness of detail is meant to cover significant omissions and distortions. Only after omissions have been filled in and distortions have been corrected, can access to the repressed material be gained [p. 653].

Kris adds that unless the "screen is pierced," the patient's life will continue under the spell of his fantasy. While Kris himself temporized, referring only to, as he says, "certain cases," his more modest prescription, as expressed here and in other papers (e.g., 1956a), has been generalized by some as an attitude toward all conscious autobiographical memories offered by all patients before the analysis is really under way and before additional memories have been recovered.

Now this position has certainly served psychoanalysis well, providing an enormous clinical yield. But, of course, as with any unvarying stance, there has been a price; here the price has been encouragement to the analyst to listen to his or her patient with a skeptical—if not, at its worst, a downright suspicious—frame of mind.

Kris (1956a) contends that the general power, force, and import of the screen memories originate from "nuclei of memories shaped into fantasy form . . . from a time when fantasy and reality were not sharply divided, when fantasy was still fully invested as a relatively integral and un-distinguishable part of the self" (p. 680). Kris is undoubtedly referring here to Freud's unchallenged position that primary process thought predominates in infancy. In turn, the persuasiveness of Freud's argument concerning the sequence of fantasy-producing primary process thought arduously proceeding to rational secondary process thought only by virtue of persistent disappointment is based on its reputed connection to normal development. That is, a movement from the early hegemony of primary process to the later hegemony of secondary process was postulated as the universal, unvarying, age-related sequence of psychological maturation. It is only by virtue of the recent revolution in infant observational research that this view has been seriously challenged and that Stern can argue that the basic assumption of primary process preceding secondary process is not only arbitrary but most likely backwards, that is, that secondary process develops first (Stern, 1985, pp. 239–240, pp. 254–255). It seems to us, then, that it is secondary process thought and action, grounded in a subjectively perceived and processed reality, that is the bedrock of normal development and that primary process thought, grounded in fantasy, comes later. The infant and young child are understood in this new view to be quite adept observers of reality, subjectively perceived, of course, with distortion being a function of immaturity and trauma (Stern, 1989). Fantasy elaboration and creative invention become the province of the older toddler and are not the basic building blocks of the infant's cognition, perception, and affectivity. Lichtenberg (1989), using this same experimental infant research, postulates a different definition of primary and secondary process thought, both of which are characterized by symbolic representation and neither of which, therefore, becomes possible for the infant before 18 months of age. Lichtenberg, too, conceptualizes the infant before 18 months and the advent of symbolic thought as a surprisingly adept observer and recorder of reality, a reality encompassed by lived experience. Of course, both Stern and Lichtenberg, along with the infant researchers upon whose work their own speculations are based, recognize that infants, by virtue of their cognitive immaturity, make egocentric errors in their understanding of reality. But their point is that infants do not—and indeed cannot—for their own defensive purposes deliberately, magically, and inventively override that reality.

So with this different view of thought in infancy and childhood, a view that postulates a reduced and delayed role for defensive fantasy formation in normal infant development, there is an additional reason to respect the patient's subjective experience of his early life. Clearly, defensive functions and the sequestered and distorted memories that such functions create can never be ignored; they *are* primary in pathology and in the clinical situation, but more weight is due, in our opinion, and more respect as well, to the patient's conscious memories of childhood, including the patient's subjective assessment of his or her significant early relationships with others.

Stern has also challenged the classical model of normal development that presumes that the infant begins life without the ability to distinguish self from other and remains without that capacity for a considerable period of time. Mahler based her view of the first phases of normal development, the normal autistic phase and the normal symbiotic phase, on this same classical belief, as did Kohut in regard to normal self–selfobject relationships. With Stern's assumptions, based on significant experimental findings, some of Kohut's followers were moved to reevaluate and to redefine the selfobject concept, deleting from that concept its normal merger aspect (e.g., Basch, 1988). We believe, as we have written elsewhere (1985, 1988), that Mahler's view of the first phases of development is similarly open to question, a perspective that, in turn, would require a modification of the subsequent subphases of normal separation–individuation. Individuation remains a valuable concept to describe the normal developmental progression to relatively independent selfhood. Separation, too, remains a valuable concept; the lifelong vulnerability to separation anxiety and the need for continual mastery of that anxiety from the first year of life on are clearly evident and most certainly clinically relevant. There is no doubt that the capacity to function adequately despite the awareness of absence of the other, to be comfortable outside the presence of that other, is a most significant developmental task. However, it seems to us that an appreciation of the significance of separation does not require the assumption of a symbiotic phase in normal development.

In our opinion, when one takes into consideration the observational data from which it is possible to infer a capacity to distinguish self from other in the early months of life, the infant is not best conceptualized as spending important developmental time in a prolonged state of merger with another; nor is the infant best understood as having to expend important developmental efforts to achieve adequate separation from fusion with that other. Even Pine (1988), who had been an important collaborator of Mahler's, now agrees that merger as a prolonged symbiotic phase is unlikely, postulating instead heightened moments of blurred self–other boundaries, with such moments being of great developmental significance as ideal states to which the person longs to return. In any case, when we reconstruct in Ms. Stone's life narrative an interference in the process of individuation, we are speaking of an interference with *normal* development. When we refer to a symbiotic transference, however, we do not mean a regression to an earlier, normal symbiotic phase of development; nor do we think of it as a failure to negotiate such a normal phase. Rather, we think of symbiosis as a pathological construction of the patient requiring the defensive abrogation of some measure of reality-testing function to facilitate an experience of the other as partially merged with the self. That is, separation anxiety is defended against by what Mahler has called a delusion of fusion or by what one might term a transference illusion of fusion.

We turn now to the primary motivational systems exhibited by this patient, conceptualized in classical theory as the drive derivatives of the id (e.g., Brenner, 1982). It is not surprising that Dr. C, as a classical analyst, utilized the dual drive theory to explain what moved or motivated Ms. Stone. For example, her efforts to hold onto her analyst were conceptualized in a sadomasochistic framework integrating libido and aggression as the primary motivators of her actions. Similarly, Ms. Stone's childhood in interaction with her parents was reconstructed as the little girl being driven by sensual-sexual and destructive-aggressive drive derivatives. If Dr. C perceived evidence for attachment needs or desires in this patient, these must have been seen as secondary and were certainly less important to Dr. C's major interpretations, at least as Ms. Stone later remembered them. Thus, for example, Ms. Stone's stated motives for wishing to protect her sister from her father, which she remembered as based on a wish to assert herself and to get affirmation from a significant other, were dismissed by

Dr. C and reformulated as a manifest screen memory for the latent, defended-against content of sadomasochistic, sensual-sexual, and destructive-aggressive drive satisfaction.

Psychoanalytic views of human motivation have been changing gradually over the past half century, with Fairbairn (1952), Winnicott (1956), and Hendricks (1942) taking the lead, joined later by Bowlby (1960), White (1959), Kohut (1977), and a host of infant observers, the latter of whom conclude that drive itself is not a useful concept to describe motivation in the human infant or young child—or, for that matter, in the adult. For example, Kohut's motivational system is based primarily on attachment needs, or the need to maintain selfobject ties; sensuality and aggressivity are conceptualized in Kohut's self psychology as secondary to the need for connectedness and preservation of the self. While Kohut's contribution is a useful corrective to the exclusive attention of classical analysis to the dual drives in relation to basic motivation, nevertheless his view at its most narrow application can also be reductionistic. Emde (1988a) describes four basic motivational principles that are inborn, universal, and operate throughout life: activity; self-regulation; social fittedness; and affective monitoring. Later on, more complex motivational structures become manifest, for example, the affective use of the self and early moral motives.

Still more recently, Lichtenberg (1989) has introduced into the psychoanalytic literature his own synthesis of the gradual changes in psychoanalytic motivational theory. His work, like Emde's and Stern's, is based on considerable research data, predominately infant and toddler observation. Lichtenberg postulates replacing both the dual drive theory of classical analysis and the unitary focus on attachment of self psychology with five different motivational systems. These encompass the psychological effects of physiological regulation, attachment-affiliation, exploratory-assertiveness, aversiveness, and sensuality-sexuality. Lichtenberg makes a special point that these motivational functional systems all have neurophysiological correlates; all remain active throughout life, having distinct developmental lines moving from need to wish to desire; and each system affects the others in a mutually interactive way. Further, while ordinarily one system may be dominant, they all exist as potentially on par with one another and no one system takes overall, lasting priority. We have some disagreements with his formulations, specifically his use of an aversive motivational system to cover all fight and flight reactions without specifying this system's intimate connection to the ego's defensive organization in response to dysphoric affects; nevertheless, we believe that Lichtenberg has preserved the best of classical analytic understanding of motivation while at the same time making that understanding consistent with modern psychological and ethological thinking (Bowlby, 1958, 1960; Modell, 1990).

Broadening our understanding of motivation and extending the range of motivational possibility open to the clinician as he or she attempts to understand the patient can be quite useful. In the case of Ms. Stone, for example, it is possible to conceptualize her as having been motivated at times by strong attachment needs directed both toward her parents in her childhood and toward her analysts in her treatment situations. One does not need to always conceptualize the primary motivation of a dual drive system. We postulate that Ms. Stone's attachment needs went significantly unmet during her childhood, and in response she showed a surface compliance, with an underlying, unconscious, persistent rage and concomitant shame and guilt. In Lichtenberg's terms, the frustration of her needs in the attachment motivational system brought the aversive motivational system into prominence. In the transference, therefore, Ms. Stone had attempted to defend herself from her destructive, rageful feelings by a surface compliance with the analyst's interpretations, a compliance that was primarily an expression of the attachment motivational system. Her underlying destructive aggression can be understood most accurately, we believe, in its interrelational context as an aversive reaction to frustration (Kohut, 1972, 1980; Parens, 1979; Shane and Shane, 1982; Stechler and Holton, 1987). In summary, Lichtenberg's multimotivational schema, like Emde's, permits us to perceive caretakers in the totality of their provision of the infant's self-regulatory functions, that is, as providing for all of the motivational need states of the young child, which variety may be reflected, to varying degrees, in the psychoanalytic situation.

We would like to add one more set of considerations pertinent to our model of an integrative developmental orientation and approach. This conceptualization is based both on Stern's organization of self development during infancy and Basch's (1988) organization of affect regulation and affect development during infancy. Specifically, Basch uses Stern's organization of domains of self–other relatedness in his own contribution, identifying for each self domain a specific difficulty in affect development, a resultant pathological character structure, and an appropriate therapeutic approach. He argues that it is not sufficient to respond to all patients with a universally applied palliative of empathic affect attunement, as if every patient were suffering from a narcissistic personality or narcissistic behavior disorder, which disorder is connected to Stern's domain of the subjective self in relation to an intersubjective other. Rather, what is necessary, Basch avers, is to assess the specific arrest or vulnerability in the sense of self in a given patient and to respond to that patient in a manner that meets the domain-specific selfobject (or object) need.

Leaving aside the concerns we have with Basch's challenging but problematic and undoubtedly overschematized system, we do agree that the selfobject concept is not sufficiently particularized; it does not identify closely enough the specific kind of need satisfaction required from the other to support either a developing or a pathological self. Moreover, as it stands it is difficult to integrate the selfobject concept with other developmental frameworks. One solution is to do what Horowitz (1988) has done and replace both *object* and *selfobject* with the term *other*, but we suspect that *object* is too familiar a term in psychoanalysis to be replaced in this way. The alternative is to retain this term but to describe in what way the object is perceived and utilized by the individual and how that object is represented in the psyche. We could then speak of a self-regulating object (or other), a self-affirming object, an intimacy-sharing object, a sensual-sexual object, a fantasy-distorted object, a limit-setting object, an ideal-setting object, and so forth. In this way one might particularize the function of an object utilized by the self both in normal development and in its emergence in the transference.

We believe that such a change might serve to integrate developmental frameworks from object relations theory, self psychology, classical analysis, separation–individuation theory, and infant research. Moreover, this schema, as modified by us, is applicable to the clinical situation, as can be exemplified in the analysis of Ms. Stone. She can be best characterized as a narcissistic personality disorder whose pathology would seem to derive from experiences with parents who did not provide adequate self affirmation. In the clinical situation with E. S. attachment needs at first appeared to predominate. Ms. Stone benefited from eventual interpretation of the transference illusion of self affirmation from an idealized object (in part fantasy-distorted) that served to support an infirm and needful self, as well as from actual attunement and affirmation from the analyst, who provided her with a new, development-enhancing object experience. At present, in the oedipal transference that is now in the foreground of the analysis, sensual-sexual needs appear to predominate, with the analyst serving as an intimacy-sharing, sensual-sexual object, as well as a fantasy-distorted and standard-setting object. This is in contrast to the view of this patient that we postulate was held by Dr. C. He apparently conceptualized Ms. Stone at the outset of the analysis as suffering from an oedipal-level neurotic disorder and related to her in the transference exclusively in his role as an intimacy-sharing sexual object, a fantasy-distorted object, and a standard-setting object. He therefore missed the options and complexities made available through a developmental orientation and approach.

In conclusion, we have presented a summary comparison of Kohut's and Mahler's developmental postulates, assessed from the vantage point of current infant observation. We then present a clinical case designed to demonstrate an integrated developmental orientation and approach.

REFERENCES

Basch, M. (1988), *Understanding Psychotherapy*. New York: Basic Books.

Bowlby, J. (1958), The nature of a child's tie to his mother. *Internat. J. Psycho-Anal.*, 39:350–373.

———— (1960), Grief and mourning in infancy and early childhood. *The Psychoanalytic Study of the Child*, 15:9–52. New York: International Universities Press.

Brenner, C. (1982), *The Mind in Conflict*. New York: International Universities Press.

Emde, R. N. (1988a), Development terminable and interminable: 1. Innate and motivational factors from infancy. *Internat. J. Psycho-Anal.*, 69:23–42.

———— (1988b), Development terminable and interminable: 2. Recent psychoanalytic theory and therapeutic considerations. *Internat. J. Psycho-Anal.*, 69:283–296.

Fairbairn, W. R. D. (1952), *An Object Relations Theory of the Personality*. New York: Basic Books.

Freud, S. (1900), The interpretation of dreams. *Standard Edition*, 4 & 5. London: Hogarth Press, 1953.

———— (1911), Formulations on the two principles of mental functioning. *Standard Edition*, 12:218–226. London: Hogarth Press, 1958.

———— (1915), Instincts and their vicissitudes. *Standard Edition*, 14:117–140. London: Hogarth Press, 1957.

Friedman, L. (1988), The clinical popularity of object relations concepts. *Psychoanal. Quart.*, 57:667–691.

Goodman, S., ed. (1977), *Psychoanalytic Education and Research: The Current Situation and Future Possibilities*. New York: International Universities Press.

Greenson, R. R. (1965), The working alliance and the transference neurosis. In: *Explorations in Psychoanalysis*, ed. New York: International Universities Press, pp. – .

———— (1966), That "impossible" profession. In: *Explorations in Psychoanalysis*, New York: International Universities Press, pp. – .

Hendrick, I. (1942), Instinct and the ego during infancy. *Psychoanal. Quart.*, 11:33–58.

Horowitz, J. (1988), *Introduction to Psychodynamics: A New Synthesis*. New York: Basic Books.

Kernberg, O. F. (1984), *Severe Personality Disorders*. New Haven, CT: Yale University Press.

Kohut, H. (1966), Forms and transformations of narcissism. *J. Amer. Psychoanal. Assn.*, 14:243–272.

_____ (1968), The psychoanalytic treatment of narcissistic personality disorders. *The Psychoanalytic Study of the Child*, 23:86–113. New York: International Universities Press.

_____ (1971), *The Analysis of the Self*. New York: International Universities Press.

_____ (1972), Thoughts on narcissism and narcissistic rage. *The Psychoanalytic Study of the Child*, 27:360–399. New York: Quadrangle Books.

_____ (1977), *The Restoration of the Self*. New York: International Universities Press.

_____ (1980), Summarizing reflections. In: *Advances in Self Psychology*, ed. A. Goldberg. New York: International Universities Press, pp. 473–554.

_____ (1984), *How Does Analysis Cure?* Chicago: University of Chicago Press.

Kris, E. (1956a), The recovery of childhood memories in psychoanalysis. *The Psychoanalytic Study of the Child*, 9:54–88. New York: International Universities Press.

_____ (1956b), The personal myth. *J. Amer. Psychoanal. Assn.*, 4:653–681.

Lichtenberg, J. D. (1983), *Psychoanalysis and Infant Research*. Hillsdale, NJ: The Analytic Press.

_____ (1989), *Psychoanalysis and Motivation*. Hillsdale, NJ: The Analytic Press.

Lifton, R. J. (1971), Protean man. *Arch. Gen. Psychiat.*, 24:298–304.

Mahler, M. (1971), A study of the separation–individuation process and its possible application to borderline phenomena in the psychoanalytic situation. *The Psychoanalytic Study of the Child*, 26:403–424. New Haven, CT: Yale University Press.

Mahler, M. S., Pine, F. & Bergman, A. (1975), *The Psychological Birth of the Human Infant*. New York: Basic Books.

Modell, A. H. (1988), The centrality of the psychoanalytic setting and the changing aims of treatment. *Psychoanal. Quart.*, 57:577–596.

_____ (1990), Some notes on object relations, "classical" theory and the problem of instincts (drives). *Psychoanal. Inq.*, 10:182–196.

Parens, H. (1979), *Aggression in Childhood*. New York: Aronson.

Piaget, J. (1951), *Play, Dreams and Imitation in Childhood*. New York: Norton.

_____ (1954), *The Construction of Reality in the Child*. New York: Basic Books.

Pine, F. (1988), The four psychologies of psychoanalysis and their place in clinical work. *J. Amer. Psychoanal. Assn.*, 36:571–596.

_____ (1989), Motivation, personality organization and the four psychologies of psychoanalysis. *J. Amer. Psychoanal. Assn.*, 37:31–64.

Sandler, J. (1976), Countertransference and role-responsiveness. *Internat. Rev. Psychoanal.*, 3:43–47.

Schwaber, E. A. (1983), Psychological listening and psychic reality. *Internat. Rev. Psychoanal.*, 1:379–392.

_____ (1986), Reconstruction and perceptual experience: Further thoughts on psychoanalytic listening. *J. Amer. Psychoanal. Assn.*, 34:911–932.

Shane, M. & Shane, E. (1980), Psychoanalytic developmental theories of the self: An integration. In: *Advances in Self Psychology*, ed. A. Goldberg. New York: International Universities Press.

_____ (1982), The strands of aggression: A confluence of data. *Psychoanal. Inq.*, 2:263–282.

_____ (1985), Change and integration in psychoanalytic developmental theory. In: *New Ideas in Psychoanalysis*, ed. C. F. Settlage & R. Brockbank. Hillsdale, NJ: The Analytic Press.

_____ (1986), Self change and development in the psychoanalysis of an adolescent patient: The use of a combined model with a developmental orientation and approach. In: *Progress in Self Psychology, Vol. 2*, ed. A. Goldberg. New York: Guilford Press.

_____ (1988), Pathways to integration: Adding to the self psychological model. In: *Frontiers in Self Psychology & Progress Self Psychology, Vol. 4*, Hillsdale, NJ: The Analytic Press.

_____ (1989a), Mahler, Kohut, and infant research: Some comparisons. In: *Self Psychology: Comparisons and Contrasts*, ed. D. W. Detrick & S. P. Detrick. Hillsdale, NJ: The Analytic Press.

_____ (1989b), The struggle for otherhood: Implications for development in adulthood. *Psychoanal. Inq.*, 9:466–481.

_____ (1990), Unconscious fantasy: Developmental and self psychological considerations. *J. Amer. Psychoanal. Assn.*, 38:75–92.

Socarides, D. & Stolorow, R. (1984/85), Affects and selfobjects. *The Annual of Psychoanalysis*, 12/13:105–119. New York: International Universities Press.

Stechler, G. & Halton, A. (1987), The emergence of assertion and aggression during infancy: A psychoanalytic systems approach. *J. Amer. Psychoanal. Assn.*, 35:821–838.

Stern, D. N. (1985), *The Interpersonal World of the Infant*. New York: Basic Books.

_____ (1989), The representation of relational patterns: Developmental considerations. In: *Relationship Disturbances in Early Childhood: A Developmental Approach*, ed. A. J. Sameroff & R. N. Emde. New York: Basic Books, pp. 52–69.

Stolorow, R., Brandchaft, B. & Atwood, G. (1987), *Psychoanalytic Treatment: An Intersubjective Approach*. Hillsdale, NJ: The Analytic Press.

Strenger, C. (1989), The classic and romantic vision in psychoanalysis. *Internat. J. Psycho-Anal.*, 70:595–610.

White, R. (1959), Motivation reconsidered: The concept of competence. *Psychoanal. Rev.*, 66:297–333.

Winnicott, D. W. (1956), Primary maternal preoccupation. In: *Collected Papers*. London: Tavistock, 1958, pp. 300–305.

4

The Stages of Ego Development:
Implications for Childhood and Adult Psychopathology

Stanley I. Greenspan

Central to all areas of clinical practice is an understanding of the development of the basic ego functions. Nevertheless, general personality and clinical theory have not yet formulated a systematic integrated model of the stages in early ego development.

In the history of psychoanalysis, dynamic psychiatry, and clinical practice the ego is confused with such constructs as object relations, self, identity, personality, character, and coping. The construct of the ego designates the mental functions that perceive, organize, elaborate, differentiate, integrate, and transform experience. Experience, in this context, includes drive–affect derivatives, various levels of internal self and object organizations, and interpersonal relationships, as well as interactions with the relatively impersonal object world. As the aspect of the mind that abstracts and categorizes experience, the ego, through its functions, organizes the various qualities attributed to mental phenomena, such as self and object representations, a sense of self, and identity. Understanding how the ego develops is central to comprehending both healthy (adaptive organization of experience) and psychopathological (deficits, constrictions, or conflictually derived encapsulations in the organization of experience) functioning.

A model of early ego development allows us to see the relationship between early patterns of development and later ones in adulthood.

Characteristic ways of organizing and differentiating experience can be compared across time. Such comparisons should not imply a causal or even sequential relationship. They should, however, reveal when functions of the ego normally are established, their purpose and structure, and the nature of compromise in them that may play a role in psychopathology.

The clinical interest in early ego development and psychopathology in infancy and early childhood is based on an impressive foundation. Perhaps most widely known are Spitz's (1945) report on anaclitic depressions in institutionally reared infants and Bowlby's monograph *Maternal Care and Mental Health* (1952), describing the now well known "syndromes" of disturbed functioning in infancy. Child psychoanalysts' interest in disturbances in infants, as indicated by the work of Bernfeld (1929), Winnicott (1931), A. Freud and Burlingham (1945, 1965), and A. Freud (1965), as well as the work of Erik Erikson (1959), amplified the complexity or multidimensional nature of early development. Important for current approaches was the work relating individual differences in infants (constitutional and maturational patterns) to tendencies for psychopathology, highlighted by the reports of Sybille Escalona and Lois Murphy and their colleagues (Escalona, 1968; Murphy, 1974) and by those of Cravioto and DeLicardie (1973).

Several existing developmental frameworks have provided enormous understanding of individual lines of development in infancy and early childhood, frameworks suggested by, for example, Sigmund Freud (1905), Erikson (1959), Piaget (1962), Spitz and Cobliner (1965), Anna Freud (1965), Kohut (1971), Kernberg (1975), and Mahler, Pine, and Bergman (1975). In addition, there has been a great deal of empirical research generating useful developmental constructs, such as the work of, for example, Sander (1962), Emde, Gaensbauer, and Harmon (1976), and Sroufe (1979). These foundations, together with the rapidly growing body of clinical experience with infants and their families (Fraiberg, 1979; Provence, 1983; Provence and Naylor, 1983), provided direction for a much needed integrated approach encompassing the multiple lines of development in the context of adaptive and disordered functioning.

Mahler's work, in particular, has guided clinicians through the intricacies of early object relationships and helped them see the connections between these early relationship patterns and later intrapsychic organizations. But the traditional views of Mahler and, to some degree, Spitz (1945) have been challenged by some empirical researchers (e.g., Stern, 1985, 1988) who characterize the early stages of infancy as being dominated by differentiated self–object representational systems.

Both the traditional and empirically derived views have important assets and limitations. The traditional views, from observations of infants under different circumstances of emotional stress, characterize selected aspects of in-depth psychological experience. Understandably, however, these views do not incorporate findings regarding individual differences in sensory-affective and cognitive reactivity and processing from recent observational and experiential studies. Some of the empirically derived views of how early experience is organized usefully highlight the different ways the infant comprehends his world. But they fail to distinguish in-depth emotional experience from other types of experiences. They focus on impersonal cognition or aspects of affect under structured experimental conditions. The infant's ability to make cognitive discriminations are mistakenly assumed to characterize the infant's way of organizing in-depth psychological experience. The clinical challenges that would reveal the ego's operations under stress (the ego's true contour) are not taken into account.

With different clinical and developmental views stemming from a lack of understanding of early ego development, it is essential to formulate a systematic, integrated perspective on the stages in the growth of the ego. The model presented in this chapter postulates six stages in the development of the ego and is based on both in-depth clinical and normative observations and studies of infants and young children and their families. These stages are examined from the point of view of the development of the infant's underlying physical capacities (e.g., sensory-affect reactivity and processing, motor tone, and motor planning); the sequence of early relationship patterns; and progressive levels in the child's ability to organize experience. The model posits how areas of the infant's experience become organized, symbolized, and differentiated in terms of drive–affect dispositions, defenses, internal self and object representational patterns, and emerging intrapsychic structures. It looks simultaneously at the biological (physical) and the interactive (relationship) underpinnings of the ego, as well as at the stages that the ego uses to organize itself, namely, its own experience. The model presented here builds on the pioneering work of Mahler and others on intrapsychic organizations and incorporates insights about differences in sensory reactivity, processing, motor tone, motor planning, and the sequence of early emotional development.

In this chapter developmental levels are described for both early childhood and adulthood. A more detailed discussion of this subject, including principles of psychotherapy and psychoanalysis, can be found in *The Development of the Ego* (Greenspan, 1989).

BACKGROUND

In an attempt to understand early development, my colleagues and I undertook a clinical descriptive intervention study of multirisk infants and families as well as of normal infants and families (Greenspan, 1981; Greenspan et al., 1987). The study of each family began prenatally with the anticipated birth of a new infant. Because there were already severe emotional disturbances in the older children in the family, we expected there would be a high likelihood of a range of psychopathologies in the newborn infants. Infants and families with expected adaptive patterns were also observed for comparison.

From this study, together with clinical work with older children and adults, we formulated six stages in early ego development. These will be described and their implications for psychopathology discussed.

HOMEOSTASIS: SELF-REGULATION AND INTEREST IN THE WORLD (BIRTH TO THREE MONTHS)

During this stage, one may postulate a self–object relationship character-ized by a somatic preintentional world self–object. Ego organization, differentiation, and integration are characterized by a lack of differentiation between the physical world, self, and object worlds. Ego functions include global reactivity, sensory-affective processing, and regulation, and sensory hyperreactivity/hyporeactivity, and disregulation.

During homeostasis, regulation and a multisensory interest in the world are the infant's two major goals. Clinically, we observe a range of patterns of sensorimotor discrimination and integration in clinical and normal groups of infants and their families, including hyperarousal and hypoa-rousal (both extreme apathy and hypotonicity). And one observes these patterns in reaction to both animate and inanimate stimuli. For the most part, the infant is using what may be considered "prewired," rather than learned, approaches to his world. In addition to the well-known primitive reflexes, the sensory and sensorimotor abilities referred to earlier allow the infant to cuddle, follow his caregiver's voice and face, and copy selected facial expressions, including tongue protrusion. The child will show preferences for different vocal patterns (e.g., mother's), show visual preferences for objects that have been explored orally (cross-sensory integration), and so forth. Yet even though these and other behaviors can come under operant control (e.g., respond to reinforcements), there is no reason to assume that these basic abilities are not part of the functional capacities many infants are born with.

It may be postulated, therefore, that there are adaptive sensorimotor patterns that are part of the "autonomous" ego functions present shortly after birth. It is then useful to consider how these capacities (e.g., the autonomous ego functions of perception and discrimination) are used to construct an emerging organization of an experiential world, including drive derivatives, early affects, and emerging organizations of self and object(s). It would be a logical error to assume that these seemingly innate capacities are themselves a product of early interactional learning or structure building, even though secondarily they are influenced by experiences.

One cannot yet postulate differentiated self–object experiential organizations. This is because the infant's main goals appear to be involved in a type of sensory awakening and interest and regulation without evidence of clear intentional object seeking or self-initiated, differentiated affective interactions. In our observations of both at-risk and normal infants, it was observed that they responded to the overall stimulus qualities of the environments, especially human handling. Likewise, there is little evidence for a notion that the infant is impervious to his emotional surroundings. In fact, in our studies of multirisk families (Greenspan et al., 1987) the quality of self-regulation, attention, and sensory-affective interest in the world in the first month or two of life was influenced to a great degree by the physical and emotional qualities of the infant–caregiver patterns (i.e., soothing and interesting caregiving patterns rather than hyperstimulating or hypostimulating ones).

One must not simply look at the infant's capacities but at how he organizes around age-specific critical psychological tasks. Because these tasks involve complex spontaneous and, at times, highly challenging or even stressful interactions with emotionally important caregivers and because the infant cannot control the behavior of the caregiver, his pattern of in-depth psychological growth is different from his pattern of cognitive growth. It must be described in its own right and not assumed or generalized from his functioning in other domains.

In terms of the tasks of this stage, regulation and interest in the world, both animate and inanimate experiences are used by the infant to further his aims. As both types of experience help the infant calm and regulate himself and attend to and process sensory information, one could argue that in terms of phase-specific tasks there is a physical world–human world sensory unity at this time.

Therefore, one may consider a preintentional stage of object relatedness (i.e., prewired patterns gradually come under interactive control) and a stage in the organization of experience where the sense of self and object are not yet organized as distinct entities. At this stage the experience of self and other is closely intertwined and unlikely to be separate from other sensory experiences involving the physical world. It is worth repeating that differential infant responses do not necessarily mean differentiated internal experiences, because responses or behaviors can simply be constitutional, reflexive (e.g., to heat or cold), and/or conditioned responses according to respondent (Pavlovian) or operant learning.

Therefore, the concept of an experiential organization of a *world object,* including what later will become a differentiation between self and other and the physical world, may prove useful. This state of ego organization may be considered to be characterized by two central tendencies: to experience sensory and affective information through each sensorimotor channel and to form patterns of regulation. Furthermore, these tendencies may be further characterized by the level of sensory pathway arousal (i.e., sensory hyperarousal and hypoarousal) in each sensorimotor pathway and by emerging sensorimotor discrimination and integration capacities.

What are the implications of the faulty formation of these capacities in adult and child psychiatric conditions? These are basic regulatory capacities, including the ability to process stimulus input and organize it (without shutting down, becoming hyperactive, or hyperreactive). In many conditions, this capacity is not well established. For example, the child with severe attentional difficulties cannot process information well, and those who are most seriously affected may clinically look withdrawn, retarded, or both. Some children who have only mild attentional difficulties, which are labeled attentional deficit disorders, actually have more problems in one sensory mode than in another. Some children are more distracted by sounds, others by visual stimuli; still others have tactile overreactivity, a pattern that is not described well in the psychiatric literature.

In many clinical populations there are individuals who are hyperreactive to light touch. Sensory processing difficulties are also seen in child and adult schizophrenic populations who have been studied experimentally. Separating and studying each processing capacity in terms of the sensory pathway involved, in relation to both impersonal and affective stimuli (i.e., the auditory, tactile, vestibular, olfactory, and proprioceptive systems) is an important research area. We are starting such studies with infants and also hope to study the same phenomena in adult and child psychiatric populations.

Sensory processing difficulties may also involve problems in making discriminations. In addition to a sensory system being hypoarousable or hyperarousable, we have observed infants in the first few months of life who seem unable, although not at these extremes, to tune in to the environment. Instead of decoding her rhythmic sound and brightening up (as most infants do) when mother talks to them, they almost look confused. We have observed clinically that this is present in some children with regard to one sensory pathway but not another. For example, an infant with intact hearing but unable to focus on rhythmic sound may be able to focus on facial gesturing. When an infant looks confused in reaction to vocal stimuli, we may coach a mother to slow down, to talk very distinctly, not to introduce too much novelty too quickly (most infants love novelty), and to use many animated facial expressions, movements (to encourage the use of vision), and tactile sensations. Often the infant will become alert, brighten up, and become engaged. Thus, by profiling individual sensory processing differences and motor and affect patterns in infancy, it has become possible through counseling to improve the flexibility or intuitive patterns of the caregiver.

ATTACHMENT (TWO TO SEVEN MONTHS)

During the attachment stage one may postulate a self-object relationship characterized by an intentional part self-object interaction. Ego organization, differentiation, and integration are characterized by a relative lack of differentiation of self and object. There is, however, differentiation of the physical world and human object world. Ego functions include part-object seeking, drive–affect elaboration or drive–affect dampening or liability, object withdrawal, rejection, or avoidance.

The attachment stage, characterized by clear pleasurable inclinations toward the human world, also evidences enormous variation; infants who are apathetic or mechanical may prefer the physical world. They may be passively compliant, not joyful, and/or active avoiders of their caregiver's gaze and vocalizations. They may be indiscriminating or, past the age of eight months, unselective or even promiscuous in their object ties. In this stage, under optimal circumstances, all the senses and the motor system become coordinated toward the aim of pleasurable interaction with a caregiver. Not only pleasure but distress and curiosity also are beginning to emerge in a more organized fashion.

The pleasurable preference for the human world suggests interactive object seeking. Apathy in reaction to caregiver withdrawal, preference for the physical world, and chronic active aversion in clinically disturbed populations also suggest emerging organized object-related patterns, although in the maladaptive direction.

Yet there is no evidence of the infant's ability to abstract all the features of the object in terms of an organization of the whole object. Infants seek the voice, smiling mouth, twinkly eyes, or rhythmic movements alone or in some combination, but not yet as a whole. In addition, the tendency toward global withdrawal, rejection, or avoidance suggests undifferentiated reaction patterns, as compared to differentiated patterns where the influence of a "me" on a "you" is occurring. The four-month-old does not evidence the repertoire of the eight-month-old in "wooing" a caregiver into a pleasurable interaction. The four-month-old, under optimal conditions, evidences synchronous interactive patterns, that is smiling, and vocalizing in rhythm with the caregiver; when in distress, he evidences global reactivity. In comparison, the eight-month-old can explore alternative ways of having an impact on his caregiver. This suggests that not until the next stage is there a full behavioral (prerepresentational) comprehension of cause and effect or part self-object differentiation. Representational comprehension does not occur until late in the second year of life.

Most likely, during this stage the infant progresses from the earlier stage of a self-other-world object (where both human and not-human worlds are not yet distinct and the human self and nonself are not distinct) to a stage of intentional, undifferentiated self-human object organization. There is a sense of synchrony and connectedness to a human object that suggests the infant's experiential organization differentiates the human object from physical objects. But even at a behavioral level there is not yet evidence of a self–object differentiation. In this sense the concept of symbiosis (Mahler et al., 1975) is not at odds with the clinical observation of a lack of self–object differentiation.

The functioning of the ego at this stage is characterized by intentional object seeking, differentiated organizations of experience, that is, differentiation of human from nonhuman and global patterns of reactivity to the human object. These patterns of reactivity include the seeking of pleasure, protest, withdrawal, rejection (with a preference for the physical world, based on what appears to be a clear discrimination), hyperaffectivity (diffuse discharge of affects), and active avoidance.

As indicated, if the infant's early experience of the world is aversive, the affective interest in the human world may be compromised. A total failure of the attachment process is seen in autistic patterns, in certain types of withdrawn and regressed schizophrenics, and, intermittently, in children who are diagnosed as having pervasive developmental disturbances.

We also see shallow attachments. There is some involvement with the human world, but it is without positive affect or emotional depth. We see a compromise in the depth of connectedness in some of the narcissistic character disorders, illustrating a subtle deficit in the range of emotion incorporated into an attachment pattern. A severe lack of regard for human relationships is seen in what used to be called the chronic psychopathic personality disorder (now the sociopathic or antisocial personality disturbance).

SOMATOPSYCHOLOGICAL DIFFERENTIATION: PURPOSEFUL COMMUNICATION (THREE TO TEN MONTHS)

During the stage of somatopsychological differentiation one may postulate a self–object relationship characterized by a differentiated behavioral part self-object. Ego organization, differentiation, and integration are characterized by a differentiation of aspects (part) of self and object in terms of drive–affect patterns and behavior. Ego functions include part self-object differentiated interactions in initiation of, and in reciprocal response to, a range of drive–affect domains (e.g., pleasure, dependency, assertiveness, and aggression); means–ends relationship between drive-affect intensification and inhibition; constrictions of range of intrapsychic experience and regression to stages of withdrawal, avoidance, or rejection (with preference for the physical world), or object concretization.

In this phase, characterized by cause-and-effect interactions, one observes the infant take initiative and participate in reciprocal (rather than synchronous) interchanges. These occur across a range of sensorimotor pathways and affective patterns.

The intentionality of the infant in both adaptive (reaching out, protesting, etc.) and maladaptive (rejecting) modes suggests at least a behavioral comprehension of a "self" influencing an "other." It also suggests self–object differentiation at the behavioral level. Behavioral level in this context means the organization of behavioral patterns or tendencies rather than the later organization of symbols. Only late in the second year does a child begin to have the ability to create mental representations, through higher level abstractions. In the somatopsychological differentiation stage, however, the "I" is likely an "I" of behavior ("If I do this, it causes that") rather than the "I" of a mental representation ("If I feel or think or *am* a certain way, it will have this or that impact"). The capacity to construct mental representations will allow the growing child to organize and even rearrange different elements of the "self" or "other" into mental images. Because there is behavioral cause and effect or differentiated interaction, one can think of this as a behavioral or prerepresentational type of reality testing.

There is no evidence yet for the child having the ability to abstract all aspects of the "self" or "other." Experiences are still in fragmented pieces. Temporal and spatial continuity, while rapidly developing, are not yet fully established.

During this stage the affect system is differentiated to the degree to which the caregiving environment subtly reads the baby's emotional signals. Some infants do not experience reciprocity at all; others experience selective limitations. Cause-and-effect feedback in one or another thematic or emotional area is missing; no family will be equally sensitive and responsive in all areas. Some families are conflicted around dependency, others around aggression. Thus, there will be more anxiety in some areas than in others, and children will receive different feedback for different emotional areas. This is, in part, what makes people different, but when a whole area like dependency, pleasure, or exploration does not receive reciprocal, purposeful cause-and-effect feedback, early presymbolic (prere-presentational) differentiations may be limited.

It is also useful to think of this stage of development as a first step in reality testing. At this time, prerepresentational causality is established. The child is learning that reaching out, smiling, vocalizing, pleasurable affect, and aggressive affect all have their consequences. Later in develop-ment, ideas or representations are also organized according to the cause-and-effect patterns. It may prove interesting to separate psychotic patients who have a failure of reality testing at the level of behavioral causality (four to eight months) from those who have a failure of reality testing at the later representational level (i.e., the level of representational causality of the two- to four-year-old). For example, some psychotic individuals tend to think and talk in a crazy way (they can hallucinate, be delusional, and have thought disorders), but they behave realistically.

At the stage of somatopsychological differentiation, the fundamental deficit is in reality testing and basic causality. There are also subtle deficits that may be part of a lack of differentiation along a particular emotional-thematic proclivity. In various character disturbances and borderline conditions, we observe patients who are undifferentiated when it comes to aggression but not dependency, or vice versa. Certain areas of internal life remain relatively undifferentiated, yet in other areas differentiation and reality testing are very good. This uneven pattern is part of many definitions of borderline syndromes.

A variety of symptoms may be seen in disorders of somatopsychological differentiation. They include developmental delays in sensorimotor func-tioning, apathy, intense chronic fear, clinging, absence of exploratory activity and lack of curiosity, lack of emotional reactions to significant caregivers, biting, chronic crying and irritability, and difficulties with sleeping and eating. Additional symptoms may be evident if there are compromises in the infant–primary caregiver relationship (e.g., the infant becomes frustrated and irritable as his new capacities for contingent interactions are ignored or misread) secondary to the failure to form differentiated patterns. If the basic comforting and soothing functions that support the baby's sense of security begin to falter, we may then see compromises in attachment and homeostatic patterns leading to physiologic disorders and interferences in already achieved rhythms and cycles such as sleep and hunger. Where disorders of differentiation are severe and are not reversed during later development, they may set the foundation for later disorders. These disorders may include primary personality (ego) defects in reality testing, the organization and perception of communication and thought, the perception and regulation of affects, and the integration of affects, action, and thought.

THE STAGE OF BEHAVIORAL ORGANIZATION, INITIATIVE, AND INTERNALIZATION: A COMPLEX SENSE OF SELF (9 TO 18 MONTHS)

During this stage, one may postulate a self–object relationship characterized by a functional (conceptual) integrated and differentiated self-object. Ego organization, differentiation, and integration are characterized by an integration of drive–affect behavioral patterns into relatively whole functional self-objects. Ego functions include organized whole self-object interactions (in a functional behavioral sense). These functions are characterized by interactive chains, mobility in space (i.e., distal communication modes), functional (conceptual) abstractions of self-object properties, and integration of drive–affect polarities (e.g., shift from splitting to greater integration). Alternatively, ego functions may be characterized by self-object fragmentation, self-object proximal urgency, preconceptual concretization, polarization (e.g., a negative, aggressive, dependent, or avoidant self-object pattern), and/or regressive states. The latter may include withdrawal, avoidance, rejection, somatic dedifferentiation, and object concretization.

The capacities for behavioral organization, affective integration, and behavioral sense of self and object in functional terms (a conceptual stand toward the world) characterizes this stage of ego development. Now there is what may be thought of as a conceptual self–object relationship because different self behaviors and object behaviors are not only differentiated from each other (as in the earlier stage) but are now viewed as part of a whole. Teasing behavior, jokes, anticipation of emotional reactions, and awareness of how to get others to evidence different emotional proclivities all point to this new conceptual affective ability. But even more important is how the toddler uses his ability to organize in all dimensions of life. This is illustrated by his tendency, under stress, to organize his negativism, use sophistication in his clinging dependency, develop intricate aggressive patterns, and exploit or manipulate peers and adults in new interpersonal patterns. One also observes the toddler regress in worrisome situations from organized behavioral patterns to highly fragmented patterns or become withdrawn or rejecting. Here, complex adaptive and maladaptive patterns suggest the emerging whole-object patterns.

A severe disorder at this phase affects the basic capacity for organizing behavior and affects, a defect of which is seen in many borderline conditions and severe personality disorders. Most worrisome is the toddler who pulls away entirely from emotional relationships in the human world or remains fragmented as he develops his affective-thematic proclivities. A less severe disorder at this stage will be reflected in the narrowness of the organization of the child's range of experience, as seen in extreme character rigidities (e.g., children who never assert themselves, those who are always negative, those who have difficulties in affiliative behavior, and those who cannot use imitation in the service of temporary gratification and delay). Because such children are tied to concrete and immediate states of need fulfillment, they may never form the intermediary warning and delay capacities that complex internal affects facilitate. They often tend to see people only as fulfilling their hunger for physical touch, sweets, or other concrete satisfactions.

Symptomatic problems at the stage of behavioral organization are chronic temper tantrums; inability to initiate even some self-control; lack of motor or emotional coordination; extreme, chronic negativism; sleep disturbance; hyperirritability; withdrawal; delayed language development; and relationships characterized by chronic aggressive behavior. In addition, if basic attachments and comforting functions are secondarily disrupted, one may see attachment and homeostatic disorders.

REPRESENTATIONAL CAPACITY (18 TO 30 MONTHS)

During the stage of representational capacity one may postulate a self–object relationship characterized by a representational self-object. Ego organization, differentiation, and integration are characterized by an elevation of functional behavioral self-object patterns to multisensory drive-and affect-invested symbols of intrapersonal and interactive experience (mental representations). Ego functions include representational self-objects characterized by mobility in time and space (e.g., creation of object representation in the absence of the object) and drive–affect elaboration (themes ranging from dependency and pleasure to assertiveness and aggression are now elaborated in symbolic form as evidenced in pretend play and functional language). There is a gradual stabilizing of drive–affect patterns (self-object representations survive intensification of drive–affect disposi-tions). Or there is behavioral concretization (lack of representation); representational constriction (only one emotional theme at a time); drive–affect lability; regressive states, including withdrawal, avoidance, rejection, and behavioral dedifferentiation; and object concretization.

This stage of ego organization is characterized by the capacity to elevate experiences to the representational level. Current experience can be organized into multisensory affective "images," and these images are mobile in time and space (e.g., children imagine images of objects in the absence of the object). The representational system can also construct multisensory images of sensations or patterns from within the organism that may have occurred in the past. These earlier patterns of somatic sensation and simple and complex chains of behavior and interaction will not be "interpreted" via representation. How well formed, accurate, or distorted these representations of earlier prerepresentational experience will be will depend on the character of the early patterns, their repetition in the present, the abstracting ability of the ego, and the emerging dynamic character of the ego, that is, its ability to represent some areas of experience while others remain and prerepresentational levels.

The ego at this stage evidences the adaptive capacity for representational elaboration. It also evidences a range of maladaptive options, including a lack of representation where the physical world can be represented but the drive–affect invested in the interpersonal world is not represented. This global lack of representational capacity is often associated with interper-sonal withdrawal and/or regressive behavioral and somatic discharge patterns. Where there is support for representational elaboration in some areas but not others, or where certain child-initiated themes lead to parental anxiety and/or parental undermining behavior, one observes representational constrictions. One also observes in some instances that these constrictions can be accompanied by intense patterns of behavioral and affective expression.

Although self and object relationships are being organized at a repre-sentational level during this stage, they are not differentiated, even though, paradoxically, the early prerepresentational behavioral and so-matic organizations are differentiated. That is, differentiation at an earlier level exists alongside emerging differentiation at the new higher level.

For this stage we can postulate an undifferentiated representational self-object built on a foundation of somatic and behavioral differentiated self-objects. The behaving child is clearly intentional and behaviorally understands that his actions have impact on others. Yet he is learning to give meanings to his behaviors and feelings and is only beginning to learn about intentionality and consequences at the level of meanings. Thus,

awareness, in a symbolic sense, is expanding rapidly and is in evidence in
the elaboration of pretend play and the functional use of language. Yet we
are also observing how symbolic awareness or consciousness may be
concretized, constricted, or encapsulated, or selectively exaggerated, depending on the opportunities the child has to engage his new ability in
appropriate interpersonal contexts.

Children with disorders of this phase include those who remain concrete
and never learn to use the representational mode (i.e., they use only
fragments of play or language). Impulsive or withdrawn behavior often
accompanies such a limitation. The child's relationship patterns are also
usually fragmented.

At a somewhat less severe level we see children who have developed a
representational capacity in both the inanimate and animate spheres but
show severe limitations or regressions with even minor stress in certain
areas of human experience. For example, they may be able to use symbolic
modes only around negativism, dominance, and aggression and consequently look solemn, stubborn, or angry, showing little range of representational elaboration, in the pleasurable or intimate domain. When
frustrated or angry, some children may quickly regress to behavioral
modes. These patterns are similar to what we see in many severe character
disorders and higher functioning borderline states.

REPRESENTATIONAL DIFFERENTIATION
(24 TO 48 MONTHS)

For the stage of representational differentiation one may postulate a
self–object relationship characterized by a differentiated, integrated representational self-object. Ego organization, differentiation, and integration
are characterized by an abstraction of self and object representations and
drive–affect dispositions into a higher level representational organization,
differentiated along dimensions of self–other, time, and space. Ego
functions include representational differentiation characterized by the
following:

1. Genetic integration (early somatic and behavioral patterns organized
   by emerging mental representations)
2. Dynamic integration (current drive–affect proclivities organized by
   emerging mental representations)
3. Microstructural integration (i.e., affect, impulse, and thought)

4. Structure formation (self-object representations abstracted into stable patterns performing ongoing ego functions of reality testing, impulse control, mood stabilization, etc.)
5. Self and object identity formation (i.e., a sense of self and object that begins to integrate past, current, and changing aspects of fantasy and reality)
6. Representational fragmentation (either genetic or dynamic or both)
7. Lack of, or unstable, basic structures (e.g., reality testing, impulse control)
8. Defective, polarized, or constricted (global or encapsulated) identity formation

As ego development progresses in its capacity to create and elaborate mental representations, it abstracts representational units into groupings leading to representational differentiation. These groupings occur along a number of dimensions including physical, spatial, and temporal aspects of experience. Self-representations are differentiated from nonself or object representations along all the relevant dimensions. But most important, these groupings also occur along the lines of affective *meanings*. Now, drive-affect colored self–object patterns coalesce into representational organizations according to the characteristics of the drive–affect dispositions as they both define and are defined by early relationship patterns.

It is useful to clinically observe and assess the representational capacity along the two simultaneous dimensions of representational elaboration and representational differentiation. Clinically one observes defects and constructions in both domains. These are evidenced by the child who

1. remains concrete, that is, prerepresentational, and never learns to use the representational mode to elaborate "inner sensations" to the level of meanings;
2. is severely constricted and is only able to represent a few of the affective-thematic domains characteristic of human functioning;
3. shows the full range of representational affective-thematic life but remains undifferentiated along the dimensions of ideas or thoughts (thought disorder), affective proclivities (mood disturbances), self and object organizations (reality testings and "self" and "other" boundary disturbances), intentionality (impulse disorders), and sense of time space (disorders of learning, concentration, and planning); and
4. Avoids affective-thematic realms that are potentially disruptive (character disorders) in order to differentiate.

Contributing to these limitations is the caregiver who cannot engage representationally in all domains because he or she is fearful of certain affective-thematic realms and therefore withdraws or becomes disorganized. Another is the caregiver who engages in all realms but has difficulty operating at a representational level in a contingent manner. The child's own limitations from earlier maturationally based processing problems and psychosexual difficulties also contribute to representational disorders. Each of the four limitations described in the preceding paragraph is seen in neurotic and character disorder levels of psychopathology in adults as well as in borderline states.

In this chapter we have considered how the ego grows in its ability to organize experience. Somatic and behavioral experience is abstracted to a higher plane, that of representation. We have seen how at each of the early stages of ego development, experience is organized in ways that contribute to either adaptation or psychopathology.

REFERENCES

Bernfeld, S. (1929), *The Psychology of the Infant*. New York: Brentano.

Bowlby, J. (1952), *Maternal Care and Mental Health* (WHO Monograph No. 2). Geneva: World Health Organization.

Cravioto, J. & DeLicardie, E. (1973), Environment correlates of severe clinical malnutrition and language development in survivors from kwashiorkor or marasmus. In: *Nutrition, the Nervous System and Behavior*. Washington, DC: PAHO Scientific Publication No. 251.

Emde, R., Gaensbauer, T. & Harmon, R. (1976), Emotional expression in infancy: A biobehavioral study. *Psychological Issues*, Monogr. 37. New York: International Universities Press.

Erikson, E. (1959), Identity and the life cycle. *Psychological Issues*, Monograph Series No. 1. New York: International Universities Press.

Escalona, S. (1968), *The Roots of Individuality*. Chicago: Aldine.

Fraiberg, S. (1979), Treatment modalities in an infant mental health program. Presented at the training institute on Clinical Approaches to Infants and Their Families sponsored by the National Center for Clinical Infant Programs, Washington, DC.

Freud, A. (1965), Normality and pathology in childhood. In: *The Writings of Anna Freud, Vol. 6*. New York: International Universities Press.

_____ Burlingham, D. (1945), *Infants Without Families*. New York: International Universities Press.

_____ _____ (1965), *War and Children*. New York: International Universities Press.

Freud, S. (1905), Three essays on the theory of sexuality. *Standard Edition*, 7:135–243. London: Hogarth Press, 1953.

Greenspan, S. I. (1981), *Psychopathology and Adaptation in Infancy and Early Childhood: Principles of Clinical Diagnosis and Preventive Intervention*. New York: International Universities Press.

———— (1989), *The Development of the Ego*. Madison, CT: International Universities Press.

———— Wieder, S., Lieberman, A., Nover, R., Lourie, R. & Robinson, M., eds. (1987), *Infants in Multirisk Families: Case Studies in Preventive Intervention*. (Clinical Infant Reports, No. 3.) New York: International Universities Press.

Kernberg, O. (1975), *Borderline Conditions and Pathological Narcissism*. New York: Aronson.

Kohut, H. (1971), *The Analysis of Self: A Systematic Approach to the Psychoanalytic Treatment of Narcissistic Personality Disorders*. New York: International Universities Press.

Mahler, M. S., Pine, F. & Bergman, A. (1975), *The Psychological Birth of the Human Infant*. New York: Basic Books.

Murphy, L. (1974), *The Individual Child* (DHEW Publication No. (OCD) 74-1032). Washington, DC: U.S. Government Printing Office.

Piaget, J. (1962), The stages of the intellectual development of the child. In: *Childhood Psychopathology,* ed. S. Harrison & J. McDermott. New York: International Universities Press, pp. 157–166.

Provence, S. (1983), *Infants and Parents: Clinical Case Reports* (Clinical Infant Reports, No. 2). New York: International Universities Press.

———— Naylor, A. (1983), *Working with Disadvantaged Parents and Their Children: Scientific and Practical Issues*. New Haven, CT: Yale University Press.

Sander, L. (1962), Issues in early mother–child interaction. *J. Amer. Acad. Child Psychiat.,* 16(4):480–484.

Spitz, R. (1945), Hospitalism. *The Psychoanalytic Study of the Child,* 1:53–74. New York: International Universities Press.

Spitz, R. & Cobliner, W. (1965), *The First Year of Life*. New York: International Universities Press.

Sroufe, L. (1979), Socioemotional development. In: *Handbook of Infant Development,* ed. J. Osofsky. New York: Wiley.

Stern, D. (1985), *The Interpersonal World of the Child*. New York: Basic Books.

Stern, D. (1988), Affect in the context of the infant's lived experience: Some considerations. *Internat. J. Psycho-Anal.,* 69(2):233–238.

Winnicott, D. W. (1931), *Clinical Notes on Disorders of Childhood*. London: Heinemann.

5

Some Comments
on Early Development

Otto F. Kernberg

Contemporary psychoanalysis is facing an explosive development of new theories. As the scientific and professional interchange among psychoanalysts from different continents has increased, the mutual influences of alternative psychoanalytic approaches are transforming the field of psychoanalytic inquiry and practice. Margaret Mahler's (1971, 1975; Mahler, Pine, and Bergman, 1975) revolutionary direct observation, on one hand, and her exploration of the psychostructural consequences of early development, on the other, have brought profound changes to the theory of ego psychology.

In the past, new ideas and challenges have often been perceived as a threat to the new science of psychoanalysis, an internal threat added to the external challenge from alternative personality theories and from the antipsychodynamic views of biological psychiatry. I believe that the cross-fertilization currently derived from alternative psychoanalytic theories may be an important stimulus for scientific inquiry, empirical research, and clinical developments that may strengthen psychoanalysis as a science.

There are, undoubtedly, both psychoanalytic fashions and facile combinations of incompatible theories that are implicitly damaging to psychoanalytic depth. How to maintain the difference clearly, avoid premature closure, and keep the dialogue open is an exciting task of psychoanalytic education. Here I wish to explore the implications of Mahler's developmental theories and the challenges from alternative theoretical approaches in order to highlight what seem to me some crucial contributions of psychoanalytic developmental theory and their technical implications.

OEDIPAL AND PREOEDIPAL DETERMINANTS OF UNCONSCIOUS CONFLICTS

Both Jacobson (1964) and Mahler (Mahler and Furer, 1968) emphasized the preoedipal determinants of early ego and superego structures and the relationship between early oral and anal conflicts, on one hand, and the general patterning of internalized self and object representations on the other, a patterning that determines the normality or abnormality of the evolving tripartite structure. Under their influence, American ego psychology has integrated the theories of early development and internalization of object relationships in a manner parallel to the integration of the relationship between preoedipal conflicts and internalization of object relationships of the British object relations school. In fact, in spite of their vast differences in metapsychological orientation, the developmental schemata of Jacobson (1964) and Fairbairn (1952) strikingly overlap, as also do with them, the ideas of interpersonal psychoanalysts such as Searles (1986), in his writing on the transferences of schizophrenic patients.

Mahler demonstrated dramatically how the fusion of self and object representations in symbiotic psychosis, and the differentiation of self and object representations in the pathology of separation–individuation determine, respectively, the structural frames of childhood and adult psychosis in contrast to borderline conditions. The developmental timetables Mahler outlined put the shifts from infantile symbiosis to separation–individuation and from separation–individuation to object constancy at a point in development that is earlier than the entrance into the oedipal phase. Thus, fundamental structures of the mind and their corresponding unconscious conflicts predate oedipal conflicts and might even overshadow them in determining unconscious conflict. In this area, the controversy between classical ego psychology and developmental and object relations theory seems to be moving toward an integration of apparently opposing views.

The psychotherapeutic interaction with adult patients with schizophrenic illness who are amenable to a psychoanalytic approach and the psychoanalytic exploration of patients with borderline personality organization and narcissistic personality disorders consistently reveal oedipal as well as preoedipal psychopathology. In fact, when early life experiences are highly traumatic and ego distortions are gross, oedipal conflicts appear at their most intense and devastatingly pathological. In these patients, a characteristic pathological condensation between preoedipal and oedipal conflicts can be observed; in clinical practice, combinations of conflicts from many levels of development may be expressed in one dominant object relationship in the transference.

In fact, as Selma Kramer (1980) has pointed out, ". . .the psychic structures forming in the preoedipal child not only create the Anlage upon which the Oedipus 'settles' but determine the fashion in which the sexual drives interact with the state of self and object differentiation and with self and object relationships reached by the child" (pp. 246–247), a formulation she convincingly illustrates with clinical examples. Agreeing with Kramer, I have found that the earlier the origins of past conflictual fixation points, the more they are expressed in the actual behaviors activated in the transference. Conflicts of later origin tend to be manifest in transference fantasies.

While ego psychology object relations theory and British object relations theories tend to converge, there are two mutually exclusive theoretical positions that, however, agree in questioning Mahler's formulation. One is the French psychoanalytic mainstream viewpoint—perhaps most articulately formulated by Chasseguet-Smirgel (1986)—which sees the archaic Oedipus complex as a primary structure determining the overall frame within which the dyadic infant–mother relationship evolves. A related viewpoint is presented in more radical fashion by Lacanian psychoanalysis (Lacan, 1966; Benvenuto and Kennedy, 1986). The other challenge to Mahler's formulations comes from Kohut's (1971, 1977) self psychology, which, in practice, relegates oedipal psychopathology to a secondary place in the psychopathology of narcissistic personality disorders and borderline conditions. In fact, insofar as self psychology tends to consider even significant oedipal psychopathology as a possible consequence of predating preoedipal pathology, the importance of oedipal conflicts in this approach fades very much into the background. In reviewing the published case material from self psychology, it is my impression that one finds very little attention to oedipal conflicts in the work with the transference throughout a broad spectrum of cases.

From the perspective of Mahler's developmental theory, significant clinical evidence may be pointed to in rejecting both the radical Lacanian affirmation of the very early organization of the dynamic unconscious under the influence of the oedipal structure and the neglect of oedipal conflicts of self psychology. As mentioned before, in patients with the most severe forms of psychopathology who are still amenable to psychoanalytic exploration—including a segment of schizophrenic patients, the entire spectrum of borderline and narcissistic psychopathology, and the most severe cases of sexual perversion and psychoanalytically approachable psychosomatic illness—one finds, again and again, a typical condensation of preoedipal and oedipal conflicts. However, in advanced stages of the treatment, in which significant structural change has taken place and part-object transferences have been replaced by total-object transferences, one finds types of transference regression that closely resemble the psychological structure of separation–individuation.

Consider, for example, the "need–fear dilemma" (Burnham, Gibson, and Gladstone, 1969) of schizophrenic patients; one may observe the development in the transference of a search for symbiotic fusion, on one hand, and a fear of aggressive, engulfing involvement on the other, precisely when the patient has become able to differentiate himself more clearly from the analyst. This transference dilemma points to the earliest stage of separation–individuation. Or, at a time of increasing differentiation, the patient may show an elated sense of security provided by the protective concern and care from the transference object, a sense of security that leads to an increasing capability to expand and deepen object relationships in general; this points to practicing-phase developments. Or, finally, the typical conflict of borderline patients who oscillate between aggressive and invasive demands for total dedication from the therapist, on one hand, and haughty and arrogant rejection of his influence on the other, points to the dynamics of the rapprochement subphase. In other words, the original condensation of oedipal and preoedipal conflicts tends to resolve, as treatment advances, into the discrete transferences reflecting the early stages of development that predate object constancy.

A central flaw in the clinical approach of self psychology is ignoring the introjection of "bad object" representations, replicated in the transference both by enactment on the patient's part of the identification with a bad internal object, and the projection onto the therapist of such a bad object representation as a part of paranoid transference development. Insofar as self psychology, in its interpretation and management of the negative transference, neglects such hostile identifications—what might be called one half of the human experience in internalizing object relations— questions arise about the extent to which both preoedipal and oedipal phases of development can be fully diagnosed, let alone analytically worked through, with this approach.

Thus, the fact that we always do find both oedipal and preoedipal determinants of development clinically, with a particular condensation of them in cases of severe psychopathology, seems to me a fundamental empirical finding eminently compatible with Mahler's developmental theory.

DRIVE THEORY AND OBJECT RELATIONS THEORY

Insofar as Mahlerian developmental theory considers Freud's dual drive theory of libido and aggression as the basic motivational system, those who reject drive theory naturally raise the same question regarding developmental theory. It is particularly the object relations theoreticians who reject drive theory who strongly criticize developmental theory, precisely because it constitutes a synthesis between drive theory and object relations theory. The close relationships between Mahler's, Jacobson's, and my own views in integrating drive theory with object relations theory (Kernberg, 1976, 1980) have led to a decided criticism of that integration, particularly on the part of interpersonal psychoanalysis. This criticism is reflected, for example, in Greenberg and Mitchell's (1983) work and by followers of Fairbairn's (1952) and Guntrip's (1971) rejection of aggression as a primary drive, a view shared by interpersonal psychoanalysis, the Fairbairnian approach, and self psychology.

Here, I believe, is an area of significant potential resolution of long-standing problematic aspects of Freud's drive theory, particularly those reflected in the English translation of the *Standard Edition,* and the relationships among drives, affects, and object relations. On the basis of Jacobson's (1971) psychoanalytic studies of affects and of Mahler's research on childhood symbiosis and separation–individuation, I have reached conclusions that reformulate Freud's drive theory while maintaining, in essence, the concept of the dual drives as hierarchically supraordinate motivational systems. At the same time, I do propose a change in our formulation regarding the relationship between affects and drives, which differentiates my view from Jacobson's and Mahler's. I believe, however, that at the clinical level these new formulations are essentially compatible with Jacobson's overall metapsychological formulations and with the developmental theory of Margaret Mahler. I summarize these proposals in the following paragraphs.

Freud described specific biological sources of the sexual drive, according to the excitability of the erotogenic zones, but not of aggression. He characterized the aims and objects of both sexual and aggressive drives as changing throughout psychic development, in contrast to his concept of fixed sources of libido; the developmental continuity of sexual and aggressive aims could be recognized in a wide variety of complex psychic developments. Freud clearly differentiated drives from instincts (see Holder, 1970). He saw the drives as supraordinate and constant, rather than intermittent, sources of motivation. He saw instincts, on the other hand, as biological, inherited, and intermittent in the sense that they are activated by physiological and/or environmental stimulation. Freud conceived of drives as on the boundary between the physical and the mental; they were psychic processes rooted in biological dispositions. He proposed (1915a, b) that the only way we can know about drives is through their psychic representatives—ideas and affects. Libido is a drive, hunger is an instinct.

Holder (1970) and Laplanche and Pontalis (1973, pp. 214–217) have stressed the purely psychic nature of Freud's dual drive theory and have pointed to the loss of this distinction between psychological drives and biological instincts in Strachey's consistent translation of both *Instinkt* and *Trieb* as *instincts*. Laplanche and Pontalis (1973) appropriately remind us that Freud always referred to instincts as discontinuous, inherited behavior patterns that vary little from one member of the species to another. I am struck by how closely Freud's concept of instinct relates to modern instinct theory in biology, as represented, for example, by Lorenz (1963), Tinbergen (1951), and Wilson (1975), who consider instincts biologically determined perceptive, behavioral, and communicative patterns that are released by environmental factors activating inborn releasing mechanisms. Such a biological–environmental system is considered to be an epigenetic phenomenon. As Lorenz and Tinbergen illustrated in their animal research, the maturational and developmental linkage of discrete inborn behavior patterns, their overall organization within a particular individual, is very much determined by the nature of environmental stimulation: hierarchically organized instincts represent the integration of both inborn dispositions and environmentally determined learning. Instincts, accordingly, are hierarchically organized biological motivational systems.

Freud proposed (when he formulated his second affect theory) that drives are manifest by means of psychic representations or ideas—that is, the cognitive expression of the drive—and an affect. In this second theory of affect Freud proposed that affects are discharge processes that may reach consciousness but do not undergo repression and that only the mental representation of the drive may be repressed, together with a memory of or a disposition to the activation of the corresponding affect (1915a, b).

In clinical psychoanalysis, the idea that affects could not be dynamically unconscious has been a conceptual problem, and one could ask to what extent Freud's exclusive stress on the discharge aspects of affects in his second theory was a consequence of the then-dominant James–Lange (James, 1884; Lange, 1885) theory of affects. In any event, Arnold (1984, Chapters 11 and 12) has given us important neuropsychological evidence to show that affects may be stored in the limbic brain structures as affective memory.

In accordance with the clinical observations of Brierley (1937) and Jacobson (1953), as well as the empirical findings of Arnold (1970a, b),

Izard (1978), Knapp (1978), and Emde (1987, Emde, Katz and Thorpe, 1978), who have conducted neuropsychological empirical research on affective behavior, I define affects as psychophysiological behavior patterns that include a specific cognitive appraisal; a specific facial expression; a subjective experience of a pleasurable, rewarding, or painful, aversive quality; and muscular and neurovegetative discharge. The facial expression is part of the general communicative pattern that differentiates each particular affect.

There exists today fairly general agreement that affects from their very origin have a cognitive aspect, that is, that they contain at least an appraisal of "good" or "bad" of the immediate perceptive constellation, an appraisal that, in Arnold's (1970a, b) formulation, determines a felt motivation for action either toward or away from a certain stimulus or situation. Unlike James (1884) and Lange (1885), whose theories posited that the subjective and cognitive aspect of affects follow or derive from the perception of muscular and neurovegetative discharge phenomena, and unlike Tomkins (1970), who thought that the cognitive and felt aspect of affects follow or are derived from the perception of their facial expression, I believe—for reasons I will spell out—that the subjective quality of felt appraisal is the core characteristic of each affect.

Affects may be classified as primitive or derived. The former appear within the first two to three years of life and have an intense, global quality, with the cognitive element diffuse and not well differentiated. Derived affects are more complex. They consist of combinations of the primitive affects, cognitively elaborated; unlike primitive affects, they may not show all their original components with equal strength and their psychic aspects gradually come to dominate the psychophysiological and facial communicative ones. For these more complex phenomena I would reserve the term *emotions* or *feelings*, a distinction corresponding to the clinical observations regarding primitive affect states and complex emotional developments in the psychoanalytic situation.

If affects and emotions are complex structures, including subjective experiences of pain or pleasure with particular cognitive and expressive-communicative implications and neurovegetative discharge patterns, and if they are present—as infant research has demonstrated (Emde, Katz, and Thorpe, 1978; Izard, 1978; Stern, 1985; Emde, 1987)—from the earliest weeks and months of life, are they the primary motivational forces of psychic development? If these structures include both cognitive and affective features, what is left in the broader concept of drive that is not contained in the concept of affect? Freud implied that the drives are present from birth on but also that they matured and developed. We may argue, of course, that the maturation and development of affects are expressions of the drives underlying them, but if all the functions and manifestations of drives can be included in the functions and manifestations of developing affects, a concept of independent drives underlying the organization of affects would be difficult to sustain. In fact, the transformation, combination, and integration of affects throughout development; their integration with internalized object relations; and their overall developing dichotomy into pleasurable ones constituting the libidinal series and painful ones constituting the aggressive series all point to the enormous richness and complexity of their cognitive as well as affective elements. I believe the following complementary considerations are relevant.

To begin, the traditional psychoanalytic concept of affects solely as discharge processes and the assumption that diminution of psychic tension leads to pleasure, whereas increase of such tension leads to unpleasure, have unnecessarily complicated the analysis of affects in the clinical situation. Jacobson (1953) drew attention to the fact that tension states (sexual excitement, for instance) may be pleasurable and discharge states (anxiety, for instance) may be unpleasurable; she concluded, in agreement with the idea suggested by Brierley in 1937, that affects are complex and sustained intrapsychic tensions as well as discharge processes.

Jacobson also described in great detail how the cognitive aspects of affects refer to their investment of self and object representations in both ego and superego. She concluded that affective investments of self and object representations constitute the clinical manifestations of drives. In other words, whenever a drive derivative is diagnosed in the clinical situation, the patient's total experience, at that point, includes always an image or representation of the self relating to an image or representation of another person ("object") under the impact of the corresponding sexual or aggressive affect. And whenever an affect state of the patient is explored, a cognitive aspect to it is found, usually, in a relation of the self to an object under the impact of the affect state. The cognitive elements of drives, Jacobson went on, are represented by the cognitive relations between self and object representations, and between self and actual objects.

I propose that early affective development is based on the fixation of early, affectively invested object relations in the form of affective memory. The empirical research of Emde (1987; Emde, Katz, and Thorpe, 1978), Izard (1978), and Stern (1985) points to the central role of object relations in the activation of the infant's affects. Contemporary affect theory emphasizes the signaling function of affects in the relationship of the infant to the caregiver. This connection of object relations with the activation of affects supports the proposal that early affect states fixed in memory always involve an object relation. The activation of different affect states toward the same object takes place as the infant or child performs different developmental tasks under the influence of biologically determined instinctive behavior patterns. The variety of affect states directed to the same object may provide an economical explanation for how affects are linked with each other and are gradually integrated into a supraordinate motivational system that becomes the sexual or aggressive drive. Libido, or the sexual drive, results from the integration of positive, or rewarding, affect states such as elation and sexual excitement. Aggression as a drive results from the integration of negative, or aversive, affects such as hatred, rage, and disgust. This concept of aggression differs from other views, such as that of Parens' (1979, 1989), who includes "nondestructive aggression" and "nonaffective destructiveness" as components of the aggressive drive, together with "hostile destructiveness": I consider only the last one as the origin of aggression as a drive. Rage may, in fact, be considered the central affect of aggression. It is under conditions of intense, peak affect states, both pleasurable and painful, that the infant's relationship to the caregiver is highlighted and the intensity of the affect reinforces the establishment of affective memory.

The unconscious integration of affectively invested early object relations assumes the existence of a higher level motivational system than that represented by affect states per se, a motivational system provided by the libidinal and aggressive drives. This concept of drives does justice to the complexity of the affective developments in relation to the parental objects. In summary, I propose that affects are the link between biologically determined ("wired-in") components, on one hand, and intrapsychic organization of these into the overall drives, on the other. The correspondence of the series of pleasurable, or rewarding, and painful, or aversive, affect states with the lines of libido and aggression makes both clinical and theoretical sense.

Memory structures acquired during peak affect states will be very different from those acquired during quiescent or low-level affect states. When the infant is in a quiescent or low-level affect state, the memory structures established will be largely of a cognitive, discriminatory nature and contribute directly to ego development. Ordinary learning thus occurs when alertness is focused on the immediate situation and tasks, with little distortion derived from affective arousal and no particular defensive mechanism interfering with it. These memory structures constitute the early precursors, we might say, of more specialized and adaptive ego functioning—the affective memory structures of early consciousness. Affect, in short, also guides and facilitates memory organization under conditions of low-level affect activation. Here, memory is apt to be continuous and schematic, procedural rather than declarative (Emde, 1990, personal communication).

In contrast, peak affect experiences facilitate the internalization of primitive object relations organized along the axes of rewarding, or "all good," and aversive, or "all bad," objects. The experiences of self and object under the impact of extreme affect activation acquire an intensity that facilitates the laying down of affectively impregnated memory structures; these have an episodic, declarative quality. These affective memory structures, constituted in essence of self and object representations in the context of a specific peak affect experience represent the earliest intrapsychic structures of the symbiotic stage of development (Mahler and Furer, 1968). They mark the beginning of structure formation of internalized object relations, as well as the beginning of the organization of libidinal and aggressive drives. Peak affect states represent, by definition, extremely desirable or undesirable experiences that motivate wishes to repeat or avoid similar affective experiences. These wishes, gradually elaborated in unconscious fantasy, determine the motivational repertoire of what eventually constitutes the organized id.

I trust I have adequately conveyed the reasons for concluding that psychoanalytic drive theory not only has eminent clinical heuristic value but theoretical value as well. One might say that internalized object relations go on to eventually constitute the tripartite structure, while the integration of affects go on to eventually constitute the hierarchically supraordinate motivational system of drives.

DYADIC ORIGINS OR AUTISTIC ORIGINS?

It is probably fair to say that early psychoanalytic theories that considered the newborn infant an isolated, self-contained entity have given way to considering the infant a "wired-in" participant in a dyadic relationship. Within the infant–caregiver relationship, as contemporary infant researchers have convincingly demonstrated, the infant evinces a surprisingly early capacity to differentiate objects from each other and to develop a specific object relationship with the primary caregiver. The highly discriminating quality of early sensory perceptions reinforces the impression of a much earlier sense of self and of object than was formerly assumed. By the same token, the contemporary concept of affect as a phylogenetically recent neuropsychological system having as its primary function the establishment of an early and urgent communication system between infant and caregiver also points in the same direction.

Autism, earlier thought of as a primary phase of normal development, is now thought to be only a severe psychopathology. In fact, given the evidence of severe organic disturbances in the large majority of autistic patients, one might raise the question to what extent a primary biological disorganization of the cognitive and affective structures that ordinarily serve infant–caregiver communication undermines the very pillars of ordinary primary object relatedness.

A major question remaining, however, is whether the early building up of an internal world of object relationships starts out with the infant having discrete and differentiated concepts of self and of object or whether the original structures of internalized object relations are symbiotic—in other words, characterized by lack of differentiation between self and object representation. Infant research has questioned the assumption of a stage of normal symbiosis. Here, paradoxically, the assumption of a primary differentiation of self and object in the model of infant researchers and in Kleinian theory (Klein, 1946) contrasts with the model of early symbiosis derived from Mahlerian theory, with Loewald's (1970, 1974) formulation of earliest development, with Winnicott's (1965) viewpoint, and with the self psychology (Kohut, 1971, 1977, 1984) approach.

I think it is important to differentiate the experiences of the infant under conditions of peak affect states of extreme elation and pain, on one hand, and of ordinary, low-level affect states—under which most empirical research on infant observation takes place—on the other. In essence, I propose that at the level of low or modulated affect states characteristic of preconscious and conscious subjectivity, the early differentiation of self and object representations takes place simultaneously with the setting up of fused or undifferentiated self and object representations under conditions of peak affect activation. These fused self and object representations will constitute the primary object relations structures of the dynamic unconscious. In what follows, I spell out in somewhat greater detail these views of the parallel development of early consciousness and the dynamic unconscious.

It would seem reasonable to assume that an assembly of memory structures under the impact of peak affects may spur the earliest symbolic activities, in the sense that one element of such a peak affect constellation stands for the entire constellation (for example, a light going on in the room represents the presence of the feeding mother even before she herself is perceived). One could ask at what point simple association and conditioned reflexes become transformed into symbolic thinking, in the sense that one element stands for an entire constellation of evoked experience outside the rigid linkage of conditioned associations. In any case, it would be reasonable to assume that the earliest symbolic function would occur when the infant is in peak affect states.

Peak affect states, then, would signal the transformation of affective subjectivity into mental activity with symbolic functions. These symbolic functions can be clinically represented by affective memory structures that reflect pleasurable relations of infant and mother. In these pleasurable infant–mother relations, in spite of their highly differentiated cognitive inborn schemata, self and object representations are as yet undifferentiated. Affective memory structures derived from the unpleasurable or painful peak affect states in which self and object representations are also undifferentiated are built up separately from the pleasurable ones.

Mahler's symbiotic stage of development would correspond to these two parallel series of early states of consciousness, which do not yet include awareness of one's awareness (or self-awareness), that is, a categorical self. Perhaps of particular importance here is the gradual development of two parallel series, one of "all good" and the other of "all bad" fantasied characteristics of this symbiotic world. The "all good" world is expressed through the excited pleasure connected with the evoked and realized presence of the "good" mother. The "all bad" symbolic world concerns the evoked and fantastically imagined "bad" mother under conditions of extreme frustration, pain, or rage.

I mentioned before that infant observation is carried out mostly under conditions of the infant's "alert inactivity," a state facilitated by pleasurable affective states in mother–infant interaction. With the exception of Mahler's original work, Parens' (1979) longitudinal observational research, Fraiberg's (1983) observations, and a few others, most infant observation has not focused sufficiently on the nature of behavioral developments under conditions of serious frustration. This restricted investigative strategy creates a problem in understanding the infant's subjectively painful, frightening, and enraged experiences, which are so prevalent under conditions of severe psychopathology (Kaplan, 1987).

By the same token, the transformation of painful experiences into the symbolic image of an undifferentiated "bad self–bad mother" obviously contains an element of fantasy that transcends the realistic character of the "good" self-object representation. The aggressively invested line of internalized object relations may be more unrealistic; it is also traumatic, more difficult to tolerate in consciousness, and more difficult to elaborate into the realm of the ego. Early splitting mechanisms may defend the ego against the full awareness of these traumatic experiences and foster their repression later on. Therefore, the original fantasy material of what is to become the repressed unconscious later on may reflect a predominance of aggressive imagery and affects over the libidinal ones (Kernberg, 1990).

I believe that although the autistic phase of normal development now needs to be put to rest, the concept of the symbiotic stage of development should be maintained. In fact, the psychoanalytic exploration of psychosis, particularly the psychoanalytic psychotherapy of schizophrenia, provides evidence for the crucial importance of early, symbiotic development. The psychoanalytic study of the most intensely desired and feared human experiences—of sexual fusion in orgasm and dreaded dedifferentiation under extreme forms of persecution—point to the symbiotic core of unconscious human experience. Psychopathology of separation–individuation reveals the abiding desire to reestablish a presumed lost symbiosis with an ideal object and the abiding terror of invasion or engulfment by a persecutory one.

THE RECOVERY AND RECONSTRUCTION OF PREOEDIPAL DEVELOPMENT

Two problems converge regarding recovery and reconstruction of the preoedipal phase: first, whether early experience, particularly preverbal experience, may be recaptured in the transference and, second, whether reconstructions are reflections of "historical truth" or merely the replacement of one set of myths with another, resulting in the construction of "narrative truth" (Spence, 1982). Behind these issues stands the fundamental question of the nature of earliest unconscious experience and the question of whether symbolic thinking is initiated by language or before—and if before, the nature of prelinguistic logic.

The concept of linear developments to be pursued in psychoanalytic exploration has been questioned (André Green, 1987, personal communication). The French psychoanalytic mainstream, in particular, has questioned linearity—as contrasted with synchronicity—development pointing to diachronic sequences as instances of particularization of general synchronic development. The French believe that an archaic, primitive structuring of a basic oedipal frame influences development throughout the classical oral, anal, and oedipal stages and that the observable developmental sequences should not be confused with the completely different fantastic organization of intrapsychic psychogenetic development.

In this connection, Freud's concept of *Nachträglichkeit* has been amply utilized by both Lacanian and French mainstream psychoanalytic approaches. Regarding *Nachträglichkeit,* it needs to be pointed out that the *Standard Edition's* translation of "deferred action" is a definite mistranslation of the meaning of this German term, which refers to a retroactive modification of a past experience (so that, for example, under the impact of later development an earlier memory may acquire, a posteriori, a highly invested, even traumatic impact). This mistranslation has been thoughtfully criticized by Thoma and Cheshire (1989).

In my view, the defensive condensation of preoedipal and oedipal conflicts under the dominance of preoedipal aggression in patients with borderline personality organization and narcissistic pathology clearly illustrates synchronic condensations as an essential aspect of development. Premature oedipalization as an escape from preoedipal conflicts is the counterpart to the retrospective reinterpretation of the preoedipal past under the impact of oedipal developments. These defensive condensations and temporal shifts tend to decrease and to be resolved in advanced stages of psychoanalytic treatment, thus providing the opportunity for detailed analysis of, for example, early separation–individuation experiences in the transference of patients who for many years struggled with intimately condensed oedipal–preoedipal conflicts.

Regarding the broader question of the nature of psychoanalytic reconstruction, a recent review by Michels (1990) provides a helpful frame to explore this issue. Michels, in a comprehensive overview, suggests that the concept of reconstruction within psychoanalytic methodology has undergone a series of successive changes. Reconstruction originally referred to the recovery of traumatic childhood memories; then it referred to the recovery of repressed infantile wishes and drives; third, it referred to the genetic and structural aspects of development under the impact of such drives and the defenses against them and clarified these in the individual's developmental history; fourth, it referred to the developmental antecedents of the currently enacted transference paradigms, that is, to the translation of present structures into past developmental motivations; and fifth, reconstruction referred to the replacement of unconscious myths about the past with new, narrative myths about the past as understood in the light of transference analysis.

Michels's comprehensive list clearly encompasses current controversies regarding psychoanalytic theory: the importance of the here-and-now interpretation as against the there-and-then; the focus on the present versus past unconscious, historical truth versus narrative truth; and the implications of these issues for psychoanalytic technique.

My experience coincides very much with the conclusions by Selma

Kramer referred to earlier. As the condensations of preoedipal and oedipal conflicts are interpretively resolved in the transference, the preoedipal structures emerge clearly in the transference. Paulina Kernberg (1980) illustrated with both child and adult cases how derivatives of early nonverbal developmental events of the symbiotic and differentiation stages may be reflected not only in the patient's transference to the analyst as mother but also to the psychoanalytic setting, with the physical surroundings and analytic routine as representations of very early surroundings and routines. Within Michels's list of concepts of reconstruction, it is the fourth one, namely, reconstruction as the translation of present transference structures into past developmental structures (which incorporate traumatic childhood memories, repressed infantile wishes and drives, and the genetic and structural aspects of early development), that represents what I would consider a valid approach to reconstruction. By the same token, and I believe this dovetails with Kramer's observations, I mentioned before that the earlier the traumatic event and the consequent structural influence of that event, the more likely it is that the reproduction of this early experience in the transference may occur in nonverbal fashion and in the form of the activation of a particular behavioral pattern rather than in the recovery of a concrete memory from the past.

Also, the earlier the developmental period activated in the transference, the more likely it is that it may present itself not in an ordered sequence of memories from the past but in an apparently disparate emergence of experiences and fantasies, behaviors and memories, which reveal their common characteristics only by means of their interpretative integration, so that an unconscious pattern with a particular meaning is gradually assembled in the here-and-now before it can be retranslated into the there-and-then. This is a particular application of the general principle that the road to the unconscious experience of the past usually must traverse the unconscious experience in the here-and-now of the transference (Sandler and Sandler, 1984). It amplifies that general principle by pointing to the increasingly disparate nature of the material, its behavioral and patterned quality reflecting earliest experiences rather than the more specific, discrete, serially related memories from the past that permit reconstructions of later, particularly advanced oedipal conflicts. The practical implication of all of this is an application of Mahler's developmental approach that does not mechanically translate present-day transferential developments into theoretically assumed past antecedents but is alert to the combination or condensation of experiences, enactments, and memories that emerge in the context of transference analysis.

REFERENCES

Arnold, M. B. (1970a), Brain function in emotion: A phenomenological analysis. In: *Physiological Correlates of Emotion,* ed. P. Black. New York: Academic Press, pp. 261–285.

———— (1970b), Perennial problems in the field of emotion. In: *Feelings and Emotions,* ed. M. B. Arnold. New York: Academic Press, pp. 169–185.

———— (1984), *Memory and the Brain.* Hillsdale, NJ: Lawrence Erlbaum Associates.

Benvenuto, B. & Kennedy, R. (1986), *The Works of Jacques Lacan.* London: Free Association Books.

Brierley, M. (1937), *Trends in Psychoanalysis.* London: Hogarth, 1951, pp. 43–56.

Burnham, D., Gibson, R. & Gladstone, J. (1969), *Schizophrenia and the Need–Fear Dilemma.* New York: International Universities Press.

Chasseguet-Smirgel, J. (1986), *Sexuality and Mind.* New York: New York University Press.

Emde, R. (1987, July), Development terminable and interminable. Plenary presented at the 35th International Psycho-Analytical Congress, Montreal.

———— Katz, E. & Thorpe, J. (1978), Emotional expression in infancy: 1. Initial studies of social signaling and an emergent model. In: *The Development of Affect,* eds. M. Lewis & L. Rosenblum. New York: Plenum, pp. 125–148.

Fairbairn, W. R. D. (1952), *An object-relations theory of the personality.* New York: Basic Books.

Fraiberg, A. (1983), Pathological defenses in infancy. *Psychoanal. Quart.,* 60:612–635.

Freud, S. (1915a), Repression. *Standard Edition,* 14:141–158. London: Hogarth Press, 1957.

———— (1915b), The unconscious. *Standard Edition,* 14:159–215. London: Hogarth Press, 1957.

Greenberg, J. & Mitchell, S. (1983), *Object Relations in Psychoanalytic Theory.* Cambridge, MA: Harvard University Press.

Guntrip, H. (1971), *Psychoanalytic Theory, Therapy and the Self.* New York: Basic Books.

Holder, A. (1970), Instinct and drive. In: *Basic Psychoanalytic Concepts of the Theory of Instincts, Vol. III,* ed. H. Nagera. New York: Basic Books, pp. 19–22.

Izard, C. (1978), On the ontogenesis of emotions and emotion–cognition relationships in infancy. In: *The Development of Affect,* ed. M. Lewis & L. Rosenblum. New York: Plenum, pp. 389–413.

Jacobson, E. (1953), On the psychoanalytic theory of affects. In: *Depression.* New York: International Universities Press, 1971, pp. 3–47.

———— (1964), *The Self and Object World.* New York: International Universities Press.

———— (1971), *Depression: Comparative Studies of Normal, Neurotic and Psychotic Conditions.* New York: International Universities Press.

James, W. (1884), What is an emotion? *Mind,* 9:188–205.

Kaplan, L. J. (1987), Discussion. *Contemp. Psychoanal.*, 23(1):27–44.

Kernberg, O. F. (1976), *Object Relations Theory and Clinical Psychoanalysis.* New York: Aronson.

————— (1980), *Internal World and External Reality.* New York: Aronson.

————— (1990), New perspectives in psychoanalytic affect theory. In: *Emotion, Psychopathology and Psychotherapy,* ed. R. Plutchik & H. Kellerman. New York: Academic Press, pp. 115–130.

Kernberg, P. (1980), The origins of the reconstructed in psychoanalysis. In: *Rapprochement,* ed. R. F. Lax, S. Bach & J. A. Burland. New York: Aronson, pp. 263–281.

Klein, M. (1946), Notes on some schizoid mechanisms. *Internat. J. Psycho-Anal.,* 27:99–110.

Knapp, P. H. (1978), Core processes in the organization of emotions. In: *Affect: Psychoanalytic Theory and Practice,* ed. M. B. Cantor & M. L. Glucksman. New York: Wiley, pp. 51–70.

Kohut, H. (1971), *The Analysis of the Self.* New York: International Universities Press.

————— (1977), *The Restoration of the Self.* New York: International Universities Press.

Kramer, S. (1980), The technical significance and application of Mahler's separa-tion–individuation theory. In: *Psychoanalytic Explorations of Technique,* ed. H. Blum. New York: International Universities Press, pp. 241–262.

Lacan, J. (1966), *Écrits.* Paris: Editions du Seuil.

Lange, C. (1885), *The Emotions,* (trans. Dr. Kurella). Baltimore: Williams & Wilkins, 1922.

Laplanche, J. & Pontalis, J. B. (1973), *The Language of Psycho-Analysis.* New York: Norton.

Loewald, H. (1970), Psychoanalytic theory and the psychoanalytic process. *The Psychoanalytic Study of the Child,* 25:45–68. New York: International Univer-sities Press.

————— (1974), Current status of the concept of infantile neurosis. *The Psychoan-alytic Study of the Child,* 29:183–188. New Haven, CT: Yale University Press.

Lorenz, K. (1963), *On Aggression.* New York: Bantam Books.

Mahler, M. D. (1971), A study of the separation–individuation process and its possible application to borderline phenomena in the psychoanalytic situation. *The Psychoanalytic Study of the Child,* 26:403–424. New York: Quadrangle Books.

————— (1975), On the current status of the infantile neurosis. *J. Amer. Psychoa-nal. Assn.,* 23:327–333.

————— & Furer, M. (1968), *On Human Symbiosis and the Vicissitudes of Individu-ation: Vol. 1. Infantile Psychosis.* New York: International Universities Press.

————— , Pine, F. & Bergman, A. (1975), *The Psychological Birth of the Human Infant.* New York: Basic Books.

Michels, R. (1990), Psychoanalytic reconstruction. Presented at the Arden House Retreat of the Faculty of the Columbia University Center for Psychoanalytic Training and Research.

Parens, H. (1979), *The Development of Aggression in Early Childhood*. New York: Aronson.

———— (1989), Toward a Reformulation of the Psychoanalytic Theory of Aggression. In: *The Course of Life, Volume II*, S. Greenspan and J. Pollick, eds. New York: International Universities Press, 2nd edition, pp. 643–687.

Sandler, J. & Sandler, A. M. (1984), The past unconscious, the present unconscious and interpretation of the transference. *Psychoanal. Inq.*, 4:367–399.

Searles, H. (1986), *My Work with Borderline Patients*. Northvale, NJ: Aronson.

Spence, D. P. (1982), *Narrative Truth and Historical Truth*. New York: Norton.

Stern, D. N. (1985), *The Interpersonal World of the Infant*. New York: Basic Books.

Thoma, H. & Cheshire, N. (1989, April), Freud's *Nachtraglichkeit* and Strachey's "deferred action"; Trauma, constructions and the direction of causality. Paper presented at the international conference Translation in Transition: The Case of Sigmund Freud and James and Alix Strachey, London.

Tinbergen, N. (1951), An attempt at synthesis. In: *The Study of Instinct*. New York: Oxford University Press, pp. 101–127.

Tomkins, S. S. (1970), Affect as the primary motivational system. In: *Feelings and Emotions,* ed. M. B. Arnold. New York: Academic Press, pp. 101–110.

Wilson, E. O. (1975), *Sociobiology: The New Synthesis*. Cambridge, MA: Harvard University Press.

Winnicott, D. W. (1965), *The Maturational Processes and the Facilitating Environment*. New York: International Universities Press.

6

Contemporary Infant Research and the Separation–Individuation Theory of Margaret S. Mahler

Patricia A. Nachman

Margaret S. Mahler's conceptualization of separation–individuation is one of the most clinically utilized theories of development of the past quarter century. During the years immediately following the publication of her work on separation–individuation (Mahler, Pine, and Bergman, 1975) there has been a burgeoning of infant developmental research relating to mother–child interaction, to cognitive, affective, and perceptual abilities, and, most recently, to the patterns of relationships between infants and their caregivers. These contributions have shed new light on the abilities and early functioning of infants and young children. The implications of some of this work have led to theoretical and clinical debates, and in some cases basic theoretical assumptions have been questioned. Mahler's work in particular, as a major psychoanalytic conception of early development, has been scrutinized in the light of these recent findings.

While some of these debates (Peterfreund, 1978; Lichtenberg, 1983; Stern, 1985; Horner, 1988) have stimulated much thought, they have also led to considerable frustration because they try to compare and synthesize ideas that, although similar in name, are remarkably different in conceptualization. From a philosophical and a methodological perspective, it is apparent that psychoanalysis and academic developmental psychology are different disciplines; moreover, the relationship between these two disciplines has undergone considerable change over the past 40 years. At one

121

time there was almost no communication between the two fields. Now, after several decades of research in child development, it is becoming increasingly apparent that the interests of these disciplines are beginning to converge; the work of a sample of authors and researchers whose work in developmental psychology is relevant to psychoanalysis is summarized in the following pages. The purpose of this chapter is to trace the changing patterns in the relationship between these two disciplines and to identify the developmental research that has contributed to these changes. The separation–individuation theory of Mahler and contemporary infant research will be discussed from this point of view.

HARTMANN

Hartmann's "Psychoanalysis and Developmental Psychology" (1950) provides a good entry point for this discussion because it anticipated some of the issues that are currently being debated. The term *psychoanalysis* in his paper and in general refers to a theory of personality development using a method based on reconstructive techniques. Data were obtained primarily from therapeutic work with adults and children based chiefly on pathological conditions. Developmental psychology offered a different approach to the study of personality and development. Its methods were based on the direct observation of children, particularly normal ones. Hartmann saw developmental psychology as a "scientifically" based theory of general psychology, one that was "objective" and closely allied with the methods of the natural sciences. Psychoanalysis, on the other hand, was methodologically more suited to the study of meanings, intentions, and events associated with unconscious conflicts.

Hartmann's central idea was that the advancement of psychoanalysis as a science requires the integration of these two perspectives into a single discipline. This conceptualization of Hartmann's instituted a shift in emphasis to the ego and to what he referred to as the "conflict-free sphere of development," which involved considerations of normality and adaptation.

MAHLER

Mahler's interest in the differentiation of the psychic structure from the perspective of the ego, her reliance on direct observation of the very young child, and her emphasis on normality attest to Hartmann's influence and to her exposure to the European psychologies of the period.

Mahler based her study of the separation–individuation subphases on psychoanalytically informed direct observation of normal children during the first three years of life. Her formulations of the earliest years of life relied heavily on metapsychological concepts, and although she might have shifted emphasis toward the ego, she worked entirely within a metapsychological framework.

The Psychological Birth of the Human Infant[1] (Mahler, Pine, and Bergman, 1975) is a book outstanding for its time because it constitutes an attempt to understand the formation of psychic structure. Mahler chose to explore the establishment of self and object representations. The book focuses on the problem of the differentiation of these representations and in understanding the genetic aspects of psychoanalysis. Central to Mahler's thesis is the idea of the infant's ability to use the mother for structuralization of its newly developing ego. Separation–individuation is the process in which the infant gradually diminishes its dependence on the mother figure, a process that culminates in established object and self representations.

Many others besides Mahler were engaged in empirical research during this period and were also aligned with psychoanalysis (Leichtman, 1990). Such major figures as Bowlby (1944, 1958, 1960) and Spitz (1945, 1965) sparked an interest in developmental research, which gained increasing momentum. They were joined by a number of researchers who were analytically trained, many of whom became interested in the earliest periods of development (Brody, 1956, 1970; Lustman, 1956; Sander, 1962, 1964; Provence and Lipton, 1962; Wolff, 1963; Escalona, 1963, 1968; Call, 1964; Decarie, 1965; Kestenberg, 1965; Robson, 1967; Emde and Harmon, 1972; and Fraiberg, 1977). These analytically oriented researchers of this period can be divided into two groups (Leichtman, 1990). The type of research that Mahler did and that continues to be done by, for example, Galenson and Roiphe (1971), McDevitt (1975) and Parens (1979) can be described as psychoanalytic developmental research. Work of this kind focuses on specific questions raised by psychoanalytic theory and utilizes the method of naturalistic observation to validate or expand on analytic notions.

A second type of research related to psychoanalysis is represented by the work of Benjamin, Emde, Sander, Settlage, Stern, and Wolff; this body of work is best described as developmental research undertaken by psychoanalysts. This work is essentially based on methods characteristic of

---

[1]Mahler's earlier papers on separation–individuation can be found in Mahler (1979).

empirical researchers, but in general the findings lead to an elaboration of psychoanalytic principles.

By 1975, the year *The Psychological Birth of the Human Infant* was published, a third important trend in developmental research had begun. This was work being done by academic developmental psychologists that was relatively remote from, and had little impact on, psychoanalysis. This work lent itself to established empirical methodologies; in addition, new methodologies were developed that rapidly advanced the study of infants and young children. Cognition, affects, perception, memory, language, and mother–child interaction were the areas of study most suitable for this type of investigation. With few exceptions, academic researchers had little or no discourse with psychoanalysis. Psychoanalysts all but ignored the developments in academic child and infant research, with the exception of a few useful ideas from Werner and Piaget.

BOWLBY

John Bowlby's place is of major significance in this discussion of psycho-analysis and academic developmental psychology. His initial psychoana-lytic orientation was integrated with the biological discipline of ethology and its focus on behavior in an evolutionary context. He provided a crucial link between the two disciplines that has had lasting impact on the field of developmental psychology. When in the early 1950s there was much controversy in England concerning the nature of early object relationships, Bowlby was alone in approaching the problem from the standpoint of academic developmental psychology. He recast basic psychoanalytic themes having to do with attachment, separation, and loss in the form of potentially testable hypotheses. He examined these phenomena using empirical methods based on the direct observation of children and suggested an alternative theory based on conceptualizations derived from ethology, a more empirically based theory. Captivated by ethological ideas based on the work of Lorenz, Bowlby now had a biological basis for his beliefs that a child needs a viable ongoing attachment to a primary caregiver and that profound suffering ensues if that attachment is inter-rupted or lost. He developed the concept of "internal working models" to describe how the infant's sense of self and others unfolds through interaction with the primary caregiver. To understand the pivotal role Bowlby played, it is necessary to see that he was the first to put forth a comprehensive alternative theory derived from concepts basic to psycho-analysis.

While his alternative theory may have isolated Bowlby from his psycho-analytic community, it set the stage for a line of inquiry that profoundly transformed the field of developmental psychology. Far more than in the past, academic developmental psychology came to focus on issues central to psychoanalysis that had to do with the mother–child relationship, separation, and loss. By employing a new methodology more in keeping with the procedures of academic psychology, academic developmental psychology eventually set itself completely apart from psychoanalysis.

AINSWORTH

The work of Mary Ainsworth, an American research assistant of Bowlby's, marked the beginning of a critical shift in developmental psychology in America. Before Ainsworth's work was published in 1969 almost no procedures using the more rigorous methodology of academic psychology were available for assessing an infant according to the concepts Bowlby set forth. Ainsworth et al. (1978) developed the most widely used measure of mother–child attachment relationships: a laboratory paradigm known as the Strange Situation. This standardized experimental procedure for assessing attachment behavior in infants aged approximately one year comprises eight increasingly stressful episodes involving the infant, its mother, and a stranger. On the basis of the infant's reunion behavior with the caregiver following a brief separation, it is possible to classify the infant's pattern of attachment to that caregiver. Infants are classified as "secure" if they seek comfort, proximity, and contact and then gradually return to play when the caregiver returns. They are classified as "insecure–avoidant" if they actively avoid and ignore the caregiver when she returns by turning or moving away. Infants who show anger and resistance to a caregiver's return, a need for proximity and contact, and an inability to be comforted are classified as "insecure–ambivalent." The significance of this laboratory procedure lies in its standardization, which allows for an assessment of complex interactive behavior patterns that are related to a young child's sense of security to attachment figures.

The Strange Situation has proved successful in stimulating further studies. Two decades of research using this procedure has generated significant information about maternal and infant contributions to the quality of attachment relationships, about stability and change in attach-ment relationships, and about the social and emotional sequelae of the secure, insecure–avoidant, and insecure–ambivalent patterns of attach-ment to the mother.

This line of investigation stemming from Ainsworth's work has been steadily progressing in a direction that was inconceivable two decades ago. Currently, academic psychologists are attempting to think more complexly about subjective experiences in parents and infants (Zeanah and Anders, 1987), about the internal construction of relationships (Sroufe and Fleeson, 1986), about the sense of self in the context of parent–infant relationships (Stern, 1985) and about how relationship patterns are carried and transmitted from parent to child (Main, Kaplan, and Cassidy, 1985). This shift in emphasis represents a change from interest in the external to the internal life and from objective to subjective experience.

The new direction in which attachment theory is now taking us means that instead of focusing on the external behavioral elements of the mother–child interaction and the correspondence to the attachment classifications of secure, insecure–avoidant, insecure–ambivalent, investigators are beginning to take interest in intrapsychic factors within mothers that promote secure relationships in their children. This shift in emphasis implies a rekindling of interest in psychoanalysis and in concepts that are basic to psychoanalytic theory, particularly those having to do with the process of internalization.

MAIN

In 1985 Mary Main and her colleagues began to examine the quality of mothers' (and fathers') "internal working models" of their own early attachment relationships and were able to document some of the ways in which the organization and content of the mothers' representational models corresponded to the quality of their infants' attachment to them. This work is significant because it offers a framework for understanding associations between parents' past history and present parent–child relationships (Bowlby, 1980; Bretherton, 1985).

The idea behind "internal working models" of self and others is that they are developed in infancy and childhood and are generalized representations of the events experienced with the caregiving figures. These conceptualizations or models become incorporated into the personality structure of the individual and serve as templates or guides for the child's future interactions (Bretherton, 1985; Sroufe and Fleeson, 1986). Internal working models and subsequent patterns of interactional behavior are predicted to be relatively stable over time and to exert influence in adult life, particularly with respect to parenting behavior.

In Main's research the quality of parents' internal working models of attachment was assessed using the Adult Attachment Interview (George, Kaplan, and Main, 1985), a structured, open-ended interview that probes for parents' recollections of their own parents as attachment figures, as well as for thoughts about the significance of attachment relations in general. Following the attachment classification system of the Strange Situation for infants, Main classified three patterns of attachment in adults that correlated with the infant classifications described by Ainsworth. Parents rated as "secure" on the basis of their interview responses were found to be more likely to have children who are themselves secure. These mothers tend to value both attachment relationships and autonomy. They were at ease when discussing the influence of their own attachment to their parents. They also were able to talk about the way those relationships influenced their own personality, and they were able to integrate both the positive and negative affects associated with their early experiences in a way that was coherent and realistic.

Main and her colleagues found that parents rated as "dismissing" were more likely to have children who were insecure–avoidant. These parents in their interview responses made light of the value of attachment relationships, feeling that early attachment experiences had little effect on their own development. They frequently claimed that they had little or no memory of incidents from childhood. When specific memories were recalled, they were not likely to support the description they had given of their parents. These descriptions tended to be idealized so that negatively tinged memories were avoided or denied.

In Main's research, parents who were rated as "preoccupied" were more likely to have children who were previously classified as insecure–ambivalent. These parents seemed overly preoccupied with earlier family attachments. They were able to recall many specific, often unhappy incidents about early childhood attachment experiences but could not integrate them into an overall cohesive picture. Their interview responses revealed that they were still enmeshed in dependencies on their own parents and used inordinate effort to please them. Their representations of early experiences were often quite inconsistent, since they had difficulty integrating the negative affects that pervaded their memories. One of the most significant ways secure adults differ from dismissing or preoccupied adults is in their ability to recognize and integrate negative affect (Kobak, 1987). Dismissing adults aim at excluding these experiences and deny them whereas preoccupied adults are inclined to be overwhelmed by them.

The organization of the young child's emotional life has been given a position of central importance in determining what has been transmitted to the child from the parents (Kobak, 1987; Kobak and Shaver, 1987; Kobak and Sceery, 1988). The "secure" pattern reflects the feeling that fear, distress, or anger can be openly communicated without risking a sense of security. "Dismissing" strategies in the adult (and avoidant strategies in the child) reflect the feeling that negative feelings will disrupt the attachment relationship.

Mental Representation

An important question that follows from the research of Main and her colleagues concerns the issue of how the parents' "messages" become internalized. The concept of the construction of mental representations is important in this context because many developmental psychologists see this as the key to further understanding of the internalization process. Mental representations as organizing structures provide the means for the integration of current experience with past experience. They are essentially memory structures that represent a version of an experience that guides behavior. Recent research has demonstrated that these mental representations are not memories of specific events but, rather, abstract "averages" of related events. This is analogous to the natural development of the concept of categories of objects in memory, which has been described in the developmental research literature. Rosch (1978; Rosch et al., 1976) has referred to these as "protypic memories," Nelson and Gruendel (1981) call these "generalized event representations," and Stern (1985a) speaks of "representations of events that are generalized" or RIGs.

This concept of the representation of experience goes significantly further than any other conceptualization to date in providing information regarding the processes taking place in the minds of infants who are not yet verbal. These conceptualizations of how representations are constructed are also the key to how schemas of the self and other are derived. The constructs of representation of event knowledge (Nelson and Gruendel, 1979), of "scripts" (Schank and Abelson, 1977), and of "episodic" memory (Tulving, 1972) all reflect the recent surge of interest in the representation in memory for events having to do with self, with other, and with autobiographical knowledge.

Several investigators of mother–infant interaction now concur that self and object representations originate prior to the emergence of symbolic capacity (Emde, 1981; Sander, 1983a, b; Stern, 1985; Horner, 1985; Beebe and Lachmann, 1988). Evidence for some basic form of representational capacity for infants under 7 months comes from experiments on recognition memory (Fagan, 1974), cued recall tasks (Fagen et al., 1984), early imitation (Meltzoff, 1985), and affect memory (Nachman, 1982; Nachman and Stern, 1983; Nachman, Stern, and Best, 1986); the creation of prototypes later in the first year has been studied by Strauss (1979). But even three-month-olds can generate "rules" to govern their expectancies as to whether an event will occur after two encounters. These "rules" are based on a determination that a pattern is the same or different (Fagen et al., 1984). This early capacity to store in memory the distinctive features of stimuli and to order events as more or less similar implies that some form of nascent or rudimentary representational system is operative even during the first months of life.

Very young infants are also apparently inherently able to perceive natural categories of events important for participating in human interaction. For example, infants have a propensity for participating in eye-to-eye contact and for alerting to the stimulus features contained in the human voice and face (see reviews by Emde and Robinson, 1979; Papousek and Papousek, 1981; Campos et al., 1983; Stern, 1985). The work on intersubjectivity (Trevarthan, 1979, Bretherton, McNew, Beeghly-Smith, 1981), affect attunement (Stern, 1985), and mother–child "matching" (Beebe and Lachmann, 1986, 1988) provide examples of a finely tuned communication system between caregivers and infants. We can assume that representations of these self and object interactions are formed as readily as those for other events (Stern, 1985).

There is increasing evidence that infants use their ability to represent social interactions in the development of expectancies about how the interactions will go (see Lewis and Goldberg, 1969; Lamb, 1981; Stern, 1985; Beebe, 1986; Beebe and Lachmann, 1988). The neonate has a remarkable capacity to perceive time and temporal sequence, to detect contingencies between its own behavior and external events, and to develop expectancies of when events occur (Allen et al., 1977; Watson, 1985). Interestingly, these studies provide empirical support for the idea Benedek (1938) proposed several decades ago about the development of "confident expectation" in very young infants. There is widespread agreement among current day infant researchers, based on an abundance of experimental evidence, that very young infants are capable of some form of self and other representation and that they also have the capacity to represent their experiences of social interaction. These studies, then, lend support to Bowlby's idea of the early formation of "internal working models" of relationship experiences.

Separation–Individuation Theory and Attachment Theory

Weaving together the diverse strands of academic developmental psychology and the metapsychological concepts of development set forth by

Mahler, one can see connections between attachment theory and Mahler's theory despite significant methodological and philosophical differences.

Central to both theories is the idea of the mother as a secure base from which the infant explores the world. Ainsworth referred to the infant's "proximity-seeking" behavior, and Mahler (1966) described the mother as "a beacon of orientation." Both conceptualizations give central importance to the idea of the emotional availability of the caregiver. For Mahler this means the infant is able to use the maternal ego as an external source of help and reassurance until its own ego matures and is less vulnerable. For Ainsworth and other attachment theorists the idea of maternal emotional availability is organized in terms of the effects of the mother's availability on the infant's exploration and play.

For Mahler separation is a gradual developmental process. Her theory of separation–individuation is primarily concerned with describing a developmental intrapsychic process through which the human infant is born in a psychological sense.

Attachment theorists, in contrast, are more concerned with the psychobiological aspects of separation than with separation as a developmental process. Their focus, until recently, has been on receptor processes that interact with environmental stimuli to activate and terminate the activity of behavioral systems, particularly those having to do with parental protection. The new shift in interest toward the internal or subjective aspects of attachment is generating a new area of inquiry that promises to bring further convergence between developmental psychology and psychoanalysis. Recent work on the organization of negative feelings (Kobak, 1987) as revealed in the Adult Attachment Interview suggests that Mahler's conceptualizations of ambivalence and the vicissitudes of the aggressive drive that are central to understanding separation–individuation (McDevitt, 1983) will find some interesting correspondences in the empirical findings from attachment research.

Our task would be much easier if we were to find no overlap or intermingling of ideas, but this is never the case. The infant researchers almost unanimously accept the concept of "predesigned emergent structures," that is, of the biological organizing processes of development. If Mahler is read carefully, it can be seen that biological concepts also informed her thinking about early development. Her notion of symbiosis was based on the idea that the child initially is ill prepared for life on its own and that a biological system prepares the mother–child for their early interactive behavior. In Mahler's work the ideas of adaptation and "social preparedness" and even the pivotal role given to walking as an impetus toward independence are rooted in an appreciation of those biological processes that are of central importance to attachment researchers and other infant researchers who have a strong biological orientation (for example, Emde and Sander).

EMDE

Robert Emde is in the group of psychoanalytically trained researchers who work within the framework of academic developmental psychology. Emde's interest in psychoanalytic research is rooted in his early work with René Spitz on infant observation. His work deserves special comment because the empirical studies coming from his laboratory are based on psychoanalytically informed observations of early development; Emde is outstanding for his capacity to cast psychoanalytic concepts in the form of testable research hypotheses. Also, he has provided the only body of empirical research that specifically tests some of the ideas set forth by Mahler. Some of these studies will be considered in the following paragraphs.

Influenced by developmental biology, Emde's research centers around the infant's innate capacities for participating in human interactions. The themes of Emde's work are affectivity (1983), emotional signaling between infant and caregiver, and moral development. He proposes that it is our affective life that gives continuity to our experience, in spite of the many other ways we change. This is so because its central organization is biological and its vital relations are unchanging. Our affective core ensures that we are able to understand other human beings.

From an adaptational point of view, affects have social signaling functions in infancy, which makes the affective core one of central importance. Emotional signaling between the infant and caregiver provides the basis for communicating needs, intentions, and satisfactions. Indeed, the emotional availability of the caregiver in infancy seems to be among the most central growth promoting features of early experience. Through her behavior more than through her mere physical presence the caregiver communicates that she is aware of the infant's emotional expressions and is monitoring ongoing activity in such a way that she is available to respond empathically and to offer her own emotional expressions as information when the infant is uncertain and looks to her for guidance. In a playroom study (Carr, Dabbs, and Carr, 1975) it was determined that 18- to 30-month-old infants positioned themselves to keep their mother's face in view even when it was at the expense of leaving interesting toys. It was inferred that infants need to refer to mother's face to be assured of her emotional availability.

Sorce and Emde (1981) found striking effects of mothers' emotional availability on infants' exploration and play in a study of five-month-olds; infants whose mothers were not preoccupied in the reading of a newspaper showed more pleasure across all activities than did infants whose mothers were reading. Not only was there more pleasurable interest exhibited by those infants whose mothers were not reading but they also smiled significantly more frequently and uttered more nondistressed vocalizations.

A second major finding of this study concerns a difference in exploratory activity. Infants whose mothers were not reading a newspaper during the observation period took an increased number of steps during various uncertain situations; that is, in all measures of exploratory behavior there was increased venturing forth in infants whose mothers were not reading. In addition, there were more looks at mother and more positive bids toward mother in the infant group where mothers were not reading. Interestingly, in terms of "refueling" behavior (Mahler et al., 1975), the infants whose mothers were reading came over to them less often but lingered longer when they came. Thus, this experimental situation gives empirical support to Mahler's claim that parental figures' emotional availability fosters enjoyment, curiosity, and enhanced opportunities for learning.

In another set of experiments Emde and his group investigated the importance of emotional signaling through a phenomenon they have termed "social referencing" (Campos and Stenberg, 1981; Feinman and Lewis, 1981; Sorce and Emde, 1985; Klinnert et al., 1986). Typically, in this series of experiments an infant explores a playroom environment and encounters one of several experimental situations of uncertainty (e.g., a toy robot, an apparent drop-off on a crawling surface, an unusual toy); the infant then looks to the mother. If mother signals fear or anger, the infant avoids the new situation; if mother signals joy or interest, the infant approaches and explores the new situation. Social referencing begins in the middle of the first year and is especially prominent during the second year of life. Uncertainty about new situations occurs frequently, and the infant looks to another (usually mother) in order to resolve the uncertainty and regulate behavior accordingly.

This notion of the importance of emotion and emotional signaling between infant and caregiver leads to Emde's recent work on moral development. One can see in following the development of very young children that approval and disapproval of behavior is successfully conveyed by means of the social referencing (exchange of emotional signals) observed during the latter part of the first year.

One- to three-year-olds are particularly sensitive to the affect signals caregivers convey when meaningful rules and standards are formulated. Infants just over one year old are, on occasion, able to obey certain rules even in their caregiver's absence, which implies that some sort of "internal" system is operative.

Emde, more than any other developmental researcher, has made use of Mahler's theories to guide aspects of his own work. The principle of emotional availability, central to Mahler's work, is prominent both implicitly and explicitly in his investigations. The striking effects of maternal emotional availability on an infant's exploration and play, have already been described. The concept of social referencing in Emde's work is very close to what Mahler described as "emotional refueling" and "checking back." Most recently, in a series of experimental studies Emde tested a hypothesis put forth by Mahler and others that the onset of walking is accompanied by a period of elation or high positive affect. These studies (Biringen et al., 1989; Biringen, 1990; Jones, Henderson, and Emde, 1990) compared walking infants with nonwalking infants of the same age. Preliminary results from these studies indicate that there is a pattern of increased positive affect as well as increased negative affect, particularly fearfulness, in the infant after the onset of walking. It is not yet clear, as additional data remain to be analyzed, whether there is also a decrease in overall negative expression, such as irritability and generalized distress, after an infant begins to walk.

STERN

Daniel Stern, like Emde, was trained in psychiatry and psychoanalysis and has worked primarily in the field of infant research using methods that are in accord with academic psychology.

Most information about the inner life of very young children comes from reconstructive reports of adults in analysis, from children in analysis, from the observation of young children, or from speculation drawn from metapsychological principles. Stern was aware that if psychoanalytic developmental theory was to be convincing, a greater correspondence between what he called the "observed" infant and the traditional psychoanalytic view of early development was needed. His work is outstanding for his creative ability in developing a methodology for getting closer to the subjective or inner experience of the prelinguistic child.

Stern's work can also be singled out from a host of other psychoanalytically informed investigators interested in developmental theory (Emde, Gaensbauer, and Harmon, 1976; Emde, 1980a, 1981, 1983; Greenspan,

1979, 1981, 1989; Settlage, 1980; Lichtenberg, 1981, 1983; Sander, 1983a; Stechler and Kaplan, 1980; Pine, 1985; and others) because he has used his research to advance a critique of psychoanalysis whereas his colleagues are more inclined to think in terms of revisions, elaborations, and refinements (Leichtman, 1990) of psychoanalytic theory.

Stern's (1985) book *The Interpersonal World of the Infant* has had significant impact in part because the position he presented was carefully laid out and clearly stated as an alternative view. He made no claims to presenting a ''finished'' theoretical position and admitted that the ''value of this working theory remains to be proved and even its status as a hypothesis remains to be explored'' (p. 275). What is of importance is that Stern's proposal can stand on its own and that it is different enough from psychoanalysis that the juxtaposition of the two views creates a tension that is useful for argument and debate. With two neatly delineated theoretical camps based on different but clearly definable assumptions, the way was paved for a challenge to the traditional psychoanalytic view of developmental theory.

Mahler's theory is at the center of this critique because she presented one of the most complete theories of early development based on psychoanalytic principles. Her central thesis is that during the separation–individuation subphases, which begin in the third quarter of the first year, the child slowly becomes able to separate self from mother and to differentiate intrapsychically its primitive self and object representations from the hitherto more ''fused'' self and object representations. With further integration and stabilization of these representations, there is the beginning establishment of (libidinal) object constancy and self-identity.

Stern's (1985) book also concerned the development of the infant's sense of self. For Stern the central developmental line from among those followed in other stage theories of development (e.g., Spitz, 1965; Mahler et al., 1975; Greenspan, 1981; Sander, 1983a) is the formation of the ''senses of self'' and correlated ''senses of others.'' The phrase *sense of self* refers to the subjective experience of the self. Stern describes four relatively distinct senses of self, each of which emerges in conjunction with new maturational capacities. It is important to understand that Stern's approach, unlike Mahler's, involves first formulating what capacities would be needed in order for the infant to consolidate the sense of self and then presenting empirical evidence culled from a vast array of current research studies to demonstrate the existence of those capacities.

Stern's major points are that infants begin to experience a *sense of an emergent self* from birth, are inherently aware of self-organizing processes, and do *not* enter the world in a state of self–other undifferentiation. Stern cites studies that make use of such behaviors as head turning, sucking patterns, and gaze to demonstrate the neonate's active need for stimulation; he uses an abundance of other studies from the developmental literature to show that from birth on there appears to be an inborn rudimentary tendency to form and test hypotheses about what is experienced in the world. From about two to six months the infant consolidates the *sense of core self* and learns how to organize the experience of "self-being-with-another." Union experiences are viewed as the successful result of actively organizing the self–other experience rather than as the result of undifferentiated representations. By way of establishing empirical evidence for the consolidation of a core sense of core self, a variety of infant studies are cited that describe infants' abilities to detect invariant features of the self. Stern calls these "self invariants" and provides examples from recent research describing the infant's nascent capacities for what he calls self-agency, self-coherence, self-affectivity, and self-history. Central to these concepts is research that provides information about memory and, in particular, the capacity of the infant to maintain a preverbal memory of himself or herself or, in other words, a self-history continuous in time. This is where the idea of mental representation that was discussed earlier is important; Stern has postulated a scheme, based on other work in developmental psychology, for conceptualizing the nature of mental representations in preverbal infants. Understanding the ways these representations are constructed is key to gaining further knowledge about the inner experience of the young child, which is why this area of research has become central for Stern and other developmental researchers (e.g., Beebe, Bretherton, Main, Nelson).

In addition, Stern cites a wealth of studies that show that the infant quickly learns that the regulation of his or her own emotional states is dependent on others (adult caregivers) and that show that during the latter part of the first year some rudimentary but profound sense that others can understand and share in their intentions, thoughts, and feelings brings about a new level of "intersubjective" experience (see Trevarthan, 1979). Around this time a *sense of subjective self* begins to evolve. Infants become aware that others can match or mismatch their mental states.

When language develops, a *verbal sense of self* emerges, and infants develop the capacity to communicate about themselves to others. While language is an extraordinary achievement, it can also be limiting in that it represents experience symbolically and not as it is actually lived. According to Stern, the preverbal infant perceives the surround as more "real" than does the verbal child, who, with the development of the capacity for symbolization, uses fantasy to temper reality. Thus language brings with it what Stern calls the narrative self, a new domain of experience in which children begin to construct their own life story, which becomes their autobiographical history.

Unlike most other stage theories of development these senses of self postulated by Stern are continuous and develop throughout the life span. One sense of self does not supersede the others, although each emerges at a different point in development.

It can be seen from this account that Stern's position suggests disagreement with the basic developmental assumptions of traditional psychoanalytic thought. Called into question are the ideas that developmental stages supersede one another, that the oral, anal, or phallic psychosexual stage is dominant during any particular developmental period; that the pleasure principle necessarily precedes the reality principle; and that drive theory is necessary to understand development. Stern disagrees with such central psychoanalytic concepts as the stimulus barrier, the undifferentiated phase, and the normal autistic and symbiotic subphases of the separation–individuation process.

DIVERGENT POINTS OF VIEW

From Stern's perspective the infant matures toward merger relationships and is not in a merged or undifferentiated state during early infancy. Related to this idea is the notion that reality is least distorted during the first months of life; thus, the reality principle is operative from birth and does not necessarily evolve from the pleasure principle.

Lest one feel that basic psychoanalytic assumptions have been turned on their heads, it is important at this juncture to recall again the different scientific and philosophical traditions from which both these points of view emerge. Seen in the broadest context, the difference between academic psychology and psychoanalysis is the difference between empiricist and rationalist epistemologies (i.e., whether we can explain knowledge solely in terms of sense experience in the form of objective research or solely in terms of reason and the workings of the mind). Although discussion of this particular point is beyond the scope of this chapter, epistemological differences such as these partially account for the polarities in perspective in the two positions.

To argue each of the aforementioned points of difference would probably yield little more than a restatement of the positions. Semantic difficulties abound when we treat ideas from each of these viewpoints as if they shared a common language and conceptual understanding. As Anna

Freud (1969) once commented when talking about attachment theory, "one simply can not make comparisons as if they were mental phenomena of the same order" (p. 176).

Academic psychologists have expressed similar opinions. After many years of work as an academic experimental psychologist attempting to test psychoanalytic propositions, Sears (1944) wrote the following conclusions:

> It seems doubtful whether the sheer testing of psychoanalytic theory is an appropriate task for experimental psychology. Instead of trying to ride on the tail of a kite that was never meant to carry such a load, experimentalists would probably be wise to get all the hunches, intuitions, and experience possible from psychoanalysis and then, for themselves, start the laborious task of constructing a systematic psychology of personality, but a system based on behavioral rather than experiential data [p. 329].

Stern's work and the research in the entire field of developmental psychology during the past two decades embody what Sears had in mind. There is no doubt that an independent and methodologically substantial body of work now exists in the field of child development. Also, within the field of developmental psychology there are many contending theories. Developmental psychology is not a theoretically unified body. Just how to understand these new research studies and how the findings from this body of work relate to Mahler's psychoanalytic developmental theory is a question of considerable complexity.

This issue is probably best conceptualized in theoretical terms. What needs to be considered is the problem of how change is made in theory, which relates to the question of whether contemporary infant research will be a challenge to psychoanalytic developmental theory or whether the findings from academic psychology will lead to a refinement of psychoanalytic developmental theory (Leichtman, 1990). In other words, do we challenge the theory and present an alternative position, as Stern proposed; or do we elaborate, expand, and refine the theory by using empirical studies to fill in the gaps in our understanding as Emde, Greenspan, McDevitt, Parens, Sander, Settlage, and others have sought to do? It is likely that both approaches provide a basis for bringing about a change in viewpoint about the infancy period.

CHANGING VIEWS OF EARLY DEVELOPMENT IN LIGHT OF RECENT INFANT RESEARCH

Many child psychoanalysts would agree that infant research has brought about slight shifts in emphasis in psychoanalytic developmental thought concerning the earliest phases of development. What has filtered down from a large number of studies is a set of ideas that gives a slightly different cast to our view of the human infant than was previously the case. Emde (1981) has identified four changing developmental concepts that are worth noting.

The Infant As Active and Stimulus Seeking

There is now an appreciation of the fundamental activity of the infant, an appreciation based on a view that is slightly different from the previous way of thinking about newborns and the earliest periods of life. A number of research studies have shown infants to be more active, particularly in seeking stimulation, than was previously thought. Naturalistic observations have documented the amount of organization and endogenous control present in the days immediately after birth (e.g., Wolff, 1959, 1966; Korner, 1969). Numerous studies have shown that the newborn possesses clearly circumscribed and highly organized behaviors that are related to internal state; the rhythmic features of the newborn's sleep–wake cycles and rest–activity cycles are a good example. Other developmental research studies have demonstrated the young infant's stimulus needs for both soothing and arousal. These needs eventuate in very active and complex encounters with the human and inanimate objects in the infant's world.

The Infant's Representational World

Another view of early development that seems to be changing as a result of infant research concerns the infant's capacity for representation. There is general agreement that very young infants have the capacity to make order out of stimuli, to store the distinctive features of stimuli in memory, and to generate rules about stimuli. These abilities have been repeatedly demonstrated. Such findings imply that infants have some form of rudimentary representational system even during the first months of life.

Stern's (1989) most recent work is relevant because he, more than any other infant researcher, is attempting to define and systematically analyze representational structures in the infant and very young child. He is postulating how different units of representation become organized into larger units. His research concerns a series of developmental questions about the categorizing process and about successive levels of organization. Only recently has such an outline of representational units and their ordering with this degree of precision been possible.

The Infant's Interpersonal and Social World

A third changing view of early development concerns the infant's interpersonal and social capacities. There are many studies that address the infant's organizational capacities for initiating, maintaining, and terminating interactions with others. These studies have demonstrated the infant's propensity for engaging in eye-to-eye contact; for responding to holding, touching, and rocking; and for showing alert attentiveness to the human voice and face. Such behaviors can all be considered an aspect of the infant's "preadaptiveness" for the purpose of human interaction (see reviews by Emde and Robinson, 1979, and by Papousek and Papousek, 1981).

There have also been studies that suggest a biologically based behavior system on the parents' side that ensures the participation of the adult social partner. Papousek refers to "intuitive parenting behaviors" as a biologically based system. Studies have analyzed parental greeting responses, parental imitation of the newborn's facial and vocal expressions, and the "baby talk" phenomenon with its exaggeration of musical features and repetitive patterns of speech as examples of intuitive parental behaviors (see Snow, 1972; Stern, 1977; Papousek and Papousek, 1979).

In addition, there have been many studies devoted to the analysis of the synchrony between parental and infant behaviors. These studies have documented the predisposition of parent and infant to mesh their behaviors in a timed, mutual interchange during social interaction. Most of these studies are microanalytic and analyze looking and arousal behavior (Stern, 1977; Brazelton and Als, 1979; Scaife and Bruner, 1975); voice and movement (Condon and Sander, 1974); infant state (Sander, 1975); and communicative connectedness or what has been called "intersubjectivity" (Trevarthan, 1979; see also Brazelton et al., 1974; Bretherton et al., 1981; Call, 1980; Stern, 1977). Interestingly, in order to demonstrate the reciprocal interaction between the mother and infant these studies use two- to four-month old infants, because the height of mother–child synchronamous behavior appears to occur at this age, a period that Mahler identified as the symbiotic phase for that reason.

Affect as an Organizer of Experience

A fourth changing view of the nature of early development concerns the infant's affective life. Considerable research has been done on affect development, affect recognition, and affect regulation (see for example, Ekman, Friesen, and Ellsworth, 1972; Emde, 1983; Izard, 1971; Izard et al., 1980; Klinnert et al., 1983). As a result of this research many new ideas are being formulated. For example, affect change often accompanies developmental shifts so that affects can be thought of as helpful in promoting the integration of experience (Emde, 1989). Due to this research we have acquired considerable information about the universality of affect expressions and also about the universality of the recognition of affects (Izard, 1971; Ekman et al., 1972). Other studies have described six discrete emotions (anger, fear, sadness, disgust, happiness, and interest) and their developmental pattern throughout the course of infancy, childhood, and adulthood (see review in Emde, 1980b). These findings have led to new ideas about affects and their role in organizing experience. Emde's work has been central to these conceptualizations, and his formulations have called attention to the importance of affective experience in providing a sense of coherence over time. This notion is the basis for his ideas about affects and the continuity of self-experience that were discussed earlier.

Even such a brief description as is provided in this chapter demonstrates that much more is known about the infant's state and its capacity for regulation and organization than was known only a few decades ago. An important result of this work has been the claim that the infant has a greater capacity for early self and object differentiation than was previously thought.

The phenomena of differentiation is at the heart of Mahler's work. Her views of the differentiation of self and object representations are clinical in nature, and in this respect Mahler's thinking differs significantly from the ideas set forth by developmental psychologists. The biological unpreparedness of the human infant to maintain its life separately is what conditions the prolonged phase Mahler designated the "mother–infant symbiosis." Her interest was in the process in which the infant gradually diminishes its dependence on the mother figure and becomes increasingly differentiated from her. As the reception of Mahler's work attests, her interest in the early formation of psychic structure has had, and continues to have, a powerful impact on clinical thinking up to the current day. Object relations theorists (e.g., Guntrip, 1961, 1969; Fairbairn, 1954; Klein, 1975) were influenced by her work, as were other psychoanalysts (e.g., Jacobson, 1964; Kohut, 1971; Kernberg, 1975, 1976) who placed strong emphasis on the genetic aspects of psychoanalysis in their theories and practice. New conceptualizations about the origins and treatment of depression, borderline conditions, and narcissistic disorders were no doubt influenced by Mahler's contribution.

CONCLUSION

Psychoanalysis is above all a genetic theory that assumes that events in early development are decisive in the formation of personality. Charting the manner in which psychic structures emerge and the process by which self and object representations arise is an essential task. As Hartmann (1950) argues, "the study of the preverbal stage is a testing ground for many of our most general assumptions, and also a prerequisite for theoretical advances in a variety of aspects" (p. 10).

Mahler's conceptualization of separation–individuation is essentially a clinical theory that describes the earliest phases of development. Her contribution is of major significance because she formulated one of the most complete theories of early development based on psychoanalytic principles. Academic research psychologists are also interested in determining the manner in which psychic structures emerge, but their methods are more concerned with the measurement and quantification of these phenomena.

Hartmann (1950) concludes his paper "Psychoanalysis and Developmental Psychology" with a plea for integration of the two disciplines, a goal he viewed as a natural evolutionary process well suited to the study of the "non-conflictual sphere."

During the past 40 years there has been an increase in communication between certain quarters of academic developmental psychology and psychoanalysis, although the interaction between these two disciplines has not been as harmonious as Hartmann envisioned. There have been debates and disputes (as well as agreements and confirmations). The moments of disquietude, however, have also prompted interesting discussion. Currently, academic infant researchers are providing a context for examining many aspects of developmental psychoanalysis that have often been taken for granted. These researchers have stimulated a different form of argument primarily because a number of psychoanalysts are beginning to look outside the boundaries of their discipline for ways to resolve questions that used to be answered within it.

At this point it is difficult to predict which ideas in one field will be brought to bear on the other. Evidently, academic developmental psychology and psychoanalysis are disciplines that can learn from each other and can utilize the differences between them to check and guide their inferences. Information from both infant research and psychoanalysis will most likely continue to inform our thinking about the earliest phases of development in the future. Whether or not infant research will have any appreciable impact on specific aspects of psychoanalytic theory and practice is a question of greater magnitude. If contemporary academic psychology succeeds in providing a greater understanding of a child's internal life during the earliest phases of psychic development, then it will have lived up to its early promise and, as with Mahler's contribution, another significant frontier will have been crossed.

REFERENCES

Ainsworth, M. D. S., Blehar, M. C., Waters, E. & Wall, S. (1978), *Patterns of Attachment: A Psychological Study of the Strange Situation*. Hillsdale, NJ: Lawrence Erlbaum.

––––––– & Wittig, B. (1969), Attachment and exploratory behavior in one-year-olds in a strange situation. In: *Determinants of Infant Behavior*, ed. B. M. Foss. New York: Wiley, pp. 113–136.

Allen, T., Walker, K., Symonds, L. & Marcell, M. (1977), Intrasensory and intersensory perception of temporal sequences during infancy. *Develop. Psychol.*, 13:225–229.

Balint, M. (1968), *The Basic Fault*. London: Tavistock.

Beebe, B. (1986), Mother–infant mutual influences and precursors of self and object representation. In: *Empirical Studies of Psychoanalytic Theories, Vol. 2*, ed. J. Masling. Hillsdale, NJ: The Analytic Press, pp. 27–48.

––––––– Lachmann, F. M. (1986), The organization of infant experience: The contribution of mother–infant mutual influence. Presented at the meeting of the American Psychological Association, Washington, D.C.

––––––– ––––––– (1988), The contribution of mother–infant mutual influence to the origins of self and object representations. *Psychoanal. Psychol.*, 5:305–337.

Benedek, T. (1938), Adaptation to reality in early infancy. *Psychoanal. Quart.*, 7:200–214.

Biringen, Z. (1990), Changes in emotional availability as related to the onset of infant walking. Presented at the International Conference on Infant Studies, Montreal.

––––––– Emde, R., McNutty, D., Trierweiler, G., Lewis, M. (1989), Infant walking onset affects the quality of the mother–infant relationship. Presented at the World Association for Infant Psychiatry and Allied Disciplines (WAI-PAD), Lugano, Switzerland.

Bowlby, J. (1944), Forty-four juvenile thieves: Their characters and home life. *Internal. J. Psycho-Anal.*, 25:19–52.

––––––– (1958), The nature of the child's tie to its mother. *Internal. J. Psycho-Anal.*, 39:350–373.

––––––– (1960), Separation anxiety. *Internat. J. Psycho-Anal.*, 41:89–113.

––––––– (1980), *Attachment and Loss: Vol. I. Attachment*. New York: Basic Books.

Brazelton, T. B. & Als, H. (1979), Four early stages in the development of mother–infant interaction. *The Psychoanalytic Study of the Child*, 34:349–369. New Haven, CT: Yale University Press.

_____ Koslowski, B. & Main, M. (1974), The origins of reciprocity: The early mother–infant interaction. In: *The Effects of the Infant on the Caregiver*, ed. M. Lewis & L. A. Rosenblum. New York: Plenum Press, pp. 49–76.

Bretherton, I. (1985), Attachment theory: Retrospect and prospect. In: *Growing Points in Attachment Theory and Research,* ed. I. Bretherton & E. Waters. Society for Research in Child Development Monographs, Vol. 49, No. 6, Serial no. 209.

_____ McNew, S. & Beeghly-Smith, H. (1981), Early person knowledge as expressed in gestural and verbal communication: When do infants acquire a "theory of mind"? In: *Infant Social Cognition,* ed., M. E. Lamb & L. R. Sherrod. Hillsdale, NJ: Lawrence Erlbaum, pp. 333–373.

Brody, S. (1956), *Patterns of Mothering.* New York: International Universities Press.

_____ (1980), Transitional objects: Idealization of a phenomenon. *Psychoanal. Quart.,* 48:561–605.

_____ (1982), Psychoanalytic theories of infant development and its disturbances: A critical evaluation. *Psychoanal. Quart.,* 51:526–597.

_____ Axelrad, S. (1970), *Anxiety and Ego Formation in Infancy.* New York: International Universities Press.

Call, J. D. (1964), Newborn approach behaviors and early ego development. *Internat. J. Psycho-Anal.,* 45:268–294.

_____ (1980), Some prelinguistic aspects of language development. *J. Amer. Psychoanal. Assn.,* 28:259–289.

Campos, J. J., Barrett, K. C., Lamb, M. E., Goldsmith, H. H. & Stenberg, C. (1983), Socioemotional development. In: *Handbook of Child Psychology, Vol. II,* ed. M. Haith & J. J. Campos. New York: Wiley, pp. 783–915.

_____ & Stenberg, C. (1981), Perception, appraisal, and emotion: The onset of social referencing. In: *Infant Social Cognition,* ed. M. E. Lamb & L. Sherrod. Hillsdale, NJ: Lawrence Erlbaum, pp. 273–314.

Carr, S. J., Dabbs, J. M. & Carr, S. T. (1975), Mother–infant attachment: The importance of the mother's visual field. *Child Development,* 46:331–338.

Condon, W. S. & Sander, L. W. (1974), Synchrony demonstrated between movements of the neonate and adult speech. *Child Dev.,* 45:456–462.

Decarie, T. G. (1965), *Intelligence and Affectivity in Early Childhood.* New York; International Universities Press.

Ekman, P., Friesen, W. V. & Ellsworth, P. (1972), *Emotion in the Human Face: Guidelines for Research and an Integration of Findings.* New York: Pergamon Press.

Emde, R. N. (1980a), Ways of thinking about new knowledge and further research from a developmental orientation. *Psychoanal. Contemp. Thought,* 3:213–234.

_____ (1980b), Emotional availability: A reciprocal reward system of infants and parents with implications for prevention of psychosocial disorders. In: *Parent–Infant Relationships,* ed. P. M. Taylor. Orlando, FL: Grune & Sratton, pp. 87–115.

_____ (1980c), Toward a psychoanalytic theory of affect, I & II. In: *Infancy and*

Childhood: The Course of Life, Vol. I, ed. S. I. Greenspan & G. H. Pollock. Washington, DC: National Institute of Mental Health, pp. 63–112.

———— (1981), Changing models of infancy and the nature of early development. *J. Amer. Psychoanal. Assn.*, 29:179–219.

———— (1983), The prerepresentational self and its affective core. *The Psychoanalytic Study of the Child*, 38:165–192. New Haven, CT: Yale University Press.

———— (1989), The infant's relationship experience: Developmental and affective aspects. In: *Relationship Disturbances in Early Childhood*, ed. A. Sameroff & R. N. Emde. New York: Basic Books, pp. 33–51.

————, Gaensbauer, T. J. & Harmon, R. J. (1976), Emotional expression in infancy: A biobehavioral study. *Psychological Issues*, Monogr. 37. New York: International Universities Press.

————, Harmon, R. J. (1972), Endogenous and exogenous smiling systems in early infants. *J. Amer. Acad. Child Psychiat.*, 11(2):177–200.

————, Robinson, J. (1979), The first two months: Recent research in developmental psychobiology and the changing view of the newborn. In: *Basic Handbook of Child Psychiatry: Vol. I. Development*, ed. J. D. Noshpitz. New York: Basic Books, pp. 72–105.

Escalona, S. K. (1963), Patterns of infantile experience and the developmental process. *The Psychoanalytic Study of the Child*, 28:197–244. New Haven, CT: Yale University Press.

———— (1968), *The Roots of Individuality: Normal Patterns of Development in Infancy*. Chicago: Aldine.

Fagan, J. F. (1974), Infant recognition memory: The effects of length of familiarization and type of discrimination task. *Child Develop.*, 45:351–356.

Fagen, J. W., Morrongiello, B. A., Rovee-Collier, C. & Gekoski, M. J. (1984), Expectancies and memory retrieval in three-month-old infants. *Child Develop.*, 55:936–943.

Fairbairn, W. R. D. (1954), *An Object Relations Theory of Personality*. New York: Basic Books.

Feinman, S. & Lewis, M. (1981), Maternal effects on infants' responses to strangers. Presented at meeting of the Society for Research in Child Development, Boston.

Fraiberg, S. (1977), *Insights from the Blind: Comparative Studies of Blind and Sighted Infants*. New York: Basic Books.

Freud, A. (1969), A discussion of John Bowlby's work on separation, grief, and mourning. In: *The Writings of Anna Freud: Vol. 5. Research at the Hampstead Child Therapy Clinic and Other Papers, 1956–1965*. New York: International Universities Press, pp. 167–186.

Galenson, E. & Roiphe, H. (1971), Impacts of early sexual discovery on mood, defensive organization, and symbolism. *The Psychoanalytic Study of the Child*, 26:195–216. New York: Quadrangle Books.

George, C., Kaplan, N. & Main, M. (1985), An adult attachment interview. Unpublished manuscript, University of California at Berkeley.

Greenspan, S. (1979), Intelligence and adaptation. *Psychological Issues*, Monogr. 36. New York: International Universities Press.

_____ (1981), *Psychopathology and Adaptation in Infancy and Early Childhood (Clinical Infant Reports, No. 1)*. New York: International Universities Press.

_____ (1989), *Development of the Ego: Implications for Personality Theory, Psychopathology, and the Psychotherapeutic Process*. New York: International Universities Press.

Guntrip, H. (1961), *Personality, Structure, and Human Interaction*. New York: International Universities Press.

_____ (1969), *Schizoid Phenomena, Object Relations, and the Self*. New York: International Universities Press.

Hartmann, H. (1950), Psychoanalysis and developmental psychology. *The Psychoanalytic Study of the Child*, 5:7–17. New York: International Universities Press.

Horner, T. M. (1985), The psychic life of the young infant. *Amer. J. Orthopsychiat.*, 55:334–344.

_____ (1988), Rapprochement in the psychic life of the toddler. *Amer. J. Orthopsychiat.*, 58:4–15.

Izard, C. E. (1971), *The Face of Emotion*. New York: Meredith & Appleton-Century Crofts.

_____ , Huebner, R., Risser, D., McGinnes, G. C. & Dougherty, L. (1980), The young infant's ability to produce discrete emotional expressions. *Dev. Psychol.*, 16:132–140.

Jacobson, E. (1964), *The Self and the Object World*. New York: International Universities Press.

Jones, D., Henderson, C. & Emde, R. N. (1990), Temperament differences and age of walking onset. Poster presented at the 6th Biennial Developmental Psychobiology Research Group Retreat, Estes Park, CO.

Kernberg, O. (1975), *Borderline Conditions and Pathological Narcissism*. New York: Aronson.

_____ (1976), *Object Relations Theory and Clinical Psychoanalysis*. New York: Aronson.

Kestenberg, J. S. (1965), The role of movement patterns in development: I. Rhythms of movement. *Psychoanal. Quart.*, 24:1–26.

Klein, M. (1975). *Envy and Gratitude and Other Works: 1946–1963*. London: Hogarth Press.

Klinnert, M. D., Emde, R. N., Butterfield, P. & Campos, J. J. (1986), Social referencing. *Dev. Psychol.*, 22:427–432.

_____ , Campos, J. J., Sorce, J. F., Emde, R. N. & Svejda, M. (1983), Emotions as behavior regulators: Social referencing in infancy. In: *Emotions, Theory, Research, and Experience, Vol. 2*, ed. R. Plutchik & H. Kellerman. New York: Academic Press, pp. 57–86.

Kobak, R. (1987), Attachment, affect regulation, and defense. Presented at the biennial meeting of the Society for Research in Child Development, Baltimore.

_____ & Sceery, A. (1988), Attachment in later adolescence: Working models, affect regulation, and representations of self and others. *Child Dev.*, 59:135–146.

_____ & Shaver, P. (1987), Strategies for maintaining felt security: A theoretical analysis of continuity and change in styles of social adaptation. Presented at the conference in honor of John Bowlby's 80th birthday, London.

Kohut, H. (1971), *The Analysis of the Self.* New York: International Universities Press.

Korner, A. (1969), Neonatal startles, smiles, erections, and reflex sucks as related to state, sex and individuality. *Child Dev.,* 40:1039–1053.

Lamb, M. (1981), The development of social expectations in the first year of life. In: *Infant Social Cognition,* ed. M. Lamb & L. Sherrod. Hillsdale, NJ: Lawrence Erlbaum, pp. 155–176.

Leichtman, M. (1990), Developmental psychology and psychoanalysis: The context for a revolution in psychoanalysis. *J. Amer. Psychoanal. Assn.,* 38:915–950.

Lewis, M. & Goldberg, S. (1969), Perceptual and cognitive development in infancy: A generalized expectancy model as a function of mother–infant interaction. *Merrill-Palmer Quart.,* 15:81–100.

Lichtenberg, J. D. (1981), Implications for psychoanalytic theory of research in the neonate. *Internat. Rev. Psycho-Anal.,* 8:35–52.

_____ (1983), *Psychoanalysis and Infant Research.* Hillsdale, NJ: The Analytic Press.

Lustman, S. L. (1956), Rudiments of the ego. *The Psychoanalytic Study of the Child,* 11:89–98. New York: International Universities Press.

Mahler, M. S. (1979), *The Selected Papers of Margaret S. Mahler, Vols. I & II.* New York: Aronson.

_____ Pine, F. & Bergman, A. (1975), *The Psychological Birth of the Human Infant.* New York: Basic Books.

Main, M., Kaplan, N. & Cassidy, J. (1985), Security of attachment in infancy, childhood, and adulthood. In: *Growing Points in Attachment Theory and Research,* ed. I. Bretherton & E. Waters, SRCD Monogr. Vol. 49, No. 6, Serial no. 209.

McDevitt, J. (1975), Separation–individuation and object constancy. *J. Amer. Psychoanal. Assn.,* 23:713–743.

_____ (1983), The emergence of hostile aggression and its defensive and adaptive modifications during the separation–individuation process. *J. Amer. Psychoanal. Assn.,* 31(Suppl.):273–300.

Meltzoff, A. (1985), The roots of social and cognitive development: Models of man's original nature. In: *Social Perception in Infants,* ed. T. Field & N. Fox. Norwood, NJ: Ablex, pp. 1–30.

Nachman, P. (1982), Memory for stimuli reacted to with positive and neutral affect in seven-month-old infants. Unpublished doctoral dissertation, Columbia University.

_____ Stern, D. (1983), Affect retrieval: A form of recall memory in prelinguistic infants. In: *Frontiers of Infant Psychiatry, Vol. I,* ed. J. D. Call, E. Galenson & R. Tyson. New York: Basic Books, pp. 95–100.

_____ _____ & Best, C. (1986), Infants' affective reactions to stimuli and novelty vs. familiarity visual preferences. *J. Acad. Child Psychiat.,* 25:801–804.

Nelson, K. & Gruendel, J. M. (1979), From personal episode to social script.

Presented at the biennial meeting of the Society for Research in Child Development, San Francisco.

—— —— (1981), Generalized event representations: Basic building blocks of cognitive development. In: *Advances in Developmental Psychology, Vol. 1,* ed. M. E. Lamb & A. L. Brown. Hillsdale, NJ: Lawrence Erlbaum, pp. 131–158.

Papousek, H. & Papousek, M. (1979), Early ontogeny of human social interaction: Its biological roots and social dimensions. In: *Human Ethology: Claims and Limits of a New Discipline,* ed. M. von Cranach, K. Foppa, W. Lepenies, & P. Ploog. Cambridge: Cambridge University Press, pp. 456–489.

—— —— (1981), How human is the human newborn, and what else is to be done? In: *Prospective Issues in Infancy Research,* ed. K. Bloom. Hillsdale, NJ: Lawrence Erlbaum, pp. 137–155.

Parens, H. (1979), *The Development of Aggression in Early Childhood.* New York: Aronson.

Peterfreund, E. (1978), Some critical comments on psychoanalytic conceptualizations of infancy. *Internat. J. Psycho-Anal.,* 59:427–441.

Pine, F. (1985), *Developmental Theory and Clinical Process.* New Haven, CT: Yale University Press.

Provence, S. & Lipton, R. C. (1962), *Infants in Institutions.* New York: International Universities Press.

Robson, K. S. (1967), The role of eye-to-eye contact in maternal–infant attachment. *J. Child Psychol. Psychiat.,* 8:13–25.

Rosch, E. (1978), Principles of categorization. In: *Cognition and Categorization,* ed. E. Rosch & B. B. Lloyd. Hillsdale, NJ: Lawrence Erlbaum, pp. 28–48.

—— Mervis, C. B., Gray, W. D., Johnson, D. M. & Boyes-Braen, P. (1976), Basic objects in natural categories. *Cognitive Psychol.,* 8:382–439.

Sander, L. W. (1962), Issues in early mother–child interaction. *J. Amer. Acad. Child. Psychiat.,* 7:141–165.

—— (1964), Adaptive relationships in early mother–infant interaction. *J. Amer. Child Psychiat.,* 3:231–264.

—— (1975), Infant and the caretaking environment: Investigation and conceptualization of adaptive behaviors in a series of increasing complexity. In: *Explorations in Child Psychiatry,* ed. E. J. Anthony. New York: Plenum, pp. 129–166.

—— (1983a), Polarity, paradox, and the organizing process in development. In: *Frontiers of Infant Psychiatry, Vol. 1,* ed. J. D. Call, E. Galenson & R. Tyson. New York: Basic Books, pp. 315–327.

—— (1983b), To begin with: Reflections on ontogeny. In: *Reflections on Self Psychology,* ed. J. Lichtenberg & S. Kaplan. Hillsdale, NJ: The Analytic Press, pp. 85–104.

Scaife, M. & Bruner, J. S. (1975), The capacity for joint visual attention in the infant. *Nature,* 253:265–266.

Sears, R. R. (1944), Experimental analysis of psychoanalytic phenomena. In: *Personality and the Behavior Disorders, Vol. I,* ed. J. McV. Hunt. New York: Ronald Press, pp. 306–332.

Settlage, C. (1980), The psychoanalytic understanding of psychic development during the second and third years of life. In: *The Course of Life: Vol. 1. Infancy and Early Childhood,* ed. S. Greenspan & C. Pollock. Washington, DC: U.S. Gov't Printing Office, pp. 523–539.

Schank, R. C. & Abelson, R. P. (1977), *Scripts, Plans, Goals, and Understanding.* Hillsdale, NJ: Lawrence Erlbaum.

Snow, C. E. (1972), Mothers speech to children learning language. *Child Dev.,* 43:549–565.

Sorce, J. & Emde, R. N. (1981), Mother's presence is not enough: The effect of emotional availability on infant exploration and play. *Dev. Psychol.,* 17:737–745.

_____ & _____ (1985), Maternal emotional signaling: Its effect on the visual cliff behavior of 1-year-olds. *Dev. Psychol.,* 21:195–200.

Spitz, R. (1945), Hospitalism: An inquiry into the genesis of psychiatric conditions in early childhood. *The Psychoanalytic Study of the Child,* 1:53–74. New York: International Universities Press.

_____ (1965), *The First Year of Life.* New York: International Universities Press.

Sroufe, A. & Fleeson, J. (1986), Attachment and the construction of relationships. In: *The Nature and Development of Relationships,* ed. W. W. Hartup & Z. Rubin. Hillsdale, NJ: Lawrence Erlbaum Assoc., pp. 51–71.

Stechler, G. & Kaplan, S. (1980), The development of the self; A psychoanalytic perspective. *The Psychoanalytic Study of the Child,* 35:85–105. New Haven, CT: Yale University Press.

Stern, D. N. (1977), *The First Relationship: Mother and Infant.* Cambridge, MA: Harvard University Press.

_____ (1985), *The Interpersonal World of the Infant.* New York: Basic Books.

_____ (1989), The representation of relational patterns. In: *Relationships and Relationship Disorders,* ed. A. J. Sameroff & R. N. Emde. New York: Basic Books, pp. 52–69.

Strauss, M. S. (1979), Abstraction of proto typical information by adults and ten-month-old infants. *J. Exper. Psychol.,* 5:618–632.

Trevarthan, C. (1979), Communication and cooperation in early infancy: A description of primary intersubjectivity. In: *Before Speech: The Beginning of Interpersonal Communication,* ed. M. M. Bullowa. New York: Cambridge University Press, pp. 321–347.

Tulving, E. (1972), Episodic and semantic memory. In: *The Organization of Memory,* ed. E. Tulving & W. Donaldson. New York: Academic Press, pp. 382–403.

Watson, J. (1985), Contingency perception in early social development. In: *Social Perception in Infants,* ed. T. Field & N. Fox. Norwood, NJ: Ablex, pp. 157–176.

Winnicott, W. D. (1965), *The Maturational Process and the Facilitating Environment.* New York: International Universities Press.

Wolff, P. H. (1959), Observations on newborn infants. *Psychosom. Med.,* 21:110–118.

_____ (1963), Observations on the early development of smiling. In: *Determinants of Infant Behavior, Vol. 2*, ed. B. M. Foss. New York: Wiley, pp. 113–167.

_____ (1966), The causes and controls, and organization of behavior in the newborn. *Psychological Issues*, Monogr. 17. New York: International Universities Press.

Zeanah, C. & Anders, T. (1987), Subjectivity in parent–infant relationships. *Infant Mental Health Journal*, 8:237–250.

II

Psychopathology as Understood in the Light of Separation–Individuation Theory

7

Contributions of Separation–Individuation Theory to the Understanding of Psychopathology During the Prelatency Years

John B. McDevitt

In what follows I use data and findings from previous studies to address separation–individuation issues not dealt with in those studies. It seems fitting that I, having observed and reported on this subject for over 20 years, should set forth my ideas on this aspect of development as it fits into a broader context. Any contribution to psychopathology in the prelatency phase made by disturbances in the separation–individuation process must be considered in relation to contributions made by other lines of development, that is, by disturbances in id and ego maturation and development and by interpersonal and intrapsychic conflict.

Some of the data that form the basis of this presentation will be recognized by those familiar with my previous writing and some of the data derive from a 25-year follow-up study now in progress. Because my data derive from several types of sources, it seems appropriate to assess the reliability of the inferences made from these various sources, which I do.

The data consist of (1) the four-times-weekly analysis of three-year-old Becky (McDevitt, 1967), (2) the naturalistic, observation research study of

Based in part on research supported by NIMH Grant MH-08238, USPHS: Margaret S. Mahler, Principal Investigator, John B. McDevitt, Co-Principal Investigator, Follow-Up Studies supported by The Rock Foundation, John B. McDevitt, Principal Investigator, Anni Bergman, Co-Principal Investigator.

153

5- to 36-month-old Donna, who was one of the 31 "normal" subjects studied in the research project on the separation–individuation process under the direction of Margaret Mahler (Mahler, Pine, and Bergman, 1975), and (3) follow-up studies conducted by Anni Bergman and me on Donna and 16 other subjects at the ages of 8 to 10 and 25 to 27. (Becky was not seen in a follow-up study.)

Becky suffered from a severe phobia with borderline features—an arrest in certain ego functions and a dearth of affectionate feelings along with an excess of aggression. Donna suffered from a severe neurosis, which had its onset as early as 19 months of age and which persisted essentially unchanged into an adulthood marked by a reasonably sound personality structure.

BECKY

Becky (McDevitt, 1971) from birth onward had had a difficult relationship with her mother. They got off to a bad start because Becky cried frequently as an infant and was difficult to comfort. She had a marked startle reaction and frequent bouts of abdominal pain; she was tense and overactive and was unable to mold easily into her mother's arms. These disturbances in the baby were most likely constitutionally determined. Pregnancy and delivery had been normal. The mother, torn between her wish for an academic career and her sense of duty toward Becky, resented the excessive demands Becky made on her and therefore felt unhappy and inadequate as a mother. As a result, she treated her baby inconsistently; she was overly permissive and then, after a long buildup of anger, exploded and withdrew from Becky both emotionally and physically. Although the father was more loving and consistent, he revealed his ambivalent feelings toward Becky in an overconcern about her care and safety—particularly at times of everyday separations—in undue permissiveness, and in seductive behavior.

The "dialogue" between parents and child continued to be disturbed throughout the preoedipal phase. In the latter half of the first year Becky developed prolonged and marked stranger and separation anxiety and at 18 months developed a severe sleep disturbance because her mother had become withdrawn and depressed during the early months of her second pregnancy and had turned the care of the child over to a strict and dominating maid.

During her third year Becky demonstrated an imbalance in a number of developmental lines; there was precocious development in some ego functions but a lag in others, particularly in the development of libidinal object constancy and the mastery of anxiety, with Becky readily regressing to the ambivalent, clinging, "toddler" relationship to her mother.

Prior to the onset of Becky's illness at the age of three, a definite change occurred in her close and affectionate relationship with her father, who frequently exposed himself to her in the shower and who vaguely sensed harboring sexual feelings toward her. Becky became frightened when he expressed the slightest anger or when he rode her on his back or tickled her—experiences that she had formerly enjoyed with excitement. For fear of being bitten, she was no longer able to play a favorite game in which her father would hand her a pill to place in his mouth. Soon after this, Becky developed a marked fear of being bitten by a man with a mustache or by a witch and was intolerant of any physical separation from her mother. Her precocious intellectual and verbal abilities were in marked contrast to her need to cling to her mother, her demandingness, and her sad and anxious expression.

The analysis revealed that the fear of being bitten by a man with a mustache expressed Becky's fear of her father, with an upward displacement in her fantasies of the penis and the pubic hair surrounding it. There were two sources of this fear: (1) the projection (onto her father) and displacement (onto mustached men) of oral-sadistic impulses directed toward her father's penis and (2) the displacement onto mustached men of the masochistically wished for, yet feared, sexual attack by the father. The fear of the witch was also the result of the projection and displacement of oral-sadistic impulses, this time directed toward her mother. Becky's dread of being abandoned was a consequence of death wishes directed toward and projected onto her mother. Although her fears of being bitten were determined in part by conflicts that were specific to the phallic-oedipal phase, the intensity of these conflicts and her failure to resolve them were also due to disturbances in the mother–child relationship that had their origin throughout the preoedipal phase.

The disturbance in the separation-individuation process was determined by and interrelated with disturbances in the development of the drives, the ego and object relations. From the viewpoint of the drives and the ego, from the start Becky's repeated, unrelieved organismic distress created a "predisposition to anxiety"—the first link in the anxiety reaction as a determining factor in her illness. Likewise, the inability of the mother to relieve Becky's distress predictably had the effect of creating a relative lack of "basic trust," thereby interfering with the earliest self- and object differentiation and influencing the subsequent nature of object cathexis, self- and object representations, and, therefore, identifications.

Becky's early distress, along with a continuing deficit in "mothering," led to an excess of aggression that was insufficiently counteracted by libido and that, when further heightened by sibling rivalry, penis envy, and oedipal death wishes, reached an intensity sufficient to exacerbate conflict, contribute to symptom formation, and adversely affect the character of her object relations. The result was a dearth of tender feelings toward the mother, or toward the analyst in the role of the mother, and a relative failure in the development of object and self-constancy and in identification. Furthermore, the provocative, ambivalent, sadomasochistic mother–child interaction, along with the father's seductive self-exposure and handling of Becky, resulted in a sadomasochistic sexualization of danger situations and of anxiety.

Becky did not have the opportunity to develop stable identifications such as could be employed in the control and modulation of impulse and anxiety, since both parents were unpredictable and inadequate in the control of their own impulses and therefore found it difficult to impose steady, consistent restraints upon her impulses.

In addition, Becky could not develop trust or confidence with regard to actual everyday experiences of separation, which also interfered with the development of libidinal object constancy. The danger of separation had been strongly impressed on her by her observation of her parents' behavior and by identification with their emotions and attitudes. For each parent, ambivalence toward Becky reached its height at the time of everyday separations from her; for example, the father warned Becky and her mother not to stand near the curb whenever they went out, for fear they would be hit by a car, and the mother always left when Becky's back was turned. For each parent, the act of separating was a disturbing event and aroused guilt and anxiety. Becky was not helped to develop a realistic appraisal of the separation experience and to discover that it need not be dangerous or frightening and that it would be temporary in any case. She continued to react to separation as a traumatic situation rather than as a potential danger. There was a failure in the ego's ability to evaluate and cope with the danger of object loss and to progress normally from primary to signal anxiety and to object constancy.

From the viewpoint of the separation-individuation process, the mother's descriptions of Becky's development corresponded closely to the disturbances and danger signs of the subphases of the separation–individuation process. Becky experienced excessive stranger and separation reactions by eight months along with the difficulties described in her relationship to her mother during the differentiation process. Her "love affair with the world" during the practicing subphase was subdued and lacking in the elation that is characteristic of that subphase. The mother's emotional withdrawal and the introduction of the maid during the rapprochement subphase constituted an acutely traumatic experience for Becky. The consequence was the return of the severe sleep and separation problems, excessive clinging to and "shadowing" of the mother, provocative darting away from her, and a depressed, angry, and anxious basic mood. This led, during the fourth subphase, to persistent ambivalence, excessive separation anxiety, low self-esteem, and narcissistic vulnerability.

Becky's representation of the mother prior to the conflicts of the phallic-oedipal phase was primitive, highly ambivalently cathected, and unstable. This arrest in development interfered with progress toward libidinal object constancy and therefore increased her vulnerability to severe conflicts during the phallic-oedipal phase. The increased aggression directed toward the mother at this time became all the more dangerous in view of Becky's doubts with regard to the mother's physical and emotional availability, doubts that formerly stemmed from their poor relationship but now had their basis in the unreliable inner representation of the mother. These doubts increased Becky's fear of object loss and thereby predisposed her to the development—in part, the reactivation—of intense anxiety on any occasion of conflict with or threatened separation from her mother. Her long history of separation anxiety had "sensitized" Becky to the experience of separation. Intense fear of object loss had persisted and was now involved in the internalized conflicts of the phallic-oedipal phase. What had earlier been a developmentally appropriate (although exaggerated) fear of object loss became, at the time of her illness, a danger of losing the mother as a consequence of her death wishes, although Becky continued to experience the danger as if it were an external one.

DONNA

In contrast to Becky's history, Donna and her mother got off to a splendid start (McDevitt, 1975, 1979). A close, mutually satisfying relation between them was apparent when Donna entered the separation–individuation study at the age of five months. Both appeared secure in the relationship, closely attuned to each other, and even-tempered. Donna's development during the differentiation and practicing subphases was advanced, and she thoroughly enjoyed her "love affair with the world." At the same time, however, she suffered much more than the usual amount of separation anxiety from 6 to 14 months when the mother left the room for her weekly interviews.

Donna's excessive fear of object loss seemed to be related to the close attachment to her mother and to the mother's close attachment to her.

Donna was always acutely aware of her mother's presence, no matter where she was; whenever Donna became upset, she immediately crawled back to her mother. The mother was similarly aware of Donna's presence and talked to her at even a hint of distress or boredom on Donna's part.

Donna's need to cling to her mother first became marked between nine and ten months, when a crisis developed. It followed a trip away from home during which time Donna's routine was disrupted; she reacted with distress and anger to the mild trauma of prohibitions and criticisms she had not previously experienced. In the nursery-like research setting she regressed and clung to her mother for several weeks, behaving as if she were afraid she would lose her mother completely. She began to anticipate with excessive anxiety the possibility that her mother might leave the room, and she became fearful of her mother's disapproval of any angry behavior she might express toward her mother or toward other children. She also became excessively sensitive to criticism. The severity of this "differentiation" crisis was the result of the unexpected trauma occurring in the context of an overly close, permissive relationship with her mother at an age when there is a normal developmental spurt in self–object differentiation and beginning object-directed aggression, both of which were advanced in Donna's development.

By her 14th month, Donna had become more independent of her mother and was described as an alert child who was more active and better able to cope with brief separations than most of her peers. This could be explained by her excellent endowment and her functional pleasure and narcissistic investment in her locomotor functions, which overshadowed any concern over her relationship with her mother at this time. The mother was pleased with and encouraged Donna's activities, which helped to overshadow any concern with the relationship on the mother's part. Donna was also described as being more consistently happy and exuberant and more self-reliant and confident than she had been at any previous time. She was among the most self-assertive of her peers, always knowing what she wanted, and her expressions of anger were more focused and directed than before.

As Donna entered the rapprochement subphase, she became less exuberant and more subject to fluctuations in her mood; she fell into frequent disagreements and fights with her mother and once again became concerned with her mother's whereabouts. She continued to tolerate her mother's absence reasonably well, however, until she suffered a mild illness and a penicillin injection when she was 19 months old. She regressed and once again clung to her mother like a baby, as she had at nine months. Although no longer openly angry with her mother, her marked ambivalence was revealed in her possessiveness and her jealousy and in the behavior of biting and chewing her fingers when she was upset, at times leaving distinct teeth marks. Donna had become a shy, inhibited, overly cautious junior toddler who suffered excessive separation anxiety and was frightened of noises. Like Becky, she had projected and displaced the aggression directed toward her mother onto others—not onto a witch but onto other adults and older children—and had become shy and fearful of them.

Donna's aggression toward her mother was the consequence of the conflicts typical of the rapprochement subphase. They were the result of the mother's inability to mitigate Donna's painful feelings of separateness, helplessness, and loss of "omnipotence" or the mother's inability to allow free reign to Donna's wish to be independent and have her own way. Donna was conflicted between her wish to do and get what she wanted and her need to please her mother. It seemed likely that her anger toward her mother brought on such serious consequences not because it was more intense than that of other children but because of the excessive closeness of the mother–child relationship and because of the mother's intolerance of aggression in either herself or Donna. Donna, who had previously been a moderately active, assertive, and aggressive infant, was now a sensitive toddler, similarly intolerant of her own aggression.

For the first year and a half Donna's mother had been considered the "perfect" mother. The infants at the Center typically picked her as their favorite mother substitute. She was a pleasant, attentive, and considerate woman in her late thirties who was also quiet, shy, and inhibited. Only in hindsight did it become apparent that she had always been much too closely and exclusively tied to Donna, as well as too lenient, too giving, too inclined to remove obstacles, and too unable to frustrate her child. During the first 18 months these traits did not seem to hamper Donna's development. They represented in part reaction formations based on unconscious ambivalent feelings toward Donna, which became only minimally observable in the mother's behavior with Donna by their exaggeration during the rapprochement crisis. They were also apparent as a personality trait on psychological testing of the mother, whom the psychologist considered to be the most normal of the mothers tested. Her ambivalence made it difficult for her to deal with Donna's self-assertion and open defiance at the beginning of the rapprochement subphase and, even more so, with the indirect, disguised ambivalence present in the child's regressive behavior and symptoms following the trauma brought on by her illness and the injection.

The nature of the mother–child relation and Donna's constitutional disposition were such that when unexpected traumatic events occurred at 9 and 19 months of age, Donna experienced them as excessively traumatic and regressed too rapidly. Donna had not sufficiently learned to tolerate frustration or disappointment, to cope with separation, to master anxiety, or to be comfortable with either her own or her mother's anger. The mother's tendency to infantilize Donna caused her to experience the conflicts and traumatic events of the rapprochement crisis with too great a disappointment and a too sudden deflation of her sense of omnipotence and self-esteem.

Only slowly and in part by identifying with the maternal, caring aspects of the mother did Donna begin to recover from the rapprochement crisis. Imaginative play in caring for and mothering her dolls, which began when she was 16 months old, had been completely disrupted by this crisis. Only after many months was Donna once again able to become a loving little "mother" of her dolls and of younger infants.

Although Donna had shown some indications of an awareness of sexual differences as early as the rapprochement crisis, concern about these differences did not seem to play a major role in her fear of object loss, loss of love, or her shyness and clinging at that time. Her concern with sexual differences, however, and her denial of this concern became increasingly apparent from her 25th to 29th month. Nevertheless, they did not significantly interfere with her ability to resolve ambivalent feelings toward her mother, for example, by identification, and to continue to tolerate separation well during these months.

This changed abruptly and dramatically, however, when she was 29 months old, following a urinary infection, a traumatic physical exam by an unfamiliar physician, and a penicillin injection, an illness and an event Donna still remembers in some detail at the age of 25. She regressed once again, clinging to her mother and sucking her thumb. She let it be known that she regarded herself as having been injured in the genital area and that she held her mother responsible for this injury. Donna's regressive behavior and symptom formation was essentially the same as that brought on by the rapprochement crisis, but now it was more severe and lasted longer. Her heightened ambivalence once again had disturbed the stability of the maternal representation. Only after many months did identification with the maternal image once again play a major role in Donna's ability to cope with separation and to begin to recover. Once again she became a "little mother" to younger infants, taking over many of her mother's attitudes, expressions, and functions. By becoming like her mother, Donna was able to maintain her tie with her internally, to function independently of her, to bind and regulate aggression, to partially resolve her severe castration reaction and her ambivalence, and to begin to resolve interpersonal and intrapsychic conflicts. Toward the end of her third year both parents reported behavior typical of the early oedipal phase: Donna showed a preference for and a sexual interest in her father.

In nursery school during her fourth year, Donna continued to be too exclusively tied to her mother and had difficulty separating and adjusting to school. She did so in part by assisting the teacher in a motherly manner, often mothering other children; she also played as a homemaker and a mother—bathing, feeding, and dressing her dolls. In weekly play sessions during that year, her continued castration reaction led to several other temporary identifications: with a boy doll; with a baby doll that would be cared for by mother and who would grow a penis; and with a girl doll that would tentatively replace mother in father's affections.

THE FOLLOW-UP STUDIES

At the time of the first follow-up study, when Donna was eight and a half years old, she insisted that her mother remain in the room with her for the first two interviews. She was extremely timid, did not speak spontaneously, and answered questions in a soft, plaintive, almost inaudible voice. When she did let her mother leave the room, she was only slightly less inhibited. But she formed a warm, positive relation with the interviewer and began to express an interest in him during doll play. Psychological testing revealed a good capacity for caring and good object relations, in part the result of her identification with the caretaking domestic functions of the mother, which had persisted essentially unchanged.

Donna showed clinically and on testing the same picture that had been characteristic of the regressions and symptoms that had occurred when she was 9, 19, and 29 months old. These had now become stable aspects of her personality organization, just as had the identification with the maternal aspects of the mother. It seems likely that they had acquired more stability as a consequence of similar regressions and compromise formations brought on by the conflicts of the oedipal phase. Psychological testing revealed that the rivalry of the positive oedipal complex, which showed itself in a passive-oral form, was experienced as too dangerous to her positive relationship with the mother. Donna feared her mother's retaliation and withdrawal of love if she asserted herself or did not conform, a fear based in part on the projection of her own hostility onto her mother, as had occurred at 19 and 29 months. The tests suggested that the use of projection and identification led to a personality organization suggestive of altruistic surrender (A. Freud, 1965). The mother and teachers reported that Donna typically was the passive partner in close relations with active, outgoing girls with whom she identified and obtained vicarious pleasure.

At the time of a second, ongoing follow-up study, the clinical picture remains essentially unchanged. Donna, age 25, is an attractive, shy, feminine young woman who formed a good relationship with the interviewer, has excellent relations with female friends, and has had two long-standing relationships with men, though in each of these she has suffered greatly by being treated badly and by eventually losing out to another woman. She continues to suffer from considerable shyness and a readiness to feel rejected, hurt, and criticized. She also continues to find it difficult to become appropriately angry, to assert herself, or to speak up for fear of object loss or loss of love, particularly in competitive situations and in the relationship with her current boyfriend. She becomes jealous too readily in this and in other close relationships.

The psychologist who tested Donna wrote the following:

> Donna is a young woman with many good resources including the capacity for empathy, introspection, and the ability to be emotionally responsive. . . . While she feels solidly able to be comfortably alone, she is now vacillating between aloneness versus being more involved with men, though her fears of oedipal rivalry, guilt and competition readily get stimulated and interfere. She is certainly capable of being warmly related. She seems to feel that to preserve the positive relationship with the women she ought not risk conflict and competition."

DISCUSSION

Each source of data presented has its advantages and limitations and suggests inferences having different levels of reliability. Used in combination, these retrospective and prospective sources of data from the analysis and research study of young children are probably the best method to gain a closer look at and a better understanding of the roots of psychopathology and of their continuity and change and the best way to provide meaningful rather than speculative links between our knowledge of early development and the genetic, reconstructive data gained in the analysis of the adult.[1] Although reconstructive data from adult analyses may provide a basis for

---

[1]We are now being aided in this effort by experimental studies (Sander, 1983; Stern, 1985; Main, Kaplan & Cassidy, 1985) and by more scientifically rigorous large scale longitudinal studies (see review by Emde, 1985).

extrapolations, they cannot provide a clear, detailed picture of early development.

Becky's analysis provided a fairly clear picture of the beginnings of her psychopathology. Both mother and child were highly verbal, both parents had been or were in analysis, both parents and Becky suffered because of her illness, and the past was not very distant. In addition, the mother's memory of what had occurred was consistent with Becky's current behavior, her illness, and the transference. This consistency strengthened reconstructive inferences, but even so, the mother's memory could provide only a limited and partially reliable picture of Becky's first three years.

Although we had the advantage of observing Donna's development in detail in the first three years, her case presented limitations of a different kind: the questionable reliability of making inferences on the basis of behavioral data alone, and the mother's inability to reveal too much about herself and her relationship with Donna because of her natural reticence, her limited psychological mindedness, and the absence of a need to seek help.

These limitations were partly overcome by the longitudinal nature of the data, which provided additional support to the validity of the inferences derived from behavioral data. Not only did we see a continuity and consistency in Donna's regressions and compromise behaviors following each of the traumas at the critical periods of 9, 19, and 29 months but the inferences based on these behaviors were confirmed at 29 months, in the symbolic play and verbal data in the weekly play sessions from ages three to four, and in the follow-up studies.[2] For example, only now do we know from verbal reports how much pain Donna suffered at the time of her urinary infection at 29 months and what her subjective experiences were when she suffered from shyness both as a three- to four-year-old and at the time of the first follow-up study.

Whether one considers the separation–individuation process to be a separate line of development or one aspect of the line of development of object relations, it is the aspect of development that leads to the gradual perceptual, cognitive, and affective evolution of self- and object differentiation and self- and object constancy. It interacts with other lines of

---

[2]Donna is one of 4 of the 17 subjects who are currently in weekly psychotherapy. She is considering entering analysis, as are 2 other subjects who are not currently in therapy. Analysis would greatly enhance the value of the follow-up study.

development and, like these, cannot be divorced from the maturation and development of the id and ego. It is both dependent on and contributes to the development of the drives, the ego, and object relations.

The foregoing clinical and observational data illustrate how disturbances in the separation–individuation process are intertwined with other lines and other aspects of development. In Becky we saw how disturbances in the dialogue between mother and child, an excess of aggression over libido, poor ego control, and failure in the mastery of anxiety contributed to a relative failure of self- and object differentiation and self- and object constancy. These failures then contributed to the development of an infantile neurosis with borderline features when combined with the contributions to that neurosis specific for the phallic-oedipal phase.

The data show that arrests resulting from disturbances in the separation–individuation process are not likely to remain static or to be encapsulated and reassert themselves later in life independent of the growth and development of the rest of the personality. They acquire psychic representation, are incorporated into the child's life, and become dynamically involved with the rest of his development. All aspects of development, in fact, become drawn into a child's feelings, impulses, and fantasies and, eventually, into the inevitable conflicts between the drives, the ego, and the superego (Arlow, 1983).

The dichotomy between the two major views of personality development and pathogenesis in the current psychoanalytic literature is misleading. One view stresses conflict and compromise formation, with particular emphasis on the oedipal phase of development and on drive and structural theory; the other stresses arrest or defect, with particular emphasis on the preoedipal phase of development and object relations theory (Arlow, 1981). Such a sharp cleavage does not exist. Structure formation and drive development occur in the context of object relations beginning in the first months of life; interpersonal conflict and compromise behaviors start in the latter part of the first year; intrapsychic conflict and compromise formations begin as early as the middle of the second year (McDevitt, 1983); arrests, defects, and distortions in development shape conflict, anxiety, and compromise formation and, in turn, conflict contributes to arrests and defects. The roles of arrest and defect, on one hand, and conflict, on the other, vary from the most severe disturbances to the milder neuroses in prelatency.

The data on Becky and Donna show that the distinctions between the preoedipal and oedipal origins of pathology are artificial. The preoedipal determinants of Becky's disturbance were probably more significant in her prelatency pathology than were the oedipal determinants, although both were necessary. Donna's symptoms began quite early, recurred with each crisis in development, and eventually became stabilized in the form of the same neurotic symptoms in prelatency, latency, and young adulthood. As these cases show, conflict and compromise formation are not necessarily confined to the oedipal phase. The compromise behaviors at the end of the first year are precursors to and continuous with the compromise formations that have their beginning in the second year of life, as was seen in Donna. And these, in turn, influence and are continuous with the conflicts and compromise formations in the phallic-narcissistic and phallic-oedipal phases in development. Although compromise behaviors may occur at any time in life as solutions to interpersonal conflicts, I am using the term here to refer to modifications of behavior during the sensori-motor or preverbal period, for example, playfully patting the mother's hair rather then angrily pulling it or playfully pinching in place of biting. Compromise formations are much more complex mental solutions to intrapsychic conflicts that may also modify behavior.

Most investigators believe that disturbances in the separation–individuation process lead to severe psychopathology—for example, psychoses (Mahler, 1965), borderline conditions (Bergman, 1971; Mahler, 1971; Kernberg, 1975), and some cases of homosexuality and perversion (Soca-rides, 1988). Pine (1979) considers failures in the cognitive aspects of the acquisition of self- and object differentiation and object constancy to be rare and to signify serious pathology, and failures in the affective and qualitative aspects to lead to severe disturbances.

In contrast to these views, Kramer (1979) and Settlage (1977) describe how less severe failures to resolve the rapprochement crisis may lead to less severe disturbances, such as an infantile neurosis or a narcissistic disorder. Mahler includes both points of view in her writings on the infantile psychosis and borderline conditions on one hand and the infantile neuroses on the other. She believed that "the infantile neurosis may have its obligatory precursor, if not its first manifestation, in the rapprochement crisis" (Mahler et al., 1975, p. 227).

Becky and Donna illustrate that, as is the case with any developmental disturbance, the severity of the ensuing pathology will depend on the nature of the disturbance and on subsequent events; that separation–individuation disturbances and their outcome not only vary in degree but also differ in nature; that their determinants and even their first manifestations may occur prior to the rapprochement crisis; and that the outcome is not necessarily severe pathology. Both the degree and the nature of the disturbance differed in Becky and Donna. For example, Becky's disturbance involved most aspects of the development of object constancy, Donna's was limited to difficulties with aggression. The vulnerability of the maternal representation to aggression made it difficult for Donna to manage conflicts brought on by aggressive impulses, caused excessive regression at times of trauma and crisis, and resulted in compromise formations that acquired additional stability during the conflicts of the phallic-oedipal phase, a stability that has persisted to the present.

The failure in the development of self and object constancy was much more marked in Becky than in Donna. A reassuring inner representation of the mother was not sufficiently available to provide Becky with protection, to aid her in coping with conflicts and anxieties, to diminish her sense of helplessness, and in all these ways to gradually help her master separation experiences and to develop signal anxiety. Becky also was not able to use identification to strengthen object and self-constancy and to resolve her struggle with her actual mother and with the intrapsychic representation of the mother to the same extent that Donna was. Instead, she projected the maternal representation onto the external world in the form of a witch. Disturbances in identification also left Becky lacking in confidence, fearful of her impulses, and with a feeling of hopelessness.

The progressively increasing stability in Donna's symptoms suggests that not only do the interpersonal and intrapsychic conflicts that occur during the separation–individuation process bring on changes in the infant's and toddler's behavior and personality at the time but that characteristic patterns of conflict resolution become established early in life and that children, provided that environmental influences do not change significantly, tend to use the same defensive patterning to cope with anxieties in subsequent phases of development that they had used in earlier phases. In the face of new danger, external or internal, the ego tends to cope or defend itself by using the same or similar behavioral and psychological defenses. In between periods of crisis, children partly recover from the particular compromise behaviors and formations that have been used to resolve each crisis; nevertheless, these may persist and be recognizable later in behavior and personality makeup. With each succeeding crisis, the same or similar defensive organization tends to become more fixed, more stable, and more structured. The compromise formations, however, change according to the wishes, fantasies, and conflicts, as well as the defenses, characteristic of the phase in development at the time of each crisis. The earlier conflict resolutions determine in part the nature, severity, and outcome of conflicts during the prelatency phase and later.

It is not clear from this study whether or to what degree or in what manner the suggestion that characteristic patterns of conflict resolution early in life tend to persist is also applicable to other types of disturbances. Becky and Donna had phobic illnesses that are more common in girls than boys and are determined both by a constitutional predisposition—a sensitivity to and avoidance of anxiety—and by a particular type of mother–child interaction. In analytic practice a similar kind of persistence, based on a different set of constitutional and environmental determinants, is seen in behavior disorders based on identification with the and in gender identity disorders in three- and four-year-old boys who identify with the mother. Further study of the 16 other research subjects may throw additional light on the question of the persistence of patterns of conflict resolution.

What would have happened if Donna's environment had improved markedly during her early childhood? If we leave aside constitutional factors, I assume that she would have managed better. I base this assumption on the resiliency and return to normal development she showed in overcoming the regressions and symptoms at 9, 19, and 29 months. The sooner the improvement in the environment, the better, however. With each crisis Donna became less resilient, since internal forces in the form of defense and compromise formation played an increasingly larger role in stabilizing her symptoms and personality structure.

We might ask two more questions: Were Becky's and Donna's compromise formations toward the end of the separation–individuation phase stable enough so that they played a significant role in determining the nature and severity of the conflicts of the phallic-oedipal phase and the ability to resolve these conflicts? And were they stable enough to significantly shape symptom formation and personality makeup prior to and (hypothetically) irrespective of the conflicts of the phallic-oedipal phase? These questions should be answered in the affirmative in these two cases, but not necessarily in the 16 other subjects in the research and follow-up studies. We see different kinds of disturbances and different sorts of outcomes, as well as change instead of continuity, in their development and functioning. Our research and follow-up studies show, for example, that subphase problems often subside and do not contribute to prelatency pathology; that prelatency pathology may be determined largely by internal and external events specific for that phase; that defects do not necessarily occur early in life only and are not necessarily related solely to particular phases in development; and that difficulties in the mother–child interaction usually continue and may even have their major adverse influence later in development.

SUMMARY

In this chapter I have used data specifically selected for the purpose of examining the influence of disturbances in the separation–individuation process on prelatency pathology. I have described how such disturbances, along with events occurring during the phallic-oedipal phase, may play a significant role in determining the severity, nature, and resolution of the conflicts typical of that phase. It is no longer helpful to think in terms of preoedipal versus oedipal determinants of prelatency pathology. Both are important. Even though the child may recover from earlier subphase disturbances, these may recur in subsequent subphases if the environment that contributed to the initial disturbance does not change. In time, these difficulties in the form of regressions, symptoms, and compromise behaviors and formations may acquire a beginning stability that shapes the nature of prelatency pathology.

REFERENCES

Arlow, J. (1981), Theories of pathogenesis. *Psychoanal. Quart.,* 2(4):488–514.
_____ (1983), Panel on "The relationship of the mind to clinical world." Presented at December meeting of the American Psychoanalytic Association, New York City.
Bergman, A. (1971), "I and you": The separation–individuation process in the treatment of a symbiotic child. In: *Separation–Individuation,* ed. J. B. McDevitt & C. F. Settlage. New York: International Universities Press, pp. 325–356.
Emde, R. (1985), From adolescence to midlife. *J. Amer. Psychoanal. Assn.,* 33(Suppl.):59–112.
Freud, A. (1965), *Normality and Pathology in Childhood.* New York: International Universities Press.
Kernberg, O. F. (1975), *Borderline Conditions and Pathological Narcissism.* New York: Aronson.
Kramer, S. (1979), The technical significance and application of Mahler's separation–individuation theory. *J. Amer. Psychoanal. Assn.,* 27:201–263.
McDevitt, J. B. (1967), A separation problem in a three-year-old girl. In: *The Child Analyst at Work,* ed. E. R. Geleerd. New York; NY: International Universities Press, pp. 24–58.
_____ (1971), Pre-oedipal determinants of an infantile neurosis. In: *Separation–Individuation, Essays in Honor of Margaret S. Mahler,* ed. J. B. McDevitt & C. F. Settlage. New York: International Universities Press.
_____ (1975), Separation–individuation and object constancy. *J. Amer. Psychoanal. Assn.,* 23(4):713–742.
_____ (1979), The role of internalization in the development of object relations during the separation–individuation phase. *J. Amer. Psychoanal. Assn.,* 27(2):327–343.
_____ (1983), The emergence of hostile aggression and its defensive and adaptive modifications during the separation–individuation process. *J. Amer. Psychoanal. Assn.,* 31(5):273–300.

Mahler, M. S. (1965), The early infantile psychosis: The symbiotic and autistic syndrome. In: *The Selected Papers, Vol. I.* New York: Aronson, pp. 155–169.

——— (1971), A study of the separation–individuation process and its possible application to borderline phenomena in the psychoanalytic situation. In: *The Selected Papers, Vol. II.* New York: Aronson, pp. 169–187.

——— Pine, F. & Bergman, A. (1975), *The Psychological Birth of the Human Infant.* New York: Basic Books.

Main, M., Kaplan, N. & Cassidy, J. (1985), Security in infancy, childhood and adulthood: A move to a level of representation. In: *Growing Points of Attachment Theory and Research: Monographs of the Society for Research in Child Development,* ed. I. Bretherton & E. Waters, Serial No. 209, Vol. 50, No. 1–2; pp. 66–107.

Pine, F. (1979), Pathology of the separation–individuation process as manifested in later clinical work. *Internat. J. Psycho-Anal.,* 60:225–242.

Sander, L. W. (1983), To begin with—reflections on ontogeny. In: *Reflections on Self-Psychology,* ed. J. Lichtenberg & S. Kaplan. Hillsdale, NY: The Analytic Press, pp. 85–104.

Settlage, C. F. (1977), The psychoanalytic understanding of narcissistic and borderline disorders: Advances in developmental theory. *J. Amer. Psychoanal. Assn.,* 25:805–833.

Socarides, C. W. (1988), *The Pre-Oedipal Origin and Psychoanalytic Therapy of Sexual Perversions.* Madison, CT: International Universities Press.

Stern, D. N. (1985), *The Interpersonal World of the Infant.* New York: Basic Books.

8

Transformations in Normal and Pathological Latency

Jules Glenn

Mahler (Mahler, Pine, and Bergman, 1975), concentrating on separation–individuation, did not devote her full energy to the influence of the earlier periods on the oedipal and latency stages, but she certainly was aware of this issue. She noted the

> broad spectrum regarding efforts to understand the preverbal period. At one extreme stand those who believe in innate complex oedipal fantasies. . . . At the other end of the spectrum stand those Freudian analysts who look with favor on stringent verbal and reconstructive evidence . . . yet who seem to accord preverbal material little right to serve as the basis for even the most cautious and tentative extension of our main body of hypotheses. . . . We believe that there is a broad middle ground among analysts who, with caution, are ready to explore the contributions to theory that can come from inferences regarding the preverbal period . . . [p. 14].

Some analytic theorists trace "earlier and earlier verbalizable memories, and ultimately . . . connect these memories to preverbal . . . phenomena in infancy" (p. 14). Indeed, Mahler observed that Freud himself did this in connecting the child's being swooped up by grown-ups and adults' dreams of flying. Blum (1977) has also shown that Freud described superego precursors during the rapprochement subphase.

171

The Oedipus complex does not appear de novo in the third or fourth year of life. There are maturational–biological as well as environmental–familial–social forces that evoke its appearance and structure. Preoedipal, internal, and external events also play a significant role in determining its character. According to Mahler (Mahler, Pine, and Bergman, 1975):

> Our limited study gave us an inkling as to why even preliminary development toward the Oedipus complex and the infantile neurosis is so unpredictable. But it also gave us a kind of mandate to build with unrelenting, cautious optimism better instruments, more sophisticated psychoanalytical developmental theories for understanding the 'unrememberable' and the 'unforgetable' realm of the mind, which we believe holds the key for prevention [p. 226].

> Not even the most normally endowed child, with the most optimally available mother, is able to weather the separation–individuation process without crises . . . and enter the oedipal phase without developmental difficulty. . . . In fact . . . the fourth subphase . . . has no single definite permanent terminal point. . . . Through cross-fertilization of the structural and refined development theories, we already possess instruments which, if used to amplify the libido theory, might bring us further in our understanding of the widening scope of neurotic symptoms in childhood as well as during the entire life cycle [p. 227].

> The tendency toward splitting, which may ensue as the child's solution to the pain of longings and losses of the rapprochement crisis, must make for greater difficulty in the resolution of the complex object-related conflicts of the oedipal period, promoting ambivalence and throwing an ominous cast on the oedipal and postoedipal personality development [p. 230].

Kramer and Byerly (1978) state the issue somewhat differently:

> It is the specific manner in which the "intertwining of the developmental lines of separation and individuation" occurs during the normal separation–individuation process that accounts for the manner in which the "reverberations of the separation–individuation process" will occur throughout the life cycle. . . . The reverberations of the "rapprochement crisis," [the child's] ambivalence and the ambitendencies experienced during the normal separation–individuation process *will* condition the manifest way [the child] progresses through latency . . . [p. 212].

This paper attempts to clarify some of the relationships of preoedipal development, including that of separation–individuation, and later development, both normal and pathological. Development involves not simple continuity of patterns but an increasingly complex integration of earlier and later states in which earlier states are transformed. As Kennedy and Moran (1989) state in a summary of Anna Freud's (1965) developmental views, there is a "transition from the numerous and various conflicts of the pre-oedipal organizations and transformation of these conflicts into the oedipal constellation" (p. 2). They add that nonconflictual preoedipal constellations can influence oedipal conflict and resolution as well.

Transformations are more complex in seriously ill patients, including those suffering from psychoses. In such patients we see symbiotic and separation–individuation and oedipal phases that are not the usual ones; they are pathological formations. The oedipal influences and organizing activity are distorted.

TRANSFORMATION DURING THE OEDIPAL AND LATENCY STAGES

An analysand in her thirties, Mrs. S had made considerable progress as a result of the analysis of her oedipal conflicts. She then suffered a setback in her fourth year of treatment: she experienced alternate periods of extreme idealization of the analyst and irrational, unexplained intense rage at him. Her love and hatred seemed perfectly justified to her, and oedipal interpretations had no effect on this pattern. After a half year of such alternations, the analyst gathered enough information to offer a reconstruction of conflicts during the rapprochement subphase (Mahler, Pine, and Bergman, 1975), which, he suggested, the patient repeated in the transference. At around 18 months, he asserted, Mrs. S had tried, as is usual, to become independent of her mother, to whom she was very attached. As she broke away from her mother emotionally, she felt deserted by her, became furious at her, felt anxious about her feelings, and returned to her mother, whom she again felt one with and whom she idealized. But after reuniting with her mother, in fantasy and actuality, she once more wanted to break away. As she detached herself from her parent, she again felt left and became furious. This cycle repeated itself in her rapprochement subphase and again during the analysis. The analyst represented the mother whom the patient idolized and loved, tried to become independent of, and then became furious at. As anxiety over fantasies of desertion appeared, the patient defended against this by again idealizing and loving the analyst/mother.

The phenomena described, splitting (Mahler, Pine, and Bergman, 1975;

Kernberg, 1975), consists of the patient's temporally alternating loving and antagonistic feelings toward an object instead of experiencing these states simultaneously. Splitting may also involve displacing hatred to another person while loving (or hating) the analyst or, originally, the mother. Splitting has been described as a typical defense during the rapprochement subphase.

The reconstruction made sense to Mrs. S and the splitting in the transference ceased. She recovered memories that appeared to confirm the interpretation. However, she did not recall the events reconstructed during the second year of life. Instead, she remembered her struggle over closeness with and antagonism toward her mother during latency.

The patient stated that her mother was very attached to her during latency; she was very interested in her relationships with friends and wanted to know the details of their interactions. The patient, who loved her mother, wanted to comply but also wished to keep her thoughts to herself. She tried to become independent, by not telling her mother of her intimate experiences, and became furious at her mother. After a while she reverted to her closeness to mother and felt happy in her love for her.

This analytic experience raises significant questions. Had the analyst correctly reconstructed conflicts at 18 months? If so, why did the patient not recall her rapprochement subphase? Why did she remember similar difficulties during latency instead? Had the analyst inadvertently reconstructed meaningful latency experiences rather than meaningful rapprochement occurrences but provided the wrong age? Had the memories of the latency years appeared defensively to avoid more painful memories of the second year? Is the seeming reappearance of the rapprochement experiences through nonverbal means rather than the reporting of conventional memory a result of cognitive inability to recall very early events? Schachtel (1949), discussing the oedipal stage and dream states, has suggested that inability to recall early events or dreams occurs because the adult's psychic state is so different from that of the young child, as well as because of repression. Certainly, preoedipal experiences are even more alien to the adult than are oedipal states, and certainly, repression of the painful preoedipal period experiences also plays a basic role.

I do not think we can rule out either of these explanations, all of which may play a part in the patient's remembering latency rather than preoedipal occurrences. I believe, however, that the occurrence of transformation of preoedipal experience during the oedipal period and latency accounts, for the most part, for the clinical observations described. I suggest that patients go through the rapprochement subphase at about 15–20 months, as children typically and normally do. With the appearance of the Oedipus complex, libidinal and *quasi*-symbiotic, not true symbiotic, longings for mother persist and acquire a genital sexual significance, and oedipal sexual desires for the father appear. Further, the clinging to mother intensifies, since it serves as a defense against forbidden wishes for father. These positive and negative oedipal attachments of both boys and girls become forbidden, and the growing superego requires punishment in the form of bodily injury, including fantasied castration, and desertion. The fantasies and fears of abandonment of the rapprochement subphase thus acquire oedipal significance.

This statement is essentially the same as Mahler's but the emphasis is different. According to Mahler, Pine, and Bergman (1975), "In these, and perhaps in other diverse ways, we believe, the infantile neurosis becomes manifestly visible at the oedipal period; but it may be shaped by the fate of the rapprochement crisis *that precedes it*" (p. 230). I emphasize the oedipal organization whereas Mahler stresses the separation–individuation phase.

The schema I described is consistent with Freud's (1923) description of the genital organization, in which preoedipal aspects are incorporated into but remain subservient to the newly formed oedipal complex. I am including separation–individuation issues in the preoedipal and then in the oedipal organization. Mahler's work and conceptualization thus contribute to our understanding of transformation during the oedipal period.

In latency transformations continue; separation–individuation is not completed at three, when libidinal object constancy is achieved. At three, children can maintain an image of their absent parents so that they, in the oedipal stage, are able to separate from them for a time. Latency children tolerate separation for longer periods; hence, they can attend school for longer periods than can younger children. Most children are not able to leave home for two months of camp until they are about ten, and even then they may become homesick. (Some do well at sleepaway camp at eight, but for many this is a difficult period to leave home.) However, as noted for the oedipal stage, separation anxiety possesses a significance different from that of the separation individuation phase.

Unconscious oedipal conflicts persist in latency, but they are less intense due to more effective defensive and adaptive activity and resultant compromise formation. A biological diminution of drive strength may also occur. The sublimation (involving neutralization) of sexual and aggressive urges for constructive educational and social purposes, in conjunction with nonlibidinal autonomous drives, helps resolve conflict. Specific defenses typical of latency (such as reaction formation and isolation) give children of that age a compulsive quality.

However, even during latency there are interruptions of the ideal state (Freud, 1905); drive derivatives periodically break through, masturbatory desires are expressed, and conflict, with attendant anxiety, becomes manifest. In pathological states the conflict may be persistent and stronger, anxiety more manifest, and defenses less adaptive. When preoedipal problems are not sufficiently resolved, the oedipal and latency configurations bear a preoedipal mark in which fears of separation dominate.

I suggest that in the patient described earlier, increased attachment to her mother, a result of the mother's earlier clinging to the patient, possibly due to symbiotic states in the mother, left a prominent imprint on her oedipal complex. The patient responded with homosexual attachment to her mother, whom she idealized, a desire to break away from this forbidden attachment, and a reactive fury when she was threatened with loss of mother. The latency pattern the patient recalled was thus not a simple repetition but, rather, a derivative of rapprochement experiences.

TRANSFORMATIONS IN CHILDREN'S GAMES

Similar transformations appear in children's pre-games and games, such as peekaboo (Kleeman, 1967; Mahler, Pine, and Bergman, 1975) and its derivatives (Phillips, 1960; Opie and Opie, 1969; Glenn and Bernstein, 1990). During the differentiation subphase of separation–individuation (at five to ten months, approximately) the mother often initiates peekaboo games, and the child responds happily. The mother covers her face or otherwise places an obstacle between the infant and herself, thus making it seem that the mother has disappeared. When the mother removes the barrier, she reappears before the child. Her reappearance serves as a reassurance to the child that mother can be recovered after loss. Mother is similarly reassured; indeed, her need for reassurance against loss is a prime motive for her initiating the game. Having, caring for, and identifying with a child revives recollections of childhood fears of losing mother and requires the institution of defenses against the anxiety and depressive affect that may appear. Further, the mother's inevitable antagonism toward the demanding child she loves also brings about fears that the child will disappear and consequent defensive activity such as the peekaboo game. Through the play, mother also experiences feelings of fun and closeness to the infant she loves.

Later, in the practicing and rapprochement subphases, the child initiates the game and creates the reassuring situation. The infant produces the barrier to seeing his mother, and removes it with delight. Mastery continues. The peekaboo game also serves as a source of pleasure in "exercising ego apparatuses" (Mahler, Pine, and Bergman, 1975, p. 71) and in separating from mother, an "elated escape from fusion with, engulfment by mother" (p. 71). The child finds pleasure in finding mother and in the mother's finding him. "To be found by mother, to be seen by mother (to be mirrored by her) seems to build body–self awareness" (pp. 221–222).

Freud (1920) described his grandson's playing a game similar to peekaboo that did not require his mother's participation. The child at 1 ½ years (the height of the rapprochement crisis) would say "o-o-o-o" (gone) as he tossed toys out of sight and then say "da" (there) joyfully as he retrieved them. He would also attempt to master his mother's absence through actively making himself seem to disappear by crouching under a mirror so he could not see his reflection.

Children in analysis delight in derivatives of such games; the reassuring quality prevails but the significance of the separation changes in the oedipal stage and in latency. The child is reassured that he will not lose his mother to a rival and is reassured that he will not be punished through desertion. If a child in the throes of castration anxiety equates mother and penis, he may defend against that anxiety by actively making mother disappear. Mahler (Mahler, Pine, and Bergman, 1975) describes a boy who, in addition to playing peekaboo games, played a similar game in which he covered and uncovered his genitals (p. 179).

The peekaboo game requires relatively simple cognitive ability. At its most complex it is based on the child's capacity for object permanence (Piaget and Inhelder, 1969), that is, an awareness that things still exist even when hidden. It requires a degree of recognition of the mother as a separate person and of the possibility that she can return if she's absent. Only limited motoric ability is necessary.

Oedipal children, with their greater capacity for locomotion, can hide, encourage mother (or therapist) to find them, and delight in revealing themselves or being found. Sometimes oedipal or latency children in analysis (or therapy) hide objects for the adult to find or have the therapist hide the objects. The objects may symbolize people they yearn for or who are lost or parts of the body they fear losing.

In latency oedipal wishes join with improved cognition and motor capacity to create the game of hide-and-seek, a marked transformation of the peekaboo game but one that retains elements of the earlier game. Frequently in latency the setting is the playground or the street and the participants are friends rather than parents and other adults. Latency is a period of further breaking away from parents. Other children and teachers play more important roles, but the child still requires his father and mother; full libidinal object constancy has not yet been achieved.

In hide-and-seek one child covers his eyes while standing at "home" base and counts to 100 while his friends hide. Upon reaching 100 he shouts, "Here I come, ready or not" and tries to locate the hiders. When he does find one, he races "home" before the hider, who tries to beat him there. The child who touches home first is the victor. The loser becomes "it" and becomes the seeker in the next game. The game now has complicated rules the group agrees to abide by, a result of increased cognition and moral development (Piaget, 1932).

In hide-and-seek the disappearance and reassuring reappearance of the loved person occurs, but another child rather than the parent is the lost one, a displacement. The seeker finds the missing one, thus reassuring himself against loss; but a competitive element enters. The seeker competes with the one he finds, who becomes the rival parent. They race for home, symbolizing mother or father; the first one there wins. Oedipal has now integrated pre-oedipal; separation issues are now incorporated into oedipal desires.

In addition, sibling rivalry, which often originates before the oedipal period and then becomes part and parcel of oedipal conflicts, expresses itself in the game, which also attempts mastery of competition. Even only children have to deal with sibling rivalry, which exists in fantasy when reality does not create it (Arlow, 1972).

New cognitive and motor capacities are necessary to play hide-and-seek. The latency child is motorically able to hide from others and run with skill. Moreover, he must be sufficiently able to put himself in the place of the seeker to avoid the seeker's finding him. Transition from egocentrism to this capacity to put oneself in another's place occurs at about seven or eight years (Piaget, 1932). The child must, of course, be able to count to engage in hide-and-seek. Further, the child must achieve a concept of the rules of the game (possible at about eight years of age), must have the ability to learn them, and a superego that insists on adhering to them. The child and his peers share the rules and require their enforcement, ostracism being the penalty for violaters. Again, the threat of separation becomes instrumental to an oedipal game that contains modified preoedipal elements.

Phillips (1960) recognized that the peekaboo game stops at age two, that hide-and-seek is a latency game, and that both are attempts to master separation. He observed that the child playing hide-and-seek at times reverses roles with the parent who loses the child. Although he did not explicitly recognize the oedipal features of the game, he did note the punishment and competitive aspects of hide-and-seek. He stated that although there is no competition in primitive games like peekaboo, it occurs in nearly all games played by older children. He added that the "boo" part of "peekaboo often survives in adolescence, but it then has a

quite different significance" (p. 203), thus implying a type of transformation. Even younger children love to appear suddenly and frighten the one
they confront by shouting, "Boo!"

THE CONCEPT OF TRANSFORMATION

In this paper I am using the concept of transformation (Freud, 1905;
Abrams, 1977; Glenn, 1979, 1989) to describe certain developmental
changes, that concept being essential for understanding development,
although it has other significance as well.

The *American Heritage Dictionary, Second College Edition* (1982) defines *to
transform* as (1) "to change markedly the form or appearance of; (2) to
change the nature, function and condition; to convert" (p. 1287). The
definition implies that basic qualities persist but change significantly their
form, appearance, nature, function, or condition.

Freud (1905) used the concept of transformation when he described the
developmental alterations that take place in puberty. He also used it to
describe nondevelopmental alterations of anal-erotic impulses and the
developmental changes at the time of the Oedipus complex (Freud, 1917).
He wondered about the later history of anal-erotic and other pregenital
impulses after the genital organization is established and they have lost
their importance. He noted that pregenital drives become assimilated into
but subservient to the genital organization of the oedipal stage (Freud,
1923).

During transformations old elements join with or are integrated with
new elements to produce a new gestalt or organization. Transformations
can be of the id, ego, or superego. Freud (1905) early on emphasized *drive*
transformations, but even before the appearance of the structural theory
he discussed defenses and adaptive mechanisms, that is, sublimation. In
"On Transformations in Structure as Exemplified in Anal-Eroticism"
(1917) he asks whether anal-erotic impulses are sublimated or assimilated
by transformation into character traits. "Or do they find a place in the new
organization of sexuality characterized by genital primacy?" (p. 127–128).
In "A Child Is Being Beaten" (1919), in which he describes changes of
such fantasies as development proceeds from the pregenital through the
oedipal stages, he says an "infantile perversion can . . . be transformed by
sublimation" (pp. 181–182).

Hartmann (1964) did not use the term *transformation*, but its meaning
is implied in his discussion of alteration through neutralization or dein-

stinctualization of drives and instinctualization or aggressivation of non-drive elements and his concept of "change of function." Hartmann stated that early structures can change their functions. Defenses can become autonomous ego functions, as when reaction formation, originally instituted to combat forbidden anal impulses, is used to achieve adaptive orderliness, or when defensive isolation serves adaptively to help concentration. Hartmann observed the not infrequent error of confusing a developmentally earlier structure with a subsequent one with a different function. As Arlow (1970) pointed out, a child's fantasy of ingesting Captain Marvel through eating marble cake and thereby becoming powerful can be misidentified as an oral stage fantasy when it is actually an oedipal fantasy based on a wish to acquire father's power.

Transformations of drive can result from integration—assimilation, Freud says—into a later organization; transformation to character traits; sublimation (which involves neutralization and displacement); deinstinctualization or deaggressivation; and instinctual fusion. Indeed, defenses generally transform drives, since the defenses tend to incorporate and express drives (Brenner, 1982). Transformations of the ego can also result from change of functions of defenses that become adaptive mechanisms. In what may be a nonadaptive way, ego aspects—including anxiety, autonomous ego functions, and defenses—may be instinctualized (aggressivized or libidinized).

The superego consists of the ego-ideal and punitive and approving parts of the superego. It results from integration of superego precursors utilizing defenses such as identification and turning aggression toward the self or aspects of the self.

Latency's transformations result from an increased capacity to neutralize, newly found cognitive capacities, the utilization of sublimation, reaction formation, and isolation. Integrations established in the oedipal period persist but are defended against. Drive satisfaction, now displaced to school and peer achievements, utilizes newly established cognitive capacities (Gesell and Ilg, 1946; Piaget and Inhelder, 1969), ability to read and write, serialization, reversibility, and motor abilities. But separation–individuation is not complete; latency children worry about parental desertion and need their parents' care. At the same time, the fears and fantasies of abandonment become a punishment for violation of superego demands. The ego-ideal expands to include not only a barrier to oedipal gratification but other demands as well, such as those for scholastic achievement. At times there is conflict within the superego. The ego-ideal may stipulate that the child not compete with father yet simultaneously require high academic achievement.

PATHOLOGICAL TRANSFORMATIONS

Thus far I have emphasized normal transformations; I now turn to the pathological. In a paper titled "From Protomasochism to Masochism: A Developmental View" (Glenn, 1989), I differentiated preoedipal proto-masochism from masochism proper. I defined protomasochism, a term used by Loewenstein (1957), as a conflictual or nonconflictual structure or pattern of interaction with others that may later be incorporated into a masochistic fantasy. In masochism proper, oedipal fantasies organize and transform the preoedipal experiences. In the 1989 paper I noted that Mahler (1966) had not used the term but did observe protomasochistic outcome during separation–individuation in recognizing that a toddler may experience "impotent resignation and surrender (in some cases with marked masochistic coloring)" (p. 71). I suggest that there is a *universal* protomasochism, which may or may not eventuate in oedipal masochistic fantasies. During the course of separation–individuation the infant feels powerful in his fantasied symbiotic union with his mother. But as he recognizes his dependence on her and her wishes and whims in the rapprochement subphase, he experiences a sense of weakness and submission. The seeds of subservience, a kind of protomasochism, will thus invariably be planted. In addition, rage generated during rapprochement may be turned against the self, another form of protomasochism.

Clinical Illustration: Eddie R

Eddie R, the patient I described in the 1989 paper, had a disturbed, borderline mother. The mutual clinging of mother and child was intense but inconsistent. Eddie was even willing during latency to sacrifice his genitals partially for the sake of continuing closeness. When the boy was approaching 10, his mother offered him a circumcision as a birthday gift. He readily agreed, and developed a masochistic masturbation fantasy: I will please my (sadistic) mother by an operation on my penis.

In addition to the early symbiotic intensity and subsequent clinging during separation–individuation (which I reconstructed) and later, there were other preoedipal contributions to the boy's masochism. Mrs. R told me that she had devoted a great deal of time to Eddie as an infant but could not relax and cuddle him since she was continually exhausted. Although she intended to employ "demand feeding," Mrs. R often awoke Eddie to feed him. She worried about his health and thus weighed him frequently. Eddie had been bottle fed and weaned at one year. Soon thereafter he started to bite his older sister. Mrs. R taught him to stop this behavior by biting him. The child experienced painful anal and abdominal sensations due to his harboring an ascaris worm, which he passed anally at the age of two years. In addition, he identified with his parents, whom he watched fight from early on. He recognized that each parent was both an attacker and a victim. Oedipal love for his mother organized and transformed the recalled and reexperienced preoedipal occurrences.

Clinical Illustration: Dr. P

Another patient of mine (Glenn, 1984), Dr. P, underwent a severe shock trauma during the oedipal stage at age five that organized his masochistic sexual fantasies and a masochistic character. During analysis when he was an adult, symbiotic fantasies became conscious and Dr. P experienced a modified Isakower phenomenon (Isakower, 1938), suggesting powerful preoedipal difficulties with separation–individuation.

The patient's mother had allowed him to lie on top of her and suck her breasts until he was five. She walked him in a carriage and wiped his behind until he was eight, far into the latency years. Preoedipal togetherness became integrated into genital excitement, which was experienced by both participants. When Dr. P was a latency child and a teenager, he and she would play a game in which she chased him around a table until she, red-faced, screamed that she would *platz* (faint) with excitement.

At five, after being attracted to a little girl (according to his memory), Dr. P became ill with a retropharyngeal abscess. The operation was performed without anesthesia; after the surgeon pierced and burst the abscess, the patient lost consciousness. During latency and beyond, the patient repeated this procedure in disguised form and in reverse: he stabbed magazines blindly and then looked at them to see how many heads he had pierced; as an adult he could not have intercourse with his wife because that involved stabbing her with his penis; he became the surgeon who does the piercing rather than the victim who is pierced.

During his analysis Dr. P experienced a variant of the Isakower phenomenon, associated in his mind with oral feeding, closeness to his mother, and sexual excitement with her. He felt a balloonlike structure, which he associated with his mother's breast, over his face as his entire body, except for his penis, became tense. This phenomenon was not a simple memory of a nursing symbiotic state of infancy: it was a transformed experience that incorporated memories of an operation and anesthesia—a tonsillectomy at three in which a mask was placed over his face. The oedipal stage operation on his retropharyngeal abscess was also integrated into the Isakower phenomenon. And the taut body represented a body–phallus equation (Glenn, 1971) through displacement from his genitals. When the patient was sexually excited on the analytic couch, his entire body would feel tense.

A symbiotic-like fantasy appeared during the analysis. Dr. P conjured up a research project in which a mother mouse and baby mouse were attached to each other through the umbilical system. As the baby grew, the mother decreased in size and vice versa; the mother could sap the infant's strength, creating an illness. Again, this was not a simple repetition of a series of preoedipal experiences, including the child's being fed by his mother. When the patient was in latency, his mother would enter the bathroom while he bathed, grasp his scrotum, and feel for his testicles, which she feared would disappear. The patient experienced this as a castration for, as well as gratification of, oedipal wishes. Thus, in analysis, memories of preoedipal and oedipal experiences were closely associated.

Clinical Illustration: Arthur D

The next illustration is more problematic because the patient reached an extremely pathological and disturbed oedipal stage, one in which separation–individuation disturbances persisted, intertwined with the oedipal. One is at a loss whether to emphasize the oedipal or preoedipal when development is so abnormal. This is an example of distorted and pathological development, not merely developmental arrest or regression.

Arthur D, 11 years old when he entered therapy, had not yet developed physical signs of prepuberty. Many years ago I diagnosed him as a victim of childhood schizophrenia; currently he might be classified as pervasive developmental disorder or borderline disorder. He entered therapy because of periods of anxiety that he sometimes relieved by tapping four times. His mother's reassuring presence could also help him calm himself. In school he had trouble concentrating, was restless, and had temper tantrums.

Indeed, the mutual closeness of mother and child was extreme and had been since Arthur's infancy. Mrs. D was a flirtatious but frigid, frightened woman who feared sexual attachment. She had never had intercourse. Mr. D suffered from impotence; he could not sustain an erection or penetrate his wife. Mrs. D became pregnant with her only son after her husband ejaculated onto her vulva. The couple did not sleep together. Because of Arthur's fears, Mrs. D said, she shared a room with her son. She bottle-fed him until he was four and spoon-fed him until six. She held him a great deal because he reportedly cried a lot from three months on, at which age he had received X-ray treatment for a skin disorder. (Neurological examination did not reveal brain damage.) Arthur's father would not allow him to go onto the street alone until he was seven because he feared he might be injured. The boy had few friends.

The patient's intimate attachment to his mother—at first symbiotic, later perhaps best called symbiotic-like—remained but changed in character as he grew into an oedipal and then a latency child. Although Arthur was a skillful artist, thus revealing his capacity for sublimation, his latency was restricted by the intensity of his drives and his inability to control hostile impulses and activity. He drew rockets—manifestations of libidinal and aggressive urges—with excitement. He required a special school with individual care because he was restless, disobedient, and attacking. He experienced sexual excitement in his mother's presence and recognized her seductiveness.

After a year of treatment Arthur started to become independent but was still quite fearful of leaving his mother. When treatment enabled mother and child to start to separate and to occupy different rooms at night, both mother and child panicked. Arthur's rage and restlessness grew as he became frightened at home and at school, he required a night light, and his compulsions became more intense for a brief period.

Over the summer Arthur calmed down. His mother said it was his best time ever, since he spent more time with mother at a vacation house and saw father less. Being away from his father meant that Arthur no longer witnessed father and mother arguing with each other viciously. At the same time, he traveled into the city to see his therapist, thus maintaining the therapeutic contact. But when September arrived and he returned to home and school, Arthur's fear, aggression, and restlessness recurred. The school had difficulty controlling the boy, now 13. Mother, feeling the therapy was breaking up her relationship with Arthur and fearing that he required institutionalization, pulled him out of treatment.

Throughout his once-weekly therapy, Arthur's fears of injury were prominent. During his therapy sessions, Arthur's grandiosity and bizarreness appeared. In a session shortly after his mother stopped sleeping in his room, he became quite disorganized. At first he built a model plane in an organized way, but then ate the decals. He described his excitement in school where he and a friend, Bill, teased and hit Jane, another student. Bill, Jane, and Arthur and another girl, who had become angry at the mistreatment of Jane, talked about planets, Arthur said. Arthur was the king.

A few sessions later, he was preoccupied with going away with his mother for the summer. He said he believed that men from Mars came to Earth in flying saucers (these delusional beliefs were firmly held as true); they may be belligerent or friendly. He added that getting to the summer place would make life peaceful. I understood Arthur's fantasies as expressions of his desire to be close to his mother and of his fear of it. She could be loving or attacking. Arthur was also glad to get rid of his father, as he openly told me, but feared his anger; father would object to his intimacy with mother, Arthur thought. At the same time, he loved his father.

In this case the child developed beyond the symbiotic stage and experienced a prolonged rapprochement crisis. The mark of symbiosis and rapprochement weighed heavily on his eventual oedipal attachment—with associated genital sensations—which appeared despite seriously faulty libidinal object constancy. Arthur experienced separation as a punishment for his oedipal attachment, with its preoedipal influence, to his mother. The paranoid nature of Arthur's disturbance led me to suspect a biological contribution to his pathological attachment. Indeed, there was a family history of psychosis in several distant relatives and clear evidence of serious pathology in the parents.

Some would assert that Arthur never entered the oedipal stage, since libidinal object constancy was not achieved; or they might say that the patient's seemingly oedipal involvement appeared prematurely as a defense against preoedipal conflicts. I suggest that maturational pressures pushed him into an oedipal stage that was seriously distorted by his previous experiences with mother and his pathophysiological predispositions. Certainly, this patient's oedipal organization was far from normal.

SUMMARY

This paper attempts to clarify some of the relationships between preoedipal development, including separation–individuation, and later development. As development proceeds, preoedipal traits are transformed and integrated into oedipal constellations. Examination of the preoedipal peekaboo game and its later variation in latency, hide-and-seek, reveals transformations.

Pathological transformations appear in serious disorders such as childhood schizophrenia, in which distortions (not merely delays) of the separation–individuation process and oedipal development occur; they also appear in masochism and psychoneurotic illness.

REFERENCES

Abrams, S. (1977), The genetic point of view. *J. Amer. Psychoanal. Assn.*, 25:417–425.

American Heritage Dictionary, Second College Edition (1982), Boston: Houghton Mifflin.

Arlow, J. A. (1970), Remarks during course on methodology at Division of Psychoanalytic Education. Downstate Medical Center, State University of New York.

———— (1972), The only child. *Psychoanal. Quart.*, 41:507–536.

Blum, H. P. (1977), The prototype of preoedipal reconstruction. *J. Amer. Psychoanal. Assn.*, 25:752–785.

Brenner, C. (1982), *The Mind in Conflict*. New York: International Universities Press.

Freud, A. (1965), *Normality and Pathology in Childhood*. New York: International Universities Press.

Freud, S. (1905), Three essays on the theory of sexuality. *Standard Edition*, 7:135–243. London: Hogarth Press, 1953.

———— (1917), On transformations in structure as exemplified in anal eroticism. *Standard Edition*, 17:125–133. London: Hogarth Press, 1955.

———— (1919), "A child is being beaten." *Standard Edition*, 17:179–204. London: Hogarth Press, 1955.

———— (1920), Beyond the pleasure principle. *Standard Edition*, 18:7–64. London: Hogarth Press, 1955.

———— (1923), The infantile genital organization. *Standard Edition*, 19:139–145. London: Hogarth Press, 1961.

Gesell, A. & Ilg, F. L. (1946), *The Child from Five to Ten*. New York: Harper.

Glenn, J. (1971), Regression and displacement in the development of the body-phallus equation. In: *The Unconscious Today*, ed. M. Kanzer. New York: International Universities Press, pp. 274–287.

———— (1979), The developmental point of view in adult analysis: A survey and a critique. *J. Phila. Assn. Psychoanal.*, 6:21–38.

———— (1984), Psychic trauma and masochism, *J. Amer. Psychoanal. Assn.*, 32:357–386.

———— (1989), From protomasochism to masochism: A developmental view, *The Psychoanalytic Study of the Child*, 44:73–86. New Haven, CT: Yale University Press.

———— & Bernstein, I. (1990), The fantasy world of the child as revealed in art, play and dreams. In: *The Neurotic Child and Adolescent*, ed. M. H. Etezady, New York: Aronson, pp. 319–347.

Hartmann, H. (1964), *Essays on Ego Psychology*. New York: International Universities Press.

Isakower, I. (1938), A contribution to the pathopsychology of falling asleep. *Internat. J. Psycho-Anal.*, 19:331–345.

Kennedy, H. & Moran, G. S. (1989), The impact of developmental considerations on the aims of child and adult psychoanalysis. Presented at the Eleventh International Scientific Colloquium, Hampstead, London.

Kernberg, O. (1975), *Borderline Conditions and Pathological Narcissism*. New York: Aronson.

Kleeman, J. A. (1967), The peek-a-boo game. *The Psychoanalytic Study of the Child*, 22:239–273. New York: International Universities Press.

Kramer, S. & Byerly, L. J. (1978), Technique of psychoanalysis of the latency child. In: *Child Analysis and Therapy,* ed. J. Glenn. New York: Aronson, pp. 204–236.

Loewenstein, R. M. (1957), A contribution to the psychoanalytic theory of masochism. *J. Amer. Psychoanal. Assn.,* 5:197–234.

Mahler, M. S. (1966), Notes on the development of basic moods. In: *Psychoanalysis: A General Psychology,* ed. R. M. Loewenstein, L. M. Newman, M. Schur, & A. J. Solnit. New York: International Universities Press, pp. 152–168.

_____ Pine, F. & Bergman, A. (1975), *The Psychological Birth of the Human Infant.* New York: Basic Books.

Opie, I. & Opie, P. (1969), *Children's Games in Street and Playground.* Oxford: Clarendon Press.

Phillips, R. H. (1960), The nature and function of children's formal games. *Psychoanal. Quart.,* 29:200–209.

Piaget, J. (1932), *The Moral Judgment of the Child.* Glencoe, IL: Free Press.

_____ & Inhelder, B. (1969), *The Psychology of the Child.* New York: Basic Books.

Schachtel, E. G. (1949), On memory and childhood amnesia. In: *A Study of Interpersonal Relations,* ed. P. Mullahy. New York: Hermitage Press, pp. 3–49.

9 Separation–Individuation and Adolescence with Special Reference to Character Formation

Louis A. Leaff

Adolescence consists of the psychological concomitants of the stage of sexual maturation. The biophysiologic changes of adolescence ultimately result in the potential for procreation, and the psychological transformations supposedly lead to the consolidation of character. For both these reasons, adolescence is a profoundly important developmental phase to understand, and yet many unanswered questions about it remain. In this chapter I review the boundaries of adolescence, its metapsychology, and the unique place it holds in understanding the development of the individual from a psychological as well as cognitive point of view. I compare the unique developmental features of the adolescent to those of the adult and younger child and explore the often difficult differentiation of normalcy and pathology in adolescence. I review and compare the views of various significant contributors, especially Margaret Mahler and Peter Blos, to our understanding of adolescence and attempt some integration of their theoretical frameworks. I examine the language and conceptualizations of their theories, including their potential for confusion as well as clarification of the psychology and metapsychology of adolescence. I examine the significance of preoedipal constructs and self–object differentiation as it applies to adolescence. Finally, I explore the concept of "character" as currently conceived, particularly the origins and development of character and whether its adult form is an integration of late adolescence, as some theorists contend.

EARLY LITERATURE

In a comprehensive review of Freud's contributions to the psychology of adolescence, Klumpner (1978) could find no evidence that Freud's own adolescent development contributed to his theories of adolescence. Freud's clinical work with adolescents is not well reported or documented as to number, duration, or outcome. Klumpner concluded that Freud's remarkable insight into the psychology of adolescence as set forth in "Three Essays on the Theory of Sexuality" resulted from the balance and interaction between his self-analysis, his clinical experiences, and his scientific style. "The manner in which Freud arrived at his concept of the psychology of adolescence is one example of the way in which his self-analysis was the existence of infantile wishes and fantasies . . ." (Klumpner, 1978, p. 18). Klumpner proposed that "Freud's concepts of the psychology of adolescence were arrived at deductively as a logical extension of the transformations of infantile sexuality which had to be understood if the varieties of sexuality found in adults normal, neurotic or perverse were to be understood. The comprehensive summary of the psychology of adolescence "in the Three Essays suggests a deductive tour de force which was then tested against clinical evidence" (p. 21).

Our record of Freud's self-analysis, however, contains only one brief mention of adolescence. Likewise, in case reports of adult patients only isolated adolescent memories are mentioned. Klumpner concluded that the gap in Freud's exposition of adolescence, with its turbulence and sexuality, was initially the result of infantile amnesia in terms of his usual inductive technique. Only later, through a deductive approach viewing adolescence as "a logical extension of the transformations of infantile sexuality" (p. 21) and of the vicissitudes of sexuality in adults, could the hypotheses concerning adolescence put forward in "The Three Essays" be tested against clinical data.

As intriguing as Klumpner's thoughts are regarding the origins, difficulties, and methodologies Freud may have struggled with regarding adolescence, they seem to me in the absence of further documentation to be highly speculative and to essentially lead to hypotheses that can neither be proved nor refuted.

Anna Freud (1969) summarized adolescence as an expectable transitional phase of disturbance between the relatively stable worlds of childhood and adult life. Usually we clinicians are confronted in childhood with developmental upsets or imbalances in one or another area of a child's personality. In adolescence the upheavals in personality and character are often sweeping and involve changes in drive, ego organization, and object relations and alterations in ideals and social relations. However, in spite of its turmoil, adolescence is nevertheless the normal continuation of childhood (Osterrieth, 1969, pp. 11–21).

LATER CONCEPTUALIZATIONS OF ADOLESCENCE

The boundaries of adolescence, however, as we know from clinical experience as well as observation, are highly fluid. There are no precise markers for the transition from childhood to adolescence. The end of adolescence and beginning of adulthood are similarly ambiguous (Panel, 1959). Puberty itself has defined and observable physiologic correlates. Phenomena occurring in adolescence have roots that may be traced clinically into childhood and sequelae that may exert lasting influence.

For example, one adolescent who presented with problems of anxiety, social withdrawal, and poor school performance had problems that could be traced to his difficulties with a narcissistically preoccupied mother who viewed him as an agent and executor of her grandiose fantasies. His father attempted to set realistic limits but could not follow through in a consistent manner; in addition, father was frequently absent. When first seen, this adolescent was considered to be a behavior problem and nonconformist. While on one hand he was driven to live out his mother's fantasies of greatness, such attempts resulted in intense anxiety guilt and paralysis, stemming from the unconscious fulfillment of what would have amounted to an oedipal victory over an already devalued father. At the same time, this youth yearned for a male with whom he could identify in terms of masculine pursuits and with whom he could establish a warm, stable, nurturing relationship. This clinical example is presented to illustrate the complexities inherent in adolescence. By the teenage years deprivations, arrests, conflicts, and skewed adaptations may be present, evident clinically, and coexist with or be layered upon earlier issues.

To complicate matters further, developing pari passu with the physiologic and psychologic issues of adolescence, there are actual changes in cognitive processes. Piaget (1954) underscored that while the significant change that characterizes adolescent thought starts around the age of 11 or 12, it does not reach its full development until the age of 14 or 15. The cognitive advances during adolescence permit the detaching of concrete logic from objects and include the ability to function on verbal or symbolic levels. Such cognitive development permits extending the classifications and serializations of the concrete operations of the latency era, resulting in an adolescent who is capable of constructing and understanding abstract theories and concepts.

Although the adolescent has developed certain biologic, psychologic, and cognitive capacities characteristic of adulthood, the adolescent is beset by complex and fluctuating processes that produce particular qualities that distinguish him or her from the adult (Panel, 1954). Fountain (Panel, 1959) described five qualities of adolescent functioning that would be considered unrealistic and extreme in adults and imply an impairment of the synthetic functions of the ego. The five qualities described are (1) a special intensity and volatility of feeling; (2) the need for frequent and immediate gratification; (3) selective impairment of reality testing; (4) a failure of self-criticism; and (5) an awareness of the world about them that differs from that of the adult. It will be noted, however, that the described issues relate to the breakthrough of primary process, to regression to earlier adaptive and cognitive modes, to regression to earlier defenses, and to identity diffusion as the adolescent struggles with both newly activated genital and revived pregenital issues and conflicts and with the pain of giving up the parent, a love object on both genital and pregenital levels.

The aforementioned qualities of the adolescent are also frequently used to describe the so-called borderline patient. This similarity, in addition to the normal fluidity and regressions in adolescence and the developmentally normal crisis nature of adolescence, may make it difficult to distinguish between health and disturbance. I feel at times it is best to observe adolescents over a longitudinal time frame, with periodic evaluations and reevaluations, before diagnostic labels are assigned and treatment is undertaken. Development tends to be a self-correcting process, and provided that the forces creating disturbance are not too virulent or deep-seated, a relatively nonintrusive course may be quite salutary. This is not to say that we should neglect situations that we know from experience are too far afield to expect developmental correction without some sort of therapeutic intervention. For example, an adolescent girl entered into a variety of sexualized and sexual relationships with older men. Her mature appearance made it easier for the participants to rationalize their behavior. Her father, who was quite well-off financially, was involved with a young woman and claimed poverty unless the patient renounced her relationship with her biologic mother. The biologic mother lived a dependent, manipulative lifestyle, placing the child more in the position of the mother. Repeatedly this adolescent acted out her oedipal and preoedipal conflicts.

While the theoretical frameworks provided by Blos and Mahler and associates are useful, clinical phenomena present us with the need to integrate unique configurations of development and experience that do not dovetail neatly with prescribed outlines. In other words, clinical phenomena are multilayered, multidetermined, and multifaceted and can only be understood by in-depth, painstaking analysis. We need our theoretical models; however, they exist at a different conceptual level from the clinical and should be derived from them. This is the difficulty with for example, Klumpner's paper; while unique and intriguing, the data are sufficiently sparse as to prevent conclusive hypotheses. Similarly, Blos presents many fertile concepts; at times, however, as in his concepts regarding the differences in development of the superego between males and females, he seems to depend on the writings of others rather than deriving concepts from his own clinical data.

Margaret Mahler defined separation–individuation as an intrapsychic process consisting of two intertwined lines of development. "It is the intrapsychic progression of the developmental lines of separation and individuation through the succeeding developmental stages beyond the first three years of life that result in the reverberations of separation–individuation throughout the life cycle. That is, the separation–individuation process (the first three years of life) and the manner in which the mother–infant duality was resolved will continually influence subsequent developmental stages and will in a sense serve as a prototype for future self–object differentiation. The beginning of latency and adolescence can be considered as early stages that are predominantly organized around the intrapsychic consequences and resulting manifestations of the developmental line of separation. Intrapsychic discord, affectual upheavals, and drive regression with weakened states characterize these early stages" (Byerly, 1990, pp. 185–186).

Blos (1962, 1979) viewed the separation–individuation phases of earlier childhood as laying the groundwork for the psychological adjustments necessary "for the shifts and changes in the mental life of the pubescent child" (Blos, 1962, p. 2). No attempt was made by Blos to precisely correlate the phases of separation–individuation with the stages or progressive and regressive shifts of adolescence. Although various contributors cited in the reference list of this chapter have focused on various aspects of adolescence, only Blos has attempted to conceptualize the entire process. However, he has done so largely in terms of the language of separation–individuation.

Developmental phases do not exactly correlate one with the other, in terms of earlier with later, although they may share similar characteristics and features. The psyche and developmental tasks of the three-year-old are different from those of the thirteen-year-old. The early stages do, however, set the stage, that is, lay the groundwork, for future developmental advances, integrations, and change. Mahler initially disagreed with Blos's use of her concepts in adolescence (personal communication, H. Parens, 1990). Mahler herself made sparse reference in terms of relating separation–individuation to adolescence and apparently did not think that later phases repeated the specific changes in the development of mental representations and in the investment of ego functions and activities she described for the hatching of the toddler from the symbiotic membrane (Furman, 1973, pp. 193–207). Mahler's only reference to adolescence was in 1963: in which she portrayed it as a parallel period of developmental potentialities. "The rich abundance of developmental energy at the period of individuation accounts for the demonstrated regeneration of developmental potentialities to an extent never seen in any other period of life except perhaps adolescence" (Mahler, 1963, pp. 307–324). In one of her discussions of the influence of the rapprochement subphase Mahler stated that the clinical outcome will be determined by later developments and experiences, including the "developmental crisis of adolescence" (Mahler, 1971). In spite of Mahler's initial reluctance, several panels and the contributions of a number of clinicians have viewed Mahler's concepts of separation–individuation as reverberating developmentally not only in adolescence but also throughout the life cycle, from infancy into adolescence and maturity. There is a continuity to development so that Mahler's contributions to the early phases of establishing one's identity, that is, the sub-phases of separation–individuation, permit analysts to examine the process clinically and theoretically at different segments of the developmental line (Panel, 1973). As Byerly (1990) puts it, "The developmental task of distancing ourselves from the basic dyadic relationship of life (mother–infant) at best remains incomplete, and profoundly influences our adult life as it did our childhood and adolescence" (p. 192). Schafer (1973) considered the processes of separation–individuation, as portrayed by Mahler, to consist of two sets of interdependent changes. One set involves the degree and stability of differentiation of self and object representations, regarded by Schafer as the core of the separation–individuation concept. The other set Schafer felt represented "independent activity in the object world" (Panel, 1973, p. 157). As Spiegal noted (cited in Panel, 1973, p. 166), it would be unrealistic to expect to discern the very early phases of individuation "shimmering through the present functioning of the analysand." "The ongoing need and development of representational cohesion and differentiations reflects a continuity in the developmental necessity for separation–individuation. However, once past early separation–individuation experiences, we must view the total picture:

the effects of each state of psychosexual development as well as the current clinical situation."

While Mahler and associates' (1975) separation–individuation phases and Anna Freud's (1965) developmental lines provide the cornerstones for understanding preoedipal and oedipal development, many other theorists have contributed to our understanding. S. Freud (1905), with the division of development into oral, anal, phallic, oedipal and latent phases, and later Abraham (1965), with his elaboration of them, attempted to correlate developmental phases with specific pathology. Other contributors include Piaget (1954), who traced development from the cognitive point of view; Erikson (1950), who viewed generational issues throughout the life cycle; and Melanie Klein (1949), who emphasized the instincts in early development and certain more primitive defenses and shifted various developmental timetables. Others—some disregarding the need for an instinctual base—have looked at development from a purely interpersonal or an object relations point of view. More recently, such clinicians and theoreticians as Kernberg (1970), Masterson (1972), Rinsley (1980), and Settlage and McDevitt (1971), as well as others, have included modified Kleinian, Mahlerian and object relations viewpoints into integrated developmental perspectives. Such integrated developmental views consider multifaceted impacts on future psychic structure, its integrations and implications for adaptation as well as pathology. Kohut (1970) and his followers have looked at development primarily from the viewpoint of libidinal relationships and narcissism. In addition to these clinicians and theoreticians, we have the infant/child developmentalists whose methodology and direct observations have increasingly been accepted into the main body of psychoanalysis (see Arlow, 1990). Many have contributed to our understanding of adolescence, including A. Freud (1965), Eichorn (1935), Greenacre (1971), A. Reich (1973), Solnit (1959, 1973), Harley (1934) and others. Biologic, social, cultural, and economic issues play their role in this complex developmental phase. The onset and course of puberty, with the upsurge of hormonal influences and sexual drive, is linked in most analysts' minds with its reintegrative (and disorganizing) functions and with the ultimate characterologic stamp left on the personality.

THE CONTRIBUTIONS OF PETER BLOS

In his overall conceptualization of adolescence Blos drew most heavily both in terminology and theory on the work of Margaret Mahler, although he stopped short of specifically correlating her stages of separation–individuation with those of adolescence, instead conceptualizing adolescence in a more global way as "the second separation–individuation."

The phases of adolescence explicated by Blos are (a) the latency period, (b) preadolescence, (c) early adolescence, (d) adolescence proper, (e) late adolescence and (f) postadolescence. Blos (1962) realized that viewing adolescence as a "second edition" or recapitulation of early childhood had meaning only insofar as it emphasized that adolescence contained elements of preceding phases of development and that the form, content, and tasks of adolescence were significantly affected by preceding drive and ego development. Blos stressed that entry into adolescence depended on consolidation of the latency period. Without such integration, the pubescent child experienced intensification of prelatency characteristics, exhibiting prelatency and latency characteristics of an arrested nature (Blos, 1979). Blos emphasized that the preadolescent girl did not show the same features as the boy. There is massive repression of pregenitality in the girl as she turns away from her mother and turns to boys in a driven fashion. In the male there appears to be an increase of instinctual drive during preadolescence and a resurgence of pregenitality, which in fact marks the end of the latency phase (Blos, 1979). In the boy there is an increase in restlessness, oral greediness, and anal sadistic behavior complete with dirty language and an aversion to cleanliness. Castration anxiety, which had brought the oedipal phase to its decline, becomes reactivated with puberty. The preadolescent male experiences castration anxieties related to the phallic mother, and passive longings are overcompensated for by defensive measures (A. Freud, 1966). Nothing analogous occurs in the girl, in whom the repression of pregenital drives associated with the oedipal phase is strengthened. The girl defends herself from the regressive pull to the preoedipal mother by a strong turn to heterosexuality.

Following the consolidation of latency and preadolescence, we enter adolescence proper. The latency period furnishes the child with the equipment in terms of ego and superego development that helps contain the increase in drive pressure during preadolescence and adolescence. Other important developmental lines at this time include identifications, object relations, self-esteem regulation, and fluctuations in superego and drive pressures, as well as primary and secondary autonomous ego functions (increasingly free from drive and superego pressures), for example, perception, learning, memory, and cognition. Peers and extrafamilial contacts (e.g., school, play, parties, social activities) become increasingly important. The girl enters the latency period with less conflict than the boy, since she has not had to give up her oedipal strivings as sharply. The girl struggles more than the boy toward the end of latency as her superego works overtime to contain the drives of prepuberty.

During latency and preadolescent phases, direct instinct gratification meets a disapproving superego. The preadolescent boy seeks the company of his own sex as castration anxiety and fear of the phallic female reappears. He belittles and teases girls, avoids them, or acts in a bragging, exhibition-istic, demeaning fashion (Blos, 1962). The preadolescent girl may show a denial of femininity and tomboyishness before femininity asserts itself (Deutsch, 1944). "The dissimilarity in male and female pre-adolescent behavior is foreshadowed by the massive repression of pregenitality which the girl had to establish before she could move into the oedipal phase; in fact, this repression is a prerequisite for the normal development of femininity" (Blos, 1962, p. 66).

A profound reorganization of emotional life takes place during early adolescence and adolescence proper with attendant and well-recognized states of chaos (Blos, 1962). During early adolescence there is an upsurge of same-sex close relationships. Separation from parents (primary love objects) becomes more noticeable. During adolescence proper there is a decisive turn to heterosexuality and renunciation of incestuous object choices. Blos and others (e.g., H. Deutsch, 1944) divide adolescence proper into two parts: early adolescence and adolescence proper. In early adolescence, close idealizing friendships with members of the same sex occur along with a search for new values. This is a period of repeated attempts at separation from early love objects. During adolescence proper there is a decisive turn toward heterosexuality and the final and irreversible renunciation of incestuous object choices. We note sublimation of the adolescent's love for the idealized parent; feelings of being in love; and concern with philosophical, political, and social problems as the young adolescent builds a continuity of self-experience and a gradual hierarchical arrangement of drive and ego functions. Blos recognized that his division into phases was a reification, since boundaries are fluid and regression and reorganization are important parts of the process. Moreover, the various phases are frequently, at best, only fluidly and perhaps vaguely amenable to definition.

During early adolescence the superego decreases greatly in its influence both in terms of controlling drive derivatives and regulating self-esteem. Following A. Freud (1965), Blos (1962) saw the weakening of the superego as a consequence of the withdrawal from the parents whose values as standards had been internalized at the initial resolution of the oedipal conflict. The withdrawal of investment in the parents and the widening gap between ego and superego result in an increase of narcissistic cathexes, with acting out or turning to peers as remedies for the experienced inner void and loneliness that is the experiential accompaniment of the impoverishment of the ego during early adolescence.

The ego-ideal, however, follows a different course from that of the superego (conscience). The ego-ideal, according to S. Freud (1914), absorbs narcissistic and homosexual libido. Blos (1962) adds that the ego-ideal that the adolescent's friend represents may yield under pressure of sexual urges into a stage of homosexuality, either latent or manifest. Essentially, masturbation fantasies counteract castration anxiety. Blos believed that in the male the process that led to ego-ideal formation at the decline of the oedipal stage via identification with the father is repeated in early adolescence, directly and through extended relationships wherein the ego-ideal replaces the lost narcissism of early childhood.

The early adolescent female does not exactly parallel the male. Helene Deutsch (1944) has described a strongly bisexual tendency before the conflicts of adolescence that is less repressed in girls than in boys. During this period girls are quite willing to stress their masculinity whereas the boy is ashamed of his femininity and denies it. A certain vagueness of reality and ego perception is a concomitant feature of the bisexual ambiguity.

Clinically, it is not unusual to encounter late-latency children or early adolescents who seem to stubbornly refuse to enter adolescence in a full-blown manner. They continue to avoid (repress) genitality and cling stubbornly or regress to preoedipal and oedipal conflicts, identifications, and modes of speaking and behaving, all of which lead to the appearance of a characterologic emotional immaturity. They are also unable to handle their aggressive drives with the result that accomplishment cannot be maintained, whether academically, athletically, or heterosexually. They cling to one-on-one or group relationships with persons of the same sex. Such a pattern is more characteristic of young adolescent males. Clinically, in females we see the development of the tomboy phase or perhaps of eating disorders, sexual "trophy hunting," exaggerated sexuality, and seductiveness.

Blos (1979) stressed that in the male the resexualization of ego and superego functions during adolescence at first leads to disorganization with later restructuring and differentiation. However, while the positive Oedipus may be more or less adequately resolved during childhood, the ego-ideal (Blos, 1979, p. 336), as it emerges at the termination of adolescence, is the heir to the negative Oedipus complex. The ego ideal emerges from its infantile state only when, during late adolescence, the narcissistic object attachment to which the infantile ego-ideal has become joined has lost its homosexual cathexis. Blos believes, as does Jacobson

(1954), that the ego-ideal of the girl follows a somewhat different path. According to Blos (1979):

> At the critical juncture of late adolescence, when the girl's stabilization of her femininity is to be obtained, the regressive incorporation of the paternal phallus as the narcissistic regulator of her sense of completeness and perfection has to be overcome by an enduring identification with the mother. The desexualized and deconcretized ego ideal favors the transformation of infantile penis envy into a striving for perfection as a woman. . . . The male ego ideal enshrines, so to speak, its history from primary narcissism to the merger with maternal omnipotence and beyond, to the oedipal love for the father. This last step is transcended in the ego-ideal structure. Only in terms of this last and decisive step, which integrates the various epochs of the ego-ideal history in its mature structuralization, can we speak of the male ego ideal as the heir to the negative Oedipus complex [pp. 332–336].

During adolescence proper the search for new heterosexual objects occurs, made possible by the abandonment of narcissistic or bisexual positions. Defensive and adaptive mechanisms in all their complexity come to the fore as "sex-appropriate drives" (Blos, 1962, p. 87) move into ascendancy and bring increasingly conflictual anxiety to bear (Blos, 1962). The adolescent breaks away for good from infantile love objects after earlier preludes. The withdrawal of cathexis from the parents' object representations in the boy leads to a narcissistic object choice based on the ego-ideal. In the girl there is a perseverance in the bisexual position with an overvaluation of the phallic component. A serious arrest in drive development occurs if this component is not eventually conceded to a heterosexual love object. That is, according to Blos (1962), sexual identity formation becomes the ultimate achievement of adolescent drive differentiation during this phase. Narcissistic defenses so characteristic of adolescence occur because of the inability to give up the gratifying parent on whose omnipotence the adolescent has come to depend. A distinction must be made as to whether such phenomena represent narcissistic object choice, narcissistic defenses, or the transitory narcissistic stage that normally precedes heterosexual object finding. The decline of the Oedipus complex in adolescence, as the adolescent disengages from primary love objects, is a slow process that reaches into late adolescence. Other themes of adolescence proper include the experience of tender love, the establishment of stable object relations within the family, the establishment of the superego, the elaboration of sexual identity, the partial resolution of oedipal stirrings, and a rise of hypochondrical sensations and feelings of body changes; defensive and adaptive processes are more varied and come close to an idiosyncratic conflict and drive constellation that foreshadows their ultimate selective influence on character (Blos, 1962).

Blos stated that the closing phase of adolescence, or late adolescence, has long been taken for granted. While pubescence is an act of nature, adolescence is an act of man. Blos viewed late adolescence as a phase of consolidation involving (1) the elaboration of a highly idiosyncratic and stable arrangement of ego functions and interests; (2) an extension of the conflict-free sphere of the ego (secondary autonomy); (3) an irreversible sexual position (identity constancy), summarized as genital primacy; (4) a relatively constant cathexis of object and self representations; and (5) the stabilization of mental apparatuses that automatically safeguard the integrity of the psychic organism.

The transition from adolescence to adulthood is marked by an intervening phase: postadolescence. This ending of adolescence proper is

> the period following the climax of adolescence proper and is characterized by integrative processes. At late adolescence these processes lead to a delineation of goals, definable as life tasks; while at postadolescence, the implementation of these goals in terms of permanent relationships, roles and milieu choices become the foremost concern. The ego, strengthened by the decline of instinctual conflicts, now becomes conspicuously and increasingly absorbed by these endeavors [Blos, 1962, p. 151].

A QUESTION OF TERMINOLOGY

As stated previously, Mahler originally opposed the application of her terminology by Blos to his exposition of adolescence. In spite of the fact that Mahler's contributions permit an understanding of the reverberations and influences of separation–individuation in adolescence as well as in adult life, there are a number of dangers in applying the same terms to childhood and to adolescence.

First, there is the danger of assuming an identity of processes because of an identity in terminology, even though the specific occurrences are in individuals varying greatly in age, level of development, and the developmental tasks in process.

Second, the mental life of infants and toddlers is not directly accessible through verbalization to analytic investigation. However, the direct observation of infant and child has permitted investigators to focus on the behavioral aspects of object relations and to postulate theoretical (metapsychological) constructs. The concept of separation–individuation has yet to be fully applied to all aspects of personality development from toddlerhood into adolescence and beyond—and assessed comprehensively in metapsychological terms (Furman, 1973). To apply the term *second separation–individuation* to adolescence implies an understanding that may be incomplete or incorrect in its specifics and that may inhibit research or imply levels of conceptualization that have not been confirmed clinically or through research paradigms. Blos's contributions are so rich and provocative in and of themselves that they invite confirmation, further clarification, and research by other clinicians. They should stand on their own both in terms of their depth and variety. Blos's use of terminology with multiple implications invites semantic and conceptual confusion. In retrospect, it would seem best had Blos referred to Mahler's work but used his own terminology for the particular issues of adolescence that he addressed.

Third, adolescence has as much to do with regression as progression, as the adolescent struggles to cope with emerging genitality. The preoedipal regressive phenomena in the adolescent have direct bearing not only in terms of developmental progressions but also as defense against genital incestuous strivings.

Four, to apply the same label or name to phenomena that are not identical and that may develop from or defend against issues from earlier phases that are similarly named can only lead to problems. While it is true that separation–individuation resonates through the life cycle, it does so in an individual who is increasingly complex and mature.

Five, earlier phenomena become part of later, more complex developmental configurations, and these may also be used defensively. The issues involved can only be identified and elaborated through a thorough clinical investigation of the individual, rather than through recourse to a label that may imply understanding generally but whose use in a given individual is incomplete. Schafer (1973) stressed that the giving up of love objects differs from the initial emergence of self and object representations. That is, the differences between the separation–individuation phase of infancy and the developmental tasks of adolescence are so great that we are not justified in applying the same term.

Six, in a given individual, multiple developmental lines reverberate through the life cycle. By limiting his thesis to one line, namely separation–individuation, Blos has truncated his view of adolescent development as well as pathology. Clinically, we must understand identifications, defenses, peer relationships, and multiple conflictual issues in addition to the reactivation of separation–individuation conflicts whether as a recapitulation or an attempted resolution of self–object conflict and constancy. The form, nature, and involvement in structure and conflict varies according to the initial adequacy of the multiple phase and conflict resolutions and to the natural corrections that occur with development. To reify or tease out one strand from a complex interactional matrix may be important for heuristic reasons but does not do justice to the multiple dynamic complex interactions in process.

Finally, although "adolescent individuation is the reflection of those structural changes that accompany the emotional disengagement from internalized infantile objects" (Blos, 1979, pp. 162–186), this is at a different metapsychologic level of conceptualization than the "hatching from the symbiotic membrane to become an individuated toddler" described by Mahler (1963, p. 309). Although Blos (1967) says that "in metapsychologic terms, we would say that not until the termination of adolescence do self and object representations acquire stability and firm boundaries, i.e., they become resistant to cathectic shifts," (p. 163), we are still left wondering. Terminologic individuality could only have added to the significant contributions made by Blos to our understanding of adolescence and would have prevented a confounding of his contributions with Mahler's. In summary, it is a mistake to apply the term second individuation–separation to adolescence. The adolescent is dealing with defenses against genital incestuous strivings. The significance of preoedipal genetic events, including separation–individuation, depends on how the adolescent resolves current genital conflicts, as well as on how he earlier resolved his preoedipal conflicts (Furman, 1973).

ADOLESCENCE AND THE DEVELOPMENT OF CHARACTER

In this section I wish to stress an aspect of late adolescence that gives personality its individual stamp, namely, the development of character. Blos viewed adolescence as a time for laying the foundation for a sense of self and strengthening the capacity for a structuralization of the ego, for healthy self-esteem, and for constancy of emotions. Late adolescence contains the final adolescent crisis—what Erikson called "identity crisis" (1950). Blos saw the consolidation of late adolescence leading to an ego-syntonic organization that is characterized by individuality, a stable arrangement of functions and defenses, and an enlarging conflict-free ego sphere and consolidation of the psychic structure, making possible the groundwork and components of "character." Blos (1979), writing on the adolescent passage, reaffirmed his view of character as arising from four developmental preconditions "without which adolescent character forma-tion cannot take its proper course" (pp. 171–191). Among the four adolescent developmental challenges Blos viewed as closely related to character formation are "the loosening of the infantile object ties and the adaptation to residual trauma, with character viewed as the continuance of earlier danger situations within an adaptive formation. According to Blos (1979), "from residual trauma emanates, so to speak, a persistent and relentless push toward actualization of that formation within the personality which we designate as character" (p. 183). A third adolescent developmental challenge is ego continuity; the establishment of historical ego continuity in adolescent analysis has an integrative and growth-stimulating effect that lies beyond conflict resolution. Character helps provide a sense of wholeness and inviolability in addition to affecting subjective feeling states. The fourth developmental challenge concerns the emergence of sexual identity. It is Blos's contention that while gender identity is established at an early age, sexual identity with nonfluid boundaries is a collateral development of sexual maturation at puberty. Blos (1979) emphasized that character takes over homeostatic functions from other regulatory agencies of childhood and subscribed to Greenacre's (1971) concept of trauma as any condition that is unfavorable to the development of the young individual.

Numerous authors have contributed to our understanding of character development and pathology. For example, Arlow (1960) saw character as a dynamic record of development that includes the normal processes of growth. He viewed biologic endowments and identifications as forming the basis of character, factors that are added to by the way the child learns to master his primitive sexual and aggressive impulses, with the most important group of dangers leading to intrapsychic conflict. Arlow also saw character formation tempered by experience, "especially the unpleasant experiences of sorrow and humiliation" (p. 145).

Otto Kernberg (1970) reviewed the contributions of numerous individuals to the concept of character. He proposed classification into high, intermediate, and low levels of character pathology organization and described an object relations–centered model as the crucial factor in ego and superego development. Kernberg viewed introjections, identifications, and ego identity formation as representing a progressive sequence in the process of internalization of object relationships. In his book *Severe Personality Disorders* (1984), he addressed Mahler's research on separation–individuation, particularly her specification of the rapprochement subphase as related to borderline psychopathology, and also applied Jacobson's concepts to his clinical and theoretical understanding. Kernberg (1984) saw Margaret Mahler's work as the "clinical evidence that permitted us to establish timetables for the developmental stages of internalized object relations proposed by Jacobson" (p. 190). Using Mahler's concepts, Kernberg (1984) indicated that it is "now possible, within Freudian metapsychology, to analyze developmentally and genetically the relation between various types and degrees of psychopathology and a failure to achieve normal stages of integration of internalized object relations and the self" (p. 190). Although Kernberg (1984) discusses differential diagnosis in adolescence in some detail he notes that "in the older literature on identity disturbances in adolescence, identity crisis and identity diffusion were not clearly differentiated. Therefore, one can still find the question raised whether all adolescents might present some degree of identity diffusion and hence be indistinguishable from later borderline organization" (p. 52). Kernberg believes that one can differentiate borderline and nonborderline character pathology in adolescence. Although antisocial behavior in adolescence may be "normal" or neurotic or a severe personality disorder, Kernberg differentiated the normal, neurotic, and infantile narcissistic reactions in adolescence and, finally, the emergence of multiple perverse sexual trends. Kernberg does not emphasize the formation of character in adolescence, although he refers to the diagnostic difficulties presented by normal developmental vicissitudes that may mimic or hide severe characterologic (personality) problems of a narcissistic, borderline, or even psychotic nature. In neither of the aforementioned works does Kernberg refer to Blos, although he clearly sees the work of Mahler and her collaborators as providing a scaffolding for our understanding of character and its disorders from childhood on into old age.

Baudry (1989), who has written extensively on the subject of character, prefers the more traditional view, that is, that "normal character formation follows the resolution of the Oedipus complex" (p. 675), an event that occurs close in time to the setting up of the infantile repression. Yet even at this point, character development is by no means complete, since some reworking takes place during adolescence. Baudry states that from a "developmental point of view, we are uncertain at which point it makes sense to talk about character formation" (p. 673).

My own view is that multiple factors play a role in the formation of character. First, we must consider inborn temperamental factors as well as intercurrent birth events. Assuming a physically healthy child, inborn potentials and nonconflictual or autonomous ego spheres are in daily interaction with the maternal surround, which may meet the criteria of a normal expectable environment, be woefully lacking, or perhaps overintrusive. Parental attachments are highly variable, depending on factors within the infant and within the mother as they interact under conditions of conflict, stress, frustration, contentment, gratification, and mutual pleasure. Early on, the infant begins to shape his or her responses to maximize or at times minimize input from the environment. Before birth we have the temperamental anlagen of what will later be called character. Its development depends on many factors, for example, nonconflictual or autonomous ego functions, identifications, and stable and expectable environmental factors, especially parental attachments, identifications, conflicts, and their resolutions.

Traditionally, the "noisy times" of development—for example, rapprochement crisis, oedipal conflict, or adolescence—and the nature of their resolutions have been looked at as the critical factors in character formation. Are perhaps the many and much more frequent "nonnoisy" times of latency, practicing, or even postadolescent development just as critical (or perhaps more critical) for character formation and for the form, nature, and outcome of adolescence as the more tempestuous and noticeable crises?

Developmental "epochs," rather than being organizers, may disrupt the structures and organizations that have been generally rather silently developing without much notice. In fact, such "epochs" may disrupt characterologic integrity, the organization and structuralization of the ego and superego, and their metapsychologic underpinnings. Such disorganization offers the opportunity for reorganization, which may boost development and offer additional options and courses for the development of character. Of course, disorganization may do just the opposite, that is, create a rigidity or fixity or areas of vulnerability with attendant affective signals and symptom formation, thus setting back or disrupting the structuralizations and adaptations and the role they play in the developing characterologic formations. To the particular behavioral, affective, or temperamental object relations, identifications, and adaptations that have stability and predictability over time we attach the term *character*, a concept that can then be labeled and described. Such description or labeling, however, does not substitute for an understanding of the multiple developmental factors—both conflictual and nonconflictual—that went into the formation of an individual's character. The individual is aware of a sense of self that carries a particular customary affective tone whereas *character* is a term described and applied by others.

Blos's conceptualization of character solidifying in adolescence is, I believe, an oversimplification of a much more complex process. For example, flexibility implies the ability, long after adolescence is but a memory, to set aside typical characterologic perspectives. Such flexibility or creativity (its lack is rigidity) could be labeled a characterologic attribute in and of itself; however, I believe it is clinically more useful to delineate the underlying ego functions and dynamic implications to understand why we may have, for example, characterologic flexibility (i.e., an "open mind") in one area and a characteristic unvarying response in another. To put it differently, each character trait has a development, a dynamic understanding, and a metapsychology of its own. Usually we focus on constellations of traits, but at times a particular aspect of character has become so important for the psychology and functioning of an individual that it must be thoroughly understood.

Thus, adolescence remains in part an era of enigma, in part an era of promise, in part an era of organization, and in part an era of disorganization. When we have the good fortune to know an adolescent well, we are frequently reawakened to the great vistas, idealism, and promises he or she sees in mankind and the world.

REFERENCES

Abraham, K. (1965), *Selected Papers*. London: Hogarth Press.
Arlow, J. (1960), Character and Conflict. *J. Hillside Hosp.*, 15:140–150.
Arlow, J. (1990), Psychoanalysis and the quest for morality. Presented to the Philadelphia Psychoanalytic Society, March 14.
Baudry, F. (1989), Character, character type and character Organization. *J. Amer. Psychoanal. Assn.*, 37:655–686.
Blos, P. (1962), *On Adolescence*. New York: The Free Press of Glencoe.
Blos, P. (1967), The second individuation process of adolescence. *The Psychoanalytic Study of the Child*, 22:162–186. New York: International University Press.
Blos, P. (1979), *The Adolescent Passage*. New York: International Universities Press.
Brunswick, R. M. (1948), The preoedipal phase of libido development. In: *The Psychoanalytic Reader*, ed. R. Fleiss. New York: International Universities Press, pp. 231–253.
Byerly, L. (1990), Neurosis and object relations. In: *Neurosis and Object Relations in Children and Adolescents*, ed. M. H. Etazady. Northvale, NJ: Aronson, pp. 159–195.
Deutsch, H. (1944), *Psychology of Women, Vol. 1*. New York: Grune & Stratton.
Eichorn, E. (1935), *Wayward Youth*. New York: Viking Press.
Erikson, E. H. (1950), *Childhood and Society*. London: Norton.
Fliess, R. (1948), The preoedipal phase of libido development. In: *The Psychoanalytic Reader*, ed. R. Fliess. New York: International Universities Press, pp. 231–253.
Freud, A. (1965), *Normality and Pathology in Childhood*. New York: International Universities Press.
――――― (1966), The ego and the mechanisms of defense. In: *The Writings of Anna Freud, Vol. 2*. (rev. ed.). New York: International Universities Press.
――――― (1969), Adolescence as a developmental disturbance. In: *Adolescence, Psychosocial Perspectives*, ed. G. Caplan & S. Lebovici. New York: Basic Books, pp. 5–10.

Freud, S. (1905), *Three essays on the theory of sexuality*. *Standard Edition*, 7:135–243. London: Hogarth Press, 1953.

—— (1914), On narcissism: An introduction. *Standard Edition*, 14:73–102. London: Hogarth Press, 1957.

Furman, E. (1973), A contribution to assessing the role of infantile separation–individuation in adolescent development. *The Psychoanalytic Study of the Child*, 28:193–207. New Haven, CT: Yale University Press.

Greenacre, P. (1971), *Emotional Growth*. New York: International Universities Press.

Harley, M. (1934), *The Analyst and the Adolescent at Work*. New York: Quadrangle Press.

Jacobson, E. (1954), The self and the object world. *The Psychoanalytic Study of the Child*, 9:75–127. New York: International Universities Press.

Kernberg, O. (1970), A psychoanalytic classification of character pathology. *J. Amer. Psychoanal. Assn.*, 18:800–821.

—— (1984), *Severe Personality Disorders*. New Haven, CT: Yale University Press.

Klein, M. (1949), *The Psychoanalysis of Children*. London: Hogarth Press.

Klumpner, G. (1978), A hypothesis regarding the origins of Freud's concepts of the psychology of adolescence. *The Annual of Psychoanalysis*, 6:3–22. New York: International Universities Press.

Kohut, H. (1970), *The Analysis of the Self*. New York: International Universities Press.

Mahler, M. S. (1963), Thoughts about development and individuation. *The Psychoanalytic Study of the Child*, 18:307–324. New York: International Universities Press.

Mahler, M. S. (1971), A study of the separation–individuation process and its possible application to borderline phenomena. *The Psychoanalytic Study of the Child*, 26:403–425. New York: Quadrangle Books.

Mahler, M. S., Pine, F. & Bergman, A. (1975), *The Psychological Birth of the Human Infant*. New York: Basic Books.

Masterson, J. (1972), *Treatment of the Borderline Adolescent: A Developmental Approach*. New York: Wiley.

Osterrieth, P. (1969), Some psychological aspects in adolescence. In: *Adolescence*, ed. G. Caplan & S. Lebovici. New York: Basic Books, pp. 11–21.

Panel (1959), A. Solnit, Reporter. The vicissitudes of ego development in adolescence. *J. Amer. Psychoan. Assn.*, 7:523–536.

Panel (1973), I. Marcus, Reporter. The experience of separation–individuation in infancy and its reverberations through the course of life: 2. Adolescence and Maturity. *J. Amer. Psychoan. Assn.*, 21:155–167.

Piaget, J. (1954), *The Construction of Reality and the Life Cycle*. New York: Basic Books, 1954.

Reich, A. (1973), *Psychoanalytic Contributions*. New York: International Universities Press.

Rinsley, D. (1980), *Treatment of the Severely Disturbed Adolescent*. New York: Aronson.

Schafer, R. (1973), Concepts of self and identity and the experience of separation–individuation in adolescence. *Psychoanal. Quart.*, 42:42–59.

Settlage, C. & McDevitt, J. (1971), *Separation–Individuation: Essays in Honor of Margaret Mahler*. New York: International Universities Press.

Solnit, A., J. Goldstein, A. Freud (1973), *Beyond the Best Interest of the Child*. New York: Free Press.

10

Adolescence, Sex, and Neurosogenesis
A Clinical Perspective

Newell Fischer
Ruth M.S. Fischer

Two adolescents, one male and one female, were analyzed by the same analyst at the same time. Though both struggled with many similar adolescent issues, their symptomatic presentations, their unique intrapsychic and interpersonal struggles, the unfolding transference, and the analytic experience of each of these youngsters were remarkably different.

In reviewing these two cases, we wondered how the differences in sex might have contributed to the differences in their clinical pictures. In a more general way, we speculated on how being male or being female influenced the quality and process of neurosogenesis. Related to these thoughts, but from a different perspective, is the observation that 75% of cases of childhood obsessive–compulsive disorders occur in boys (Hollingsworth, 1980) whereas anorexia nervosa is overwhelmingly a dysfunction of girls.

In this chapter our primary direction is to address the question of the influence of an individual's sex on the process of neurotic symptom formation. At the outset, we want to underscore the fact that the two adolescents to be described are different and unique individuals. Their personalities emerged from and were molded by a large number of known and unknown genetic, maturational, developmental, and environmental elements. Similarly, their particular symptomatic struggles were the result of many factors, some known and others obscure. In our presentation we are focusing on one factor, namely, how their sex significantly influenced neurosogenesis. It is important to recognize the reductionistic strategy in this study. We start by describing the two adolescents, outlining their central conflicts and noting some characteristics of their respective analyses.

CLINICAL ILLUSTRATION #1—JIM

Jim, approaching his 15th birthday, presented as an energetic, vivacious youngster bubbling with enthusiasm. His sloppy attire, manner, and slight body habitus conveyed a picture of someone in early adolescence. In a pressured manner he was spontaneous, keenly aware, and reactive to those around him. He was curious about everything. When asked directly about his worries, he abruptly looked down at the floor and became tearful. Such pauses were brief and were quickly followed by a string of questions about the office, psychiatry, psychiatrists, or whatever attracted his attention.

With a good deal of affect, Jim described his problem as "these habits which are silly, but I feel I have to do them." Then he elaborated: he had thoughts that unless he touched things or did things in "the right way" he would hurt or kill his mother. He knew this was silly, yet felt so worried that he thought of running away or even killing himself.

Since his 11th birthday, he had had fleeting ideas that he might kill his mother or stepfather. Initially, these thoughts were isolated but very frightening and repugnant. He felt uneasy and avoided using knives or seeing horror movies. He saw a picture in a magazine of a woman with an ax in her head; for many weeks, this would flash in his mind at bedtime. Several months prior to consultation he had the persistent thought that unless he swung the bat in a certain way in baseball practice, his mother would be killed. He rarely spoke of these thoughts but when he did, mother would be reassuring, telling him not to worry. Stepfather would be angry.

About two months before coming for consultation, Jim was watching a TV show in which four women were murdered. He became increasingly worried that he would kill his mother. This quickly became associated with the thought that if he touched things in a particular way or moved things a certain number of times (the specific number chosen could not contain a 4 or any multiple thereof), this would prevent him from harming her. He became increasingly terrified by his thoughts and paralyzed by his rituals. He finally told his mother that he could not go on and asked if he should run away or be locked up so that he could not hurt her.

Jim's parents had been married for five years prior to his birth. He was their first and only child. The marriage had been an unhappy one and was floundering. Mother described Jim's father as inadequate, ineffectual, and "unreal"; he could not hold a job, often seemed in another world, and treated her more like a friend than a wife. Because of this, she hesitated for five years before becoming pregnant.

Jim was a healthy, sociable child who was happy and "did everything according to schedule." He developed a mild intermittent stutter when he was 5. At age 11, around the time he had his first frightening thoughts, the stuttering became pronounced. He saw a speech therapist and the stuttering disappeared. The parents divorced when he was three and a half years old. Although the relationship had always been somewhat distant, contact was maintained with father through phone calls and regular weekend visits. Mother did not notice any reaction on Jim's part to father's moving out. When he was six, mother remarried. From the beginning Jim and stepfather, a construction worker, were "buddies." He continued to see his father on alternate weekends.

Jim's first school experience was at 2½. Separation was not a problem. Jim was outgoing and had many friends in the early years of grade school. However, in the two years prior to consultation he had become more withdrawn from peers, was watching TV a great deal, and played with children two to three years his junior. Mother was always amazed at how aware he was of things around him and how well he remembered events from early childhood.

Mother described herself as "aggressive, ambitious, confident, and at times overwhelming." She wondered if she intimidated Jim. She had been working for many years as a full-time executive secretary. The biological father was described by mother as distant, unrelated, and religious, the stepfather as "easy going and fun." The family life-style was somewhat unusual in that mother worked from 9 A.M. to 5 P.M. and stepfather worked from 10 P.M. to 7 A.M. In recent years mother noticed that Jim always went to bed before his stepfather left for work and then remained in bed. The only time that Jim would stay up later than 10 P.M. was on nights that stepfather was not working. Mother wondered if Jim was afraid to be alone with her and yet did not want to leave the parents alone together.

Course of Treatment

The analysis was conducted in a face-to-face manner, five sessions each week for three years. Following some early bubbly defensive chatter about school and friends, Jim began to confront the "disgusting" thoughts and worries from which he was trying to distract himself and the analyst. For several months in a pressured, affect-laden manner, he described in detail his terrifying fantasy life. Just beneath the playful facade, he was preoccupied with fears of stabbing, ripping apart, and destroying women. With considerable disgust and terror, he imagined stabbing his mother in the breast. He saw a girl in class and thought of having sex with her by ripping open her vagina with a huge thorny club, tearing her insides apart, and then comforting her in a maternal fashion. He was revolted by and yet could not stop thinking about a scene in the movie *The Exorcist* in which a young girl stabs a crucifix into her bleeding vagina. A flood of such fantasies, some from the past and some more recent, filled the daily analytic sessions. As Jim related these "imaginations," his manner became increasingly meek and subdued. He often had tears in his eyes and reported feeling totally disgusted with himself; he wondered out loud if the analyst found him disgusting and horrible. Despite this inner anguish, Jim was doing satisfactorily at school, and apparently none of his friends or teachers suspected that he was in distress.

In the first six months this outpouring, this painful confessional, dominated the analytic sessions. As the transference evolved, the analytic relationship became colored by certain preoccupations: (1) Jim expressed a series of thinly disguised wishes to tear the office apart and to smash the analyst's face. There was a challenging, testing quality to his questions: "If I broke your lamp, what would you do?"; "Do you worry that I'll come to your office with a knife?" A teasing, playful quality and a certain bravado were employed to deal with the anxiety stimulated by these fantasies. (2) At other times the analyst was seen as a puny, ineffectual, weak, and pitiful person like father. Jim wondered if the analyst could tolerate his "teasing" and if his wife "wore the pants." Often his sympathy had a mocking quality. At other times he expressed considerable remorse at being insulting and perhaps threatening. (3) He developed a series of symptomatic behaviors surrounding his sessions. He felt that he was contaminating the furniture with germs or skin from his body and had a strong urge to wipe off the chairs before leaving the office. For several months he intermittently came late or did not arrive at all: on the way to the office he would become engaged in ritualistic behavior, rewalking certain routes, touching certain walls, walking on cracks, all of which was accompanied with great inner anguish. He described a mental tug-of-war, knowing that the rituals and the obsessions were "crazy" yet fearing that if he did not perform them, someone—either his mother or the analyst— would get hurt. (4) At the same time, he taught himself to play the guitar. Though he could not read music, he listened to records and become quite expert at playing and singing. He brought his guitar to the office and played and sang for the analyst. The songs were predominantly love ballads. The defensive as well as the homoerotic aspects of this behavior were quite apparent.

Many memories emerged. Parental conflicts, around age three, were particularly vivid. He recalled closeness and a certain camaraderie with father. One anecdote was particularly prominent: mother sent father out to make a purchase and Jim joined him. Father bought him some candy. Mother was very angry with this indulgence and loudly berated father in front of Jim. He recalled feeling responsible for the upset, sorry for his father, and frightened by his mother. He felt that he was just like his father—a "wimp" and a "flunky"—and that he would always be like that. Indeed, Jim's initial presentation was of someone quite meek and ineffectual. He considered mother a "hard bitch"; "She threw father out," he said, "but my father was a wimp." Fantasies of the analyst's wife emerged wherein she was a "complete bitch." Clarifications and interpretations focused on the intense rage and conflict that were at the core of the presenting symptoms. The oedipal rivalry, Jim's apparent success in this struggle at age 3½ when father was sent away, and the rage at father for not protecting him from the castrating and overwhelming mother were all reflected in Jim's condescending manner toward the analyst.

The analytic material during this middle phase of the analysis was vivid and rich. Though Jim was of average intelligence and his background had not particularly fostered introspection, he had become remarkably psychologically minded and self-reflective. He thought a great deal about the sessions and often started an analytic hour by reflecting back on some thought he had had about the last meeting. He had an unusually good memory for early life events and was intensely involved in the transference. As the analysis deepened, he recalled in considerable detail events and feelings from his early years. Experiencing this in the transference led to further exploration and understanding. Resolution and working through were noted in the final six months of the analysis.

At this point there was no evidence of obsessional thinking or ritualistic behavior. He described a sense of being in control of his feelings and thoughts and, indeed, expressed anger openly and realistically. He talked with conviction about his future plans, which included music school and college. He wanted to live on campus away from home. He wanted more direct contact with his father, and he worried about getting better since that would mean leaving the analyst. He played with the idea of getting the analyst to visit his school to talk to his class about psychiatry. He saw his doctor as a "cool" dresser. He became interested in some of the girls in his class and wondered if they liked him or saw him as foolish or clumsy. He became engaged in an intensive weight lifting program to enhance his "puny" body. Rather dramatically, in six months his body changed from that of a small preadolescent to a muscular young man approaching six feet. As he grew, he covertly measured his height against that of the analyst.

CLINICAL ILLUSTRATION #2—JANET

Janet was 16 years old when she came for consultation. Her appearance was alarming: she was pale and emaciated, weighing no more than 75 pounds. She had the classical signs and symptoms of anorexia nervosa: she had dieted and lost 30 pounds over the past year and yet saw herself as fat and ugly. She had been amenorrheic for over ten months. She indulged in strenuous exercise to lose weight, harshly restricted her diet, and was disgusted with herself if there were a minor infraction of her dietary rules. She denied any concern about her weight loss or the amenorrhea but admitted being mildly depressed over the past year, which she attributed to a lack of interest in schoolwork and concerns about being fat. She was annoyed and frustrated with her parents, friends, and family doctor because they nagged at her to eat more. She did not see herself as thin and had an intense fear of being fat.

Janet was a much desired firstborn child. There were no difficulties with the pregnancy or delivery. Breast-feeding was started on a relaxed schedule but discontinued after several weeks owing to colic, which was diagnosed as an allergic reaction to mother's milk. The family pediatrician treated the colic by having the parents give Janet enemas daily for the first three months. In spite of this, Janet's weight gain was normal. She sat at five months, stood at nine months, and walked soon after one year of age; she was weaned at 2½. Bowel and bladder training were slow and "natural"; diapers were no longer needed by age three. Janet was speaking well at two; she had a favorite blanket, which she carried around until she was three. In general, the parents saw her as a bright, lively, precocious youngster.

At two years of age a urethral restriction was noted in Janet, for which she was cystoscoped several times. She was hospitalized for a number of days and repeatedly catheterized. Although mother stayed with her throughout the hospitalization, Janet seemed very distressed. Mother recalled thinking at the time that someday the trauma of the procedures would cause her daughter problems.

Between the ages of one and three years Janet suffered four or five ear infections. On each occasion the pediatrician held her down and incised her eardrum. The parents were uneasy about the treatment of the colic, the ear infections, and the bladder difficulties, but the doctor was a prominent and highly respected member of the medical community. It was only after Janet's third year that they felt confident enough to change doctors.

There were no major separations from parents until age 13. Janet entered nursery school at three; the separation did not appear particularly distressing. According to reports, her school adjustment was quite smooth; teachers described her as a very bright, sociable, delightful youngster. At age 3½ her only sibling, a girl, was born. There was an early show of resentment and some resistance to going to school but this was transient. Mother prepared her for menarche, which occurred at thirteen; her periods were regular and not associated with any appreciable discomfort. She was not upset when her menstrual periods stopped one year prior to coming for consultation.

In describing their daughter's personality over the past several years, the parents noted that Janet tended to be rather indecisive, agonizing over every decision. She was "nonaggressive," had difficulty initiating activities, and was reluctant to approach peers to make friends. Once a friendship was initiated, however, she was very well liked. This was part of a general pattern: Janet had to be coaxed and pushed into any new experience, such as going on trips or joining a group; once she was launched into a new activity, she became very involved and then self-critical because of the time she had wasted in getting started. Father also noted that Janet tended to "give you what you want"; she rarely rebelled. She came across as an ideal child with no major problems. She was never a discipline problem and appeared to enjoy a rather open and warm relationship with both parents. She was consistently on the school honor roll and tended to be a serious, hardworking student.

Janet's parents were professionals in their mid-forties, warm, articulate, intelligent, and sensitive people who were deeply concerned about their daughter. There was no family history of emotional difficulty; the marital relationship was strong.

Course of Treatment

The analysis, which lasted four years, was conducted in a face-to-face manner. From the start there was an intense, painful engagement. Soon after the initial evaluative interviews Janet presented herself as a helpless, whining, angry little girl. Though sixteen years old, her pale emaciated appearance, her ill-fitting baggy clothing, and her plaintive manner gave her the appearance of a 10- or 11-year-old petulant, injured prepubescent child. There was a steady stream of anguished complaints and requests for help: "I don't know what to say"; "Nothing is on my mind"; "What should I talk about?"; "My thoughts fly by and they don't mean anything"; "Why don't you ask questions or tell me what to talk about?" Janet's pleas for help had an edge of demanding indictment and were interspersed with long silences during which she seemed most uncomfortable, irritable, and agitated; she thrashed about in her chair. If she brought up an event, a thought, or a worry, her descriptions and elaborations would be meager and her associations minimal. Efforts to draw her out regarding details of her current life, whether of school, home, or friends or her feelings and thoughts in the analytic sessions, all were summarily dismissed as unimportant. She was annoyed, impatient, and angry with the analyst's inquiries and observations.

Criticism was not just directed at the analyst; there was a great deal of self-depreciation and self-punitive preoccupation as well. Janet was critical of everything: her passivity, her paralyzing indecisiveness; a sense of failure pervaded all sectors of her life. Her self-directed rage was accompanied by anguished crying. Occasionally, she punched her leg in disgust as she talked. Every decision, what dress to wear or what school course to take, was a major struggle with overt and covert efforts to draw the analyst into the fray. "I need advice, not analysis," she shrieked. "I need help; tell me what to do," she demanded as tears rolled down her face.

Janet was totally frustrated by whatever the analyst did or did not say. If he made a clarifying or interpretive comment, he was summarily dismissed and disdainfully told, "It isn't important. I don't agree. Forget it." If he was quiet and pensive, she raged on about how she was not being helped, how he was tormenting her.

Although Janet's behavior in the analysis was vivid and her affect intense, the actual content of what she said was repetitive, impoverished, and generally vague. She did not report dreams or fantasies and was most reluctant to elaborate or associate to thoughts and feelings. With great frustration she complained that she could not put her thoughts into words. A nebulous, vague quality prevailed.

The ensuing pleas and demands for help, the veiled threats, her crying and screaming were not experienced by the analyst as shallow manipulations or hollow histrionics. Janet was in considerable distress. Efforts to clarify and understand this distress led to further anguished crying and/or disdainful dismissal.

The first 2½ years of the analysis were dominated by this intense, anguished transference. Understanding, analyzing, and then working through this transferential engagement were essential in resolving Janet's core conflicts, which had manifested themselves in her paralyzing indecisiveness and in her life-endangering anorexia. Indeed, once this central intrapsychic conflict and manifest interpersonal struggle was analyzed and worked through, development resumed, and the last 1½ years of the analytic work proceeded rapidly. The focus of this work was on clarifying and resolving a variety of oedipal themes and conflicts.

But first it was necessary to appreciate the intense engagement, the pull–push dance, the scenario, "I feel so helpless, inadequate, and alone. You must help me to function, but if you do, I will feel more helpless and overwhelmed. You must help me." The perspective that was most helpful in clarifying this inner struggle was Mahler's conceptualization of the separation–individuation process, in particular, the negotiation of the rapprochement subphase.

This subphase spans the period from about 16 to 24 months. It has been described as the mainspring of man's eternal struggle with fusion and isolation (Mahler, Pine, and Bergman, 1975). Maturation of perceptual, cognitive, and motoric skills at this time makes the junior toddler increasingly aware of his separateness from his mother and increasingly aware of his vulnerability. His developmentally normal sense of shared parental omnipotence as well as fantasies of his own omnipotence in the dual oneness of the symbiosis are threatened and deflated. The anger stimulated toward the now separate and relatively less available parent, the object he both loves and now realizes he desperately needs, increases the threat of losing the mother or of being lost from her. On one hand, the toddler wants to fully exercise his newly found autonomy and independence; on the other, he painfully feels the loss of his former sense of omnipotence and is distressed by his relative helplessness.

With this developmental framework the expression in the analysis of Janet's intrapsychic conflicts took on clearer definition, and the enacted intense, frantic, stagnating, circular quality of her interpersonal struggles, vividly reflected in the transference, could be understood. It was the appreciation of this developmental, object-related struggle, rekindled in early adolescence and now in the regressive transference, that was in the foreground of the analytic work for the first 2½ years. The inadequate negotiation of the developmental tasks of the rapprochement subphase were historically linked to the intrusive medical traumata in her early years. This was actively reconstructed in the analytic sessions. It was these same unresolved issues, which were being expressed in the anorexia, that had brought her for treatment.

CLINICAL OBSERVATIONS

In both these young people we see major disturbances related to the onset of adolescence; developmental progression was blocked and maturation was delayed. Janet became overwhelmed by her indecisiveness and developed life-threatening anorexia; Jim was paralyzed by a severe obsessive–compulsive neurosis.

One of the primary tasks of adolescence is the resolution of oedipal conflicts. The upsurge of libidinal and aggressive drives during this developmental period is a stress requiring major adjustment, a stress that proved overwhelming for both Janet and Jim. Major regressive and defensive features came to dominate their psychic functioning and their daily lives.

Despite the broad similarities of these two dysfunctional adolescents, there were major differences in their presenting clinical pictures as well as in their respective intrapsychic and interpersonal struggles. This should be of no surprise for, indeed, Janet and Jim were quite different people coming from different backgrounds. Their maturation and developmental unfolding were different, as were their defenses and adaptations. They had unique strengths, areas of vulnerability, and foci of unresolved conflicts. They were also of different sex, and it is our aim in this chapter to focus on the importance of sex in determining the particular form in which the adolescent struggle is experienced.

Jim's disabling preoccupations were an expression of and a defense against rekindled oedipal fantasies that were significantly contaminated with preoedipal rage, in particular, that of an anal-sadistic nature. Consciously, he was terrified he would sadistically penetrate his mother, stab her in the breast, rip her apart, assault her in some terrible way. He constantly thought of her, as he regressively utilized magical thinking and ritualistic behavior to defend against erotic sadistic impulses and fantasies. Some of this struggle was displaced onto the girls in his class. Later, it was to unfold in the transference with fantasies of torturing and destroying the "puny" analyst. At times, only remorse and an increase in symptoms prevented him from going to the analyst's office and enacting his fantasies. Negative oedipal wishes were reflected in his longing to be close to his absent father and in the love songs and wooing behavior directed toward the analyst. He was enraged at his mother, since he perceived that she had emasculated and cast out his father. This was expressed in the transference in fantasies about the analyst's wife.

Jim's inner struggles were best understood and most clearly interpreted in terms of oedipal conflicts rekindled at the onset of adolescence and involving a regressive retreat to anal-sadistic wishes and conflicts. In this regression we see no loss of self-boundaries or return to a partial fusion with mother. The patient's boundaries remained well defined; compulsive behavior shored them up even tighter. There was no apparent threat of loss of self; if there was any such threat in his regression, it was defended against by relying ever more on himself and his own actions. Clinically, this was manifested by the fact that few people realized that Jim was in such turmoil. His inner struggle remained essentially an inner struggle with separate, well-defined internal object representations. The primary danger related to his wish/fear of his destructive and castrating fantasies. He feared that he would be punished for his evil thoughts and impulses and that he would become defective and impaired like his father.

For Janet, negotiation of adolescence was also at a standstill. She too was in conflict over oedipal issues, and she too showed signs of major regressive shifts in her inner struggle and in her functioning. However, her regressive and symptomatic behavior was most clearly expressed and understood in terms of the nature and quality of her object relationships. As with Jim, conflicts over anal sadism were in the analytic material. The repeated body intrusions in Janet's early childhood served to crystallize anal conflicts related to sphincter control, and the anorexia was in part an attempt at body and instinctual control.

Anal-sadistic issues, however, were not primary to Janet's experience. What was foremost was her need both to remove and to establish boundaries between herself and the important other in her life. These contradictory aims reflected poorly negotiated rapprochement conflicts of toddlerhood, conflicts related to the seeking of an optimal distance from mother so that dependency needs are met while autonomy is protected. During periods of regression, as in the transference relationship or under developmental stress, such as puberty, these poorly resolved conflicts of infancy were rekindled and came to dominate Janet's life. Thus, in the transference, she yearned for and demanded that the analyst support her and take over for her while, at the same time, she experienced any intervention as an intrusion into her unstable sense of herself as a separate individual.

What is to be underscored is that this formulation of Janet's primary conflict focuses on issues of autonomy and separateness. Feelings of disintegration and unreality emerged when her ego was severely threatened by the intensity of impulses experienced within the transference. The inadequate boundary definition, the incomplete sense of separateness, led to a threat of loss of self. This was the central struggle in Janet's anorexia and the central struggle that dominated the transference for the first 2½ years of the analysis. This was the struggle that was experienced-near for Janet and became the focus of the analyst's interpretive efforts.

For both Janet and Jim the issue of destructive aggression and its control were major concerns. This was evident in the transference as Janet raged at, abused, and felt abused by the analyst. Jim was preoccupied with fantasies of torturing and destroying the "puny" analyst. Both felt guilty, embarrassed, repulsed, and threatened by their overt and covert expressions of rage. When hostility toward the analyst was particularly intense, Janet described feelings of disintegration and unreality; she needed time and space to "collect" herself. Jim's ritualistic behavior, his walking in the "right way," increased to the point of paralysis when his "disgusting imaginations" about smashing the analyst dominated his thinking. Janet's hostility was to a greater extent directed inward and at her own body; she literally punched herself when she felt angry, and she abused her body through starvation. Jim was more in conflict over outwardly directed aggression. The interdiction against aggression was powerful for both. Their underlying personality structures were different and different responses were called forth. While turning aggression inward, Janet turned to others to take over. Jim, whose aggression was more outwardly directed, established self-contained behavior patterns, private rituals, and silent but agonizing obsessive thinking.

Some of the differences in the clinical pictures of these two youngsters seem paradoxical. Historically, Janet's trauma was more directly related to her body, Jim's to relationships. One would anticipate, therefore, that Janet's dynamics would be centered more on bodily experiences, on drive, and Jim's on relatedness to others. But the opposite was the case. Jim's symptoms were more intrapsychic, Janet's more interpersonal. She, like Jim, experienced internal anguish. However, her appearance and distress evoked and provoked response from others: people wanted to help; she demanded it; she pulled others in; she pushed them away. Her struggle was in getting others to take over and in avoiding their intrusion. Janet's aim was to get others to control her, Jim's to control himself. The issue of control was the same; the method of attaining it different. Jim was self-sufficient, unto himself. Janet looked to the outside, to others, for help with an internal need.

To summarize, in comparing the psychopathology, the inner experiences, and the transference engagement of these two adolescents, we see significant differences. Jim was besieged with conflicts related to drive derivatives. His destructive castration fantasies were central to his overwhelming anxiety. Psychosexual regression from oedipal to anal-sadistic conflicts was dominant. His struggle and compromise formations could best be conceptualized within a structural theory framework, and this guided the analyst's interpretative interventions. In contrast, Janet's character structure, dysfunction, and intense transference were best understood as reflecting a defensive regression to create or recreate an earlier mode of relatedness. An appreciation of her inner struggle as a rekindling of inadequately resolved rapprochement subphase issues was central to this understanding. Janet's conflict was over autonomy; the danger was object loss. Such considerations were closest to her experience and were the framework for the analyst's interpretive interventions.

We tease apart and speak of differences for purposes of examination and clarity. In discussing the inner struggles of these two adolescents, we contrast a developmental understanding based on an object relationship model with a triadic structural conflict schema. Such diagrammatic distinctions, by their simplification, do a certain injustice to the complexities of overlapping, intertwining, complementary issues and conflicts in the clinical material. As Arlow (1990) suggests, "Pursuit of drive gratification and the nature of object relations can not be separated one from the other. They are part and parcel of the same process" (p. 11). As Mahler emphasized, the separation–individuation process is inextricably linked with the vicissitudes of instinctual life (Mahler et al., 1975). The rapprochement subphase of the separation–individuation process can only be understood in terms of the libidinal and aggressive ties between infant and caretaker. Nevertheless, attempting to delineate primary themes and dominant conflicts in the amalgam of human experience and the formulation of this experience are important in defining and understanding differences in symptom formation. From this perspective, the struggles that underlie Janet's and Jim's respective dysfunctions are distinguishable in terms of the nature of their central conflicts and the primary danger situations.

DISCUSSION

Over the past 20 years there has been a wealth of research addressing the differences in the psychological development of girls and boys, considering genetic, hormonal, developmental, and experiential factors (Kohlberg, 1966; Money and Ehrhardt, 1972; Korner, 1973; Galenson and Roiphe, 1976; Kleeman, 1976). Characteristic differences in the developmental lines of femininity and masculinity are noted (Tyson, 1982). Of pertinence are studies in the areas of drive endowment and developmental unfolding (Bell, 1960), child–parent interaction (Stoller, 1976), body sensations (Galenson and Roiphe, 1976), and the vicissitudes of the separation–individuation process (Olesker, 1990). Girls and boys develop and mature at a different pace and in different ways. It is not surprising, therefore, that the form and quality of neurotic symptom formation in females and males also differs.

Our current understanding suggests that the girl's psychic development is embedded in attachment. The boy's experience is of greater separateness and self-definition. Two major factors contributing to this developmental difference are the nature of the genital sensations and the characteristics of the separation–individuation process—that is, the influences of drive and object relations.

Body sensations are central to the child's unfolding development.

Proceeding through the various psychosexual stages, the child appreciates and integrates the world through the experience of the body. The sense of the self and of the world is organized around these experiences (Spitz, 1965). As Erikson (1950) noted, oral sensations—the thumb in the mouth, taking in and spitting out—promote definition of inside and out, self and other. Anal sensations lead to holding on and letting go and exerting active control on the self and on the environment. In the early genital phase genital sensations organize experience in a new way. They draw the child's attention to the genitals. This leads to investigating the part of the body in which the new pleasurable sensations are being experienced. The child looks, touches, and is curious about his own genitalia and those of others. Difference is noted.

For the boy, the genitals are external organs with boundaries that can be seen, touched, and readily defined. The sensations are discrete. They lead to a thrusting outward into the world, into objects and into people. The world is now seen as a place into which one thrusts oneself and the self is further defined by the thrusting sensation. All of this promotes greater self-definition and boundary formation. A moving out into the world is promoted and, no doubt, augmented by a motoric discharge inclination and an aggressive phallic drive that, for the boy, are either more intense or more freely expressed (Parens, 1990) than for the girl.

The girl's genital sensations influence her development in their characteristic fashion (Barnett, 1966; Kestenberg, 1982; Roiphe and Galenson, 1981). For a long time we had denied that the girl has these sensations prior to puberty. More recent awareness that the girl has such specific genital sensations allows us to appreciate and to postulate her very different experience. Her sensations are diffuse, radiating, ill-defined, and located somewhere within. This is in marked contrast to the boy's experience of discrete, localized sensations and his visible and manipulable organ. The girl's genital sensations lead to a diffuse drawing inward, rather than to an outward penetration. The quality of these sensations does not contribute to self-definition and boundary formation but, instead, promotes diffuseness and connectedness. Thus, body sensations, so similar yet so uniquely different, promote divergent characteristics. In a similar manner, sexual difference promotes difference in the separation–individuation experience (Olesker, 1990).

Throughout development various forces operate that foster separateness for the boy and connectedness for the girl. The genital sensation pulling the girl inward and pushing the boy out reinforces earlier experience. From the beginning of the mother–child matrix the mother experiences the girl as "like me" and the boy as different. Thus, a sense of fusion or separateness is promoted by the very fact of the mother's experience of the infant's sex.

The child's experience of his own sex in relation to his mother also influences connection and separateness. For the girl, sexual identity is established within the mother–child matrix. Femininity is fostered within the closeness with mother; the girl's sexual identity does not require definitive separation. The boy (Greenson, 1968; Mahler et al., 1975), however, must give up his identification with the mother to establish his sexual identity. He must separate out in order to attain and stabilize his masculinity. Because his masculinity is threatened by too tenacious an identification with mother, he must make a more definitive separation. In terms of her gender identity formation, the girl experiences no such pressured organizing force; her sexual identity is safely structured within the mother's orbit. For her there is no great need to break this protective, reassuring bond. And herein lies the girl's unresolved preoedipal attachment to mother that Freud (1931) so astutely observed lying behind the unresolved oedipal attachment to father. Herein, we suggest, may lie the explanation for Jim's relative lack of regression in the sphere of object relatedness, namely, his desperate fortification of defenses keeping himself separate from mother. Any loss of separateness would have been too great a threat to his already tenuous masculinity.

In adolescence there is an upsurge in the boy's need for his father as revived oedipal strivings threaten psychic equilibrium; the seeking of the father is a commonly observed phenomenon at this time. We note it in Jim's history. Father's presence becomes important to counter the threat of engulfment with mother and to reinforce masculine identification at a time when the boy is feeling threatened by the maternal presence. The implied threat to his masculinity makes regression in object relations much more conflict-ridden for the adolescent boy than for his female counterpart.

Because adolescence fosters regression, both boys and girls retreat from oedipal conflicts and struggle with issues of control, autonomy, gender identity consolidation, closeness, and body sensations. For the boy, inasmuch as it threatens gender identity consolidation, the door to closeness with mother is barred. In a boy with weakly developing masculinization, regression in this arena becomes tantamount to a giving up of his masculine identity. It cannot be allowed. The push away from such closeness has been great; masculinity demands it. It is interesting in this light that Jim's symptoms, rather than evoking involvement from others, served instead to isolate him. It is as if they served as a defense against this dangerous pull to closeness. Jim turned to his father for support, to help him maintain his separateness from mother and maintain his masculinity. He also imbued the representation of his mother with much hostility and rejected and maligned her, in large part to protect his threatened masculinity. Despite his efforts, as noted in the transference, this movement toward father nonetheless threw him into a negative oedipal conflict of some intensity.

Some incompletion of separateness is not incompatible with femininity (Mahler et al., 1975), however, and therefore regression in this realm is not only tolerated but it is commonly observed. This is frequently what occurs in the transference, as was noted in Janet's analysis. Rapprochement conflicts are evoked, giving the girl another opportunity to rework issues of closeness, dependence, separateness, distance, and autonomy as well as of love of and competition for and with mother. This is an important task of adolescence. In order for the girl to take hold of her life, she must come to terms with her separateness and move on. Before this occurs, however, the tie to the mother once more comes to the fore, and the push–pull of the rapprochement conflict takes center stage.

We propose that male and female alike deal with oedipal conflicts and separation issues but that the manner in which they are resolved varies along gender lines. Patterns are noted. Regression in object relatedness is more commonly experienced as central in the analyses of girls and women, a reflection of its role in the girl's developmental experience. It is less prominent in analyses of boys and men, again, a reflection of its role in the developmental experience.

Furthermore, we postulate that this developmental difference underlies the significant difference noted in the greater access to regression in the sphere of object relations for girls and the greater resistance to it in boys. In an effort to substantiate this proposition, we have looked at the analyses of two adolescents. The manifestations of their dysfunctions are quite different. At the symptomatic level we noted that Jim's obsessive-compulsive disorder was kept hidden from almost all those around him; Janet's illness painfully engaged even the most casual observer. Elements of their underlying struggles differed. For Janet, the danger of object loss, with the struggle for optimal distance from the sustaining object, the pull–push struggle of the rapprochement subphase of the separation-individuation process, was of central importance. Jim's struggles related more directly to his murderous impulses within the context of the triadic infantile neurosis and were formulated most clearly in terms of an intersystemic conflict. The object representations of his struggle, though clearly intrinsic to his inner world, were less in the foreground of his dysfunction. Object representations were clearly more differentiated and separated. Intense conflict over his destructive drive derivatives best characterized his inner turmoil.

The experience of the transference for each patient was different. For Janet, it was a struggle over dependence, intrusion, and autonomy. Boundaries were ill defined and internal representations were not clear-cut.

Jim was more in conflict over feelings of love and hatred experienced toward well-defined objects. For Janet, regression in object relations was not only available to her but it was fostered by the developmental vicissitudes of her sex. Jim's masculinity promoted and fostered stable object relations; he resisted regression in this sphere.

It is important to repeat the obvious—that Janet and Jim are different and unique individuals. Their personalities emerged from and were molded by a large number of known and unknown genetic, maturational, developmental, and environmental elements. Similarly, the particular characteristics of their symptomatic struggles were the result of many factors, some known and others obscure. We are suggesting, however, that just as one's sex is an essential factor in determining developmental unfolding, it is also an important contributing factor in the organizing and shaping of psychic dysfunction. Just as the vicissitudes of her object relationships took on particular importance in Janet's normal development as a female, so, too, did the mental representations and her relationships to the important objects in her life become pivotal issues of her symptomatic conflict in the dysfunctions occurring at puberty. Jim's normal development as a male was much more focused on conflicts surrounding his drive derivatives. Regression in object relatedness was not fostered by—indeed, was threatening to—his gender identity consolidation. Castration anxiety and intersystemic conflicts were the dominant forces influencing the compromise formations and the forms of his regressive illness at puberty. For this reason, structural theory provides the clearest perspective on Jim's dysfunction. An object relations perspective is more germaine to Janet's struggle.

This chapter begins with two specific examples of adolescents in analysis and moves to more general speculations about the influence of the child's sex on the form and quality of psychopathology. We hope that the tentative formulations in this chapter will contribute to the further study of the influence of the child's sex on neurosogenesis.

REFERENCES

Arlow, J. (1990), Psychoanalysis and the quest for morality. Presented to the Philadelphia Psychoanalytic Society.

Barnett, M. (1966), Vaginal awareness in the infancy and childhood of girls. *J. Amer. Psychoanal. Assn.* 14:129–141.

Bell, R. Q. (1960), Relation between behavior manifestations in the human neonate. *Child Dev.,* 31:463–477.

Erikson, E. (1950), *Childhood and Society.* New York: Norton.

Freud, S. (1931), Female sexuality. *Standard Edition,* 21:225–243. London: Hogarth Press, 1961.

Galenson, E. & Roiphe, H. (1976), Some suggested revisions concerning early female development. *J. Amer. Psychoanal. Assn.,* 24:29–57.

Greenson, R. (1968), Disidentifying from mother. *Internat. J. Psycho-Anal.,* 49:370–376.

Hollingsworth, C. (1980), Long-term outcome of obsessive–compulsive disorders in childhood. *J. Amer. Acad. Child Psychiat.,* 19:134–144.

Kestenberg, J. (1982), Inner genital phase—prephallic and preoedipal. In: *Early Female Development,* ed. D. Mendell. SP Med/Sci Books, pp. 71–126.

Kleeman, J. (1976), Freud's view on early female sexuality in the light of direct child observation. *J. Amer. Psychoanal Assn.,* 24:3–17.

Kohlberg, L. (1966), A cognitive-developmental analysis of children's sex role concepts and attitudes. In: *The Development of Sex Differences,* ed. E. Maccoby. Stanford: Stanford University Press, pp. 82–173.

Korner, A. (1973), Sex differences in the newborn. *J. Child Psychoanal. Psychiat.* 14:19–29.

Mahler, M., Pine F. & Bergman, A. (1975), *The Psychological Birth of the Human Infant.* New York: International Universities Press.

Mayer, E. (1985), Everybody must be just like me: Observations on female castration anxiety. *Internat. J. Psycho-Anal.,* 66:331–348.

Money, J. & Ehrhardt, A. (1972), *Man and Woman, Boy and Girl.* Baltimore: Johns Hopkins University Press.

Olesker, W. (1990), Sex differences during the early separation–individuation process: Implications for gender identity formation. *J. Amer. Psychoanal. Assn.,* 38:325–346.

Parens, H. (1990), On the girl's psychosexual development: Reconsiderations suggested from direct observation. *J. Amer. Psychoanal. Assn.,* 38:743–772.

Roiphe, H. & Galenson, E. (1981), *Infantile Origins of Sexual Identity.* New York: International Universities Press.

Spitz, R. A. (1965), *The First Year of Life.* New York: International Universities Press.

Stoller, R. J. (1976), Primary femininity. *J. Amer. Psychoanal. Assn.,* 24:39–79.

Tyson, P. (1982), A developmental line of gender identity, gender role, and choice of love object. *J. Amer. Psychoanal. Assn.,* 30:61–86.

11

Neuroses and Separation–Individuation Theory

J. Alexis Burland

In 1923 Freud wrote, concerning castration anxiety, the following: "It has been quite correctly pointed out that a child gets the idea of a narcissistic injury through a bodily loss from the experience of losing his mother's breast after sucking, from the daily surrender of his faeces and, indeed, even from the separation from the womb at birth" (p. 144). A decade later Jones (1933), also wrote of the psychosexual development of boys:

> I fully agree . . . (with Horney and Klein) . . . that the boy's reaction to the critical situation of the Oedipus complex is greatly influenced by his earlier relationship with his mother. . . . Oral privations . . . are undoubtedly of the greatest importance in rendering harder the later task of coping with the parents on the genital level. . . . Why should imperfect access to the nipple give a boy the sense of imperfect possession of his own penis? I am quite convinced that the two things are intimately related, although the logical connection between them is certainly not obvious [p. 10].

Freud's and Jones's clinical experience with neurotic patients was alerting them to the importance of experiences occurring prior to the phallic-oedipal phase in terms of their impact on neurotic conflict. In the more than half a century since these thoughts were voiced, a large body of research and theory has accumulated addressing the issues raised by

Freud's observations and Jones's most prophetic question. Margaret Mahler's separation–individuation theory is one such effort at conceptualizing the developmental challenges that foreshadow the infantile neurosis. Of the impact of her research findings on the understanding of the infantile neurosis she wrote the following:

> Much of the empirical data available to us reveals that, while the concept of the infantile neurosis derives from the prototypic source of intrapsychic conflict at its most complex state—the Oedipus complex—there is much in the neurotic development we see daily that derives as well from the prephallic, preoedipal periods, during which crucial forms of psychic organization and reorganization are structured [Mahler, 1975, p. 190].

The infantile neurosis was among the first of Freud's discoveries concerning the psychogenesis and dynamic structure of adult neurotic illness (Breuer and Freud, 1893–1895). He discovered that the structure of the adult neurosis consists essentially of a reworking of the infantile neurosis, that is, those sets of conflicts and compromise formations elaborated at the time of the individual's struggle with the phallic-oedipal phase of development in childhood. The infantile neurosis as directly observed in a child (in contrast to its being reconstructed during the treatment of an adult) was first recorded in the psychoanalytic literature by Freud in his write-up of the case of the five-year-old "Little Hans" (Freud, 1909). Since then, child analysts have had the opportunity to observe and psychoanalyze many children of that age, and the appearance and dynamics of the infantile neurosis are accordingly well understood (see, e.g., Etezady, 1990).

The manifest appearance of the infantile neurosis is quite similar among children. There are the preoccupations with the sexual organs themselves: First, there is great and intense curiosity about the structure and function of the genitals—one's own and those of others, including both sexes, all ages, all animal species, and even such inanimate objects as dolls. Second, there is curiosity and much fantasy formation concerning what happens when the boy's and girl's genitals meet, that is, when penis enters vagina; such fantasies often have a manifest violent nature. Then there are the object-related preoccupations: first, there is the love triangle that gives this phase its name, with its mixture of lust, envy, and competitiveness directed toward the parents, and second, there is the wish to observe (and fantasy) the parents in sexual congress, with a wish to participate in the activity. There is also curiosity about having babies and about the role of sex in the process. And, finally, there is infantile masturbation, with its associated fantasies that express these preoccupations in some mix unique to each child. Accompanying all of these manifestations of the infantile neurosis is a variety of powerful affects, including narcissistic and erotic excitement over the exhibition of the genitals; pride related to erotic sensations in the genitals; active and passive penetration urges and anxieties; lust; excitement over angry and competitive phallic jousting; narcissistic mortification and envy in the face of defeat or of slights; and, increasingly over time, castration anxiety, shame, and eventually guilt as the internalization of the superego moves the oedipal child into latency. The child has great difficulty containing, identifying, and sorting out the stimulating fantasies, urges, and anxieties; symptom formation that is, the infantile neurosis, is a common outcome although it is often overlooked by parents or dismissed as naughtiness. Almost all of the oedipal child's activities become focused on coping with these conflicts; this is particularly true of play, which, of course, is the rationale for its use in child psychoanalysis.

   Separation–individuation theory seeks to conceptualize, in almost direct response to Freud's and Jones's observations, certain preliminary and overlapping developmental events that set the background and context for how the child will cope with the infantile neurosis. Further, it views development from the perspective of the interaction with the primary objects, not simply on the zones and aims of the drives, as is the focus of more traditional psychosexual theory. Both Freud's and Jones's reference to the lasting influence of the infant's interaction with the nipple, the presumed first libidinal object, underscores the idea that what is psycho-genetically of significance in each clinical instance is not just the drive itself but its historical interaction with the primary object. Since the Oedipus complex is in essence a struggle with objects in childhood, this focus on object relationships is tailor-made to understand the dynamics of oedipal conflicts as they exist in the minds of our older child, adolescent, and adult neurotic patients.

SEPARATION-INDIVIDUATION THEORY AND THE INFANTILE NEUROSIS

Separation-individuation theory traces several developmental lines. Three of them are of particular importance in terms of their impact on the infantile neurosis. First, the theory posits the development of a "basic mood," a manner of experiencing oneself affectively in interactions with other people. This mood relates to the balance between the excitement over autonomy and independence from the primary object and the anaclitic depressive response to the discovery of separateness from the same primary object, both of which are forced upon the child by maturational pressures. Second, separation-individuation theory recounts the process by which the child emerges from the mother–infant dyad and developes a cognitive and structural sense of himself or herself as a separate individual in a world of separate individuals, that is, self- and object differentiation. And third, it recounts the process by which destructive aggression is sufficiently tamed so that libidinal object relationships can be entered into, stabilized, and maintained. It explicates phenomena that occur in tandem with those drive phenomena that psychosexual developmental theory labels as the oral, anal, and early phallic-oedipal stages; these phenomena interact and are mutually influencing.

Basic Mood

Affects play a central role in early psychological development. It has long been assumed in psychoanalytic theory that the infant's first experiences are motivated, perceived, and ultimately organized in memory around the affective polarity of pleasure versus unpleasure; the experiences that make up the separation–individuation process are no exception. Pleasure motivates progressive movement along the developmental continuum from birth. This allows for the full investment of psychological and physical energies in the phase-specific and maturationally determined neuromuscular and cognitive skills being developed at any point in time; it also encourages the psychological organization and stabilization of ego skills. One can see it in the "function lust" experienced from the exercise of a skill once it has been mastered, an important affective source of self-esteem and self-definition.

The separation–individuation process is understood as involving two participants, mother and child. It is pleasure that motivates the child first to enter into the mother–infant dyad, then to separate and individuate out of it; pleasure can also offset the unpleasure that is experienced in response to the inevitable moments of failure that occur on the part of anyone's "average expectable environment" (Hartmann, 1939) or from a "good-enough mother" (Winnicott, 1960). The mother plays an important role in encouraging developmental accomplishment by affectively investing in it; with her affect she also defines, modulates, and eventually helps in the stabilization of the attendant affect in her child. That infants are inherently preprogrammed to live in an environment of objects is evident from the power of infantile affects to communicate. An infant engaged in "kootchy-koo" games with a doting mother, their eyes focused on one another, mother's eyes ablaze with love and pride, her infant chortling with delight, is an infectious everyday scene that makes evident how interactive affects define the essence of the dyad. The same is true of the converse: the almost lifeless, limp body of a deprived infant, the blank and unfocused look of the eyes, and the lack of interpersonal contact or interaction between the parties of a dysfunctional dyad are painfully depressing to observe (Burland, 1984).

In terms of separation–individuation, Mahler observed that the affect she called "elation" played a particular role during "practicing," the second subphase of the process (Mahler, 1966). As the toddler practices and gradually masters upright locomotion, there is a pleasurable self-intoxication that only fuels further efforts at even greater mastery. This sense of gleeful omnipotence is communicative and infectious and, indeed, stimulates empathic shared delight on the part of others—of mother, in particular, whose mirroring support of it is necessary for its perpetuation. During the subsequent rapprochement subphase, this elation is set off against an anaclitic depression secondary to the cognitive realization of separateness from the comforting dyadic object and to the consequent discovery of aloneness and vulnerability as a facet of life. At the same time, struggles over control of the toddler's defecation and resistance to submission to the will of the parent versus a need to please the parent clearly reflect not simply zonal erotic anal drive manifestations but also independence–dependence and autonomy–submission issues as described in separation–individuation theory. This interplay between the infant's inherent drives and capacities and the mother's response plays a critical role in the organization of the child's evolving self- and body-images, their stabilization, and their affective valence.

In addition to Mahler, various observers of developing children (Roiphe and Galenson, 1972; Parens et al., 1976; Bernstein, 1990) have noted the extent to which the discovery of the genitals provokes a strong affective reaction in both boys and girls. Elation resembling that seen during practicing is evident in the excited narcissistic exhibitionism of the children indulging themselves in their nakedness or gleefully giving themselves over to their sexual curiosity and exploration. Children's enjoyment of their new genital sexuality can be a part of the process of discovering and defining themselves and their bodies. On the other hand, some children can be seen to feel overwhelmed by their sexuality and to feel, instead of elation, a frightening estrangement from their supportive objects such that they regress to anxious clinging. Is that not but the expression in developmental terms of Jones's (1933) observation that "imperfect access to the nipple give[s] a boy the sense of imperfect possession of his own penis" (p. 10)?

A clinical example of what Jones was describing comes from the analysis of a young adult who complained that he felt totally devoid of any masculine attributes, physically or psychologically. He complained of feeling depressed, hopeless and helpless, and of being physically without energy, weak, and always tired. He was obsessed with looking at other men and envying what he assumed was their easy and natural pleasure with their bodies and their sexuality and their high level of energy. He longed to feel "turned on" by women in the manner he assumed all other men were and complained that on those instances when he had had intercourse with women he had experienced, though he was functional, neither excitement nor pleasure. He saw neither parent as having anything to offer in terms of sex education or as models to show him how to enjoy himself or his body. He saw them as finding no pleasure from anything in their own lives, mother because of her depressed nature, father because of his paralyzing anxiety and bland niceness. The patient seemed anhedonic about everything he tried in the hopes of generating some level of excitement within himself: sexual activity, school work, tennis, body building, sailing, tutoring the underprivileged, and, of course, the analysis. He felt alone and unsupported in his misery and therefore clung to his parents and to his analyst, convinced that only through them could he find in life what he was seeking. Indeed, self-reliance or autonomy terrified him, since he saw within himself, both in terms of his body and of his identity, nothing of any stability or pleasure to build on. The process of individuation had been abortive, in large measure because the positive affective charge that sustains it was not consciously available to him; the resultant preponderance of an anaclitic and narcissistic depressive affect prevented him from finding pleasure and self-affirmation in his phallic-oedipal sexuality.

Self- and Object Differentiation

There is some disagreement over the terminology employed in attempting to conceptualize the process by which infants first move into an intimate connection with their mothers and then separate out to become, as experienced subjectively, separate beings in a world of separate beings. Mahler's terms recounting the movement out of the "normal autistic" and into the "normal symbiotic" phase have drawn criticism for having misleading implications from their usage in other contexts, such as in descriptions of childhood psychoses. There have also been doubts raised as to how truly oblivious to external reality is the child in the normal autistic phase and how truly without a sense of separate identity is the child during the normal symbiotic phase (see Stern, 1985). Nevertheless, all observers note that there is an initial phase of seemingly greater responsiveness to internal perceptions (i.e., primary narcissism), followed by a move into a unique oneness with the mother that has been called, variously, the establishment of the libidinal object (Spitz, 1965), attachment (Bowlby, 1969), and symbiosis (Mahler, 1952). This concept is also included in Winnicott's (1960) often quoted statement "There is no such thing as an infant"—that is, the infant cannot exist apart from the maternal facilitating environment. Winnicott credits the origin of the idea to Freud's statement to the effect that the infant and the care it receives from its mother are a "psychical system" (Freud, 1911). This initial developmental accomplishment of achieving a symbiosis with the mother sets the stage for what children must then accomplish during separation–individuation, namely, grow out of that unique dyad and become, more or less, their own individual person.

Becoming one's own person is a complex process that has been traced by infant observational research, with confirmatory data from the analyses of those patients still struggling with inadequately mastered remnants of it. Spitz, for instance, traced the steps by which the newborn gradually recognizes some facial features, then a whole face, and then specifically the mother's face; he theorized that these observable behaviors indicated the gradual accretion of an intrapsychic representation of the mother. This process is accompanied by a deepening affective investment in the mother and culminates in what Spitz termed "the establishment of the libidinal object"; this is indicated early in the latter half of the first year by the child's selective response of anxiety to faces other than the mother's (Spitz, 1965). Mahler's observational data revealed how in the second half of the first year of life, after the peak of the mother–infant symbiosis, the infant explores mother's face and body and then compares his own to hers, a behavior she concluded indicated the accumulation of perceptual and cognitive impressions of what is himself and what is his mother (Mahler, Pine, and Bergman, 1975). Starting at about the same age, musculoskeletal maturation energizes the toddler's sense of his own powers; with the growing capacity for self-reliance—including, importantly, the ability to approach and distance from mother—there is further elaboration of the sense of self as active agent in confronting reality.

A patient in analysis who had a unique capacity to remember events from the first two years of life suggested another interesting dimension to the elaboration of internal images early in life. We had become used to noting that in his dreams the larger the images of other people or inanimate objects, the earlier the childhood memory being tapped. We assumed this expressed the perspective of a little child in a world of grown-ups and adult-size furniture. But as he began to recapture memories from the end of the first and the second year of life of his mother's, his nurse's, and the family cook's faces, the faces seemed even larger than large. He soon noted that these images of faces seemed so large that they filled the entire visual field, side to side and top to bottom. We were able to note that memories of these same faces from later in his childhood increasingly included background scenes and objects, so that the faces became an increasingly smaller part of the total picture. We took this to reflect a libidinal investment that was initially exclusively in the caretakers but then gradually diffused to include the nonhuman environment as well.

As the child elaborates richer and richer internal representations of himself and his mother, then of others, such as father, siblings, pets, as well as of the important and constant inanimate objects in his world, the way is paved for the central conflict of the rapprochement subphase, namely, mastering the maturationally derived cognitive awareness of one's separateness—that is, the differentiation between the internal representation the child has of himself or herself and the representation of his or her primary objects. On the basis of this new awareness of their separateness, the child's attitude toward mother and their relationship must change from the unquestioned implicit assumption that mother is an extension of the self, all-knowing, ever present, and omnipotent, to the realization that she is autonomous, intermittently unavailable, and not omnipotent.

Although in the rapprochement crises the child longs for the increasingly lost illusion of symbiotic safety and bliss, there are also the developmental thrust and narcissistic gains of increasing autonomy, self-reliance, and self-definition. The elaboration of a more self-reliant and autonomous internal representation of the self, that is, individuation, is accompanied by the further elaboration of the maternal and paternal internal objects as separate beings. As Mahler has pointed out (Mahler, 1975, p. 192), there is also the internalization of parental demands and expectations, that is, the beginning of superego development, with its heightened concerns about parental approval and disapproval.

The resolution of the rapprochement crisis involves the creation over time for each person of his or her "optimal distance" from others, a distance that renders the person neither so dependent that autonomy is threatened nor so self-contained that separation anxiety is generated. There is some selective flexibility to this optimal distance, as well as more or less stability, depending on the nature of each child's individual developmental accomplishments and the specifics of any day-to-day situation.

These efforts at modulating the comfortable distance from the primary objects affect and are affected by the newly unfolding, conflicted phallic-oedipal relationships. New and intensified erotic sensations from, first, anal and then genital zones are altering the child's experience of himself or herself and the way the primary objects are perceived, used, and experienced. In other words, the struggle to achieve self and object differentiation and constancy occurs at a time when self experiences and object desires are undergoing powerful transformations. The two processes impact upon and influence one another.

For example, a late adolescent in analysis described a recurrent dream in which he was on a Rube Goldberg–like stretching machine. His first associations were to his wishes to be taller, which meant to him becoming more of a man and achieving greater independence from his intrusive and domineering mother. Further associations led him to the realization that behind this wish was the wish that his penis be made longer. But further associations uncovered another facet to this fantasy: the bigger the penis, the more of him is inside the woman with whom he is having intercourse and the more, therefore, they are fused into one being, his idealized and "romantic" conception of lovemaking. Over the subsequent months these thoughts led to a deepened realization of how terrified he was of any distance between himself and his overidealized and omnipotent mother and of how without her presence and support he felt small, unimportant, and vulnerable, too alone to tolerate. He recovered a memory from infancy: he was crying in his crib and no one came; that is, his mother did not respond. He grew to realize that in his most active sex life he was reuniting, in his mind, with the infantile dyadic mother. His phallic-oedipal wishes were contaminated by persistent self-doubts and longings for safety due to inadequately achieved individuation; castration anxiety, in other words, was compounded by separation anxiety, just as Jones had observed, with a resultant need to recapture the safety of the lost dyad in illusion.

The anhedonic young man mentioned earlier was haunted by a particular memory: one night he, as an oedipal-age child, awakened, needing to go to the bathroom. He had an erection, however, and was terrified that as he crossed the hall, his parents—especially his mother—would see him through their open bedroom door. The reaction he feared was no reaction; what he wanted was some form of recognition and affirmation, some sense that his having a penis was a comfortable, if not joyful, part of his parents' image of him. In a similar vein, he was frightened of revealing to me his sexual fantasies and masturbatory practices for fear I would interpret what he said as though from a distance—that is, in terms of coldly "scientific" and possibly incorrect theories instead of hearing what he said empathically, in his terms and from his perspective. He could not accept or integrate his genital sensations—or his oedipal longings—into his own self-image without the participation of a dyadic partner's affirmation of them at the same time. It is of interest that when masturbating he would fantasy the sexual excitement of masculine heterosexual men, using them as envied proxy outlets for his own phallic excitement. At a deeper level, he was also recreating a dyadic relationship with a fantasied man, attempting to erase the self and object differentiation that placed a gulf between them and replacing it, in effect, with a dyadic maternal transference such that their bodies were perceived in illusion as undifferentiated. By that means he could heal his own defective and castrated body image by the illusion that he was expropriating the body, the genitals, and the exciting phallic narcissism of the fantasied man. I suspect that an important dynamic in all instances of a pathologically intense negative oedipal constellation involves a dyadic maternal transference to the Oedipal parent of the same sex; this could explain the not uncommon oedipal fantasy in male patients that their father's penis inserted in their rectum "becomes" their penis inserted in their mother.

The Vicissitudes of Aggression

A variety of theoretical models has been offered over the years to explain the common clinical observation that the strength of the libidinal ties to others is inversely related to the quantity of expressed destructive aggression. Separation–individuation theory offers a model for understanding this process in terms of the developing child's relationships to the primary objects.

Prior to rapprochement, adequately attuned and attentive parenting has allowed for the elaboration within the child of a preponderance of internal images of loving and available parents and of a loving and lovable self, all intertwined in images of a reciprocating interaction that is stable and supportive of feelings both of safety and dawning individuality. Coexisting are also memory traces of painful and frustrating experiences, with the affects of hurt and anger, associated with images of a bad self and bad parents; under the best of circumstances these negative images have less influence on day-to-day interactions than do the positive ones. That the child has, therefore, developing intrapsychic images of what could be called a good mother and a bad mother can be seen in the rages toward the mother that normally alternate with those moments of love and joy felt toward her. In rapprochement, the realization of the separateness from mother and of her limited availability generates narcissistic injury, frustration, and anger, and the attachment to mother becomes intermittently an anxious one, in which she is seen as withholding and distanced. The split-off negative images of the frustrating mother are evoked sympathetically, and during the period of the rapprochement crises the alternation of good and bad perceptions of mother (and self) can be intense and rapid. Typical in rapprochement is the behavior in which the child pulls at mother in a distressed and whiny manner, demanding to be picked up, only to then push her away and demand to be put down; it is the good but now distanced mother into whose lap the child wants to crawl, but it is fear of the still undifferentiated mother the child rejects lest she threaten his autonomy. Over time, the child experiences the mother's affective investment even in the face of his hostility and her greatly decreased omnipotence. The child also continues to experience growing physical, cognitive, and emotional self-definition and self-reliance. The presence of father as a less conflictual parental object plays a further important role in promoting a diminution in the exclusivity of the affective bond to the mother. There is an increased awareness of and comfort with separateness as individuation proceeds and the child develops a more comfortable sense of autonomous self.

With the increased differentiation and demarcation between internal object images, part object images coalesce into whole object images. The good mother and the bad mother, less powerful in their impact on now more stable and sophisticated internal structures, are understood to be two sides of the same person. "Fusion" of libido and aggression, long noted as a developmental phenomenon but poorly understood in terms of alterations in the drives themselves, is better conceptualized as the by-product of the coalescence of the internal part objects, some of which are emotionally invested with libido and some with destructive aggression. The final whole object is therefore invested with a mixture of affects, positive and negative, each serving to moderate the impact of the other. Ambivalence replaces splitting. Normally, the positive affects predominate; that is, the good portions of the new, whole internal objects are sufficiently stable to withstand any hostility that might be evoked as the result of a passing conflict.

There is much interplay between this newly stabilizing relationship to the parents at a post-rapprochement level and the destabilizing influence of the developmental push forward into triadic relationships. The oedipal parents are now increasingly invested with an exciting and frightening array of lustful and competitive affects. There is support and safety for the child if the capacity for stable whole object relationships has been achieved, for with ambivalence what is good and strong in the relationship with the parental object can counterbalance the more conflicted aspects of these same relationships. Inadequately neutralized anger directed at still split-off negative internalized part objects, on the other hand, can threaten to destabilize a child's benign libidinal attachment to the loving "real" parent, an attachment needed to support the traversal of the stormy seas of the Oedipus complex. For instance, there can result a sadistic coloring to the new erotic fantasies, or a primitive destructive quality can be added to the new urges for competitive jousting such that the wish to be the victor over the object becomes a wish to destroy the object. Castration anxiety can thus trigger separation anxiety as the child experiences the instability of the internalized good part objects; in severe cases, the separation anxiety can then regressively trigger annihilation anxiety (Winnicott, 1960). Further, as the still split-off and negatively cathected parental internal images can be internalized as part of the process of the crystallization of the superego, the resultant ego–superego relationship perpetuates the excessive destructive charge.

The following clinical vignette is of a young woman whose relative failure to "heal the split" during rapprochement left her with quantities of unneutralized destructive aggression that interfered with her successful negotiation of the infantile neurosis. In analysis she complained that she did not feel like a woman, that she needed to experience a penis in her vagina to be "made" into a "real" woman. Yet her desperate attempts to find a man with whom to have intercourse all met with failure for reasons she was initially convinced were external and real. Although ardent in her pacifism—she was a '60s antiwar activist—she had many pleasant and exciting dreams about war; in one, about a year and a half into the analysis, cherries were being used as ammunition. Her first associations were to cherries as a slang reference to the female genitalia, but as her associations continued she recalled cherries as food and cherry pie as a favorite of hers in childhood; she also recalled her angry struggles with her parents concerning her overeating.

Over subsequent months the material shifted from manifestly genital sexual to dyadic issues as she recovered previously repressed childhood memories of feeling deprived and angry instead of happily "liberated" by her "progressive" and "nondirective" parents; in fact, her mother was depressed and her father was isolated. Her initial idyllic images of her childhood and of her parents changed into one characterized by suppressed and subversive hurts and hostilities. She discovered that behind the wish for a penis in her vagina was the wish for her mother's nipple in her mouth, as she had seen it in the mouth of her five-years-younger sister, and that her wish was that sexual intercourse/breast-feeding would make her into a person, not just a woman. She also became aware of an urge to bite off both nipple and penis so that the changes in her would be permanent and under her control, an urge that was also an expression of her envy of the power of those upon whom she depended. These insights were followed by a flood of memories of her rage in childhood, including its expression in play. A favorite fantasy of hers, while sitting in the backseat of the family car, was that she would hold out her arms as though they were giant scythes extending out beyond the car's side windows, cutting down all that they passed—pedestrians, buildings, trees; the fantasy ended with her feeling alone and wretched in a sea of rubble of her own making.

The patient's sociopolitical activism took a violent turn, and she joined the local branch of a national terroristic student organization and participated in several of their more destructive activities. What was striking in her ideology was how she increasingly viewed the world in all-black or all-white terms, political figures, for instance, being either the incarnation of evil, deserving of assassination, or overidealized and saintly. Dreams she had had previously of intercourse were replaced by dreams of being raped or torn apart by the insertion of huge penises in her vagina. From the analysis of her rage at me and her fear that it would drive me away, turn me against her, or even destroy me, it became clear that she had herself undermined all of her efforts at finding a sexual partner, and why—it was her fear of the power of her own destructive forces, which she could not control.

CONCLUSION

Separation–individuation theory has played a role in reshaping the way analysts listen to their patients. The mental models of significant childhood developmental challenges and accomplishments are deepened and broadened so that derivative material in our patient's productions can be understood and interpreted, when appropriate, in more than simply oedipal terms; the resolution of the Oedipus complex is the capstone of childhood mental life, but it is not its totality. The clinical utility in understanding the developmental processes that precede the child's entry into the infantile neurosis from the perspective of separation–individuation theory is due in large measure to its focus on object relationships. The infantile neurosis, though instinctual in its origin, is in fact interpersonal in its experience, with conflicts arising within the intrapsychic remnants of the relationships to the primary objects, who are the direct targets of a complicated mixture of yearnings and fears, oedipal and preoedipal. Separation–individuation theory explicates the significant prehistory to the development of a capacity for such relationships as well as offers a model for understanding their dynamics.

Clinically, separation–individuation theory broadens our understanding of the transference by viewing it in terms of more than simply drive derivatives displaced onto the analyst; it is also the object of those drives that is projected onto the analyst, as patients seek to reenact the specifics of their conflicted infantile past. The analyst feels therefore not simply a pressure from the patient to gratify conflicted oedipal and preoedipal drive derivatives; the analyst feels a pressure from the patient to conform to the specifics of the primary objects in relationship to those drives, to thereby enter into reenactments of the critical early childhood interpersonal experiences that generated conflict within the patient's psyche. Further, in raising our consciousness concerning the richness and affective expressivity of preverbal mental life, we are no longer limited to attending only to the verbal content of our patients' communications; they tell us much about their earlier history with their affects and with the form of their communications; their behavior implies how they experience their relationship with us. Being attuned to those feelings and attitudes the patient is attempting to evoke within us is perhaps the most valuable source of information concerning the dynamics of the transference and the psychogenesis of the patient's neurotic illness. This makes possible interpretations that in their exact choice of language are closer to the subjective experiences of the child within the psyche of the patient, the child who is struggling with remembered interpersonal conflicts selectively evoked in the transference by the regressive and interpersonal nature of the analytic process.

REFERENCES

Bernstein, D. (1990), Female genital anxieties, conflicts and typical mastery modes. *Internat. J. Psycho-Anal.*, 71:151–165.

Bowlby, J. (1969). *Attachment and Loss: Volume I. Attachment*. New York: Basic Books.

Breuer, J. & Freud, S. (1893–1895), Studies on hysteria. *Standard Edition*, 2:1–311. London: Hogarth Press, 1955.

Burland, J. A. (1984), Dysfunctional parenthood in a deprived population. In: *Parenthood: A Psychodynamic Perspective*, ed. R. Cohen, B. Cohler & S. Weissman. New York: Guilford Press, pp. 148–163.

Etezady, H., ed. (1990), *The Neurotic Child and Adolescent*. Northvale, NY: Aronson.

Freud, S. (1909), Analysis of a phobia in a five-year-old boy. *Standard Edition*, 10:5–149. London: Hogarth Press, 1955.

———— (1911), Formulations on the two principles of mental functioning. *Standard Edition*, 12:218–226. London: Hogarth Press, 1958.

———— (1923), The infantile genital organization: An interpolation into the theory of sexuality. *Standard Edition*, 19:141–145. London: Hogarth Press, 1961.

Hartmann, H. (1939). *Ego Psychology and the Problem of Adaptation*. New York: International Universities Press.

Jones, E. (1933), The phallic phase. *Internat. J. Psycho-Anal.,* 14:1–33.

Mahler, M. S. (1952), On child psychosis and schizophrenia: Autistic and symbiotic infantile psychoses. In *The Psychoanalytic Study of the Child,* ed. R. Eissler, A. Freud, H. Hartmann & E. Kris. New York: International Universities Press, pp. 286–305.

_____ (1966), Notes on the development of basic moods: The depressive affect. In: *The Selected Papers of Margaret S. Mahler, M. D.: Vol. II. Separation–Individuation.* New York: Aronson, 1979, pp. 59–75.

_____ (1975), On the current status of the infantile neurosis. In: *The Selected Papers of Margaret S. Mahler, M. D.: Vol. II. Separation–Individuation.* New York: Aronson, 1979, pp. 189–193.

_____ , Pine, F. & Bergman, A. (1975), *The Psychological Birth of the Human Infant.* New York: Basic Books.

Parens, H., Pollock, L., Stern, J. & Kramer, S. (1976), On the girl's entry into the Oedipus complex. *J. Amer. Psychoanal. Assn.,* 24 (Suppl.):79–107.

Roiphe, H. & Galenson, E. (1972), Early genital activity and the castration complex. *Psychoanal. Quart.,* 41:334–347.

Spitz, R. (1965), *The First Year of Life.* New York: International Universities Press.

Stern, D. (1985), *The Interpersonal World of the Infant.* New York: Basic Books.

Winnicott, D. W. (1960), The theory of the parent–infant relationship. In: *The Maturational Process and the Facilitating Environment.* New York: International Universities Press, 1965, pp. 37–55.

12

Psychosomatic
Phenomena

Troy L. Thompson II

Psychosomatic symptoms may represent a number of psychological conflicts and defenses, including a regression to or continuation of a merger state, an activation of inadequate self-regulation under nonspecific stress, a symbolic expression of specific object-directed fantasies derived from preoedipal or oedipal phases of development, a transitional object type of relatedness to incompletely renunciated primary objects, or a defensive heightening of a vulnerable self-cathexis. In this chapter, I discuss these dynamics and attempt to demonstrate the involvement of unresolved separation–individuation with psychosomatic vulnerability. I begin with a historical review of some "classic" psychosomatic conditions and theories. I briefly evaluate the current status of these theories, following which I comment on some contemporary psychoanalytic contributions and some recent psychophysiologic research pertinent to psychosomatic conditions.

EARLY LITERATURE

The term *psychosomatic* was first used by Heinroth in 1818 (Kaplan, 1985). However, the recognition that psychological conflicts can trigger physical illness probably is as old as the practice of medicine. Henry Maudsley

243

(quoted by McDougall, 1989, p. 139) observed that "the sorrow that has no vent in tears makes other organs weep," and much earlier, in 1539, Sir Thomas Elyot noted that "affects and passions of the mind . . . if they be immoderate . . . annoy the body and shorten the life" (p. 7). A vicious circle may be set into motion if an individual develops any type of physical illness that is also psychologically stressful. The resultant psychological stress may cause the individual to then call into play what prove to be maladaptive psychological defense mechanisms. Those maladaptive defense mechanisms may produce further conflicts that may secondarily worsen the somatic condition.

Whether the individual became physically or emotionally ill first has little effect on the ultimate outcome, which becomes dependent on the path taken by the concantenation of events based on that individual's physical and psychological strengths and vulnerabilities. Reiser (1975) termed such imbricating interactions between psyche and soma as the somatopsychic–psychosomatic model of development. These interchanges begin before birth and continue to interreact synergistically throughout the life cycle, feeding on or sometimes counterbalancing or neutralizing each other.

A review of theories espoused during the past century concerning psychosomatic phenomena should begin with Freud's contributions. In 1895 Freud published the "Project for a Scientific Psychology," in which he elaborated on the role of anatomic or biochemical characteristics as one level of cause of psychological phenomena. Freud felt that when the biomedical sciences became more advanced, they would add to the understanding of severe psychopathology that he could not explain totally through psychological mechanisms. However, Freud felt that advanced biomedical knowledge would never mean that psychological factors would not be critical from a causation perspective or that all medical conditions would be solely initiated by biomedical factors. In the case of Dora, Freud (1905) discussed his understanding of conversion hysteria operating unconsciously to cause the development of somatic symptoms.

In conversion hysteria, Freud concluded, the hysterical symptom is selected that will have a symbolic meaning relating to the conflict experienced and this symptom will be a compromise formation that provides a neurotic solution for an unconsciously conflictual situation. In other psychosomatic conditions, the individual may not specifically select the illness that develops but a pathophysiologic process may develop in an organ that is vulnerable for biomedical reasons.

During the 1920s, Cannon (Thompson, 1988) elucidated the importance that psychological events can have on the autonomic nervous system. Specifically, he formulated the "fight or flight" model of sympathetic response to an acutely perceived emergency situation. Later researchers noted that prolonged activation of the sympathetic nervous system places physiologic stress on a number of organ systems.

Another theoretical milestone relating to psychosomatic phenomena occurred when Franz Alexander published *Psychosomatic Medicine: Its Principles and Applications* in 1950 (updated in 1968 by Alexander, French, and Pollock). Alexander put forward the psychosomatic specificity theory, in which a specific type of "conflict constellation" is posited to lead to a particular medical condition, specifically one of the seven "classic psychosomatic disorders." These are essential hypertension, neurodermatitis, bronchial asthma, rheumatoid arthritis, hyperthyroidism, ulcerative colitis, and peptic ulcer. Few today doubt that psychological factors play a major role in triggering or exacerbating these conditions; however, few believe that specific personality constellations are the primary cause of these medical disorders.

As one example, Alexander felt that an asthma attack in a child symbolically represented that child crying for attention from his inadequately responsive mother. If an individual has a tendency to wheeze and become short of breath as a child, he understandably might become anxious and might need and wish to have more attention from his mother than is true of a healthy child. If the mother becomes tired and exasperated by a repeatedly demanding asthmatic child and wishes to withdraw, her behavior would be frightening to the child and might cause a vicious cycle to be set in motion. That is, the more the child cries, the more the mother might understandably become frustrated, which might frighten the child and lead him to cry more, which might further worsen the wheezing, and so on. If such a cycle is not interrupted during childhood, it might create individuals who are very anxious later in life about whether or not they can trust and depend on other individuals, even in times of emergency (Fenichel, 1945).

Most psychoanalytic theoreticians and practitioners today feel that there are multiple factors that interact in biopsychosocial spheres to create the specific psychosomatic condition the individual develops (Engel, 1977). The individual must have a physiologic vulnerability (which may be produced in a variety of ways—including genetic, traumatic, metabolic, and infectious) to a specific condition in order to have it develop. Therefore, biologic vulnerability is necessary but not sufficient for a psychosomatic condition to emerge. The physiologic vulnerabilities may become linked to personality and sociocultural factors in the individual. For example, the individual who smokes cigarettes or drinks alcohol excessively may do so for psychological or cultural reasons; however, in doing so he will predispose himself to a number of biomedical conditions.

Flanders Dunbar also became a major contributor to understanding psychosomatic conditions; she coined the term "coronary-prone personality" and wrote a classic text entitled *Emotions and Bodily Changes* (1954). Dunbar felt the specific type of psychological conflict the individual experienced is not as important etiologically for psychosomatic conditions as the specific types of personality traits and emotional reactions to stress the individual carries into adulthood.

Beginning in the late 1950s, two cardiologists, Friedman and Rosenman (Rosenman et al., 1975) elaborated on Dunbar's concepts and coined the term "type-A personality," a personality that they felt predisposed an individual to coronary artery disease (Thompson, 1988). The type-A individual became the cultural stereotype of the chronically struggling, aggressive, driven, time-pressured, hostile, and cynical business executive who is a workaholic and cannot relax and enjoy life. Such individuals characteristically do not take good care of their health—that is, they smoke cigarettes and drink alcohol excessively, fail to watch their diet, avoid exercising, and so forth—and thus their development of coronary artery disease is often multiply determined.

RECENT PSYCHOANALYTIC STUDIES

The important role that the early psychological trauma of incest may play in setting the stage for psychosomatic phenomena has received renewed emphasis in recent years. Kramer (1990) has continued her long-term studies of consequences of incest by describing a condition known as "somatic memories," a psychosomatic phenomenon that is significantly underrecognized. The phenomenon involves a variety of physical sensations and disturbances in sexual functioning that may result as a residue of sexual abuse by a parent or some other person during early childhood, latency, or adolescence. For example, in cases of mother–child incest, the sexual abuse initially may take the form of mother's being too zealous and vigorous in the hygiene of her child's perineal area. The intense "cleansing" of this area may be overstimulating to the child and, occasionally, the mother may actually masturbate the child (Shengold, 1967). Fathers have traditionally not been as involved as mothers in the changing of diapers; with house husbands becoming more common and fathers in general playing a greater role in diapering and other caretaking activities of their children, however, such sexual abuse may become more common with fathers as well. Incest may occur in infancy before the child's reality-testing capabilities are established. However, reality-testing abilities are not the major issue in the traumatizing potential of incest. Pathologic doubting is not caused by inadequate reality-testing capability but, rather, by anxiety and defenses erected to cope with the incest or other sexual abuse.

The somatic memories of incest that emerge in adulthood often arise in association with some type of sexual activity. The person might find himself experiencing anxiety or discomfort anytime he becomes sexually excited or experiences any type of sexual activity, including masturbation. Some of these patients may, beyond developing increased sensitivity or aversion to sexual stimulation, develop totally blunted feelings, frigidity, impotence, and anorgasmy (Shengold, 1967). A wide range of other emotional reactions, including profound depression and feelings of anger and aggression, may also result as a "somatic" residue of being sexually traumatized early in life. For example, Katan (1973) noted that some of her incestuously abused patients had problems integrating sexual and aggressive drives. When these individuals were sexually excited, they became aggressive in response, either taking out the aggression on themselves in self-destructive behaviors or interacting destructively with others.

Problems with learning also may result from incest. School problems and learning disabilities may result from a mental block that has occurred owing to the child's need to keep incestuous thoughts, feelings, and memories out of consciousness. It may require such an inordinate amount of mental effort to keep such thoughts repressed that a person may not have the mental processes available to learn new information and to interact effectively with others.

Intensive psychotherapy or psychoanalysis is the treatment approach best able to uncover underlying incest-related trauma and meaningfully correct them. As is often the case with sexual or other forms of marked abuse, memories of the events may not be available initially. However, somatic memories of the trauma may be brought to the surface in the psychotherapy or analysis, often initially in a derivative or metaphoric form. At times, the actual memories and the associated fears and sensations may begin to emerge into consciousness. The analysis of somatic memories may lead to the recovery and reconstruction of incest or other physical or emotional trauma from earlier in life. In a similar manner, Brenner (1988), when studying Holocaust survivors, was sometimes able to bring to the surface during psychoanalysis certain physical sensations that later led to the recovery of some of the traumatic memories of that experience.

Kramer (1990) notes that it is rare for adults to totally fabricate a story of incest or other major trauma related to their childhood. In fact, individuals usually have a stronger need to repress, deny, or otherwise minimize severe psychic trauma. If for no other reason, it is very painful for a person to realize just how damaging and destructive a parent or other significant adult in his life was when he was a child; the intense anger and rage that is often associated with resurrecting such memories is dysphoric. Some fear that if they allow themselves to relive such feelings, they might develop homicidal rage or become psychotic. It may be easier psychologically, at least in the short run, for a person to try to rationalize such events as being fantasies, bad dreams, or distorted childhood memories.

Another psychoanalytic concept related to psychosomatic phenomena has been described by Joyce McDougall as intrapsychic "theater scripts." McDougall (1989) formulated the idea that scripts are written by each individual during childhood and that reruns of those scripts occur regularly in each person's adult mind, recreating scenarios relating to the scripts throughout life. These complex psychic scenarios may surface as psychosomatic conditions or alexithymia. Especially highly emotional and preverbal trauma may later be pantomimed or symbolized by the body through psychosomatic conditions, including the somatic memories described by Kramer (1990).

Focusing attention on the body to avoid dysphoric self-awareness is one of the earliest, most primitive psychological defenses (Kohut, 1971, 1977). When one's unconscious mental efforts fail to externalize a conflict, a compromise formation often expresses the conflict within one's own body. Prior to the development of language, infants must communicate with their mother and other caretakers through somatic channels. (The word *infant* is derived from the Latin term meaning "one who cannot speak.") Therefore, McDougall (1989) believes, a predisposition for later psychosomatic preoccupation begins in scripts learned during the preverbal period of interaction between the infant, and his mother or other major caretakers.

Language is a form of symbolic expression that is often used by older children and adults in attempts at conflict resolution. Such psychological uses of language may even occur to some degree in a person "talking to himself." However, there are times when a person may feel too overwhelmed to speak or may not be able to find the words to express his feelings. At such times, since the conflict cannot be brought to higher levels of mental operation for discharge via verbalization or mediation, the body may take the brunt of that conflict.

Most individuals communicate with others through their bodies; for example, nonverbal "body language" is a valuable source of clinical information. The facial expressions of happiness, surprise, anger, disgust, and so forth are universal. In addition, other gestures have become well-known expressions of specific feeling states, such as raising the hands in front of the face and then suddenly dropping them to one's lap, a gesture that is associated in virtually all cultures with feeling hopeless and helpless and with giving up.

RECENT PSYCHOPHYSIOLOGIC RESEARCH

The *Diagnostic and Statistical Manual of Mental Disorders* (third edition, revised), or DSM-III-R, the current official text of psychiatric diagnostic nomenclature, does not include the term *psychosomatic*. Rather, it includes a category of "psychological factors affecting physical conditions." The unfortunate aspect of this category is that it does not make clear the fact that the physical condition present may not have developed had psychological factors not triggered it. Instead, this category implies that the physical condition was present and that psychological factors separate from or in response to that physical condition further affected the physical condition. The possibility of psychological factors causing the initial development of the physical condition may be overlooked if this designation continues as the only diagnostic option.

Although specific personality constellations are not the primary cause of specific psychosomatic conditions, a number of emotional factors are associated with many psychosomatic symptoms. For example, the onset and exacerbations of peptic ulcer disease in older children and adolescents is often associated with a recent loss or separation experience (Ackerman, Manaker, and Cohen, 1981). And although a specific personality type has not been reliably correlated with essential hypertension, one of Alexander's classic psychosomatic conditions, individuals who have a habitually angry approach to life and chronically suppress anger have a significantly increased risk for developing essential hypertension (Gentry et al., 1982). There also is a greater tendency in families with a hypertensive member to avoid addressing and resolving psychological conflicts, in comparison with nonhypertensive families (Baer et al., 1983). If a family member has not separated and individuated, this is often a source of psychological conflict and of habitually angry interactive styles. In addition, members of societies that are undergoing major social shifts or individuals who are moving out of or away from their traditional social matrix are at increased risk for hypertension (Thompson, 1988). Sociocultural separation from an individual's traditional family and social support matrix may be particularly stressful for someone who has had intrapsychic separation–individuation difficulties.

Psychosomatic issues are relevant for respiratory disorders, which are closely tied, metaphorically and realistically, to life and death issues and which may be exacerbated by a number of emotional states (Thompson and Thompson, 1985). Respiratory tract events are tied to both ends of the life cycle: baby's first breath and cry are associated with the beginnings of independent physiologic life, and death is often spoken of in respiratory terms, as in someone "breathing his last" or "drawing his last breath" (Thompson, 1988). Therefore, respiration is initially linked to separation from the mother and then, with death, is tied to separation from those who continue to live and with whom one has been emotionally attached. Anxiety, including that due to separation or individuation issues, frequently leads to hyperventilation, which in turn may exacerbate breathing difficulties due to asthma, chronic obstructive pulmonary disease, or other respiratory disorders. In addition, hyperventilation may precipitate panic attacks in some individuals (Gorman et al., 1984).

Exciting recent research has focused on the effects of psychological states on immune functioning (Kiecolt-Glaser and Glaser, 1986). Owing to this important research on the effects of stress on the immune system, we know that object loss and separation experiences that cannot be mastered are physiologically meaningful. Specifically, stressful separations, losses, or other emotionally laden life events may significantly lower a person's natural killer (NK) cell activity, a critical factor in the immune response. The degree of loss, grief, bereavement, and depression also have been correlated with decreases in human lymphocyte activity (Schleifer et al., 1985). Adult macaque monkeys who experienced early traumatic separation from their mothers or from important peers have been found to develop a reduction in their lymphocyte B- and T-cells. In addition, it was found that if these monkeys were able to cope with this separation stress or to avoid it in some effective manner, their lymphocyte levels remained normal (Laudenslager, Capitanio, and Reite, 1985). Geriatric individuals who have supportive social systems and who have not experienced recent losses or separations have been found to maintain higher indices of normal immune function than elderly individuals who have had recent losses or separations or do not have a strong social network (Thomas, Goodwin, and Goodwin, 1985).

Emotional stress may lead to a "fight or flight" reaction, which leads to increased production of epinephrine and norepinephrine, which in turn may decrease immunity. Emotional stress has also been found to decrease the production of interferon, a lymphocyte-produced compound that increases resistance to some viral illnesses (Stein, Schleifer, and Keller, 1985). Allergic reactions are mediated, in part, by B- and T-cell lymphocyte functioning, which is often impaired by depression or stress. Therefore, stress may increase the susceptibility to allergic reactivity. Also, some autoimmune disorders, including Hashimoto's thyroiditis, systemic lupus erythematosus, rheumatoid arthritis, myasthenia gravis, and psoriasis, are related to B- and T-cell functioning. As was true for monkeys, separation and loss experiences in humans may interfere with functioning of the immune system; such experiences have been associated with the onset of both juvenile and adult forms of rheumatoid arthritis (Thompson, 1988), coronary crises (Fischer and Dlin, 1962), leukemia and lymphoma (Greene, 1966), and other somatic illnesses (Parens, McConville, and Kaplan, 1966). There is a substantial literature in this area, including contributions by Engel (1959, 1968) and by Engel and Schmale (1967).

Positive psychological and sociocultural factors may improve immune function and have other beneficial physiologic effects. Participating in a supportive social network may even prolong cancer survival. Spiegel and associates (1989) found that women with metastatic breast cancer who had regular, supportive group psychotherapy meetings with other women who had the same condition survived about twice as long as a matched control group of women with the same condition who did not have the group therapy experience.

To summarize this section, no specific psychological traits, defenses, or life events can be definitely linked in a linear cause-and-effect manner at this time to a specific psychosomatic disorder. However, any type of significant life stress may alter the immune system and physiologically stress the organism in other ways to precipitate a pathophysiologic disorder that otherwise would not have developed, or at least not as soon, without that psychological stress serving as a catalyst. Likewise, emotional stresses may cause exacerbations of numerous somatic conditions. Spiegel and associates (1989) also suggest that positive, supportive psychological experiences may delay the progression of some somatic disorders, including metastatic breast cancer. Interventions that alter type-A behavior patterns also may lessen cardiac risks (Hackett, Rosenbaum, and Cassem, 1985; Williams, 1985). However, although seemingly paradoxical, other recent research suggests that those with more type-A characteristics (not necessarily including hostility and cynicism) may have improved survival if they do have a heart attack. That is, what may add to the likelihood of having a myocardial infarction in the first place may make survival more likely once the infarction does occur (Thompson, 1988).

PSYCHOSOMATIC PHENOMENA AND LEVELS OF PSYCHIC DEVELOPMENT

Mahler and associates (1975) characterized the first few months following birth as involving symbiosis, leading later in normal development to a period of separation–individuation. If a mother is not able to be appropriately emotionally available to her baby during symbiosis, the baby, while able to attach, may become overvigilant and develop an ongoing state of stress. A poor symbiosis may result in a person's having a lower stress tolerance level and, therefore, a greater vulnerability to psychosomatic disorders in response to multiple stressors. If a mother is not able to protect her baby from overstimulation while also assuring that the infant is not understimulated, the child may not learn to adequately separate a representation of himself from that of the mothering figure; an archaic body representation may be one result of such failure of individuation (Shengold, 1967). Focusing of conflictual psychic energy on the soma may result, leading to later exaggerated concerns in response to somatic symptoms. Any significant emotional stress during the first three years of life may produce vulnerability to psychosomatic disorders. The separation from or loss of a loved or otherwise needed individual may precipitate psychosomatic disorders, and individuals who have had major difficulties with separation and individuation issues have an increased risk of developing psychosomatic disorders (Taylor, 1987). Engel (1959, 1968) and Engel and Schmale (1967) found that loss of an important object may lead to a feeling state of hopelessness and helplessness, which may precipitate somatic illness. The degree of success with which an individual earlier addressed separation–individuation issues might determine in part the stress associated with later losses. Therefore, if an individual has a biologic susceptibility to a somatic illness, a separation will often precipitate the onset or an exacerbation of that illness (Lipowski, Lipsitt, and Whybrow, 1977; Weiner, 1977; Kaplan, 1985; Taylor, 1987; and Thompson, 1988). Mahler and her collaborators, including Selma Kramer, demonstrated that optimal development in children includes the establishment of a stable sense of self and the capacity to develop stable object relations, that is, to reasonably negotiate the separation–individuation process (Mahler et al., 1975). Separation–individuation is an intrapsychic process that occurs within the child, not between the mother and child. However, if the mother tries to inhibit the child from separating from her emotionally, in the child's psyche they may continue to be merged at a preverbal stage of development. Such a merger may include an unconscious belief that the two never physically separated, and even when the child is physically grown, he may retain the unconscious belief that he and mother share one body; psychosomatic symptoms are often a preverbal form of dialogue between such a merged twosome. Thus, psychosomatic symptoms may sometimes represent a regression to or continuation of such a merged state.

Later, the healthily progressing child develops concrete transitional objects to symbolically carry mother's caring with him while he gradually becomes more emotionally separate and distant from her (Winnicott, 1951). When the child learns to speak and can utter his own name as well as "Mommy," he then has a verbal representation of the progressively experienced separateness of the two. He then may achieve a new psychological level of abstract symbolization, represented by being able to say "Mommy" and to evoke a reassuring image of her in his mind without having to have her physically or symbolically present. The rapprochement crisis, as described by Mahler, also produces an acute state of stress in children, especially if the mother is not adequately available during that period.

Taylor (1987) proposed another perspective on early mother–infant relationships that might predispose to psychosomatic disorders. He feels there are a number of regulatory processes that are learned or transmitted through this relationship if it functions appropriately. However, deficiencies in the early mother–child relationship may produce developmental defects in the child that reduce his capacity to self-regulate numerous physiologic processes in an appropriate manner; this reduction in self-regulatory capacity may predispose the child to later develop organic disorders if he has the biologic diathesis to do so. Therefore, psychosomatic symptoms sometimes may be due to an activation of inadequate self-regulation under nonspecific stress.

Other psychosomatic symptoms are a symbolic expression of specific object-directed fantasies derived from the preoedipal phase of development. For example, psychosomatic symptoms may serve to define the limits of a person's own body and unconsciously assure him that he is not at risk of psychologically merging with someone else, in particular, his mother (Kernberg, 1975). The intensity or style of affective interactions with an inadequate mother during infancy may lead to physical and emotional needs not being met and to the development of fears, including fear of abandonment or of being engulfed.

Additionally, sometimes even primarily, psychosomatic symptoms are a symbolic expression of oedipal phase fantasies (Fenichel, 1945). A psychosomatic illness may then be an attempt to punish or provoke guilt in the mother (or other caretaking figure) for her earlier overinvolvement, underinvolvement, or inappropriate behaviors vis-à-vis the child. Although the relationship with the mother or other early caretakers may have been traumatic, the patient may feel that the rest of the world may be worse, so that the illness assures ongoing contact and caretaking from a mother who at least was healthy enough to allow the child to survive long enough to face this dilemma and to suffer an illness (Kernberg, 1975, 1984). Such issues bring us to the unclear boundaries between psychosomatic phenomena, hysterical conversion symptoms, and quasi-deliberate involvement of the body in emotional states relating to addictions and bulimia (Schwartz, 1988).

Ideally, a child will be taught by his mother and father that diverse emotional responses are normal and appropriate and that, in fact, being able to accurately perceive and express one's emotions through appropriate channels is adaptive and a sign of emotional health. However, it is possible for a child to grow up to become alexithymic (Nemiah and Sifneos, 1970; Sifneos, 1975; Nemiah, 1978; McDougall, 1982), in part because his parents will only tolerate the expression of a very constricted range of emotional reactions. The child does not learn how to tolerate rage or other strong emotional reactions. The parents in such situations may be emotionally illiterate, that is, unable to determine major emotional responses accurately within themselves and therefore unable to transmit to their children the skill of accurately perceiving various emotions in themselves and others. However, the parents' actions alone are insufficient to produce alexithymia in a child.

The child contributes to the development of alexithymia, perhaps by a constitutionally determined preference of psychological defense. If a child is punished for expressing an emotional reaction (whether it be warmth, caring, disgust, anger, etc.), then he will learn that emotional awareness is dangerous. Within such families stoicism may become idealized (Nemiah and Sifneos, 1970; Sifneos, 1975; Nemiah, 1978; and McDougall, 1982).

Another misconception in emotionally impoverished families is that emotions are a sign of mental illness. In families that teach such misinformation a child may come to fear that if he experiences any emotion too intensely, he may lose emotional control and become suicidal, homicidal, or psychotic. These children learn to fear that if they allow themselves to feel even a mild degree of appropriate annoyance, an unstoppable cascade may be catalyzed (Kernberg, 1975; Sifneos, 1975). When questioned about why they feel that emotional sensitivity and awareness is so dangerous, they may offer media reports of a quiet, passive, and seemingly nice person becoming a mass murderer. An individual may also believe emotions may be dangerous by precipitating fatal physical disorders. Again, stories may be offered of someone who died of a myocardial infarction or cerebrovascular accident shortly after getting upset emotionally. A sense of rejection, emotional distance, and disconnectedness may come to be considered as the norm of existence by individuals in such families (Kernberg, 1984).

Psychosomatic symptoms may sometimes come to serve a transitional object (Winnicott, 1951) function. In this situation, psychosomatic symptoms may provide a transitional object type of relatedness to incompletely renunciated primary objects. That is, the symptom allows the patient to symbolically maintain an attachment to a loving, caring mothering figure. The transitional object level of psychosomatic symptom may be able to be set aside periodically and to varying degrees, depending on the person's emotional needs for attachment. That is, like the teddy bear or security blanket that is clung to at night and at times of anxiety, including separation from mother, psychosomatic symptoms that serve as transitional objects may be called upon when needed and ignored the rest of the time.

A psychosomatic symptom also may protect patients from feeling as though they might act on frightening affects or impulses. For example, if a person is convinced he is ill, he may feel unable to carry out murderous or sexual impulses. A person who feels weak and disabled by his symptoms may convey that he need not be feared by others or that they need not fear that he might leave them. Complementary feelings—that is, that an ill person should be cared for by others and should not be hurt or ignored, and that only a heartless or selfish individual would abandon an ill person— may be evoked in potential caregivers by such symptoms. Creation of such emotional constellations is useful in minimizing the risks that may be felt to be associated with expressions of hostility, including the caretaker's retaliatory anger.

However, if the ill individual does periodically erupt into anger, the illness provides a socially acceptable means of explaining away the anger (e.g., "He deserves to be angry occasionally, because life has dealt him such an unfortunate blow to be so disabled"). That is, assuming the "sick role" assures or at least greatly increases the likelihood of safety and caring from others in the environment. The ill person may feel justifiably relieved from responsibilities other adults would be expected to assume. Simultaneously, the caretaker may feel increased self-esteem for caring for a seemingly poor, unfortunate, ill victim of a cruel fate and may also be relieved of other responsibilities by assuming the caretaker role in our society.

The aforementioned types of attachments through psychosomatic symptoms to mother or other caretakers will typically be repeated in aspects of the transference during the analysis of these patients (Fenichel, 1945). For example, the patient may become frightened to relinquish physical or mental symptoms during the analysis, fearing that this will lead the analyst to prematurely terminate the analytic relationship.

At a more primitive level, some psychosomatic patients may be reassured, through their ability to develop and maintain psychosomatic symptoms, that they are emotionally sensitive and reactive to others and to their environment and even that they exist and are alive (Kernberg, 1984).

They may feel that their exquisite sensitivity and reactivity is preferable, and the only alternative that they have, to feeling callous and inert (McDougall, 1989). For these patients, psychosomatic symptoms may be due to a defensive heightening of a vulnerable self-cathexis.

The loss of psychosomatic symptoms during analysis may also evoke a strong grief and mourning reaction. If patients have come to view themselves as chronically ill, symptomatic, and disabled, they are losing a major aspect of their previous self-image and the basis of many key relationships in their lives as they begin to understand and leave behind the emotional needs for such symptoms. A core of some patients' sense of being is their suffering self—a powerful masochistic image but nevertheless the self-concept around which they have organized their major relationships and life experiences (Kohut, 1971, 1977). For these reasons, Taylor (1987) feels that the use of self psychology psychoanalytic techniques is often more effective than only using classic analytic techniques with psychosomatic patients.

Even toward the end of an analysis patients may continue to somatically discharge some of their affective experiences. If they are no longer acting out outside the analytic situation, they may attempt to find a new neurotic solution to their conflicts by developing psychosomatic symptoms (even if they did not have them prior to their analysis), which is a self-punishing form of acting out (Limentani, 1966).

PSYCHOANALYTIC TREATMENT OF PSYCHOSOMATIC PHENOMENA

Recently intensified biases against psychoanalysis have diminished public and even professional opinion of its appropriateness as a therapy for a number of psychosomatic conditions. No rigorous double-blind studies, popular in comparing two drugs, for example, can ever be applied to psychoanalysis. However, numerous cases have been reported of patients with psychosomatic conditions who greatly benefited from analysis. Also, many analysands, without a psychosomatic disorder per se, report a lessening of somatizing and hypochondriacal symptoms.

Psychosomatic phenomena have become a major interest of a number of analysts, and some consult and practice in medical inpatient or outpatient clinic settings. In France analysts with these interests are called "psychosomaticiens" (Oliner, 1988). In the United States a number of analysts also have interests in consultation liaison psychiatry and regularly consult with other medical specialists concerning psychosomatic and other psychiatric disorders in their patients (Thompson, Scully, and Thompson, 1985). For the analyst, there is often a steady supply of patient consultations and referrals from specialists who fail in their efforts to manage patients with multiple somatic and hypochondriacal complaints. When we provide appropriate professional feedback, those referring physicians may begin to appreciate the benefits of psychoanalytic treatment for these patients.

Some analysts, however, fear that rigorous psychoanalytic treatment may cause acute, dangerous exacerbations of a patient's psychosomatic condition. In fact, most psychosomatic patients who have the psychological attributes that make analysis possible are able to proceed with a careful analysis without developing more exacerbations of their condition than they had during a similar time interval before the analysis. An effective analysis might lessen the psychic stresses in the individual to a degree that would diminish the number and degree of severity of exacerbations that are later triggered by emotional factors (Mumford et al., 1984).

Individuals may develop a great variety of somatic symptoms in response to seemingly similar psychological conflict constellations and life histories. For example, patients who are conflicted about sexual impulses may develop anxieties, depression, compulsive rituals, phobias, or a wide range of psychosomatic conditions (e.g., asthma attacks, colitis symptoms) in response to or as a compromise formation to deal with these conflicts. It is often unclear, even after psychoanalytic exploration, why an individual developed symptomatic expression in one specific area and someone else developed symptoms in a different organ system. The disorder or psychic symptom that appears probably has more to do with the individual's physiologic and psychologic vulnerabilities (Reiser, 1975); each individual has a hierarchy of vulnerabilities in both dimensions, and the order of appearance of symptoms relates to that hierarchy.

CONCLUDING REMARKS

In recent years biological psychiatry and the use of psychotropic agents have taken center stage in many psychiatric arenas. An unfortunate accompaniment of this rapid development of biological knowledge has been a failure to fully recognize the importance of intrapsychic factors in physical disorders. To be sure, constitutional vulnerabilities underlie practically all forms of psychopathology. It is, perhaps, also true that judicious use of medications may at times facilitate the analytic treatment of psychosomatic or other types of patients. However, all this should not tempt us conceptually into Cartesian dualism. Biological and psychological realms cannot be separated in human beings (von Bertalanffy, 1968). Biological, psychological, and sociocultural factors—including family interactions and ethnic and religious factors—constantly interact with each other to create the mental and physical state of individuals (Engel, 1977). This chapter, though emphasizing the intrapsychic factors, has been written in the spirit of such a biopsychosocial model.

REFERENCES

Ackerman, S. H., Manaker, S. & Cohen, M. I. (1981), Recent separation and the onset of peptic ulcer disease in older children and adolescents. *Psychosom. Med.*, 43:305–310.

Alexander, F. (1950), *Psychosomatic Medicine*. New York: Norton, 1987.

———, French, T. M. & Pollock, G. H., ed. (1968), *Psychosomatic Specificity*. Chicago: University of Chicago Press.

Baer, P. E., Reed, J., Bartlett, P. C., Vincent, J. P., Williams, B. J. & Bourianoff, G. G. (1983), Studies of gaze during induced conflict in families with a hypertensive father. *Psychosom. Med.*, 45:233–242.

Brenner, I. (1988), Multisensory bridges in response to object loss during the Holocaust. *Psychol. Rev.*, 75:573–587.

Dunbar, F. (1954), *Emotions and Bodily Changes* (4th ed.). New York: Columbia University Press.

Elyot, T. (1539), Of affects of the mind. In: *Three Hundred Years of Psychiatry: 1535–1860*, ed. R. Hunter & I. Malcalpine. New York: Oxford University Press, 1963, pp. 7–9.

Engel, G. L. (1959), "Psychogenic pain" and the pain-prone patient. *Am. J. Med.*, 26:899–907.

Engel, G. L. (1968), A life setting conducive to illness: The giving-up–given-up complex. *Ann. Intern. Med.*, 69:293–311.

Engel, G. L. (1977), The need for a new medical model: A challenge for biomedicine. *Science*, 196:129–136.

Engel, G. L. & Schmale, A. H. (1967), Psychoanalytic theory of somatic disorder: Conversion, specifically, and the disease onset situation. *J. Amer. Psychoanal. Assn.*, 15:344–361.

Fenichel, O. (1945), *The Psychoanalytic Theory of Neurosis*. New York: Norton.

Fischer, H. K. & Dlin, B. M. (1962), Time patterns and emotional factors related to the onset of coronary occlusion. *Psychosom. Med.*, 24:516–528.

Freud, S. (1895), Project for a scientific psychology. *Standard Edition*, 1:295–397. London: Hogarth Press, 1966.

——— (1905), Fragment of an analysis of a case of hysteria. *Standard Edition*, 7:7–122. London: Hogarth Press, 1953.

Gentry, W. D., Chesney, A. P., Gary, H. E., Jr., Hall, R. P. & Harburg, E. (1982), Habitual anger-coping styles: 1. Effects on mean blood pressure and risk of essential hypertension. *Psychosom. Med.*, 44:195–202.

Gorman, J. M., Askanazi, J., Liebowitz, M. R., Fyer, A. J., Stein, J., Kinney, J. M. & Klein, D. F. (1984), Response to hyperventilation in a group of patients with panic disorder. *Amer. J. Psychiat.*, 141:857–861.

Greene, W. A. (1966), The psychosocial setting of the development of leukemia and lymphoma. *Ann. NY Acad. Sci.*, 125:794–804.

Hackett, T. P., Rosenbaum, J. F. & Cassem, N. H. (1985), Cardiovascular disorders. In: *Comprehensive Textbook of Psychiatry* (4th ed.), ed. H. I. Kaplan & B. J. Sadock. Baltimore: Williams & Wilkins, pp. 1148–1159.

Kaplan, H. I. (1985), History of psychosomatic medicine. In: *Comprehensive Textbook of Psychiatry* (4th ed.), H. I. Kaplan & B. J. Sadock. Baltimore: Williams & Wilkins, pp. 1106–1113.

Katan, A. (1973), Children who were raped. *The Psychoanalytic Study of the Child,* 28:208–224. New Haven, CT: Yale University Press.

Kernberg, O. (1975), *Borderline Conditions and Pathological Narcissism.* New York: Aronson.

────── (1984), *Severe Personality Disorders.* New Haven, CT: Yale University Press.

Kiecolt-Glaser, J. K. & Glaser, R. (1986), Psychological influences on immunity. *Psychosomatics,* 27:621–624.

Kohut, H. (1971), *The Analysis of the Self.* New York: International Universities Press.

────── (1977), *The Restoration of the Self.* New York: International Universities Press.

Kramer, S. (1990), Residues of Incest. In: *Adult Analysis and Childhood Sexual Abuse,* ed. H. B. Levine. Hillsdale, NJ: The Analytic Press, pp. 149–170.

Laudenslager, M., Capitanio, J. P. & Reite, M. (1985), Possible effects of early separation experiences on subsequent immune function in adult macaque monkeys. *Amer. J. Psychiat.*, 142:862–864.

Limentani, A. (1966), A re-evaluation of acting out in relation to working through. *Internat. J. Psycho-Anal.*, 47:274–282.

Lipowski, Z. J., Lipsitt, D. R. & Whybrow, P. C. (1977), *Psychosomatic Medicine: Current Trends and Clinical Applications.* New York: Oxford University Press.

Mahler, M., Bergman, A. & Pine, F. (1975), *The Psychological Birth of the Human Infant.* New York: Basic Books.

McDougall, J. (1982), Alexithymia: A psychoanalytic viewpoint. *Psychother. Psychosom.*, 38:81 90.

────── (1989), *Theatres of the Body: A Psychoanalytic Approach to Psychosomatic Illness.* New York: Norton.

Mumford, E., Schlesinger, H. J., Glass, G. V., Patrick, C. & Cuerdon, T. (1984), A new look at evidence about reduced cost of medical utilization following mental health treatment. *Amer. J. Psychiat.*, 141:1145–1152.

Nemiah, J. (1978), Alexithymia and psychosomatic illness. *J. Continuing Educ. in Psychiat.*, 39:25–37.

────── & Sifneos, P. (1970), *Modern Trends in Psychosomatic Medicine, Vol. 2.* London: Butterworth.

Oliner, M. M. (1988), *Cultivating Freud's Garden in France.* Northvale, NJ: Aronson.

Parens, H., McConville, B. J. & Kaplan, S. M. (1966), The prediction of frequency of illness from the response to separation: A preliminary study and replication attempt. *Psychosom. Med.*, 28:162–176.

Reiser, M. F. (1975), Changing theoretical concepts in psychosomatic medicine. In: *American Handbook of Psychiatry, Vol. 4* (2nd ed.), ed. M. F. Reiser. New York: Basic Books, pp. 477–500.

Rosenman, R. H., Brand, R. J., Jenkins, C. D., Friedman, M., Straus, R. & Wurm, M. (1975), Coronary heart disease in the Western Collaborative Group Study: Final follow-up experience of eight and a half years. *J. Amer. Med. Assn.*, 233:872–877.

Schleifer, S. J., Keller, S. E., Siris, S. G. & Stein, M. (1985), Depression and immunity. *Arch. Gen. Psychiat.*, 42:129–133.

Schwartz, H. J., ed. (1988), *Bulimia: Psychoanalytic Treatment and Theory*. Madison, CT: International Universities Press.

Shengold, L. (1967), The effects of overstimulation: Rat people. *Internat. J. Psycho-Anal.*, 48:403–415.

Sifneos, P. E. (1975), Problems of psychotherapy of patients with alexithymic characteristics and physical disease. *Psychother. Psychosom.*, 26(2):65–70.

Spiegel, D., Kraemer, H. C., Bloom, J. R. & Gottheil, E. (1989), Effect of psychosocial treatment on survival of patients with metastatic breast cancer. *Lancet*, ii:888–891.

Stein, M., Schleifer, S. J. & Keller, S. E. (1985), Immune disorders. In: *Comprehensive Textbook of Psychiatry*, (4th ed.), ed. H. I. Kaplan & B. J. Sadock. Baltimore: Williams & Wilkins, pp. 1206–1212.

Taylor, G. J. (1987), *Psychosomatic Medicine and Contemporary Psychoanalysis*. Madison, CT: International Universities Press.

Thomas, P. D., Goodwin, J. M. & Goodwin, J. S. (1985), Effect of social support on stress-related changes in cholesterol level, uric acid level, and immune function in an elderly sample. *Amer. J. Psychiat.*, 142:735–737.

Thompson, T. L. II. (1988), Psychosomatic disorders. In: *Textbook of Psychiatry*, ed. J. A. Talbott, R. E. Hales, & S. C. Yudofsky. Washington, DC: American Psychiatric Press, pp. 493–532.

————, Scully, J. H. & Thompson, W. L. (1985), The "difficult" medical patient and the importance of consultation-liaison psychiatry. In: *Understanding Human Behavior in Health and Illness* (3rd ed.), ed. R. C. Simons. Baltimore: Williams & Wilkins, pp. 113–120.

Thompson, W. L. & Thompson, T. L. II, eds. (1985), *Psychiatric Aspects of Chronic Pulmonary Disease: Advances in Psychosomatic Medicine*. Basel, Switzerland: Karger.

von Bertalanffy, L. (1968), *General System Theory*. New York: Braziller.

Weiner, H. (1977), *Psychobiology and Human Disease*. New York: Elsevier.

Williams, R. B., Jr. (1985), Biobehavioral factors in cardiovascular disease. In: *Psychiatry, Vol. 2*, section ed. J. L. Houpt; eds. R. Michels, J. O. Cavenar, Jr., Philadelphia: Lippincott, pp. 1–9.

Winnicott, D. (1951), Transitional objects and transitional phenomena. In: *Collected Papers*. New York: Basic Books, pp. 229–242.

13

Three Fantasies Related to Unresolved Separation–Individuation
A Less Recognized Aspect of Severe Character Pathology

Salman Akhtar

Narcissistic, borderline, antisocial, paranoid, hypomanic (Akhtar, 1988), schizoid, and "as-if" (Deutsch, 1942) personality disorders represent various types of severe character pathology. Although they differ in surface presentations and, to a certain extent, in developmental backgrounds and psychostructural characteristics, all these personality disorders imply a "lower level" (Kernberg, 1970) character organization. Descriptively, such individuals exhibit chronic restlessness, unstable emotions, vacillating relationships, unrealistic goals, excessive self-absorption, defective empathy, egocentric perception of reality, impaired capacity for mourning, inability to love, sexual difficulties, and moral defects of varying degrees. Dynamically, splitting or active dissociation of mutually contradictory self and object representations is a major defensive operation in these conditions. This is accompanied by the subsidiary mechanisms of denial, primitive idealization, and projective identification. Psychostructurally, at this level of character organization there is a restriction of the conflict-free ego, poor superego internalization and integration, blurring of the ego–superego delimitation, and, most importantly, the lack of an integrated self-concept, resulting in the syndrome of identity diffusion (Erikson, 1959; Kernberg, 1967, 1980; Akhtar, 1984a).

These phenomenological, dynamic, and psychostructural similarities in various severe character disorders are partly due to the fact that unresolved separation–individuation (alongside the subsequent distortions of the Oedipus complex) underlies all of them. Now, although Mahler had declared early on that normal separation–individuation is the "first crucial prerequisite" (Mahler, 1963, p.5) for the development of personal identity and had correlated the tendency toward intense ambivalence, splitting, turning aggression against the self, and depressive mood swings with inadequate maternal availability during the rapprochement subphase (Mahler, 1966), it was not until 1971 that she specifically linked failures in separation–individuation with severe character pathology in adult life. Mahler observed that symptoms of severe character pathology resemble the object coercion, the splitting of the object world, and the rapidly alternating clinging and withdrawal of a toddler in a severe rapprochement crisis. Combining her child observation data with reconstructions from the analysis of a borderline adult, Mahler concluded that such a character constellation indicates

> that the blending and synthesis of "good" and "bad" self and object images has not been achieved; that ego-filtered affects have become inundated by surplus unneutralized aggression; that delusions of omnipotence alternate with utter dependency and self denigration; that the body image has become or remains suffused with unneutralized id-related erogenity and aggressive, pent-up body feelings and so on [Mahler, 1971, p. 181].

Of paramount importance in the genesis of such pathology was a failure to integrate the image of the "good" symbiotic mother with the representations of the potentially reengulfing, dangerous "mother of separation." Mahler acknowledged that the fate of such developmental failure during the rapprochement subphase was determined by

> (i) the development towards libidinal object constancy; (2) the quantity and quality of later disappointments (stress traumata); (3) possible shock traumata; (4) the degree of castration anxiety; (5) the fate of the Oedipus complex; (6) the developmental crisis of adolescence—all of which function within the context of the individual's constitutional endowment [Mahler, 1971, p. 179].

However, a persistent difficulty in separation–individuation does lead to severe character pathology. The latter manifests in a tendency toward unstable mood, impaired capacity for ambivalence, intense oscillations of self-esteem, poorly integrated identity, difficulty in maintaining optimal distance in relationships, and a lifelong yearning for the symbiotic mother and the "coenesthetically remembered harmony of the dual-unity stage" (Mahler, 1971, p. 186).

Over the two decades following this pioneering paper, the relationship between separation–individuation and severe character pathology was further elaborated by Mahler and her colleagues. While not attempting a comprehensive survey of this literature, I would like to mention some of its outstanding contributions: (1) Blum's (1981) concept of "inconstant object," an object that is tenaciously maintained as being untrustworthy by the paranoid person while constant fear of betrayal itself acts as the reciprocal of libidinal object constancy; (2) Burland's (1975) convincing and eloquent reconstructions in analyses of individuals striving to recapture the shared symbiotic omnipotence with their mothers; also significant is his (1986) description of the "autistic character disorder," a multifaceted developmental arrest resulting from the infant's failure to establish a libidinal object and experience a gratifying symbiotic phase due to early, severe, and sustained deprivation of maternal care, with the resulting character pathology manifested in affectionlessness, cognitive lag, fragmented identity, pathologic narcissism, and much destructive aggression; (3) Greenspan's (1977) delineation of various "areas of personality functioning" (p. 385) that need to be assessed in order to distinguish whether the character organization is predominantly oedipal or preoedipal; (4) Kaplan's (1980) reminder that adult borderline pathology is the product of both the transformations of the infantile biopsychological organizations and the organizational impact of adolescence and adulthood; (5) Kernberg's (1980) correlation of his object relations conceptualization of severe character pathology with Mahler's separation–individuation theory; (6) Kramer's (1980) exposition of continued splitting of self and object representation in adolescence; splitting of the self representation may have a protective function toward the self, yet it exerts a noxious effect upon self-esteem, identity, consolidation of ego-ideal, and overall character formation; (7) Lax's (1980) observation that turning of aggression against the self is based on an identification not only with the aggressive but also with the self-destructive elements in the aggressor (mother) and that such development often leads to a feeling that one has a "rotten core" (p. 447); (8) Parens's (1979a) observations on the origins of hostile destructiveness and a negatively valanced affective core in infants and children; his description (1979b) of two basic conflicts of ambivalence, one involving the progressive emergence of love and hate toward the libidinal object of the preoedipal period and the other involving the triadic situation of the Oedipus complex; and his (1980) exposition of the essential complementarity between the classical psychosexual theory and Mahler's separation–individuation theory; (9) Pine's (1979) distinction of two levels of psychopathology related to separation–individuation—a higher level pathology where the disturbance is linked to the process of differentiation itself and a lower level pathology that involves undifferentiated self and objects; (10) Ray's (1986) and Rinsley's (1986) outlining of various phenomenological outcomes of deficient "object permanency" (Piaget, 1936) and object constancy; and finally, (11) Settlage's (1977) hypotheses about the differences in the development of borderline and narcissistic personalities, and his correlation of rapprochement subphase phenomena with psychological formations characteristic of narcissistic personality disorder.

These contributions have profoundly enriched our capacity to understand and help patients with severe character pathology. However, there is one area that, though inherent in many of these works, does not appear to have been directly addressed by them. This involves certain specific fantasies related to unresolved separation–individuation. While this is not the place to summarize the arguments over the timing of when fantasy begins (see Hayman, 1989, for an excellent review), the fact that Freud (1926) included loss of love object as a danger perceived by the early ego suggests that he regarded a preoedipal child quite capable of fantasy. Without the capacity to imagine a situation of not actually having the love object, how could the danger from its loss be experienced? Since fantasy implies imagining a condition different from one at hand, the requirement that seems necessary is the capacity for evocative memory, which is established by age 18 months or so (Piaget, 1936). In light of this, it seems reasonable to assume that there might exist fantasies that, at least at their core, reflect wishes activated by the anxieties consequent upon insufficiently progressed separation–individuation.

SOME CAVEATS

First, and foremost, the fantasies I am about to describe should not be taken as literally representing the ideational events of the first two years of life. While vague, wordless thoughts and feelings of this period do form the building blocks of these fantasies, their specific content, requiring greater cognitive maturity, seems derived from later childhood. In a fashion analogous to writing a song on a preexisting tune, the experiences and images of later childhood give form to the nebulous notions of the preverbal period (e.g., Isakower, 1936; Spitz, 1965; Frank, 1969; Burland, 1975; Parens, 1979a, in press). Freud's designation of fantasies involving intrauterine life as "retrospective phantasying" (Freud, 1918, p. 103) is an apt reminder here.

Second, the manner in which these fantasies are communicated (by the patient) and deciphered (by the analyst) makes certainty about them difficult. Pertaining largely to preverbal experiences, these fantasies are hardly ever satisfactorily put into words. Patients often resort to allusions, metaphors, and visual images while the analyst finds himself relying on his own affective experience to a greater than usual extent (Burland, 1975). The ground is murky and all the risks attendant upon excessive reliance on empathy (Wallerstein, 1983; Akhtar, 1984b, 1989a)—including, of course, countertransference intrusions—loom large in such an interpretive undertaking.

Third, while these fantasies seem mostly related to unresolved separation–individuation, in accordance with the principle of multiple function (Waelder, 1930) they also contain drive-defense type conflicts from various psychosexual levels, including the phallic-oedipal phase. Insofar as they portray struggles over regaining infantile omnipotence, establishing optimal distance, coercion of the other, achieving authenticity, even regressive longings for merger and undifferentiation, the contextual ground is well suited for the expression of conflicts involving oral greed and incorporation, anal retentiveness and angry expulsion, and the breaking of the incest barrier in both positive and negative oedipal scenarios. The fantasies described here, therefore, must not be taken as related solely to separation–individuation, although in their technical handling this genetic determinant may take precedence over others, especially during earlier phases of analysis. Caution should also be exercised in assigning diagnostic significance to such fantasies. While their association with severe character pathology forms the focus here, the fact remains that these fantasies might exist in less disturbed, even normal, individuals. Longings implicit in these fantasies usually occur as a result of unresolved separation–individuation, but such longings may also be mobilized by developmentally later conflicts.

Finally, it should be kept in mind that, like any other material, these fantasies can be employed en bloc as defensive structures against the emergence of "newer," less familiar anxieties in the transference. Analytic attention is, therefore, to be directed at one time to the intrinsic nature and purposes of these fantasies and their various components, and at another time to their overall resistance leverage. Yet another matter to be considered is the potentially idiosyncratic relevance the specific content of these fantasies may have for a given patient. Such open-mindedness would facilitate discovery and enrich reconstructions in this area.

Having outlined some limitations and conceptual pitfalls in this realm,

let me proceed to describing three fantasies related to unresolved separation–individuation: (1) "someday . . ." and "if only . . ." fantasies, (2)
the fantasy of a tether, and (3) the fantasy of a long embrace.

"SOMEDAY . . ." AND "IF ONLY . . ." FANTASIES

Some people are dominated by the belief that there will always be some kind
person—a representative of the mother, of course—to care for them and to
give them everything they need. This optimistic belief condemns them to
inactivity [Abraham, 1924, p. 399].

Only by remaining a hope does hope persist [Bion, 1961, pp. 151–152].

If now the analyst fails to 'click in,' that is, to respond as the patient expects
him to do . . . this is simply accepted as a painful fact and it is most surprising
how little anger, still less a willingness to fight, is mobilized by it. It is still
more surprising that a feeling of hopelessness hardly ever develops. . . .
Though feelings of emptiness and deadness . . . may be very strong, behind
them there is usually an earnest, quiet determination to see things through.
This queer mixture of profound suffering, absence of cheap pugnacity, and an
unshakable determination to get on makes these patients truly appealing—an
important diagnostic sign that the work has reached the level of the basic fault
[Balint, 1968, pp. 19–20].

The first among such fantasies is the one pertaining to "someday." Like
Balint, who was led to choose the term *basic fault* because that was "exactly
the word used by many patients to describe it" (p. 21), I too am guided
by my patients and have called this fantasy "someday." This is precisely
how these individuals refer to a certain kind of expectation from themselves, from their analyses, from life in general. They undertake analysis (or
psychotherapy) with gusto, religiously keep their appointments, arrive
punctually, pay their bills promptly, and, from all outer appearances, seem
good patients. Most of them talk copiously, offering well-thought-out
formulations regarding their maladies. They earnestly express the hope of
"someday" overcoming this or that inhibition, "someday" resolving this
or that symptom, and "someday" achieving this or that life goal. They
often stir up much redemptive enthusiasm and optimism in the analyst as
well, especially during the opening phases of the analysis. Gradually,
however, some mutual disappointment sets in. A different picture now
begins to emerge that challenges the assumed industriousness on the
patient's part. They seem to be taking on too much, putting things off,

never finishing anything. Whenever they run into difficulties, "road-blocks," "situations of conflict," or "too much hassle," they withdraw. This withdrawal gives a superficial appearance of their being flexible and realistic. In actuality the case is just the opposite, since their withdrawal is not caused by their accepting realistic difficulties and the resultant mourning but is intended to negate the impact of such limits on their wishes and their vision. It is a behavioral counterpart of denial. After a brief lull in their optimistic pursuit of "someday," they begin all over again. They do not truly look for alternatives for anything since they never accept defeat in the first place. They overlook discordant aspects of reality, cut perceptual and ethical corners, and perpetually "shelve things away." Their secret hope is that "someday" all problems would vanish or they would be strong enough to deal with them. Their unrealistic optimism[1] appears to caricature the "confident expectation" (Benedek, 1938) or "basic trust" (Erikson, 1950) that results from a satisfactory infant–mother relationship.

Patients vary greatly in the extent to which they provide details of their hopes for this "someday." Indeed, many patients feel puzzled, uncomfortable, ashamed, anxious, and even angry upon being asked to elaborate on their "someday." This is especially so if they are asked what would happen *after* "someday." It is as if "someday," like God, is not to be questioned at all. Some patients use metaphors and/or visual images to convey the essence of "someday," while others remain largely silent about it. Frequently, the analyst has to fill in the blanks and surmise the nature of their expectations from "someday." In either case, it is the affective

---

[1]Psychoanalytic literature has traditionally viewed optimism, even when excessive, in relatively positive terms. Benedek's (1938) and Erikson's (1950) normatively inclined concepts were preceded by Freud's (1917) well-known correlation of "confidence in success" with being mother's "undisputed darling" and by Abraham's (1924) linking "imperturbable optimism" with an overly gratifying oral phase. In an exception to such thinking Angel (1934) noted that excessive optimism is often a defensive development. She described three female patients with chronic, unrealistic optimism and hopes of a magical event (*wunderglauben*) to improve their lots. Angel traced the origin of these patients' undue hopefulness to a tenacious denial of their lacking a penis. Their optimism defended against intense penis envy and associated feelings of inferiority. Angel, however, offered a different explanation for undue optimism in men. They had been prematurely and painfully deprived of their infantile omnipotence and were seeking its restoration by a fantasied regressive oneness with their mothers. Their optimism contained the hope of such longings being realized. I have found this latter dynamic to be operative in female patients as well. (I am thankful to Dr. Cordula Holzer for translating this paper from German for me).

texture associated with "someday" that seems its most important feature.[2] Basically, "someday" refers to a time when one would be completely peaceful and totally conflict-free. Everything would be available, or nothing would be needed. Motor activity would either be unnecessary or totally effortless. Even thinking would not be required. There would be no aggression from within or from outside. Needless to say, such a universe is also oblivious to the inconvenient considerations of the incest taboo and the anxieties and compromises consequent upon the oedipal situation.

A complex set of psychodynamic mechanisms helps maintain the structural integrity of "someday." These include (1) a tenacious denial and negation of sectors of reality that challenge it, (2) splitting off of those self and object representations that mobilize conflict and aggression, (3) a temporal displacement from past to future of a preoedipal, preverbal state of unity with the "all good" mother of the symbiotic phase (Mahler, 1972; Mahler, Pine, and Bergman, 1975), and (4) a defensively motivated feeling of inauthenticity (Gedimen, 1986) in those areas of personality where a healthier, more realistic, compromise formation level of mentality and functioning has indeed been achieved. The speculation that this fantasy alludes to a profound longing for the luxurious symbiotic phase gains strength from these patients' descriptions of relative inactivity, timelessness, wordlessness, thoughtlessness, unexcited bliss, and the absence of conflict and of all needs in this "someday." This genetic backdrop is confirmed by the observation that individuals who tenaciously clung to the wish for "someday" had invariably been suddenly "dropped" from maternal attention during their second year of life (at times due to major external events, e.g., birth of a sibling, prolonged maternal hospitalization). Topographically speaking, only the focal and externalized derivatives of "someday" are usually consciously held. The infantile fused self and object representations powerfully invested with "primitive idealization" (Kernberg, 1967) emerge only after considerable analytic work has been accomplished. The adaptive functions of the "someday" fantasy involve its fostering optimism, perseverance, even sublimation. Built as a defensive structure against the affective turmoil consequent upon less than "optimal emotional availability" (Mahler, 1971, p. 176) of the mother during the

---

[2]The meagreness of free-associative data and verbalized fantasy in such cases is partly responsible for my resorting to a composite sketch of such individuals rather than a specific case illustration in this section. Burland (1975), in describing an analysand "struggling to recapture preseparation, symbiotic bond with his mother," was also struck by the fact that "the 'raw material' pointing to interruptions early in ego development tends to be affectual rather than verbal or intellectual" (pp. 312, 317).

rapprochement subphase of separation–individuation, the idealized "someday" helps to avert more pervasive splintering of the mind, depression, and suicidal tendencies.

It should be noted that patients vary on the behavioral level in the manner in which they strive to reach this "someday." Those with a narcissistic personality (Akhtar, 1989b) actively seek to bring this "someday" to life by devoting themselves to hard work and social success. Those with an antisocial bent seek similar magic through swindling, gambling, and other get-rich-quick schemes. Paranoid individuals (Akhtar, 1990) focus on the obstacles in their path to "someday." Borderline individuals frantically look for this "someday" through intense infatuations, perverse sexuality, and the use of mind-altering drugs. Schizoid individuals (Akhtar, 1987), in contrast, adopt a passive stance in which they are constantly waiting for a magical happening, a windfall, a chance encounter with a charismatic guru, or a sexual explosion of idiosyncratic transcendental connotations. All individuals with a severe personality disorder—be it narcissistic, antisocial, paranoid, borderline, or schizoid—seem to be seeking a restitution of an inner homeostasis that was disturbed years ago. All are in chronic pursuit. To borrow terms from Settlage and colleagues (in press) in a different context, it seems that all are in the appeal phase of the infantile "appeal cycle" (adaptation-distress-appeal-interaction); only the manner of their appeals varies. Perhaps these stylistic differences contain remote echoes of early infantile experiences. Spitz (1953) points out that an infant, when separated,

> first becomes weepy, demanding and clinging to everybody who approaches it; it looks as though attempts are made by these infants to regain the lost object with the help of their aggressive drive. Later on, visible manifestations of the aggressive drive decrease [p. 133].

Could the various phenotypic variations of severe character pathology at least partly be due to their different locations on this spectrum of affectomotor responses of a betrayed child?

Finally, I would like to mention a particular variant of "someday" fantasy. This is the "if only . . ." fantasy. Individuals with this fantasy do not search for or await "someday." Indeed, they lack all interest in the future. They are constantly wringing their hands over something that happened in the past. They focus their attention on this event and insist that "if only" it had not taken place everything would have turned out all right. Life before that event is glossed over or retrospectively idealized. When a childhood event, for example, parental divorce, gets involved in the "if only" fantasy, an elaborate "personal myth" (Kris, 1956) tends to develop that, with its seductive logic, might even go unquestioned during analytic treatment (e.g., my case of Mr. A in Kramer and Akhtar, 1988). The "screen" nature of such "if only" formulations is, however, clearer where the trauma, relentlessly harped on, is from the recent past. Individuals who remain tormented year after year by the memories of a failed romance from college days, a psychotherapist who moved out of town, or an extramarital lover who withdrew his or her affection often give histories of early maternal depressions and hospitalizations that had led them to be painfully "dropped" from maternal attention.

The metapsychological structure of the "if only" fantasy is similar to that of the "someday" fantasy. It too involves splitting, denial, and primitive idealization. It too serves defensive purposes and reflects incomplete mourning over the premature and painful loss of adequate maternal attention. In the "someday" fantasy, future is idealized, leading to hope, optimism, and a search for ideal conditions. In the "if only" fantasy, past is idealized leading to nostalgia,[3] self-pity, and a certain kind of self-righteousness. Frequently, the two fantasies coexist and form a tandem theme: "if only" this had not happened, life would be all right, and "someday" this will be reversed and life will (again) become totally blissful.

THE FANTASY OF A TETHER

When the infant loses the nipple and recovers it, contact with the need-gratifying percept is lost and recovered, and lost and recovered, again and again. During the interval between loss and recovery of *contact* the other element of the total perceptual unit, *distance perception* of the face, remains unchanged. In the course of these repetitive experiences visual perception comes to be relied upon, for it is not lost; it proves to be the more constant and therefore the more rewarding of the two [Spitz, 1965, p. 65].

Despite the children's apparent obliviousness to their mothers during the early practicing period, most of them seemed to go through a brief period of increased separation anxiety. The fact that they were able to move away independently, yet remain connected with their mother—not physically, but by way of their seeing and hearing her—made the successful use of these distance modalities extraordinarily important [Mahler, 1974, pp. 157–158].

---

[3]Here my views parallel Chasseguet-Smirgel's notion of the pervert's "nostalgia for primary narcissism" (1984, p. 29).

The second fantasy betraying unresolved separation–individuation is that of a tether. While only one analysand of mine referred to it literally as such, three others reported essentially similar fantasies during their treatment. The first patient, Mr. B, a successful businessman in his mid-forties, brought up this fantasy around the third month of his analysis. He announced that he was going away to a sales meeting on the West Coast, adding in the same breath that his attendance there was optional, not mandatory. I pointed out his ambivalence and commented upon the anxiety he seemed to be experiencing with his wish to be temporarily away and thus separated from me. He agreed and said that he wanted somehow to be at both places simultaneously. Further associations during this and later sessions revealed that he frequently had difficulty leaving places, people, even ideas and options. He was never fully at one place and often carried something of where he had formerly been with him. As the day of his departure drew closer, Mr. B became more anxious. He started fearing being so far away from my office and from me. He had disturbing thoughts about feeling hungry late at night while on the West Coast, not being able to find any food, going unnourished, and dying of starvation. It was around this time that Mr. B first reported the fantasy of a tether, a long rope by which he was tied to my office while being on the West Coast. With this he could be there safely and feel much less anxiety. As he was talking about this, he "saw" a mental picture of a little boy learning to walk. As is often typical of visual images during analytic sessions (Warren, 1961), this picture was at first affectless and experienced as having little or no connection with the patient's own self. Gradually, however, Mr. B was able to more directly acknowledge both the anxiety and the pleasure in his wish to walk away from me. The imagined tether clearly served a defensive purpose insofar as it minimized the anxiety of separation while permitting him autonomous functioning. During later periods of his analysis, the fantasied tether reappeared sometimes around separations. While in the beginning its reassuring aspects were emphasized, ambivalence gradually got attached to it. At times, it appeared to be a strangulating rope or even an enslaving chain from which he wanted escape. Still later, the tether disappeared from his associations or became irrelevant. Mr. B's analysis moved on to more familiar oedipal themes. During termination Mr. B did recall the tether, however. This was associated with jocular disbelief that, at times, seemed to hide a wistful longing for continued attachment to me. At other times, his humor displayed pleasure in his increased psychic freedom both within himself and in relation to me.

Less graphic but similar themes were reported by three other patients. Ms. D felt that an "invisible fence" precluded too much movement on her part. It prevented her from taking up a better job at a location some miles farther from her current place of employment and from my office. Significant assertiveness of any sort, especially vis-à-vis her domineering and controlling mother (and later toward me), led her to feel a jolting "electric shock." She said that she felt like a dog in a front yard with an invisible electric fence. "I can only go this far but if I try to hit the street I get the shock." Her associations to "hitting the street" led to leaving home and autonomy as well as to streetwalking and loss of control of sexual impulses. Further analysis revealed a childhood of intense engulfment by an exhibitionistic, hypochondriacal, and controlling mother and a marked lack of attention from a self-engrossed, heavy drinking father. Mr. E, a young college student, who as far back as he could remember had felt "completely forgotten" by his mother, reported many social and motoric inhibitions. One among these was his anxiety about jogging. While he enjoyed jogging, he constantly worried that he would end up too far away from his home, be unable to find his way back, and get hopelessly lost. As a result he jogged only around the block, never permitting himself to go "too far away" from his apartment building. Ms. F felt a similar inhibition in the sphere of mental activities. A politically conscious attorney, who at the age of 18 months had been separated from her mother for about six to eight weeks, Ms. F had never felt close to her mother. While growing up she felt her mother to be an "all duty and no love" type of person who pushed Ms. F toward premature independence. As a child she feared acquiring skills, since this led to greater autonomy and further loss of attention from her mother.[4] During her analysis she revealed that she found reading fiction especially difficult since rapt absorption took her "away" from her surroundings. In the midst of reading she would suddenly become aware of her absorption and start to worry lest she get "lost" in reading at the expense of other chores. It was as if she had stretched her mental tether to the limit and had to return to the secure base of reality for refueling.

Common to these patients was their concern about distance, literal or figurative, from an anchoring person or environment. They felt confined to an orbit. Upon reaching the outer limit of this orbit they felt anxiety and retreated to a comfortable distance within it. Mostly they felt reassured by having a central point of reference and feared getting lost if

---

[4]As one would expect, each progressive movement in her analysis was quickly followed by fear of abandonment by me and hence a regressive loss of newly acquired insights. Recognition of such a preoedipal substrate may enrich the usual dynamic understanding of negative therapeutic reaction (Freud, 1923) as resulting largely from unconscious oedipal guilt.

they broke the tether by going "too far." At times, however, they experienced a hypomanic-like excitement at the thought of this eventuality. Mr. E, for instance, imagined that if he allowed himself to jog freely he might go on for 100 to 200 miles and—who knows?—even more. Ms. F felt that if she allowed herself to read with concentration, she might continue reading, not sleep, miss her work, and disregard her analytic appointments. In such moments, real or imagined, these patients were flooded with elation and grandiosity, covered over during the analytic sessions by slightly apologetic giggling and shyness.

These patients' concerns were strongly reminiscent of those experienced by children in the practicing subphase of separation–individuation. The main manifest issue here is that of distance versus safety. Although distancing from mother begins in the differentiation subphase, it is not until the practicing subphase that the "symbiotic orbit" (Mahler et al., 1975, p. 293) actually begins to be mapped out and the strength of the "invisible bond" (p. 25) between mother and child is truly tested. Mr. B, in feeling reassured that a tether connected him to me while he traveled, was like a toddler in practicing subphase. During this time, despite pleasurable forays in the external world, the "mother continues to be needed as a stable point, a 'home base' to fulfill the need for refueling" (Mahler et al., 1975, p. 69). Mr. E's and Ms. F's hypomanic excitement, while at the farthest extremes of their tethers, hinted at a regression to practicing subphase phenomena, but one with a "knowledge" of rapprochement subphase issues. Thus, on one hand, such phenomena resembled the practicing phase child's elation upon freely exercising his ego apparatuses and escaping from fusion with the mother; on the other hand, these patients also showed the characteristic "ambitendency" (Mahler, 1974, p. 161) of the rapprochement subphase children. They wanted to assert themselves and experiment with a wider segment of the world but feared becoming untethered and losing the "home base." At the same time, they feared moving too close to the center of their orbit as well. This was manifest in their dread of intimacy, regression, and merger with the analyst. (Mr. B, for instance, repeatedly voiced his fear of never being able to leave analysis, doing nothing but analysis, and becoming an "analytic monk.") Fearing both progression and regression, they existed in a "satellite state" (Volkan and Corney, 1968), that is, as captive bodies orbiting within the gravitational field of an intense, though ambivalent, dependency. Their distancing attempts (e.g., travels, jogging, assertiveness) reassured them against the dread of fusion while their imaginary tethers provided them "distance contact" (Mahler et al., 1975, p. 67) with the analyst who remained available despite their comings and goings. The fantasied tether also allowed them time to work out their separation–

anxiety as well as their dread of merger and to negotiate an "optimal distance" (Bouvet, 1958) from early maternal object representations and their transferential recreations during analysis.

Besides it being particularly apt as a metaphor in this regard, the fantasy of a tether may, at times, have contributions from childhood realities. The joining and bringing together functions of strings and ropes are routinely witnessed by children. They may also see domestic pets on leashes and farm animals on tethers. They play with yo-yos and other string-manipulated toys. Toddlers are sometimes taken for walks with restraining devices with tether-like cords held by parents walking behind them. Kindergarten-age children on school-sponsored field trips often hold on to a rope whose end is held by their teacher. Thus, there are ample opportunities for ropes, leashes, tethers, and strings to get incorporated in inner concerns about maintaining contact with someone while being physically apart. Colloquial wisdom seems aware of the kinship between metaphor and reality in this regard. This is evident in expressions such as "He is tied to his mother's apron strings," "She has him on a leash," and "He has not been able to cut the cord yet."

In light of this, the paucity of psychoanalytic writings on fantasies involving ropes, leashes, and tethers is striking. The papers by Winnicott and Bach are two notable exceptions. Winnicott (1960) reported the case of a seven-year-old boy who was preoccupied with strings and was constantly tying various household objects to each other. In view of the boy's many traumatic separations from his mother beginning around the age of three years, Winnicott felt that he was "attempting to deny separation by his use of string, as one would deny separation from a friend by using the telephone" (p. 154). While the "tether" aspect is clearly evident here, Bach's (1977) description of "the rope to another world" has a somewhat different emphasis. According to him, narcissistic individuals often have a fantasy that a rope hangs down from the sky and they may be lifted out of this world by it (or climb up) to the Heavens. While acknowledging that the possibilities of interpretation here are multileveled, Bach emphasized the narcissistic–omnipotent aspects of this fantasy. He viewed it predominantly in the context of the human "search for transcendence of earthly limitations." Bach did not explicate the joining and connecting aspects of the rope metaphor, a feature that is central to the tether fantasy described here.

THE FANTASY OF A LONG EMBRACE

The ability to be truly alone has as its basis the early experience of being alone in the presence of someone. Being alone in the presence of someone can take place at a very early stage, when the *ego immaturity is naturally balanced by ego-support* from the mother. In the course of time the individual introjects the ego-supportive mother and in this way becomes able to be alone without frequent reference to the mother or mother symbol" [Winnicott, 1958, p. 32].

If the needs of the regressed ego are met, first in relation to the therapist who protects it in its need for an initial passive dependence, this will mean not collapse and loss of active powers for good and all, but a steady recuperation from deep strain, diminishing of deep fears, revitalization of the personality, and rebirth of an active ego that is spontaneous and does not have to be forced and driven" (Guntrip, 1969, p. 244).

The third fantasy with links to unresolved separation–individuation is that of a long embrace that will forever quench the thirst for contact with another person. One will then be free to follow one's destined path in life. Mr. C, a bright lawyer in his mid-forties, displayed this fantasy literally as well as in myriad subtle forms. For quite some time in his twice-a-week treatment, he remained convinced that if he could hug me for a long enough time, *then* he would be forever satiated and somehow fundamentally improved. A similar situation prevailed between him and his wife. Upon reaching home each evening, Mr. C demanded that his wife drop everything and sit next to him while he talked, read his mail, or drank beer. Any delay on her part irritated him; moreover, he felt that she always returned to her chores too soon, leaving him hurt and sulking. He felt that if she stayed with him long enough, *then* he would feel deeply satisfied and "ready to face anything." As the treatment progressed, however, it became evident that no amount of time his wife spent with him was ever enough. Mr. C found it quite embarrassing, even a bit shocking, to discover his own inconsolability in this regard. Soon, however, he began noticing a similar tendency in many other areas of his life. He chronically wanted to stay in his bed or in the shower longer and left both reluctantly each morning. In all these situations, he was looking for a warm contact that would last long enough for an inner fulfillment. This never occurred and consequently Mr. C felt chronically starved and unhappy.

Mr. C's parents had been divorced when he was three years old, and he had been raised almost single-handedly by his talented, successful, and busy mother. As far back as he could remember, he was always being left, often crying, with baby-sitters. As an older child, he would devise ways to engage his mother in conversation just when she was about to leave home. One especially painful memory was his running after his mother's car, at age five or so, while she was leaving for one of her innumerable "meetings" (Mr. C despised the word). While an analytic reconstruction was not possible, this developmental background hinted that Mr. C's prolonged-embrace fantasy may have contained a powerful drive for a sustained relationship with his mother and its subsequent internalization leading to structure formation. Mr. C was clearly searching for "object constancy"—at times in a most literal sense—and, through it, for "self constancy" (Mahler, 1974), enhanced self-esteem, and greater autonomy.

Two other patients described fantasies with minor variations on the same theme. Mr. A (for details of this case, see Kramer and Akhtar, 1988) excitedly talked of huge meals that seemed to promise sustained satiety and filling up of an inner void. It was as if eating good food to his heart's content would forever obliterate the need for another meal. His actual trips to various idealized restaurants, however, were always disappointing. Yet the fantasy retained its allure. Ms. F, mentioned earlier, longed for sessions twice the length of her usual ones and believed that even one such concession on my part might greatly diminish the overall length of her treatment. At times, she wished to hypnotize me so that I would not end the session until she felt satiated and ready to leave.

Common to these patients was their longing for a sustained environmental provision, including attention from a valued person. Obtaining this seemed necessary for them to feel internally soothed and freed up to be themselves. With minor variations, all fantasies involving this desire had a biphasic theme: fusion with a dimly perceived object followed by satiety, separation, and enhanced autonomy. Moreover, there frequently was involved a certain passive, incorporative bodily pleasure (bed, meals, shower, beer) coupled with coercion of another person (mother, wife, analyst) into a narcissistically invested pseudomutuality. Such a situation would easily lend itself to becoming a "Greek tragedy," that is, a malady of two truths. The analyst, for instance, may experience the patient's entitlement, coercion, and longing (for a hug, personal information, more sessions, longer hours, extra-analytic contact, etc.) as burdensome, controlling, even sadistic. The patient, however, only feels a desperate need for the other individual's sustained presence and sees himself entitled to it. A monotonous persistence of such "needs," a special quality of directness in their expression, and affective oscillations between urgent hope and resignation are three valuable cues (Kilingmo, 1989) to the underlying state of deficit[5] in such instances.

---

[5]At the same time, I agree with Kilingmo (1989), who points out that this "does not refer to the personality as a whole, only to that *part* of the psychological

The biphasic aspect (merger–separation) of the long-embrace fantasy involves what Winnicott (1958) referred to as the essential paradox in the development of the capacity to be alone. The opportunity to be "alone" in the unobtrusive presence of the mother facilitates internalization of the soothing maternal functions. Numerous such occurrences gradually lead to the diminution of the need for the actual presence of the mother and the emergence of the capacity for peaceful solitude. The long-embrace fantasy contains both the elements involved here: to be with someone and then to be on one's own. In Mahler's (1972, 1974) terms, the long-embrace fantasy illustrates a rapprochement subphase toddler's wooing of the mother in order to reestablish the delusional omnipotent unity with her. Both regressive and progressive currents are in evidence here. On one hand, such coercion for merger ("embrace") seeks to deny the anxiety consequent upon increasing awareness of separation. On the other hand, it is also in the service of consolidating the still vulnerable inner structures, establishing object constancy, and thus promoting further separation. The individual with a long-embrace fantasy (Mr. C, for instance) feels that he needs a hug, wants one, and wants a long and sustained one—but *not* an interminable one. Even in the best of fantasized circumstances, the embrace always comes to an end, leading to separation of the two parties.

Two other elements of this fantasy deserve comment. One pertains to a certain quantitative factor that seems integral to it, and the other involves its occasional sadistic and sexual coloration. The long-embrace fantasy by its very designation implies a quantitative factor. Mr. C wanted to stay in bed longer, take longer showers, have his wife sit with him longer, and hug me for a very, very long time; Mr. A wanted to eat really large meals; and Mr. F wanted sessions twice the length of ordinary ones, at times even longer. A quantitative factor is undeniable here. Does it reflect a quantitative factor in the ontogenesis of psychic structures as well? Could the optimal emotional availability of the mother required to successfully traverse the rapprochement subphase also have a similar quantitative dimension?

The second issue pertains to how much aggression gets involved in the coercion leading to the prolonged embrace. At its most benign and literal extreme, the very idea of embrace implies an almost total lack of aggression. However, more often than not, patients' fantasies involve controlling the analyst in this regard with varying degrees of aggression. Holding on tightly to the analyst, hypnotizing him, locking his office

---

make-up which derives from deficit. Not even on hypothetical level would it be reasonable to conceive of an individual totally without conflict" (p. 72).

door, tying him down to his chair, and attaching oneself to him in a vampire-like fashion are the various gradations of aggression in safe-guarding a "long embrace."[6] These differences may be based on individual variations in constitutional levels of activity and aggression as well as on the degree (once again, a quantitative factor) of maternal unavailability during the rapprochement subphase. After all, Mahler (1972) emphasizes that "the less emotionally available the mother has become at the time of rapprochement, the more insistently and even desperately does the toddler attempt to woo her" (p. 139); this insistence and desperation may persist in adult life. Moreover, since anal stage, early genital phase, and early oedipal conflicts also sequentially come into play during rapprochement and its subsequent subphase of separation–individuation, such aggression in long-embrace fantasy might easily get condensed with wishes for sexual domination and control.[7] Sexual fantasies of immobilizing or tying someone up or being tied may have this condensation at their roots. One cannot fail to note the admixture of the tether and the long-embrace fantasies here. The bond of reassurance has here become the organ of bondage and discipline!

CONCLUDING REMARKS

In this chapter I have described three fantasies related to unresolved separation–individuation. These involve "someday . . ." and "if only . . .," a tether, and a long embrace. While I have so far discussed the genetic and phenomenological characteristics of each separately, I will now highlight their common elements and in doing so underscore the ebb and flow not only in fantasy life but in psychic development in general.

First, all of the fantasies express longings activated by separation and loss. The "someday" fantasy denies the loss of oneness with the mother. The tether fantasy acknowledges separateness but minimizes anxiety over it by

---

[6]Young children often play games in which one can be abruptly immobilized by the opponent's uttering a particular word or phrase (e.g., "statue," "red light"). Another word or gesture is then necessary in order to recover one's motor freedom. The wish for a coercive, omnipotent control of an insufficiently attentive mother of the rapprochement subphase is, perhaps, significant among the multileveled, complex determinants of such games.

[7]Even in the absence of such aggressive overtones, condensation of the fantasy of an embrace with sexual wishes is not infrequent. On a behavioral level this overlap between sexual desire and a wish to be held has been studied in a large sample of women by Hollender et al (1969, 1970).

retaining distance contact. The long-embrace fantasy acknowledges total separation but with the proviso of a profound contact prior to it. The three fantasies seem to be built as responses, respectively, to the three different emotional reactions to loss described by Freud (1926, p. 169): psychic pain, anxiety, and mourning. Insofar as these reactions refer to different facets of separation, the fantasies are different; insofar as they all do refer to separation, the fantasies are alike.

Second, all are object-related fantasies though the degree of the object's clarity and separateness varies with each of them. In the "someday" fantasy, the object, like the mother of symbiosis, is almost indistinguishable from the self and yet paramount in its "holding" (Winnicott, 1960b) functions. In the tether fantasy, the object is an anchor like the mother of the practicing subphase (Mahler, 1974; Mahler et al., 1975). In the long-embrace fantasy, satiety is sought from a reliable and sustained object representing the mother of rapprochement and of "on the way to object constancy" (Mahler et al., 1975).

Third, all three fantasies are linked to developmental issues of boundary formation, becoming oneself, authenticity, and individuation. In the "someday" fantasy, spontaneity, authenticity, and freedom are linked with a regressive and unconditionally accepting environment. In the tether fantasy, the safety of attachment comes in conflict with the mobile search for autonomy. In the long-embrace fantasy, temporary fusion with an object is followed by the establishment of a contentedly separate self.

Fourth, all three fantasies involve some reference to motor activity, whether as being unnecessary or effortless ("someday"), enjoyable but risky ("tether"), or temporarily immobilizing both the self and object and then freeing them to part from each other ("long embrace").

Fifth, "prehistoric" somatic schemata exist for each of the three fantasies. These include intrauterine life, umbilical cord and breast feeding, pertaining to "someday," tether, and long-embrace fantasies, respectively. However, in all fairness, it should be acknowledged that imagery and references pertaining to body are more clearly discernible in the tether and long-embrace fantasies than in the "someday" fantasy. Whether this implies a chronologically earlier root for the last-mentioned fantasy remains unclear.

Sixth, each fantasy contains affectomotor (and sometimes rudimentary ideational) residues from more than one subphase of separation–individuation. The "someday" fantasy seems to contain the mindlessness of autism, the bliss of symbiosis, the wonder of differentiation, and the freedom of the practicing subphase. The tether fantasy alludes to the distancing of differentiation, the refueling of practicing, and the ambitendency of the rapprochement subphase. The long-embrace fantasy hints at the fusion of symbiosis, the refueling of practicing, the ambitendency of rapprochement, and the sense of accomplishment of the "on the way to object constancy" subphase (Mahler, 1972, 1974; Mahler et al., 1975). Each of these fantasies receives tributaries from various aspects of autism, symbiosis, and separation–individuation sequence. This seems in accordance with the reminder, admittedly made in a somewhat different context, by Mahler and Kaplan (1977) that "the overriding dominance of one subphase distortion or fixation must not obscure the fact that there are always corrective or pathogenic influences from other subphases to be considered" (p. 84).

Seventh, each of the three fantasies also contains drive-related conflicts from various psychosexual levels, including the phallic-oedipal phase. The "someday" fantasy hints at oral bliss and at regressive circumvention of anal restrictions and oedipal prohibitions. The tether fantasy contains both oral incorporative (umbilical) and phallic (bridging two bodies) imagery. The long-embrace fantasy alludes to oral satiety, anal eroticism (pleasurable parting), primal scene, and oedipal transgression.

Finally, while I have described the pathologic extremes of these fantasies, it is quite likely that in muted forms these exist universally and constitute the deepest basis of certain ubiquitous human traits. The "someday" fantasy may underlie search, ambition, and hope, the tether fantasy a sense of belonging and attachment to family, country, and social organizations, and the long-embrace fantasy the lifelong human oscillations between intimacy and aloneness. Vicissitudes of the three fantasies are also found in religious motifs, mythology, and fairy tales. Such tempting speculations are, however, beyond the scope of this particular contribution.

REFERENCES

Abraham, K. (1924), The influence of oral erotism on character formation. In: *Selected Papers of Karl Abraham, M.D.* New York: Brunner/Mazel, 1979, pp. 393–406.

Akhtar, S. (1984a), The syndrome of identity diffusion. *Amer. J. Psychiat.,* 141:1381–1385.

———— (1984b), Self psychology vs. mainstream psychoanalysis. *Contemp. Psychiat.,* 3:113–117.

———— (1987), Schizoid personality disorder: A synthesis of developmental, dynamic and descriptive features. *Amer. J. Psychother.,* 41:499–518.

———— (1988), Hypomanic personality disorder. *Integr. Psychiat.,* 6:37–52.

———— (1989a), Kohut and Kernberg: A critical comparison. In: *Self Psychology: Comparisons and Contrasts,* ed. D. W. Detrick & S. P. Detrick. Hillsdale, NJ: The Analytic Press, pp. 329–362.

———— (1989b), Narcissistic personality disorder: Descriptive features and differential diagnosis. *Psychiatr. Clin. North Am.*, 12:505–529.

———— (1990), Paranoid personality disorder: A synthesis of developmental, dynamic, and descriptive features. *Amer. J. Psychother.*, 44(1):5–25.

Angel, A. (1932), Einige Bemerkungen uber den optimismus. *Internat. Zeitschr. of Psychoanal.*, 20(2):191–199.

Bach, S. (1977), On narcissistic fantasies. *Internat. Rev. Psycho-anal.*, 4:281–293.

Balint, M. (1968), *Basic Fault*. London: Tavistock.

Benedek, T. (1938), Adaptation to reality in early infancy. *Psychoanal. Quart.*, 7:200–214.

Bion, W. R. (1961), *Experience in Groups*. New York: Basic Books.

Blum, H. (1981), Object inconstancy and paranoid conspiracy. *J. Amer. Psychoanal. Assn.*, 29:789–813.

Bouvet, M. (1958), Technical variations and the concept of distance. *Internat. J. Psycho-anal.*, 39:211–221.

Burland, J. A. (1975), Separation–individuation and reconstruction in psychoanalysis. *Internat. J. Psychoanal. Psychother.*, 4:303–335.

———— (1986), The vicissitudes of maternal deprivation. In: *Self and Object Constancy*, ed. R. Lax, A. Back & J. A. Burland. New York: Guilford Press, 1986, pp. 324–348.

Chasseguet-Smirgel, J. (1984), *Creativity and Perversion*. New York: Norton.

Deutsch, H. (1942), Some forms of emotional disturbance and their relationship to schizophrenia. *Psychoanal. Quart.*, 11:301–321.

Erikson, E. H. (1950), *Childhood and Society*. New York: Norton.

———— (1959), *Identity and the Life Cycle*. New York: International Universities Press.

Frank, A. (1969), The unrememberable and the unforgetable: Passive primal repression. *The Psychoanalytic Study of the Child*, 24:48–77. New York: International Universities Press.

Freud, S. (1917), A childhood recollection from Dichtung und Wahrheit. *Standard Edition*, 17:145–157. London: Hogarth Press, 1955.

———— (1918), From the history of an infantile neurosis. *Standard Edition*, 17:1–122. London: Hogarth Press, 1955.

———— (1923), The ego and the id. *Standard Edition*, 19:1–66. London: Hogarth Press, 1962.

———— (1926), Inhibitions, symptoms and anxiety. *Standard Edition*, 20:87–174. London: Hogarth Press, 1959.

Gedimen, H. K. (1986), Imposture, inauthenticity and feeling fraudulent. *J. Amer. Psychoanal Assn.*, 33:911–936.

Greenspan, S. I. (1977), The oedipal-preoedipal dilemma: A reformulation in the light of object relations theory. *Internat. Rev. Psychoanal.*, 4:381–391.

Guntrip, H. (1969), *Schizoid Phenomena, Object Relations and the Self*. New York: International Universities Press.

Hayman, A. (1989), What do we mean by 'phantasy'? *Internat. J. Psycho-Anal.*, 70:105–114.

Hollender, M. H. (1970), The need or wish to be held. *Arch. Gen. Psychiat.*, 22:445–453.

————, Luborsky, L. & Scaramella, T. J. (1969), Body contact and sexual excitement. *Arch. Gen. Psychiat.*, 20:188–191.

Isakower, O. (1936), A contribution to the pathopsychology of phenomena associated with falling asleep. *Internat. J. Psycho-anal.*, 19:331–345.

Kaplan, L. J. (1980), Rapprochement and oedipal organization: Effects on borderline phenomena, In: *Rapprochement: The Critical Subphase of Separation–Individuation,* ed. R. Lax, S. Bach & J. A. Burland. New York: Aronson, pp. 39–63.

Kernberg, O. F. (1967), Borderline personality organization. *J. Amer. Psychoanal. Assn.,* 15:641–685.

———— (1970), A psychoanalytic classification of character pathology. *J. Amer. Psychoanal. Assn.,* 18:800–822.

———— (1980), *Internal World and External Reality.* New York: Aronson.

Kilingmo, B. (1989), Conflict and deficit: Implications for technique. *Internat. J. Psycho-Anal.,* 70:65–79.

Kramer, S. (1980), Residues of split-object and split-self dichotomies in adolescence. In: *Rapprochement: The Critical Subphase of Separation–Individuation,* ed. R. F. Lax, S. Bach & J. A. Burland. New York: Aronson, pp. 417–437.

———— & Akhtar, S. (1988), The developmental context of internalized preoedipal object relations: Clinical applications of Mahler's theory of symbiosis and separation–individuation. *Psychoanal. Quart.,* 57:547–576.

Kris, E. (1956), The personal myth: A problem in psychoanalytic technique. *J. Amer. Psychoanal. Assn.,* 4:653–681.

Lax, R. (1980), The rotten core: A defect in the formation of the self during the rapprochement subphase. In: *Rapprochement: The Critical Subphase of Separation–Individuation,* ed. R. Lax, S. Bach & J. A. Burland. New York: Aronson, pp. 439–455.

Mahler, M. S. (1963), Thoughts about development and individuation. In: *The Selected Papers of Margaret S. Mahler,* Vol. 2. New York: Aronson, 1979, pp. 3–19.

———— (1966), Notes on the development of basic moods: The depressive affect. In: *The Selected Papers of Margaret S. Mahler, Vol. 2.* New York: Aronson, 1979, pp. 59–75.

———— (1971), A study of the separation and individuation process and its possible application to borderline phenomena in the psychoanalytic situation. *The Psychoanalytic Study of the Child,* 26:403–424. New Haven, CT: Yale University Press.

———— (1972), Rapprochement subphase of the separation–individuation process. In: *The Selected Papers of Margaret S. Mahler, Vol. 2.* New York: Aronson, 1979, pp. 131–148.

———— (1974), Symbiosis and individuation: The psychological birth of the human infant. In: *The Selected Papers of Margaret S. Mahler, Vol. 2.* New York: Aronson, 1979, pp. 149–165.

_____ & Kaplan, L. (1977), Developmental aspects in the assessment of narcissistic and so-called borderline personalities. In: *Borderline Personality Disorders,* ed. P. Hartocolis. New York: International Universities Press, pp. 71–86.

_____ , Pine, F. & Bergman, A. (1975), *The Psychological Birth of the Infant.* New York: Basic Books.

Parens, H. (1979a), *The Development of Aggression in Early Childhood.* New York: Aronson.

_____ (1979b), Developmental considerations of ambivalence. *The Psychoanalytic Study of the Child,* 34:385–420.

_____ (1980), An exploration of the relations of instinctual drives and the symbiosis-separation-individuation process: Part 1. Drive motivation and psychic development with special reference to aggression and beginning separation–individuation. *J. Amer. Psychoanal. Assn.,* 28:89–114.

_____ (in press) A view of the development of hostility in early life. *J. Amer. Psychoanal. Assn.,*

Piaget, J. (1936), *The Origins of Intelligence in Children.* New York: International Universities Press, 1952.

Pine, F. (1979), On the pathology of the separation–individuation process as manifested in later clinical work: An attempt at delineation. *Internat. J. Psycho-Anal.,* 60:225–242.

Ray, M. H. (1986), Phenomenology of failed object constancy. In: *Self and Object Constancy: Clinical and Theoretical Perspectives,* ed. R. Lax, S. Bach & J. A. Burland. New York: Guilford Press, pp. 233–250.

Rinsley, D. B. (1986), Object constancy, object permanency, and personality disorders. In: *Self and Object Constancy: Clinical and Theoretical Perspectives,* ed. R. Lax, S. Bach & J. A. Burland. New York: Guilford Press, pp. 193–207.

Settlage, C. F. (1977), The psychoanalytic understanding of narcissistic and borderline personality disorders: Advances in developmental theory. *J. Amer. Psychoanal. Assn.,* 25(4):805–833.

_____ Bemesderfer, S., Rosenthal, J., Afterman, J. & Spielman, P. (in press), The appeal cycle in early mother–child interaction: The nature and implications of a finding from developmental research. *J. Amer. Psychoanal. Assn.*

Spitz, R. (1953), Aggression. In: *Drives, Affects, Behavior,* ed. R. M. Loewenstein. New York: International Universities Press, pp. 126–138.

_____ (1965), *The First Year of Life.* New York: International Universities Press.

Volkan, V. & Corney, R. T. (1968), Some considerations of satellite states and satellite dreams. *Brit. J. Med. Psychol.* 41:283–290.

Waelder, R. (1930), The principle of multiple function: Observations on multiple determination. *Psychoanal. Quart.,* 5:45–62.

Wallerstein, R. S. (1983), Self psychology and "classical" psychoanalytic psychology: The nature of their relationship. In: *The Future of Psychoanalysis,* ed. A. Goldberg. New York: International Universities Press, pp. 19–63.

Warren, M. (1961), The significance of visual images during the analytic session. *J. Amer. Psychoanal. Assn.,* 9:504–518.

Winnicott, D. W. (1958), The capacity to be alone. In: *The Maturational Processes and the Facilitating Environment*. New York: International Universities Press, 1965, pp. 29–36.

_____ (1960a), String: A technique of communication. In: *The Maturational Processes and the Facilitating Environment*. New York: International Universities Press, 1965, pp. 153–157.

_____ (1960), The parent–infant relationship. *Internat. J. Psycho-Anal.*, 41:585–595.

14

Dyadic Psychopathology and Infantile Eating Disorder
Psychoanalytic Study and Inferences

Harold P. Blum

Eating disorders are among the most frequently seen problems reported by pediatricians and child guidance clinics, and in recent years there has been a high incidence in both adolescents and adults. Cultural factors, for example, those associated with dieting, weight, and figure preoccupation, have been noted to account for the widespread forms of eating and feeding disorders. Certainly, deviant eating behavior can be found in a variety of cultures as well as in the different historical eras. Bulimia and anorexia have been noted in ancient chronicles, and food or eating avoidance has been described as part of religious rituals or as fasting for political purposes. However, in addition to sociocultural trends, constitutional factors, and innate biogenetic dispositions, psychological factors in eating disorders are fundamental.

Despite differences and difficulties in the diagnosis of feeding and eating disorders, common forms of pathogenesis or pathogenic factors have been sought as a unifying explanation for the protean manifestations of these forms of psychopathology. This chapter focuses particularly on the role of separation–individuation in the pathogenesis of eating disorder. Analytic observations and inference concerning the parent–child relationship supplement the expanding psychoanalytic literature and data from direct infant observation. Because of the magnitude and complexity of the pathophysiological disturbance that may contribute to or is consequent to

285

eating disorder or that may represent organic accompaniments of eating disorder, it is not possible here to do more than indicate an awareness of the physiological and neuroendocrine perspectives. Concomitant malnutrition may have its special significance and consequences. The psychological factors are important in their own right and are constantly interacting with other internal and external influences (Sours, 1980). At the present time a clear understanding of the pathogenesis of eating disorders has not been established, and controversies abound concerning their development and their relation to compulsions, addictions, impulse disorders, depression, and borderline syndromes.

From the psychoanalytic viewpoint, growth in psychoanalytic knowledge about these disorders has steadily increased, beginning with the pioneer emphasis on oral fixation and regression. Cannibalistic oral greed has been noted in bulimia, and defenses against such impulses to devour are prominent in anorexia. Bulimia and anorexia may alternate, and bulimia may be followed by undoing in purging, vomiting, and laxatives. Oedipal factors were early noted, and eating disorders were viewed as representing wishes for as well as defenses against incest, oral impregnation, and rivalry with the fertile mother. Elaborations of structural theory gave rise to studies of particular ego defenses, such as denial and reaction formation; the importance of body ego and body image considerations; and the nature of the earliest object relations, identifications, and internalizations. Superego factors took into account the importance of guilt and shame in these disorders and the close relationship that may occur between certain deviant eating disorders and depression or impulsive disturbance. Superego considerations also were involved in studies of the rules and regulations concerning eating and feeding, as well as of the regulation of hunger with associated feelings of deprivation and gratification.

More recently, with advances in ego psychology and in the formulation of the process of separation–individuation, there has been close attention to issues of ego discrimination, communication, and integration and to the earliest interactions and communications between parent and child (Bruch, 1982; Chatoor, 1989). Separation–individuation takes into account disposition, earliest object relations and the role of the ego, and, particularly, ego development in the course of personality growth and disorder during the period of life from approximately six months to three years (Mahler, Pine, and Bergman, 1975). While much remains for further research, developmental disturbance during the period of separation–individuation appears to play a significant role in many of the eating disorders encountered in clinical practice.

At present, it is difficult to generalize about the nature of these disorders or to provide a comprehensive explanation for their pathogenesis, even of a specific disorder such as anorexia. However, many different studies have pointed to the importance of preoedipal determinants and the role of developmental disturbance, with serious implications for the vulnerability, predisposition, and sometimes the prototype of later eating disorders and their related symptomatic derivatives.

Developmental studies of separation–individuation and, from a quite different perspective, inferences from disturbed adolescents and adults focused on early developmental failure and lack of adequate internalization of self-soothing and self-comforting function. In turn, developmental disturbance contributes to or may result from other structural deficits.

I *should* like to emphasize the importance of phase interpenetration, overlap, and reorganization. Development is not simply linear, and there may be subtle disharmonies as well as discontinuities. While the preoedipal colors and determines the later phases of development, oedipal and postoedipal factors are not minimized. The focus on separation–individuation here is not meant to indicate that oedipal development in adolescence does not have a major role in the final form of adult psychopathology and the selection and organization of eating disorder. The appearance of feeding disorder such as anorexia during adolescence is probably due to both psychological and biological factors, with constitutional predisposition important in both areas. The balance of oedipal and preoedipal issues may vary according to each individual's psychopathology and personality organization (Risen, 1982).

In my experience, the eating disorders that have extended into adulthood have been markedly influenced by the adolescent and oedipal phases, although the vulnerability to these conditions was to be found in infancy and early childhood. A history of infantile or childhood feeding disturbance in the adolescent or adult with an eating disorder is very common but not universally present. Moreover, the infantile feeding disturbance may not be isomorphic with the adolescent or adult form of eating disorder. Changes in later forms of psychopathology may be closely or loosely related to similar infantile disturbance. Further, the eating disorders themselves may overlap; for example, anorexia may be associated with food fads and food preoccupations, and bulimia with alcoholism and addiction. Some forms of eating disorder have been classified as compulsions, others as a type of substance abuse.

The roots of compulsive eating, food fads, and aberrant reactions to eating, feeding, digestion, and nutrition converge in the process of separation–individuation. It should also be noted that many infantile feeding disturbances are self-limited, that beneficial phase reorganization in later development may occur, and that developmental mastery and sublimation may replace an earlier eating disorder.

When studied analytically and in statu nascendi, the type of eating disorder described in this chapter was found to have important determinants deriving from unresolved preoedipal problems in the mother and child. The findings tended to confirm a derailment of dialogue (Spitz, 1965) and the miscuing and tendencies toward mismatch noted by Mahler and associates (1975), as well as the impact and organizing influence of unconscious oedipal conflict and fantasy. Food and feeding, as A. Freud (1946) observed, represents the object, the object's love, gratification and deprivation, reward and punishment. As a result of caregiver disturbance and the type of infant who tends to elicit that disturbance or fails to appropriately communicate with and adapt to his particular caregiver, there is failure in discrimination and regulation of hunger, feeding, and satiety. Conflicts over food and feeding develop, and the infant confuses or symbolizes such conflicts as dependence or independence, separateness or fantasied symbiosis, and control or lack of control in terms of disordered eating. The eating struggle represents the parent–child conflict; like the food itself, the conflict may become internalized, elaborated in fantasy, and ultimately far removed from the original infantile feeding situation and the early eating disorder.

The adult forms of feeding disorder, in may experience, have always involved conflict and compromise formation with important components of oedipal guilt, oral greed, and infantile dependent need. Defensive and compensatory issues are also important. Ego deficits may potentiate conflict and trauma but are also consequent to and always amalgamated with conflict. The anorexic, in particular, seeks to present a perfect façade of self-sufficient, self-contained tranquillity, as though self-starvation represented mastery and self-reliant autonomy. However, character façade does not apply to an infantile feeding disorder but to later developmental phases.

The separation–individuation and preoedipal issues discussed here were inferred from the analytic data obtained in the analysis of the mother to be presented. The mother reacted to her infant's separation–individuation and preoedipal development and reported about her infant in her analysis. Her own infantile development was subject to analytic reconstruction. Her infant was never directly observed by her analyst. The observations are consistent with and extend the formulation of tan impaired separation–individuation process described by other authors (Kramer, 1974; Chatoor, 1989; Fischer, 1989), a process that colors oedipal conflict and resolution. The primary data considered are the analytic data concerning the mother's

reports of her own involvement with her infant and the analytic understanding of the unconscious conflicts of the mother that impinged upon
the rearing of her child. In this case the area of eating, ordinarily
self-regulated according to biological need and the cycles of hunger and
satiety, became derailed and deviant. The analytic process, the analyst's
interest, and the patient's talent and preoccupation allowed a remarkably
lucid picture of this dyadic disturbance to unfold. The deviant feeding
developed in a predisposed child under the influence of maternal psychopathology.

The analytic situation permitted not only reconstruction of the mother's predisposition to feeding disorder but an understanding of her infant's
feeding disorder in statu nascendi. The unusually detailed analytic data
depicting the mother–infant dyadic disorder followed from the analysis of
the mother's pathological preoccupation with her infant, her conscious
and unconscious requests for help in parenting, and her capacity for vivid
evocation of the dyadic interaction with her infant. She readily identified
her infant with her infantile self and fluidly shifted perspectives among
those of the mother, infant, and, later, analytic observer. All mothers in
analysis make meaningful observations and judgments about their infant's
attributes and development.

I believe that the analyst's perspective is also important and is likely to
influence the data obtained. If the analyst is interested in the reported
dyadic interaction only for research or for limited transference implications, then the full clinical and research potential of the analytic situation
will be diminished.

The mother has a major investment in her infant that is lived outside the
analysis. Many aspects and nuances of this relationship do not fully appear
in the analytic transference. Mothers react differently to each infant despite
the compulsion to repeat the past evident in transference repetition. In
addition, the infant is not only a real new object but a transference object.
The analytic transference will be fractionated between the infant and the
analyst so that extratransference considerations (beyond the analytic
transference) are essential (Blum, 1983). Mothers will talk about their
infants if there is analytic interest and understanding of the mother's
feelings, fantasies, and interaction with her child. The effect of that
particular child upon the parent is reciprocally important. Crucial developmental data cannot be obtained from the analytic transference alone,
and the mother's actual attitudes and behavior toward her infant are not
simply an acting out of her analytic transference. In some respects there is
a tripartite situation for the preoccupied mother for whom the infant is a
psychological presence, the other child in the adult analysis.

The situation has transference–countertransference analogies to child analysis. The analyst may develop a complex countertransference to the infant and mother. Discussion of her infant may elicit the mother's envy, jealousy, and rivalry for the analyst's attention and affection. The infant's problems may be used to defend against awareness of other conflicts or to surrender the infant and parenting to the analyst. The analysis of these issues deepens the analytic process and further enlightens both the analytic relationship and the actual mother–infant relationship.

CASE ILLUSTRATION

At the time she began analysis, this mother, a striking, intelligent, and well-educated woman in her 30s, knew that she was having difficulties in appropriately rearing her infant but had little understanding of how or why the problems had evolved or how to correct the difficulty. She reported feeling anxious and depressed, revealing that she had always wondered about the type of parent she would become. She was a recovered anorexic, having suffered from mild adolescent anorexia nervosa that had spontaneously resolved without treatment. She thought that her early adolescent problems, particularly concerning her fears of growing up and of independence and an acceptance of herself as a woman, had been gradually mastered in her later adolescent years. As a young adult she was subject to frequent, mild, and transient depressive episodes accompanied by a tendencey toward restless sleep and sometimes insufficient sleep. She had not had the type of severe anorexia in adolescence and young adulthood that would have precluded pregnancy because of amenorrhea and/or associated lack of fertility. She had denied an interest in food while being preoccupied with food. She intellectualized a perfectionistic control over her body while her body was also an isolated, alien self. The patient had experienced her parents as usurping her corporeal autonomy while she actually struggled with her own conflicts over independence and young womanhood. These issues of autonomy and self-regulation of bodily urges resurfaced with her own child. The patient had a significant, provocative role in the disturbed relationship with her mother and in the strained relationship of her parents; she was not simply a passive, dependent offshoot of her parents (Weil, 1970; Mahler et al., 1975).

The patient had always wanted children and had expected to find considerable satisfaction in motherhood. For many anorexics, pregnancy and parenthood precipitate the eating disorder and/or depression because of demands on them for adult nurturance and caregiver responsibility and because of fears of being depleted or devoured (Garfinkel and Garner,

1982). This patient was fearful of insufficient weight gain during pregnancy and, in the last trimester, of starving her baby in utero. The baby was not at risk because of the mother's insufficient weight gain, since her weight was actually within normal limits, distinguishing this patient from those who are anorexic during pregnancy or who become pregnant during their anorexia. Some anorexic women, may seek to become pregnant in the hope of restoring a sense of well-being, which is based on a conscious or unconscious fantasy of restored idealized mother–infant relationship.

This patient actually overcompensated during the latter half of her pregnancy by eating excessively, but not to the point of bulimia. She had mild "postpartum blues," which were relatively transient. She did not, as some anorexic mothers do, gain weight in order to nourish the fetus only to then develop an anorexic eating disorder within six weeks postpartum (Mogul, 1989). During her infant's first year she became overconcerned with feeding the infant enough, while she carefully restricted her own diet to avoid weight gain. In actuality, she maintained her own weight within normal limits but began to become inwardly preoccupied with issues concerning feeding herself and the baby.

When the baby lost a little weight, early in the second year of life, following a mild infantile illness, the mother became particularly anxious about the baby's eating and weight and tendencies to overfeed the baby then appeared. Her child was far more active and willful than before, and it is quite possible that the infantile illness might not have been the necessary trigger for the struggles over eating, which might have appeared as an almost predictable conflict in the infant–mother relationship during the second year of life.

The "overfed" baby and "starved" self formed a dyad with many meanings. For example, the self-sacrifice and desire to overfeed "overcompensated" for maternal hostility and reactively defended against the mother's own unconscious dependent, devouring attitudes. This mother defended against her own wishes to eat and be eaten and wishful fantasies as well as fears of fusion and identity diffusion. The infant's representation was colored by projection and introjection and variable maternal regression. There was a split in the maternal nurturant and withholding self and object representations. The boundary between mother and infant representation in the maternal psyche could be blurred at times. But this mother's fantasies of desired and dreaded fusion were not equivalent to maternal merger with her infant. Her infant could also be regarded as an alternate and additional transference object.

Symptomically, the previously anorexic mother attempted to induce bulimia in her infant. The mother's anorexic tendencies and tendencies to overfeed her infant represented two sides of the same inner conflict. Her infant was unconsciously regarded as an incompletely separated narcissistic object. The patient's response to her infant's hunger and satiety was in many ways governed more by her fantasies than by the infant's needs. Becoming a mother revived infantile conflicts and problems with her own mother. She was unconsciously repeating and reenacting the unresolved pathological bond and identification with her own mother in her own unresolved struggles with issues of separateness, autonomy, oral greed, and narcissistic entitlement and rage. Her overfeeding engulfed her infant and also represented her ambivalent wish to narcissistically nurture herself.

The patient's husband was caring and concerned but not very available or empathic. He was a very ambitious professional, busily involved in the development of his own career. The patient had not been able to really gratify her dependent needs in her marriage and had remained highly threatened and conflicted in her relationship with her own parents, never defining a comfortable closeness or distance or easy give-and-take with her parents. Considering her regressive vulnerability, her husband's increased support and involvement were of auxiliary assistance as her analysis progressed.

This mother did not have a history of a pronounced infantile feeding disorder, but she had tended to be an overweight baby and then a chubby child. She had been described as temperamental, strong-willed, and given to temper tantrums in her own infancy prior to becoming a rather "good, conforming, and generally well behaved, studious, serious" child. She was chubby but not fat and really began to be concerned about her weight and figure only in preadolescence. Periods of dieting, with moderate weight loss followed by gaining back the weight, had preceded the onset of mild adolescent anorexia.

The patient had always thought her mother was a powerful, dominant personality with a veneer of flexibility who insisted on having things her own way. This was particularly true with respect to meals, which were elaborately planned and carefully served with an emphasis on decorum and expectations of family appreciation. The patient recalled her mother's special interest in cooking, cookbooks, and kitchen designs; her mother also had an elaborate collection of plates with various shapes and designs, collected from many nations. The patient felt her mother had fine culinary and esthetic taste but was insensitive in other areas.

While emphasizing the pleasures of motherhood, the patient's mother had done little to prepare her for menstruation and had provided no sexual education or orientation toward adult independence. The patient was and wanted to remain mother's little girl. She later sensed that many marital and familial issues had been handled with silent avoidance. Discussions of food replaced other conversations about matters that were not nearly so palatable or "in good taste." Denial of problems with her mother preceded the patient's denial of significant adolescent weight loss. She had been expected to not be challenging or complaining, to swallow her pride and anger, and to not compete with her mother as the "queen bee" of the hive—or she would be stung. She was expected to think and behave as mother wished, harmonizing their superficial attitudes. Oedipal rivalry and jealousy favored a submissive homosexual attachment and preoedipal narcissistic regression. The residues of preoedipal difficulties in the patient's separation–individuation had lasting effects on the shape and fate of her Oedipus complex (Kramer and Akhtar, 1988).

Though the patient consciously determined to be different from her own mother, there were marked areas of similarity, particularly in her concerns about feeding and nurturance. Given her own concerns about the self-regulation of dieting and maintenance of weight, as well as her adolescent anorexia, it was not surprising that she would have problems regulating her infant's feedings. She had great difficulty in allowing the infant to self-regulate his own hunger, eating, and satiety. Problems of setting appropriate limits and of defining and negotiating rules and regulations became paramount (Blum and Blum, 1990); related unresolved conflicts with her own mother were reactivated in her motherhood.

The child's slight weight loss had revived his mother's earlier concerns over her anorexic weight loss and her fears about "starving the baby." She was guilty over her jealous rivalry with the baby and her own wishes to be fed—her wishes to withhold nurturance from the baby and to reverse roles of baby and mother. She unconsciously wanted to be the nurtured baby, who was also her greedy, needy self. She attempted now to overcompensate and overfeed by bribing, cajoling, coercing, and trying to trick the child into additional food intake. When her toddler rejected the food, this mother experienced it as a personal rejection and as a blow to her self-esteem. Her toddler's good eating had meant she was a good mother and had signified their mutual love, as though eating and feeding were a barometer of good feeling and well-being.

It is noteworthy that this patient and her own mother had shared denial of external interpersonal problems and similar conflicts in the recognition and appropriate expression of aggression. Aggression and reactive defenses compromised my patient's relationship to her own mother and later to her infant and husband (Parens, 1979). Her child reacted by not "swallowing" the mother's anxiety and anger and by dawdling over his food instead; he became a highly selective and finicky eater. Her toddler ate very slowly and selected his foods very carefully, often throwing the food he did not want to eat off the table.

This mother could not say no to herself and stop the feeding fights, the protracted mealtime struggles. She was also unable to say yes to the toddler and permit him to eat what he wanted in his own way and time. Although overcontrolling with respect to her child's intake, she could not say no to his regular extension and derailing of meals. Control over eating meant control of impulse, affect, and object and was pursued with persistence and varying effectiveness. Mother and child had become a pair of "gluttons for punishment" who devoured each other and the food with a vengeance. The mother became increasingly enmeshed with the child, who maintained the mother's close involvement even as he struggled to preserve autonomy through food refusal. Feeding was not a matter of hunger and satiety but, rather, a power struggle, endowed as well with elements of good and bad. To eat mother's food was generally good as far as she was concerned, and to not eat was bad. Eating or not eating could represent her own bad self and her toddler as a bad, despised narcissistic object. The case has similarities to other eating disorder patients, (cf. Chatoor, 1989), although this mother did not report that the baby was particularly irritable or difficult to soothe. Nor was her affect flat; nor did she avoid eye contact or communication with the baby during meals. However, in both instances, the toddler appeared particularly sensitive to the mother's cues and watched the mother's moves as the food was chewed or eschewed, thrown or made part of play. Both mother and toddler seemed aware of the mutual manipulation, of the affective and behavioral responses that were part of the cyclic cause-and-effect set of behaviors. The toddler's aggressive endowment and assertive, insistent, and persistent temperament contributed to his mother's conflicts and to their pathogenic expression.

In both cases the struggle was expressed with regard to play as well as to feeding. The child's separateness and autonomy from his mother were ambivalently wished and feared, ardently avoided and bitterly defended. In my patient's toddler, thwarted in an area usually governed by self-regulation, impaired regulation intruded into other areas, with inconsistent acceptance of limits and rules. Battling his mother's coerciveness, the youngster was a "holy terror" in nursery school; he refused to accept the teacher's reasonable limits; he banged and broke toys. This toddler was not frantic but apparently controlled the teacher through his infantile behavior and manipulation, refusing instruction and limits and extending the battle at home with his mother.

During the child's third year, his impulse control and ability to respond to limits and regulations gradually and then markedly improved. This occurred consequent to beneficial beginning oedipal reorganization in the child and to parallel improvement in the mother as a positive effect of her analytic treatment. As she gained insight into her conflicts, the mother was then able to set appropriate limits, to permit appropriate autonomy, and to negotiate settlements of even minor conflicts without either partner feeling totally defeated or omnipotently victorious. The taming of infantile omnipotence in the mother's analysis contributed to realistic judgments and limits and the taming of her infant's omnipotence. The improvement in both mother and child was sequential and parallel but hardly in a lockstep progression. There were separate and spontaneous regressive reactions and progressive movement for both partners without dramatic, sudden transformations of personality or behavior. Improvement was gradual and with much testing of limits in the analytic work of the mother and in her childrearing and maternal reactions. The child's developmental achievements also had a beneficial effect on the mother, so that a benign interaction replaced the battles on multiple fronts. As mother and child were less threatened and provoked by each other, the increased tranquillity permitted an expanded relationship and playful affection and aggression.

The father had a significant influence also, though his role is not elaborated here. This father was much more involved with the verbal, older, "developed" child, aiding the child's oedipal progression. He became an alternate benevolent object and a buffer, simultaneously offering relief to the child and unburdening the mother. It is also important to note that the parental relationship improved parallel to the mother's progress and their child's improvement.

DISCUSSION

In those cases where the infantile feeding disturbance is the precursor and prototype for similar adult disorders, it may be possible to trace the development of more subtle aspects of the disorder. The developmental disturbance and interwoven infantile conflicts may become absorbed into behavior patterns, character, and symptoms that are embedded in the overall personality. Over the course of later development, the symptoms and character disturbance may take on many new meanings, profoundly influenced by oedipal conflict and reorganization. The anlage of disturbance during separation–individuation may not be apparent compared to meanings that have now become confused and laden with oedipal and later development. The separation–individuation issues have to be inferred from laborious analytic work, which will reveal the preoedipal coloring or more serious distortions of the Oedipus complex. In some cases, infantile feeding disturbances such as unusual food selectivity, food fads, or very slow eating may persist into later life. In other cases, radical transformations may occur without any adult eating disorder.

The problem of setting rules and regulations and being self-regulated may appear in the form of alternate impulse and addictive disorders—such as abuse of alcohol or drugs, or promiscuous, hyperactive sexuality—or tendencies toward exploitative manipulation of others, theft, and other delinquencies. Earlier problems of prohibition and permission and of corruption of the formative superego through bribery, seduction, or coercion may lead, when not corrected in later phases of development, to an unreliable, dysfunctional, brittle superego vulnerable to infantile regression. Many of the features usually described in the past in terms of oral imprints on character, such as impetuosity, imperative demandingness, and insatiability, are also related to lack of frustration, tolerance, and impulse control and to an inconsistent and unreliable internalization of superego standards and ideals.

From an ego viewpoint, there are often highly idealized and devalued self and object representations, body image disturbances, and an inability to discriminate between affect and sensation, particularly in the area of hunger and satiety. Having long expressed their emotional needs and conflicts through eating or not eating and through the struggles of an eating disorder, these patients may not verbalize their emotional feelings and attitudes. They are then similar to other patients with psychosomatic disorders who demonstrate tendencies toward somatization rather than verbalization. However, the patient discussed in this chapter would not closely fit the category of alexithymia (Sifneos, 1973), since her fantasy life was not impoverished. Furthermore, each patient is unique, and generalizations should invoke caution and alternative considerations.

Familial patterns of avoiding discussion of affect-laden issues also contribute to the relative inability of patients with an eating disorder to describe their emotional states. The reliance of the adult patient on more infantile defenses of denial and projection is common. An anorexic patient, for example, may deny her anxiety about weight loss and malnutrition and may, instead, report only anxiety about "being fat." The oral greed and narcissistic entitlement may be repressed. What may appear are reaction formation and concerns not about being devouring and demanding but only about the need to be generous and self-sacrificing to not have needs, and to not impose upon others. Infantile omnipotence is untamed.

In analytic work in the transference, one is impressed with how much certain adolescent issues continue to carry forward earlier problems of incest, independence, and identity. The struggle for individuation (Blos, 1965; Mahler et al., 1975) continues as a very powerful motif and, at the same time, is in the service of disengagement from the incestuous objects.

Enmeshment with the original objects is particularly powerful and dangerous, so that narcissistic and preoedipal regression is even more pronounced in these adolescents and young adults. The distortions of early development that resulted from a pathological mother–child tie and interfered with separateness and autonomy, as well as the confusion and fusion of eating and emotional struggles (Bruch, 1982), are particularly revived with the problems of achieving adulthood. It should also be noted that preoccupations with eating and feeding and often obsessions about figure or food or their derivatives have resulted from and often lead to an impoverishment of object relations; narcissistic concerns with food and figure, eating and the body, have taken the place of enriched, developmentally advanced object relations. The bodily preoccupation can be of hypochondriacal intensity, with the body representing self and object. In the more infantile personalities, the narcissistic object relationship and pathogenic residuals of separation–individuation can be inferred in the condensation and coloring of their oedipal conflicts. Struggles over autonomy and separation and over omnipotence and narcissistic object relations tend to complicate, impede, or impose limits and modifications on the analytic process.

SUMMARY

Preoedipal issues are often important, though not exclusive, factors in adult eating disorders. Analytic work with parents, especially the mother, illuminates pathogenic preoedipal problems, with particular stress on separation–individuation. Food, feeding, eating, and nutrition become enmeshed in both interpersonal and intrapsychic conflict. Many adolescent and adult eating disorders have infantile prototypes, although later developmental consequences of infantile feeding disturbance are highly variable.

These patients with severe preoedipal problems are difficult to treat because of a lack of self and object constancy and because of preoedipal fixations. Autonomy; omnipotent control of affect, impulses, and objects; and narcissistic bodily preoccupation are critical areas for analytic work. The patient's instant, insatiable, and imperative demands are not only related to their oral character but can be further understood in terms of infantile superego function. Some of these patients have inconsistent and unreliable internal regulation, with contradictory dimensions of permission and punishment. Untamed entitlement and stoic self-sacrifice may coexist or alternate or may become dramatically manifest with preoedipal and superego regression.

The analysis of this mother with an anorexic history permitted an unusual analytic "window" into the development of her infant's infantile feeding disturbance in statu nasendi. Analytic exploration revealed the interrelated psychopathology of the mother–infant dyad and reconstructed the pathogenic infantile conflicts underlying the mother's own anorexic tendencies.

REFERENCES

Blum, E. & Blum, H. (1990), The development of autonomy and superego precursors. *Internat. J. Psycho-Anal.* 71:585–595.

Blum, H. (1983), The position and value of extratransference interpretations. *J. Amer. Psychoanal. Assn.,* 31:587–617.

Bruch, H. (1982), Anorexia nervosa: Therapy and theory. *Amer. J. Psychiat.,* 139:1531–1538.

Chatoor, I. (1989), Infantile anorexia nervosa: A developmental disorder of separation–individuation. *J. Amer. Acad. Psychoanal.,* 17:43–64.

Fischer, N. (1989), Anorexia nervosa and unresolved rapprochement conflicts. *Internat. J. Psycho-Anal.,* 70:41–54.

Freud, A. (1946), The psychoanalytic study of infantile feeding disturbances. *The Psychoanalytic Study of the Child,* 2:119–132. New York: International Universities Press.

Garfinkel, P. & Garner, D. (1982), *Prognosis in Anorexia Nervosa: A Multidimensional Perspective.* New York: Brunner/Mazel.

Kramer, S. (1974), Discussion of J. Sours's "The Anorexia Nervosa Syndrome." *Internat. J. Psycho-Anal.,* 55:577–579.

Kramer, S. & Akhtar, S. (1988), The developmental context of internalized preoedipal object relations: Clinical application of Mahler's theory of symbiosis and separation–individuation. *Psychoanal. Quart.,* 57:547–576.

Mahler, M., Pine, F. & Bergman, A. (1975), *The Psychological Birth of the Human Infant.* New York: Basic Books.

Mogul, S. (1989), Sexuality, pregnancy, and parenting in anorexia nervosa. *J. Amer. Acad. Psychoanal.,* 17:65–88.

Parens, H. (1979), *The Development of Aggression in Early Childhood.* New York: Aronson.

Risen, S. (1982), The psychoanalytic treatment of an adolescent with anorexia nervosa. *The Psychoanalytic Study of the Child,* 37:443–459. New Haven, CT: Yale University Press.

Sifneos, P. (1973), The prevalence of "alexithymic" characteristics in psychosomatic patients. *Psychother. Psychosom.,* 22:255–262.

Sours, J. (1980), *Starving to Death in a Sea of Objects.* New York: Aronson.

Spitz, R. (1965), *The First Year of Life.* New York: International Universities Press.

Weil, A. (1970), The basic core. *The Psychoanalytic Study of the Child,* 25:442–460. New York: International Universities Press.

15

Form and Function in Sexual Perversion
A Contribution to the Problem of "Choice" of Perversion

Charles W. Socarides

The "choice" of perversion remains a partial mystery. Why does one individual develop one form of perversion and another a different design even though both were exposed to pathological parenting of a similar nature? In this chapter I attempt to provide a verification of a general hypothesis arrived at from 30 years of psychoanalytic study of sexual perversions: the form or "choice" of a perversion, as it has been loosely alluded to, is determined by the function that it serves. The word "form" is used to mean the life within; it gives shape and individuality to any act or piece of behavior or structure. Form is the work either of nature or of art; it results in the arrangement of the parts, and *this disposition of the parts is adopted for performing certain functions*. Function, on the other hand, is an interoperational act, either unconscious or conscious, acting according to given rules set up by the form itself. Function becomes habitual and essential, and when function is interfered with, the form disintegrates. When form is disturbed, functional ability is destroyed and the motive power of any activity, including perversion, ceases to exist, especially in those cases subject to intensive psychoanalytic therapy.

The "choice" of neurosis and perversion seemed inextricably intertwined with each other from the very beginning, since Freud's data and theories originated from a single point of reference, that is, the level of libidinal fixation or regression (instinctual framework). Freud attempted to provide an explanation of both the "choice" of neurosis and the "choice" of perversion at more than one point in his career. In a letter to W. Fleiss (ca. 1900, #125) he commented:

> Perhaps I am up against the [problem of] "choice of neurosis." What makes a person an hysteric instead of a paranoiac? My first impression at this time while we are still trying to take the citadel by storm, was that this was dependent on the age at which the sexual [incident] occurred—at the time of the experience [Freud, 1897–1902, p. 303].[1]

FREUD'S CONTRIBUTION

In "The Three Essays" Freud (1905) made the interconnection among infantile sexuality, perversions, and neuroses, concluding that the neurosis represents the "negative of a perversion." In the next five years he, along with his contemporaries, developed a formulation of the essential developmental factors of homosexuality, including the different types of narcissistic object choice (1914) and the genetic constellations responsible for this developmental inhibition, such as an overstrong mother fixation that results in running away from the mother and a transfer of excitation from women to men in narcissistic fashion. These observations led to the discovery of an early positive Oedipus complex of great intensity, in the opinion of Freud's contemporaries. It has remained for future generations of psychoanalysts, informed as to object relations theory, ego psychology, ego functions, newer concepts of narcissism and self psychology, and, especially, knowledge derived from separation–individuation phases of development supplied by Mahler and her associates, to lessen the mystery of "choice" of perversion leading to its possible solution.

Long before the advent of ego psychology, Freud (1905) had remarked that the ego functions of identification and repression play an important part in homosexuality and that in homosexuals one finds a predominance of primitive and archaic psychical mechanisms. The absence of a comprehensive theory of ego development comparable to the already established theory of libidinal development presented difficulties for many years in the application of structural concepts to homosexuality and other perversions. Freud was well aware, however, that the late determinants of homosexuality came during adolescence, when a "revolution of the mental economy" takes place: the adolescent, in exchanging his mother for some other

---

[1]This temporal factor was noted by Freud (1905, 1922) as being of central importance.

sexual object, may make a choice of an object of the same sex. In 1910 Freud pointed out that the absence of the father and rearing of a male child in an almost completely feminine environment or the presence of a weak father who is dominated by the mother promoted feminine identification and homosexuality in the male child. The presence of a cruel father, he noted, would heighten a disturbance in male identification.

It became quite clear that there was a great similarity between a neurotic symptom and homosexuality. Perversions were not simply residues of the developmental process of infantile sexuality or the conscious representatives of unconscious instinct. Moreover, there appeared to be at times an alternation between phobia and perverse gratification. Freud's work on the relation of perversion to psychosis approached the matter from the point of view of the ego. In 1925 he showed that the ego is capable of extending its boundaries to accept what would otherwise be repressed provided that it be consciously denied. In his last years, Freud (1938b) defined the splitting of the ego and the object and the role of each in perversion formation (1938a).

The concept of the role of a premature fixation of the libido in the genesis of homosexuality appeared in "Some Neurotic Mechanisms in Jealousy, Paranoia, and Homosexuality." Freud (1922) further added that an important discovery is evident in the fact that the "qualitative factor, the presence of certain neurotic formations, has less practical significance than the quantitative factor, the degree of attention or, more correctly, the amount of cathexis that these structures are able to attract to themselves" (p. 228).

Freud could not sufficiently separate perversion formation from neurosis except to say that the perversion represents an inhibition and dissociation of psychosexual development, bringing pain rather than pleasure, and is one of the pathological outcomes of the oedipal period. He commented that analytic investigation at that time could not disclose any single psychogenic or structural pattern that would apply to all or even a major proportion of the cases of homosexuality or of any other perversion. Freud (1919) returned to this vexing problem in "A Child is Being Beaten." He noted that Binet, long before the days of psychoanalysis, was able to "trace the strange sexual aberrations of maturity back to similar impressions and precisely the same period of childhood, namely the fifth or sixth year" (p. 182). Freud attempted an explanation for Binet's observations: one of the components of sexual function has "broken loose prematurely . . . developed in advance of the rest, has made itself prematurely independent, has undergone fixation and in consequence been withdrawn from the later processes of development, and has in this way given evidence of a peculiar and abnormal constitution of the individual" (p. 181). This explanation, however, was both contradictory and confusing, since it proposed that an "abnormal constitution of the individual," not "an hypertrophy" of development, resulted in perverse development. Freud conceded that

> at this point . . . [we are] confronted with limitations of our knowledge; for the impressions that brought about the fixation were without any traumatic force. They were for the most part commonplace, not exciting to other people. It is *impossible* to say why the sexual impulse had underdone fixation particularly upon them [p. 182].

What was possible in Freud's mind, however, was that the impressions "offered an *occasion for fixation* [my emphasis], (even though it was an accidental one) to precisely that component which was prematurely developed and ready to press forward. . . . [We must trace] back the chain of causal connection" (p. 182). Such a causal connection was to be based upon the "congenital constitution" that seemed exactly to correspond with what was required for a "stalking place of that kind" (p. 182).

In the same essay Freud came to two important conclusions that set the stage for future psychoanalytic researchers who would arise from the field of infant/child observational studies. First, perverse fantasies appear only toward the end of this period, that is, "two to four or five years or after its termination. So it might quite well be that they (beating fantasies) have an earlier history, that they go through a process of development, that they represent an end-product and not an initial manifestation" (p. 184). Second, Freud (1919) concluded that

> the constitutional reinforcement of premature growth in a single component is not shaken, indeed, but it is seen not to comprise the whole truth. The perversion is no longer an isolated fact in the child's sexual life, but forms a place among the typical, not to say normal processes of development which are familiar to us. It is brought into relation with the child's incestuous love object, with its Oedipus complex. It first comes into prominence in the sphere of this complex and after the complex has broken down it remains over, often by itself, the inheritor of the charge of the libido from that complex and laid over by the sense of guilt that was attached to it. The abnormal sexual constitution, finally, has shown its strength by forcing the Oedipus complex into a particular direction, telling it to leave an unusual residue behind. . . . A perversion in childhood, as is well known, may become the basis for the construction of a perversion having a similar sense and persisting throughout life, one which consumes the subject's whole sexual life. On the other hand, the perversion may be broken off and remain in the background of a normal sexual development, from which, however, it continues to withdraw a certain amount of energy. The first of these

alternatives was already known before the days of analysis. . . . We find often enough with these perverts that they too made an attempt to develop a normal sexual activity, usually at the age of puberty, but their attempt had not enough force in it and was abandoned in the face of the first obstacles which inevitably arise. Whereupon they fell back upon their infantile fixation once and for all [p. 191–193].

Nevertheless, Freud knew that a psychoanalytic understanding of perversion was not yet complete:

The additional task of making it clear why something has not taken place . . . should not be our task. The present state of our knowledge will allow us to make our way so far and not further toward the comprehension of beating fantasies [for example]. . . . In the mind of the analytic physician, it is true, there remains an uneasy suspicion that this is not a final solution of the problem [p. 183].

Despite his inability to arrive at a solution, Freud's observations were of great significance to our present state of knowledge. The following is a reemphasis with further specificity of the assumptions contained within Freud's ideas: (1) at certain points the obligatory male homosexual had an intense infantile preoedipal attachment to the mother, although he can not explain the reason for this attachment; (2) the sexual perversion may well be considered the "negative of the neurosis," since it brought pleasure, not pain, and relieved intrapsychic distress, at least temporarily; (3) a component of the sexual function, constitutionally reinforced, advanced and became independent of the remainder of the sexual function and was then confronted by or interacted with an *event* that produced a fixation; the end result is a withdrawal from later processes of development, and an abnormality, the perversion, occurs. Central to this view is Freud's (1919) conclusion that "substitutes for the penis which [men] feel is missing in women play a great part in the determination of the *form* of many perversions" (p. 195; italics added).

LATER THEORETICAL AND CLINICAL PSYCHOANALYTIC CONTRIBUTIONS

Anna Freud (1949) concluded that perverse behavior is the consequence of a perverse fantasy that occurs in latency: "One single image of a fantasy remains into which the whole past area of infantile sexuality and aggression may be compressed" (p. 80). She thereby introduced a concept of the vicissitudes of *aggression,* formerly simply thought of as a form of libidinal expression, in the formation of perversion. She noted that the "nature of this fantasy varies according to the main fixation points [returning to Freud's original theory] in the child's instinctual life, secondary to early satisfactions, frustrations, or traumatic experiences [that] had the strongest influence over development" (pp. 90–91). In 1956 Kris elaborated on this theme, concluding that the *form* of a perversion is dependent upon the specific life experiences that are usually incorporated in a camouflaged way into a fantasy.

Edward Glover (1964) asked, and offered explanations for, the following questions:

> What determines the option of perversion against the option of neurosis and what determines the particular *form* of perversion organized? The possible answer to the first question has already been suggested, namely that the individual attempts to spare himself the pressures by displacing his pathogenic conflict to the psychosexual sphere and by his partial or total renunciation of normal sexual relations. He thereby seeks to preserve himself (not always successfully, of course) from situations liable to activate the incestuous conflict and the aggressive charges incident thereto [p. 153; italics added].

Glover proposed that one spares oneself depression by displacing conflicts within the psychosexual sphere, as well as those thoughts enumerated by Anna Freud, and emphasized a warding off of incestuous conflict and aggression. A third significant factor in the more serious and intractable perversions is that they offer an option of perversion over psychosis. "By these acts of denial and displacement the pervert is able to protect his reality sense from gross interference which might otherwise give rise to psychotic or near psychotic manifestations" (Glover, 1964, p. 154). As proof of the latter, Glover cited clinical material that melancholic and schizoid individuals frequently develop transitory perverse formations with the relief of depression and with a corresponding recovery of reality sense through the use of perversions. This recovery of reality sense was preceded by an onrush of primitive sadomasochistic fantasies. Glover's observations were validated by later investigators: perversion represents an attempt to protect against anxiety and guilt associated with primitive fantasies through a process of excessive libidinization. These comments explain, in part, the function of a perverse act but not its form. Through the neutralization of sadism, for example, an individual sacrifices freedom and adult libidinal functioning, with a resultant quantitative decrease in the strength of sadism and aggression through the perversion.

In 1978 I introduced the concept of the "organizing experience" in perversion encompassing a wide range of forms, from oedipal to preoedipal to severe preoedipal and even schizoperversion. The theoretical underpinnings for my interpretations were supplied by the separation–individuation theory of Mahler and her associates (1975). All perverts present (1) a basic preoedipal nuclear conflict with a dread of and wish for merging with the preoedipal mother and a failure to traverse separation–individuation phases, with consequent merging and fusion anxiety (Socarides, 1978, 1988); (2) a predominance of archaic needs and primitive mental mechanisms; (3) deficiencies of the ego; (4) an increase in early primary and secondary aggression; (5) a disturbance in body–self schematization, particularly of the genital area; (6) a disturbance in the attainment of object constancy; and (7) a persistence of a primary feminine identification with the mother together with a faulty gender-defined self-identity, that is, an inability to disidentify from the mother and make a counteridentification with the father. It is not the erotic act *per se* that is reactivated in the perversion, whether homosexuality, transvestism, pedophilia, bug perversion (Stolorow and Grand, 1973), and so forth, or the bizarre acts themselves but the function of these acts that is reanimated in the perversion.

Organizing Experiences

Organizing experiences are those early sexual activities that not only provided orgastic release, sexual excitement, and a feeling of being alive but by virtue of the accompanying affective release supplied an initial sense of self-cohesion and means of relating to the internal world and external object. Organizing experiences reflect different compromises between simultaneous identifications with the phallic and penisless mother, the wish to maintain an optimal distance from and closeness to her without fear of her engulfment or feelings of fragmentation, faulty development of object and self representations, and an inadequate separation of self from object.

All perversions express two functions: (1) a warding off or reassuring function and (2) a reaffirming or compensatory function. To illustrate, engaging in a spanking game with his sister and neighborhood girlfriend at the age of five produced in my patient, Dr. X, a sense of "physical and emotional closeness," a sense of pleasure and well-being that he had never known before. In contrast to his usual state of helplessness, apathy, hopelessness, and despair in his family life, the experience simultaneously aroused him genitally and helped repress other aspects of his sexuality that he deplored on a religious and ethical basis. As a result, despite being high in the academic world, he would have to visit a prostitute once a week in order to engage in his spanking perversion while dressed as a little girl of eleven or twelve.

Other examples may be seen in voyeurs who begin peeping just before puberty. One stated: "I had been shy before that, but when this began I felt like I had escaped from a shell," a shell of reclusivity and an inability to sustain object relations.

A homosexual patient recalled during analysis that it was only at the age of seven, after an older boy lay on top of him while he was napping in a schoolroom during lunch time, that he became "vital" and alive and not a "sexless" kind of person. Another example is that of a fetishist who used male underwear in his later life in order to ward off fears of bodily disintegration as a female, a practice organized around the experience at three or four of being wrapped tightly by his mother before going to sleep.

Niederland (1958) described a 30-year-old overtly homosexual masochistic man who induced older athletically built men to "insult and threaten him verbally, and make him kneel before them, suck their genitals and finally have them perform anal intercourse on him" (p. 383). In this case history Niederland presented a patient who was brought up in a household overloaded with females—mother and four older sisters—in which he was made to feel like a girl. In one of the sessions the patient reported a particularly satisfactory experience of anal intercourse with an older man: "I liked the way he did it. It was a good beat." His associations to the word "good beat" led back to what was an organizing experience: a beating experience at the age of four when his father beat him in the parental bedroom with a belt for having locked his bedroom door. The patient's mother stood outside the locked door, screaming and begging to be let in, and was prevented from doing so by the enraged father. The patient was trying to "create the passion my father was in during this beating. This is what I wanted, this kind of athletic man grabbing me, holding me. . . . it was really breathtaking, father holding me with his strong arms tightly and I cringing." It was the breathtaking, passionate experience of the father's "passion," the mother's "screaming," and the patient's taking the latter's place, being beaten, that he then tried to repeat with a never-ending succession of male partners.

In a case reported by Bak (1971), a patient became a transvestite and finally attempted a transsexual solution because his sister overstimulated him at the age of two and a half, repeatedly seducing him by pushing his genitals inward and saying to him, "Now you are a girl." This decisive trauma in Bak's patient was repressed and covered over with infantile amnesia only to reappear later in the dangerous practice of pushing the genitals inside the body and in the occasional compulsive wish to cry out,

"I am a girl." The continual witnessing of his mother's dressing and undressing and the incessant photographing of his sister by the father created massive excitations of rivalrous rage, which the patient's ego had to deal with through a preordained path. The ego made use of the traumatic fixation in the defensive process and obviously used it as a solution of aggressive conflict.

To reemphasize, in general we may say that organizing experiences are those early sexual activities, not always of an obvious traumatic nature by themselves but recovered in the analysis, that play a crucial role in the later *form* of the perversion. They not only provide genital excitement but by virtue of the accompanying affective release supply an initial sense of self-cohesion, a means of relating to the internal world and external objects. Since such experiences help create the "end-product" (Freud, 1919), they may be considered to play an essential role in the "choice of a perversion" and validate and fulfill Freud's hopes concerning the understanding of this condition.

As early as 1969 I suggested that the choice of perversion is a multifactorial one, depending on a number of variables. One person finds it much easier to accept a particular aspect of infantile polymorphous sexuality than another, due to specific organizing experiences, for example, traumata occurring at vulnerable periods of libidinal-phase progression in the context of a defective early ego development. The ego's acceptance of a particular aspect of infantile sexuality into consciousness through displacement, substitution, and other mental mechanisms serves to keep deeper anxieties in repression. This suggestion was first made by Hanns Sachs in 1923. The Hanns Sachs mechanism can be observed in the formation of all perversions, giving to each perversion its surface manifes-tations while excluding from consciousness the deeper, more destructive anxieties. It is a solution by division whereby one piece of infantile sexuality enters the service of repression (i.e., is helpful in promoting repression through displacement, substitution, reaction formation, and other defense mechanisms) and thus carries over pregenital pleasure into the ego while the rest undergoes repression. This repressive compromise mechanism allows a conscious suitable portion to be supported and endowed with a high pleasure reward so that it competes successfully with genital pleasure. It is acceptable to both the ego and to the superego: a split-off part of the superego derived from the parents may sanction the perversion, and a manifest perversion gives expression to preoedipal drives in a masked form. On the other hand, a repressed portion may still remain strong enough so that in the course of life it may threaten a breakthrough, and the pervert may at any time develop neurotic symptoms. Thus, the instinctual gratification takes place in a disguised form while its real content remains unconscious. Viewed in this light, the manifest perversion can be likened to the relationship that exists between the manifest dream and latent dream content; the true meaning of the perversion can be ascertained only through the analysis of the unconscious meaning of the perverse action.

There may be fluctuations in the balance of psychic economy that force the individual to manifest now one and now another perverse practice, although perverse practices are stereotyped and obligatory, as a rule. On these occasions, the defensive value of one type of perversion appears insufficient to maintain the mental equilibrium, and multiple perversions or fantasies may appear. The alternation between perverse practices, or the inability to form a well-structured perversion in the face of intense primitive anxiety, may in some instances indicate that we may be dealing with an underlying schizophrenic process or that there has been an unsuccessful splitting of the ego and object, a precondition for the formation of sexual perversions (Gillespie, 1956); on the other hand, the perverse activity may be completely unacceptable to the superego so that perverse fantasy is reacted to only with dread rather than with pleasure.

Affects, Need-Tension Gratification, and Narcissism

Greenacre (1968) predicted that studies of early infant development would indicate that in all perverts the fundamental cause of the disturbance is that the defectively developed ego uses the pressure of the maturing libidinal phases for its own purposes in characteristic ways because of the "extreme and persistent narcissistic needs" (p. 484). What are these "extreme and persistent narcissistic needs" and what is their significance for the choice or form of the perversion? Greenacre (1968) correctly noted that there are children who have had to undergo variable feelings of deadness and chronic states of depletion who then attempt to counteract their sense of emptiness when their requirements for selfobject responsiveness are chronically unmet. They attempt to rescue their depleted selves "via the forced stimulation of their own body, particularly the erogenous zones, their function, and products" (p. 115). The result is sadomasochism, homosexuality, narcissistic stimulation of one's own body, anal practices, compulsive cleaning of the anus, and so forth. In the history of sexual deviants we find retention of feces, soiling, smearing, lonely and depressed masturbation, addiction-like sucking, overeating, food avoidance, passivity, and even hypersexuality. According to Tolpin (1979), "the pervert is driven to sexual enactments with figures or symbols to give him a feeling of being wanted, real, alive and powerful, just as the drug addict needs an escape from the realization that he feels devoid of sustaining self-confidence and sustaining ideals" (p. 135). These enactments increase the feeling of being alive, of existing in the world. In perversion there is a search for sexualized reassurance: acts are repeated unremittingly without producing a cure. Such patients have a need for a parent to be a calm self-esteem regulator (Socarides and Stolorow, 1985). The mothers of such patients produce in the child a *phase-hunger* for touch, love, and vision.

Mahler and colleagues' (1975) description of the subphases of separation–individuation allowed us to examine each perversion under several headings: (1) the acceptance or rejection of appropriate gender-defined self-identity, including that of disidentification with the primary feminine identification with the mother in early childhood and a counteridentification with the father in boys; (2) the severity and degree of neutralized aggression, primary or secondary; (3) the form of the perversion itself, for example, perverse telephoning, voyeuristic behavior, homosexuality, transvestism; (4) the attitude toward the presence and/or absence of the penis; and (5) specific organizing life experiences (Socarides, 1988) incorporated and camouflaged into a fantasy derived from infantile sexuality and aggression, together with reassuring affective aspects of the original experience.

Excessive stimulation and frustration help decide the *form* of perversion. Greenacre (1968) suggested that excessive erotization in early life takes place because of the need to control or diminish emotions of a purely aggressive kind. Serious physical operations between the ages of three and four should be avoided, since they have a particularly devastating effect owing to the threat of the loss of the object or of the object's love.

Other mental mechanisms may be important. For example, through displacement the eye may come to stand for the genitals, a displacement that produces visual disorders of the sadomasochistic type, expressed in a disguised way. The symbolic expression of the castration complex arising from the Oedipus complex is often experienced as a fear of damage to the eye or of blindness. Rosen (1964a, b) stated that although visual instinct and function are so central to human behavior as to be linked developmentally with all other instinctive behaviors and to the relationship with objects, there are two special linkages that it has with other drives. The first is the wish to show or exhibit one's self, the second to touch what is seen. Looking and showing belong to a duality felt at the conscious and unconscious levels of the mind in the way that sadism and masochism coexist. There are different degrees to which sadism and masochism or both are present in any particular individual, depending on the amount of hypercathexis, repression, or reaction formation against the exhibitionistic or scopophilic tendencies. Acts of exhibitionists, according to Rosen, have unconscious voyeuristic wishes and acts of voyeurs have an exhibitionistic component. Rosen believes the sexual perversions are the living out of pieces of infantile sexual behavior that have been retained in the personality in order to hold in check other, more undesirable, elements or to defend the individual against the threat of castration or the effects of object loss.

Vision becomes concentrated and directed onto the bodies of the parents and in particular onto the genitals, excretory, copulatory behavior, or any other surgical or physical abnormalities. A successfully treated underwear fetishist was frequently exposed to the sight of the mother's cesarean-section scar before the age of four. Witnessing parental intercourse or excretory behavior greatly increases the scopophilic sexual fantasies in the already predisposed.

From many years of clinical observation I have concluded that perverse activity is likely to occur when there is a lack of satisfactory maternal care (need-satisfaction), the mother being either depriving or overwhelming (Greenacre, 1968). This solution tends to produce a "prolongation of the uncertainty about the 'I' and the 'other,' with a consequent situation conducive to continuing oscillation in relationships. The condition makes for an impairment or slowing of object relationships and a greater retention of primary aggression with an increase in secondary aggression secondary to frustration" (p. 305).

Another determinant of perversion is the child's observation of a lack of a phallus in girls. Children are not likely to be disturbed by the sameness of body or genital schema but by the absence of a particular bodily part. They then may imagine, for example, that the phallus "must have been torn out of me while I was asleep." Such an observation is ubiquitous and requires a predisposition to give it much force. It is especially strong and persistent in many perverse conditions and clearly attains a compelling importance in fetishism. The consequent belief in the phallic mother (Bak, 1968) must be preceded by disturbances in the first two years of life; this belief dramatically affects the progress of the separation–individuation phases with a consequent interference in the development of appropriate gender-defined self-identity and appropriate object relations, and with a disturbance in ego function (e.g., body-ego definition, self-concept).

A further determinant of perversion was suggested as early as 1905 by Freud when he alluded to weakness in the sexual apparatus that had been especially affected by some trauma of childhood. But he could not describe its specific nature or how it influenced the "special character" of the perversion.

An additional matrix for perversion was that supplied by Mahler and colleagues (1975) and also by Abelin (1971). These authors were of the opinion that the following factors are important: (1) a lack of respect for the father by the mother[2] (important for the development of homosexuality in a male child); (2) a failure of satisfaction in maternal care in a seemingly overprotective and domineering mother who does not allow the phallic qualities of her son to emerge owing to her own sex-related conflicts. The mother, according to Mahler, may be either overdepriving or overwhelming, thus producing a prolongation of the separation of the "I" and the "other," as noted by Greenacre.

Still other possible factors leading to perversion are the following: (1) "visual focusing," which may play a role that we have not yet fully investigated; (2) frequent exposure to the opposite sex, which may confuse the child about anatomical differences and impair his perception of his own body, particularly his genitals; (3) the belief in the phallic mother, which may be preceded by disturbances in the first two years of life affecting the progress of separation–individuation and consequently interfering with developing object relations, disturbances along the lines suggested by Kernberg (1975); (4) too-early separation from the mother and father, which may lead to voyeurism (object loss, according to Almansi, 1983, may also have pronounced effects on the development of genital body schema in later life); (5) direct injury to the child in the fourth year, which may produce serious shock and collapse (Greenacre, 1968).

To summarize, early disturbances in the mother–infant relationship, severe impairment in object relations combined with precipitously determined weakness of the self- and body-image, especially of the genitals, may occur in situations where the maturing sexual drives are distorted in the interests of bolstering the body image. There is then a vicious circle of recurring castration panic for which the fetish or ritualized behavior seems almost a stopgap. (Perverse development may also occur in individuals with good character structure, especially in creative ones.)

Mahler, Pine and Bergman (1975) noted that the accomplishment of enduring individuality consists of the attainment of two levels of the sense of identity: an awareness of being a separate and individual entity and the beginning awareness of a gender-defined self-identity. These authors observed that difficulties in gender-identity development are revealed more by their failures than by normal variations. They noted that gender-identity in the male develops with less conflict when the mother respects and enjoys the boy's phallicity, especially in the second and the third year. An identification with the father or possibly with an older brother facilitates the early beginning of a male's gender identity. The mother must

---

[2]Chasseguet-Smirgel's (1986) monograph refers to and explores the importance of this factor.

not interfere with the boy's developing autonomy, or his gender-role identity may be threatened or disturbed.[3] She must be able to relinquish her son's body and give ownership of his penis to him. Crushing activity or forcing passivity is extremely damaging to the development of gender-defined self-identity. Rapprochement unquestionably takes on the character of a more or less desperate biphasic struggle on the part of the boy to ward off the dangerous mother after separation.

While Mahler and her associates' major interest was to achieve an understanding of the development of the human infant and child in the course of normal separation and individuation processes, a development leading to the establishment of object constancy, self-constancy, and enduring individuality (the attainment of a separate and individual self), Galenson and Roiphe (1973) have illuminated factors in the preoedipal phase that lead to the awareness of gender-defined self-identity. Roiphe (1968) made a definitive connection between the fear of object loss and early castration anxiety, noting that the major thrust of development during the early months is of concern for the differentiation of the self from the object and the internalization and assimilation of the object representation. This early period of genital interest and activity takes place entirely during the preoedipal phase. "Early experiences that tend to challenge the child unduly with a threat of object loss or bodily dissolution result in a faulty and vacillating genital outline of the body at the time when a genital schematization normally undergoes a primary consolidation" (Roiphe, 1968, p. 357).

FORM AND FUNCTION IN PERVERSION: AN ATTEMPTED CORRELATION

My thesis is that the variable forms and protean manifestations of a sexual perversion are dependent on Freud's general rule (1915–1916): "Let us once more reach an agreement upon what is to be understood by the 'sense' of a psychical process. We mean nothing other by it than the intention it serves in its position in the psychical continuity" (p. 40). Correspondingly, the *form* is dependent on the unconscious and unconscious motivation of the act, that is, its functional importance. Both form and function are furthermore dependent on the stage of development—

---

[3]Important contributions to this subject have been made by Stoller (1964, 1966, 1968, 1975, 1982) and Volkan (1979, 1982), among others.

that is, the level of libidinal fixation; the presence or absence of developmental arrest, either partial or complete; the status of object relations; the
successful or unsuccessful traversing of the preoedipal phases of separation–individuation leading to object constancy; and the "organizing
experiences" (Socarides, 1978) undergone by the subject during preoedipal, postoedipal, and even pubertal years.

All perversions reflect the intention to achieve sexual orgasm, a primary
trait of perversion, and autoerotic satisfaction through orgastic experience.
Normally, this is accomplished in the standard sexual pattern (Rado,
1949), characterized by (1) the sexual act occurring between adult male
and adult female and (2) a possibility for the penis to enter the vagina
before orgastic release, although this activity may not be preferred at the
moment. Perverse sexual practices occur between same-sex adult pairs,
adult–child pairs, and/or in deficient sexual acts such as sadism, masochism, transvestism, and transsexualism. All the latter imply a deficiency in
the possibility of male/female penetration and, of course, are ineffective for
reproduction.

It is becoming increasingly evident that it is not the fixated neurotic
experience *per se* (the instinctual derivative)—its polymorphous perverse
derivative—that is regressively reanimated in the patient's perversion;
rather, it is the early function (Stolorow and Lachmann, 1980) of this
erotic experience that has been retained and regressively relied upon. In
this way, through erotization, the patient attempts to maintain a structural cohesion and implement the stability of threatened self and object
representations.

Through erotization, anxiety and depressive affects are also eliminated.
Depression is turned into its opposite through a "manic defense" or flight
to antidepressant activity via sexuality (Socarides, 1985). By acting out, the
pervert further stabilizes his sense of self, reinforces object relations—even
though they are pseudo object relations—overcomes destructive aggression
and feelings of vulnerability, and brings pleasure to an internalized object.
The symptom represents an overcoming of earlier severe intrapsychic crises
by displacing and projecting the inner need and tension onto another
person or object. It is an attempt to master a traumatic internal problem
through controlling actual external objects by concocting what Khan
(1965) has termed "active ego-directed, experimental play-action object
relations" (p. 409) in which the "technique of intimacy" plays a major
role. Affective release into the external world diminishes internal threats
provoked by destructive aggression. Pathological internalized object relations that have led to despair and hopelessness are mitigated. The
perversion is experienced as a creative and reparative act. Similarly, the

absence of healthy self-esteem and the pathological relation to internal parental objects is lessened through "creating a pseudo object relationship and mutual pleasure," which reestablishes a "rudimentary mode of communication with the external object" (Khan, 1965, p. 408). Because no true object relation is achieved through the perverse act and no internalization of the object takes place, there is no true ego enhancement and the perversion must be incessantly repeated, often with numerous partners.

Perverse acts are facilitated by (1) deficiencies in the ego due in part to a lack of neutralized energy, deficiencies impairing the ability to control immediate responses and to neutralize instinctual discharges of both primary and secondary aggression; (2) a lack of internalization of superego functions, resulting in a horizontal or vertical split (Kohut, 1971), so that an individual of high character and morals may behave in one moment according to his public self and another according to his private sexual self; and (3) splitting of the ego, making it possible for a perversion to be sanctioned by the split-off part representing parental attitudes themselves. In a primitive manner, acting out helps to maintain the cohesiveness of the ego and supplies it with an opportunity to initiate reparative moves toward a real object, therefore making it seem "quite normal" to engage in perverse activities, even of the most bizarre type. (One of the strangest perversions on record is that of a man who could only achieve orgasm by allowing his legs to be run over by a young woman driving a convertible car in such a way that his legs were not shattered but simply pressed into a soft mat or soft material (Keeler, 1960).

The form of perversion is dependent on early childhood experiences and seductions; on the degree of need and control of aggression; on the need to meet certain narcissistic needs; on the need to create, even in fantasy, suitable "parenting," to find empathy, to find a "holding environment" (Winnicott, 1965); and on the need to provide internal structure that was in the process of formation but became frustrated.

Above all, the *form must be restorative,* in the psychological sense of making good that which was unjustly taken away. Restitution may be provided through an archaic form via the sensoriperceptive apparatus—the eye and the mouth, for example. The need to cover up a defect in ego boundaries may lead to sensory stimulation from the outside against body surfaces to produce a feeling of being alive. The defect in gender-defined self-identity leads to an inability to know what sex one is consciously and/or unconsciously (gender-defined self-identity confusion). The need to control aggression may lead via libidinization to play activities engaged in with an active, supportive partner in which aggression is controlled by actively supporting and inducing it rather than passively enduring it.

Clinical Examples

In male transvestism there is an unconscious wish to be a female; aggression is neutralized by the perversion. The mechanism employed is visceral and tactile introjection with identification; the attitude toward the absence of a penis is denial. In fetishism the need to control and have one's own ego boundaries may lead to a reestablishment of the sense of self through the concretization of a symbol, the female phallus. In male transsexualism, where there is a nonacceptance of a female gender-defined self-identity, aggression is neutralized through becoming a woman; the mechanism employed is both surgical and endocrinological recasting, together with all the mechanisms present in male transvestism. In preoedipal type II narcissistic homosexuals (Socarides, 1978), the homosexual encounter is related to pathological narcissism, representing a search for both the narcissistic and grandiose self-representation. In uniting with another man there is a fusion of the self with various images of both mother and father with their associated emotions. Suffering from a severe loss of normal narcissistic self-esteem and filled with pathological object relations, these patients remedy their sense of emptiness and inertia by giving pleasure to an external object and self simultaneously. In the homosexual act, they induce dependence in the partner, compel an external object into instinctual surrender, augment a sense of power, and reduce a sense of isolation. The aim of the act is to shore up a failing self-representation and ward off regressive fragmentation. The homosexual encounter provides a place to put emotions so that the patient is made to feel alive and whole, at least for the moment. In contrast, in preoedipal type I homosexuals (Socarides, 1978), the pursued partner is a representation of the patient's own self (narcissistic) in relation to an active phallic mother. The patient identifies with and incorporates the partner's masculinity through the sexual act. An unconscious reenactment of the mother–child role via the breast–penis equation tends to undo separation.

In a case of fetishism I (1960) analyzed, the underwear (boxer shorts) fetish had many functions: (1) it protected the patient's entire body against change, delivering him from bodily disintegration anxiety; (2) it afforded him orgastic release; (3) it provided a symbolic wish to have a child; (4) it assured him in his belief in the phallic mother; (5) it defended him against homosexual desires; (6) it warded off the activation of more primitive bodily destruction fears intimately connected with separation anxiety and his own (unconscious) wish to have a child himself; (7) it displaced damage to his own body in that the clothing, rather than his own body or the body of the mother, could be ripped; (8) it represented not only the imagined penis of the mother but also her breast, her swollen pregnant abdomen, and other parts of her body from which he did not wish to be separated; (9) it recaptured the early object relationship with his loved mother—the sameness in the continuation of the primary feminine identification with her; (10) it helped terminate the savagery of fantasied attacks against the maternal body and breast, bringing sexual arousal and orgasm—the fetish was a stand-in for the mother when he felt all alone and very unhappy (the primary feminine identification with the mother and the excessive splitting-off of parts of himself, their lack of formation into a cohesive self, and the anxiety attendant in this state of confusion and threat of self-disintegration were alleviated by the invocation of the fetish); (11) it symbolically protected him against the hostile impulses toward changes in form and shape of the female body (since the fetish covered the penis, it became clear that the sight of the penis reminded him of an impending mutilation; thus, the fetish served a warding-off function); (12) it both gratified and protected him from his own wishes to have a child; (13) it showed, as revealed in his dreams, a strong defensive function—it provided restitution for the desired destruction of the maternal body and helped continue the union with his mother in order to prevent her loss.

The analysis of a telephone perversion revealed that the function of heterosexual perverse telephoning was to achieve masculinity and self-object differentiation through eliciting and hearing the verbal/emotional and sexual responses to sexual/obscene/aggressive words at a distance. Verbalization was the equivalent to exhibiting one's sexual organs and, in complimentary fashion, to viewing those described by the object (*form* of the perversion). The introjection of the female's response was achieved through the auditoriperceptive apparatus. The object's sexual response and the description of female sexual organs and reactions provided the subject with a sense of masculinity, since they reassured him of the anatomical differences between the sexes. Telephoning reassured against and lessened castration fear, diminished separation anxiety, and promoted and simultaneously disavowed the identification with a powerful mother. It neutralized fear of her while unconsciously, at an oedipal level, gratifying the infantile wish for sexual closeness to her. The psychosexual motivation for the act was orgastic desire beneath many other desires. The patient stated: "If I picture myself as the man and the woman reacts, then I am a man and I do not desire men [denial of homosexuality] and I am not a female [defense against feminine identification]."

Another illustration may be provided by a case of voyeurism: in a patient I (1974) analyzed, the voyeur and sadist was seen to have suffered from a basic preoedipal nuclear conflict found in all perversions: the fear of merging and fusing with the mother. This was accompanied by a predominance of archaic and primitive psychical mechanisms, especially projective and incorporative anxieties. The failure to separate from the mother caused a disturbance in gender-defined self-identity and the patient developed an intense primary feminine identification that was unacceptable to him consciously. The *function* of voyeurism was to reinforce masculinity through the visual reassurance of viewing the female body at a distance and as distinct from his own. By viewing intercourse that took place outside himself the patient was sure that it was not he who was being penetrated (*form*): the entire event took place externally to himself. He wished also to reassure himself by means of distancing that he was not being swallowed up or enveloped by the woman's orifices. He masturbated while viewing his victim from outside the bedroom window. Often during his voyeuristic acts he exhibited his penis (in later stages of his condition) so that the woman would react with fright (exhibitionistic component). My patient's voyeurism proved to be a defense against unconscious homosexual wishes that he found too threatening and disturbing, with their connotation of being damaged by men in anal intercourse (in prison he did not allow any men to approach him homosexually). He was reassured against his primary female identification and his fear of castration. The occurrence of the sexual event outside himself prevented a deep fear of being invaded by the body of the mother. For this patient the engulfment by the female could occur in the eye of the female (a substitute for her genitals) through the mechanism of ocular introjection. Her eyes could penetrate into his eyes, into his body, and become an internalized persecutory object that threatened to destroy the insides of his body, to tear them out, to rob and deplete him of strength and masculinity, to weaken and depress him, to divest him of well-being. These fears originated in childhood with the fear of his mother robbing him of everything he possessed. Frequently, as he closed his eyes and attempted to sleep, he fantasized a dream of an enormous hawk-like bird flying through the window and attacking him. He dared not close his eyes to stop looking, fearing he would then be attacked and destroyed. The voyeur wishes to retain the optimal distance from and/or closeness to women (mother) without fear of engulfment; he yearns for masculinity and dramatizes his masculine strength through his voyeuristic activities. Voyeurism, an act of invading others' sexual privacy, can proceed from looking to touching, from seeing to assaulting and ultimately destroying (sexual sadism).

In 1919 Freud alluded to the *function* of the sexual experience by asserting that the four aims of sexual experience were longing for love, relief from loneliness, a yearning for a reunion with the loved one, and a desire for ecstasy. Certainly perversions satisfy these requirements, although fleetingly and impermanently. It is the power of the orgasm to create or confirm conviction: one of the unique functions of sexual perversions, as well as of normal sexuality, is the establishment and reaffirmation of the incontrovertible truth of the reality of personal existence. Sexuality is the most archaic mode, closely related to primary process, that can convey this emotional truth in both sexually deviant individuals as well as in those with more standard sexual patterns.

REFERENCES

Abelin, E. L. (1971), The role of the father in the separation–individuation process. In: *Separation–Individuation,* ed. S. B. McDevitt & C. F. Settlage. New York: International Universities Press, pp. 229–253.

Almansi, R. J. (1983, April 28), Research and clinical psychoanalytic findings in voyeurism. Presented at the discussion group for the Sexual Deviations: Theory and Therapy at meeting of the American Psychoanalytic Association, New York, NY.

Bak, R. C. (1968), The phallic woman: The ubiquitous fantasy in perversions. *The Psychoanalytic Study of the Child,* 23:15–36. New York: International Universities Press.

_____ (1971), Object relations in schizophrenia and perversion. *Internat. J. Psycho-Anal.,* 52:235–242.

Chasseguet-Smirgel, J. (1986), *Sexuality and Mind.* New York: New York University Press.

Freud, A. (1949), Certain types of stages of social maladjustment. *The Writings of Anna Freud,* 4:75–94. New York: International Universities Press.

Freud, S. (1897–1902), *The Origins of Psychoanalysis: Letters to Wilhelm Fleiss,* ed. M. Bonaparte, A. Freud & E. Kris. New York: Basic Books, 1954.

_____ (1905), Three essays on the theory of sexuality. *Standard Edition,* 7:135–243. London: Hogarth Press, 1953.

_____ (1910), Leonardo da Vinci and a memory of his childhood. *Standard Edition,* 11:3–137. London: Hogarth Press, 1957.

_____ (1914), On narcissism: An introduction. *Standard Edition,* 14:73–102. London: Hogarth Press, 1957.

_____ (1915–1916), Introductory lectures on psycho-analysis. *Standard Edition,* 15 & 16. London: Hogarth Press, 1963.

_____ (1919), A child is being beaten. *Standard Edition,* 17:179–204. London: Hogarth Press, 1955.

_____ (1922), Some neurotic mechanisms in jealousy, paranoia, and homosexuality. *Standard Edition,* 18:223–232. London: Hogarth Press, 1955.

_____ (1925), Negation. *Standard Edition,* 19:233–239. London: Hogarth Press, 1961.

_____ (1938a), An outline of psychoanalysis. *Standard Edition,* 23:144–207. London: Hogarth Press, 1964.

_____ (1938b), Splitting of the ego in the process of defence. *Standard Edition*, 23:271–279. London: Hogarth Press, 1964.

Galenson, E. & Roiphe, H. (1973), Object loss and early sexual development. *Psychoanal. Quart.*, 22:73–90.

Gillespie, W. H. (1956), The general theory of sexual perversion. *Internat. J. Psycho-Anal.*, 37:396–403.

Glover, E. (1964), Aggression and sadomasochism. In: *The Pathology and Treatment of Sexual Deviation*, ed. I. Rosen. London: Oxford University Press, pp. 153–154.

Greenacre, P. (1968), Perversions: General considerations regarding their genetic and dynamic background. In: *Emotional Growth, Vol. 1*. New York: International Universities Press, 1971, pp. 300–314.

Keeler, M. H. (1960), An unusual perversion: The desire to be injured by an automobile operated by a woman. *Amer. J. Psychiatry,* 11:1032.

Kernberg, O. F. (1975), *Borderline Conditions and Pathological Narcissism*. New York: Aronson.

Khan, M. M. R. (1965), Intimacy, complicity and mutuality in perversions. In: *Alienation in Perversions,* New York: International Universities Press, 1979, pp. 18–30.

Kohut, H. (1971), *The Analysis of the Self*. New York: International Universities Press.

Mahler, M. S., Pine, F. & Bergman, A. (1975), *The Psychological Birth of the Human Infant*. New York: Basic Books.

Niederland, W. G. (1958), Early auditory experiences, beating fantasies and primal scene. *The Psychoanalytic Study of the Child,* 13:471–504. New York: International Universities Press.

Rado, S. (1949), An adaptational view of sexual behavior. In: *The Psychoanalysis of Behavior, Vol. 1,* rev. ed. New York: Grune & Stratton, 1956, pp. 186–213.

Roiphe, H. (1968), On an early genital phase. *The Psychoanalytic Study of the Child,* 23:348–365. New York: International Universities Press.

Rosen, I. (1964a), Looking and showing. In: *Sexual Behavior and the Law,* ed. R. Slovenko. Springfield, IL: Thomas, 1965, p. 487–515.

_____ (1964b), Exhibitionism, scopophilia and voyeurism. In: *The Pathology and Treatment of Sexual Deviations,* ed. I. Rosen. London: Oxford University Press, pp. 293–350.

Socarides, C. W. (1960), The development of a fetishistic perversion: The contribution of preoedipal phase conflict. *J. Amer. Psychoanal. Assn.,* 8:552–556.

_____ (1969), The psychoanalytic therapy of a male homosexual. *Psychoanal. Quart.,* 38:173–190.

_____ (1974), The demonified mother: A study of voyeurism and sexual sadism. *Internat. Rev. Psycho-Anal.* 1:187–195.

_____ (1978), *Homosexuality*. New York: Aronson.

_____ (1985), Depression in perversion. With special reference to the function of erotic experience in sexual perversion. In: *Depressive States and Their Treatment,* ed. V. Volkan. New York: Aronson, pp. 317–334.

_____ (1988), *The Preoedipal Origin and Psychoanalytic Therapy of Sexual Perversions*. Madison, CT: International Universities Press.

Socarides, D. D. & Stolorow, R. D. (1985), Affects and selfobjects. *The Annual of Psychoanalysis*, 12/13:105–119. New York: International Universities Press.

Stoller, R. J. (1964), A contribution to the study of gender identity. *Internat. J. Psycho-Anal.*, 45:220–226.

_____ (1966), A mother's contribution to infantile transvestite behavior. *Internat. J. Psycho-Anal.*, 47:384–395.

_____ (1968), A further contribution to the study of gender identity. *Internat. J. Psycho-Anal.*, 49:364–368.

_____ (1975), Happy parental influences on the earliest development of masculinity in baby boys. *Psychoanal. Forum*, 5:234–240.

_____ (1982), Transvestism in women. *Arch. Sexual Behav.*, 2:99–115.

Stolorow, R. D. & Grand, H. T. (1973), A partial analysis of a perversion involving bugs. *Internat. J. Psycho-Anal.*, 54:349–350.

_____ & Lachmann, F. M. (1980), *Psychoanalysis of Developmental Arrest: Theory and Treatment*. New York: International Universities Press.

Tolpin, M. (1979), Remarks on pathogenesis and symptom formation in disorders of the self. In: *The Course of Life*, ed. S. Greenspan & G. Pollock. Washington, DC: U.S. Government Printing Office.

Volkan, V. D. (1979), Transsexualism: As examined from the viewpoint of internalized object relations. In: *On Sexuality*, ed. T. B. Karasu & C. W. Socarides. New York: Aronson, pp. 189–222.

_____ (1982), The transsexual search for perfection: Aggression reassignment surgery. Presented at the discussion group on Psychoanalytic Considerations about Patients with Organic Illness or Major Physical Handicaps at the annual meeting of the American Psychoanalytic Association, New York City.

Winnicott, D. W. (1965), *The Maturational Process and the Facilitating Environment*. New York: International Universities Press.

III

Treatment Implications

16 Treatment of Psychological Disorders of Early Childhood
A Tripartite Therapeutic Model

Eleanor Galenson

While many therapeutic approaches to the psychological problems encountered in very young children have been utilized during the past two decades, there is a striking paucity of information in the literature on the rationale for the specific therapeutic modality, the details of the therapeutic work itself, and the clinical results. The consequence has been a burgeoning of methods of treatment of young children and their parents that cannot be evaluated systematically. We hope to encourage others to present their methods for evaluation and comparison by outlining the rationale as well as the clinical application of the tripartite therapeutic model that we began to employ in the late 1970s.

Our therapeutic model grew out of our experience in two contiguous fields: (1) infant observational research on early sexual development (Galenson and Roiphe, 1971, 1976, 1980; Roiphe and Galenson, 1981) and (2) the treatment of psychological disorders of very young children and their parents in several therapeutic nurseries in hospital clinic settings (Galenson, 1984, 1986). Our own model was based on Mahler's (Mahler, Pine and Bergman, 1975) tripartite method of treating autistic children, modified to suit the requirements of other types of psychopathology. Mahler's inclusion of the mother as an integral member of the treatment unit, a unique and original approach, has remained an element central to our type of therapy.

Mahler's subsequent research concerning the complexities of the mother–infant relationship laid the groundwork for others in the field who began to treat young infants and their parents. Fraiberg (1980) and others (Fraiberg, Adelson, and Shapiro, 1975) found that the birth of a new baby revives important preoedipal memories and regressive tendencies in all parents, along with new parental capacities. In this chapter we emphasize the pathological rather than the normal aspects of the parent–infant relationships that we have encountered in the infants and parents who have been our patients. It should be emphasized, however, that our familiarity with normal developmental unfolding was an essential prerequisite for the therapeutic work we carried out.

Beginning in 1978 all children under four years of age who were referred to us for treatment in our private practice were seen in conjoint treatment with their parents. Forty-five infants from the middle and upper socioeconomic sector constitute the group from which our clinical experience with this particular therapeutic model has been drawn. Most of the infants were not yet two years old when they were brought for consultation. Their presenting symptoms included disturbances in sleeping and eating, problems involving impulse control, excessive fearfulness, failure to develop speech, and difficulty in establishing social relationships with their peers. Six were adopted children; ten were the children of divorced parents or of parents who were contemplating divorce. Most of the mothers of the infants we have treated were in their early or midthirties, and almost all had a professional commitment outside the home. All but three of the pregnancies had been planned; several mothers were referred to us by therapists with whom they were then in treatment, because of their intense anxiety about their impending delivery and fears that the infant would be malformed, despite negative findings in the prenatal investigative procedures that had been carried out.

This failure to engage the mothers with issues relating to their unborn or young infants in the course of individual parental treatment appears to support Bibring's (1959) hypothesis that pregnancy brings shifts in the maternal psychic structure. It also supports Fraiberg's (1980) view that the baby is a special kind of "transference object" for all parents beginning at the time of conception, an object with whom some of the parents' early experiences and conflicts may be acted out for the first time. Our clinical experience with parents of very young children, accumulated in the course of 15 years of infant observational research (Galenson and Roiphe, 1971, 1976, 1980), had already convinced us that conjoint treatment of the infant in the company of at least mother, and preferably both parents, was far more effective as a therapeutic model than individual therapy with one member of the family in addressing the various psychological disturbances of young infants. Fraiberg and her group were simultaneously developing an intervention technique in the Child Development Project at the University of Michigan. She found that data obtained when both mother and infant toddler were present differed from those obtained from the mother alone, a finding amply corroborated by our data.

Blos (1985) described the dynamics underlying the maternal psychic changes that appear to accompany the biological changes of pregnancy and the postpartum period. As the baby becomes the object upon which the mother unconsciously displaces her own early strong and conflicted feelings, remnants of forgotten but affectively charged memories become evident in her actions with her baby.

The primitive nature of the need states and the helplessness of the very young infant are probably responsible for reactivating the archaic remnants of the parents' unresolved early needs. This ego-syntonic maternal and paternal regression accounts for the enormous suggestibility and the intense quest for support that are encountered in so many new parents. We believe it is therapeutically unwise to accentuate this parental regression by authoritative counseling, a procedure that undermines the parents' already faltering sense of parental competence. Unfortunately, young parents who have consulted us had already relinquished their parental prerogatives to a nurse, housekeeper, or a parental guidance professional with whom they had established a strongly dependent relationship. This division in primary maternal caretaking leads to confusion in the infant's relationship to both caretakers. The confusion is increased when the mother continues to retreat from her role as primary caregiver. Although some mothers continue to share the caretaking role with the surrogate mother on more or less equal terms, in most cases the stability of this double maternal representation appears to be adversely affected by the split in caretaking between two people. Separation problems of many types and degrees of severity appear to be related to this splitting of the maternal role.

In contrast to mothers who surrender their babies to a caretaker are those whose early experiences with their own mothers lead to an overintense and exclusionary relationship with the infant. The latter group of mothers nurse the baby well beyond the first year and tend to exclude the father from involvement with the infant as well as with themselves. Marital disruption often ensues as the mother's earlier tie to her mother is now reenacted with her baby.

In view of the fact that so many psychological disturbances of infancy are due to a disturbance of the mother–child relationship, whatever the nature of the maternal psychopathology may be, therapeutic intervention must be aimed at a firmer establishment of a more harmonious balance in this dyadic system. If this is to be accomplished, the emotional investment in the therapist on the part of both parent and infant must be a temporary one. The therapist should never displace the mother, except under those unusual circumstances where the mother is likely to remain emotionally unavailable to her infant. Maintaining an optimum balance in joint therapy is difficult; offering initial support to the mother without usurping her role goes contrary to the tendency of mothers of young infants who identify with the therapist. The mothers' identification with their own mothers is revived within the transferences that develop between therapist and mother on the one hand and between mother and baby on the other. However, it is the development of precisely these transference relationships that allows old, unresolved parental conflicts to be approached and more successfully resolved as mother, child, and therapist interact in the joint sessions. While in some mothers early maternal identifications serve to strengthen aspects of the sense of oneself as a mother, in other mothers this revival of archaic maternal and self-representations during pregnancy and following the birth of the child often contributes to confusion and conflict, with the new mothering role allowing old unresolved conflicts to surface once again.

One young woman whose mother had remained at home as the sole and intensely involved caretaker could not decide whether or when to leave her child to go back to work. She was overcome by guilty feelings at "abandoning" her infant if she left but was irritable and angry whenever she remained at home. This conflict spread to involve other areas, all of which involved the issue of separation. She could not decide when to stop nursing, when to decrease the number of bottles, when to allow her baby to negotiate the separation involved in falling asleep alone in his crib rather than in her arms, when to encourage her baby to play alone, walk alone, be alone, and so forth. Every variety of interchange between mother and child that involved some degree of separation had become a crisis.

For another mother whose mother had worked outside the home during her infancy, another type of conflict characterized the relationship with her infant. She had decided to rear her child herself, since her own childhood had been spent so unhappily, constantly yearning for her working mother. However, she soon came to realize during joint psychotherapy that she was jealous of her baby, who was now receiving the very maternal attention of which she had felt so deprived.

As to the effect of the birth of a child upon the father, it is probably true that no marriage is unchanged thereafter in its basic psychological structure. In several of our patients, marriages that were described as stable and harmonious before the pregnancy began to deteriorate even before the actual delivery occurred. In other instances the deterioration followed the birth of the child. Many fathers have described their feelings of being excluded from their former intimacy with their wives, feelings that could then be traced to the revival of ancient sibling rivalries that had never been resolved. These fathers found themselves competing with the baby for their wife's attention, especially if the mother left the home to work and divided her emotional investment between her baby and her work. Such fathers felt particularly guilty about expecting attention for themselves from their already stressed wife, while the wives rationalized their intense commitment to their infant as necessary for the establishment of a sound relationship with the child. In many instances these rationalizations concealed the mother's revival of her attachment to her own mother and the fulfillment of an unsatisfied yearning for her, a regression from the heterosexual oedipal attachment that had prevailed before the pregnancy.

Our psychotherapeutic model consists of two or three joint sessions per week with the young child, the mother or father, and one of the two therapists, and a weekly session between the parent(s) and the second therapist. An unexpected finding in our treatment model has been the correlation of dynamic themes that emerged in the twice- or thrice-weekly therapeutic tripartite joint sessions and those that emerged in the weekly individual sessions with the parent(s). (The parents are informed at the outset that the therapist conducting the tripartite joint sessions is in constant communication with the second therapist.) As similar themes unfolded in both therapeutic settings, clarification of the infant's psycho-pathology in the light of the parents' unresolved preoedipal conflicts has been astonishing in its mutative effect on both infant and parental psychopathology.

While this therapeutic model is both costly and time-consuming, it has produced therapeutic results that one would not have believed possible in some of the severely disturbed young children we have treated. Further-more, despite the complexities of this psychotherapeutic structure, there have been surprisingly few transferential problems—which one might expect when two therapists are involved in the treatment of both infant and parents. Close collaboration between the two therapists not only has provided rich material that was then utilized in interpretive work but also undoubtedly prevented serious transferential problems from developing.

The major variants in our approach to each of the cases involving the 45 infants and young children from which our clinical data are drawn have been the intensity and type of parental treatment, adjusted according to the nature of parental psychopathology we found. In almost all instances the presenting complaint concerned the young child and the child–parent interaction remained the primary focus of the dynamic material we pursued with the parents until the treatment had taken hold sufficiently for the parent(s) to be invested in the work with the therapist who was treating the child and parent(s) jointly. For some parents this focus on the parent–infant interaction had to continue for the duration of therapy. Most of the parents, however, became accessible after some months to greater exploration of their own inner conflictual childhood residues, which were, of course, central to their child's psychopathology. About one-third of our parents gradually developed an interest in more intensive individual treatment for themselves and continued psychotherapy with the individual therapist (E. G.), the person whom they had consulted originally about the child. It is this therapist (E. G.) who remains responsible for the many decisions that arise; it is self-evident that the transferential problems would be severe without an arrangement in which the ultimate responsibility rests with one therapist who considers the suggestions and tentative decisions of the therapist conducting the joint child and parent(s) sessions before arriving at an ultimate decision.

Regarding the age group for which this joint model of therapy has been appropriate, we have found the following to be true: separating parents from children who are less than three and a half or four interferes with, rather than aids, the treatment process. Much is gained when the mother and father alternate in joint sessions with their child, and this continues to be the case well into the middle of the third year of age of the child in treatment, or even beyond. It is only when oedipal material constitutes the major aspect of the child's dynamic themes that the child himself begins to request exclusivity with the therapist. And since most of our child patients reach oedipal phase development relatively late because of their preoedipal psychopathology, we have begun individual treatment of the child at a later age than is ordinarily the practice in either psychotherapeutic or psychoanalytic treatment of children.

CLINICAL ILLUSTRATION

The clinical material that follows illustrates the application of our treatment model to a rather severely disturbed young child and her equally disturbed parents.

Janet was brought for consultation at 21 months because she had never been heard to utter a word. Her gestures and other behavior indicated that she understood even complex spoken language, and prior testing had ruled out an organic hearing impairment. The only child of a professionally successful mother and father past his professional prime and 15 years the mother's senior, Janet had been left to the care of a nursemaid from the time of her birth. In addition to the delay in her language, Janet had been a very poor eater from her earliest months and was particularly recalcitrant on the rare occasions when her mother tried to feed her. At 21 months she sucked on her bottle often during the day, refused solids, and used several pacifiers at night.

The mother, Martha, had decided to have a child since "I was getting old and couldn't wait much longer"—a decision with which the father complied without much objection but with little enthusiasm. Once the child was delivered, Martha had little wish to see her newborn infant in the hospital, and she returned to full-time work within six weeks of Janet's birth. Janet had not developed a special attachment to her mother nor had she shown stranger anxiety during her first year, but she did cry at times during her second year when her mother sneaked out of the house each morning to go to work. She was now very easily frustrated and had begun to have severe temper tantrums.

On her first visit to our playroom with her mother, this tiny, frail, very pretty little girl left her mother immediately without a backward glance, handled a number of toys on the shelves, and appeared to ignore the therapist (E. G.). She made not a sound but communicated by gestures to her mother and then to the therapist exactly what she wished them to do. Furthermore, she complied with a number of quite complex requests from the therapist, indicating that she already possessed a well-developed capacity for receptive language. Our initial clinical impression of this clearly intelligent, auditorily intact child was that her marked delay in expressive language was secondary to a severe disturbance in the mother–child relationship. We hypothesized that there had been a split in her maternal mental representations between the strict nanny and the emotionally and physically distant mother. Because of these circumstances our treatment model was modified to include the nanny, who participated with therapist B. F. in one of Janet's sessions each week; the mother joined Janet in the two other sessions. In addition, the mother was seen individually twice-weekly by therapist E. G., who also met with the father whenever he was available.

The Mother's History

Martha, the firstborn of two children, had been her mother's "perfect child" in every respect. Always obedient and helpful, Martha had been extremely close to her mother during the first ten years of her life, despite the birth of a younger sibling. Her father was rarely at home before her bedtime; he was friendly if distant. Martha's poor appetite was the only area of conflict between mother and daughter; Martha often threw food away surreptitiously and remained a poor eater throughout childhood, adolescence, and adult life. She was a totally different child in school, however, than she was at home; from her first year in nursery school at three years of age she was a fiercely disobedient troublemaker who was labeled as such until the end of high school. Yet despite this almost intolerable school conduct, she did well in her studies and her parents never discussed her deviant school behavior with her or her teachers.

Martha did well academically in college. She had a series of love affairs during her adolescence and a brief marriage in her early twenties. After the divorce she entered a profession that was closely connected with her father's career and was highly successful in this work. Several years later she married her current husband, a man considerably older than she. She knew she did not love him at the time but had decided she was ready to have a child.

Martha had suffered from many bouts of depression since her adolescence; these were not relieved by several attempts at psychotherapeutic and psychoanalytic treatment over a period of 15 years. Yet despite these recurrent periods of depression, she was able to continue to work and to enjoy much of her social life—as long as she took medication for her "headaches" and could relieve her evening moods by a rather heavy consumption of alcohol.

Martha's relationship with her mother changed at about ten years of age after a summer spent away from home. She then became quite ambivalent to her mother and continued to fight and then make up with her from then on throughout adolescence. She was extremely homesick during that first summer away from home, and her relationship with her father slowly changed after this first parting from her mother. She became closer to him and saw him daily in the course of her work, which had become the major source of satisfaction in her life. Her current marriage was unsatisfactory; she considered her husband too passive and was clearly contemptuous of him. It appeared that Martha had won out in the battle for her father, since her husband (and mother) were now the outsiders while Martha and her father were extremely close. Janet, Martha's child, seemed to represent Martha's younger sibling, who had been relegated to a nursemaid's care (just as Janet had been) while Martha and her mother maintained their intense attachment to one another during the first ten years of Martha's life.

Course of Treatment of Mother and Child Over the First Ten Months

Within two weeks of the beginning of treatment Janet's first word, "No," appeared as she played out many games involving regressive oral and anal themes during the joint sessions where either her nursemaid or her mother watched passively. The issue of separation pervaded Janet's play sessions during the next month or so, and she became increasingly angry and rebellious both at home and during her sessions. Instead of throwing her former tantrums she now directed her anger at her mother, who was both annoyed and frightened, particularly since her daughter's behavior reminded her of her own early misbehavior at school. Martha began to wonder about the contrast between her own compliance with her mother's every demand at home and her rebelliousness at school. Then, as Janet became embroiled in issues of separation during the treatment sessions and wanted to have her mother sit close to her at all times, Martha began to think seriously for the first time about leaving her husband. But now for the first time she was acutely aware of her own fears of separation, as she saw Janet struggling with *her* separation fears during the conjoint sessions.

During the third month of treatment, Janet began to act out many forms of anal derivative play in her sessions, smearing paints and using Play-Doh and hammering toys. At the same time there was much outward-directed aggression, including resistance to having her soiled diapers removed, constipation, and overtly negative behavior, as well as efforts to control her anger. Correlated with this emerging anality was the beginning of expressive language development. (Concurrence of anal-phase unfolding and the development of expressive language has long been recognized as a clinical constellation, probably signaling the relative degree of release of the expression of aggression from its prior inhibition.) However, the advance in one aspect of Janet's psychosexual development was accompanied by intense regression in other spheres. She initiated a "tiny baby" game, which she played endlessly and in which she took both the active and passive roles, discarding the baby and being discarded herself—a game in which her mother was able to participate to some degree.

However, as Janet's freedom to express her aggression increased, her mother became more depressed. Memories of Martha's first prolonged and intensely painful separation from her mother, when she attended overnight camp at ten years of age, now crowded in; during her individual sessions she described her suicidal ideation when she had not been allowed to return home. She also elaborated on the rebelliousness against her mother that had begun at that time and on the relationship with her father, which slowly flowered into a solid and often secret alliance with him against her mother.

During the fourth month of treatment, 24-month-old Janet began to protest remaining with her nurse when her mother left for work. This behavior was now welcomed by Martha, in contrast to her previous feelings, and she herself decided to gradually replace the unempathic and authoritative nurse, after considerable preparation during the joint sessions. With this slight improvement in the mother–daughter relationship, new information emerged about the nature of Martha's "obsession" with her daughter since the time of her birth. Martha now described her fear of the delivery and of having a deformed child. She had been so frightened of handling the baby during her first two months lest she drop or hurt her that she had gone back to work to escape these frightening impulses; she had been only partially aware of her motivation at that time. She remembered that she had never liked young infants, since they were "unable to verbalize their needs," and she had attributed her difficulty with Janet to this lifelong intolerance of all infants. However, she now recalled that a major preoccupation as a little girl had been to remain her mother's "little girl," the price she now realized she had paid for retaining her mother's love. She said she had known that her mother would discard her if she behaved independently, and thought she had found a partial solution by splitting herself into the helpless, obedient "mama's girl" at home and the intelligent, angry, and rebellious child at school. This split became a permanent aspect of her self-representation. As an adult, the pleasant "phony" facade with which she faced the world hid her private depressed and angry feelings. She had thought everyone was like that and had never questioned this contradiction in herself.

By the fifth month of treatment, as mother and child became engaged in mutual play during the joint sessions, Martha decided to leave her work for several months while Janet became acquainted with the new nurse. This decision signaled an important shift in Martha's feelings; there was now a period of consolidation in the mother–daughter relationship, with tenderness both within and outside the sessions. It was significant that Janet developed signal anxiety for the first time now, as the libidinal ties to her mother strengthened. Also, modulation of all affects had increased; Janet was sad at times and angry at others, with many in-between states that had not been present before. Janet spoke wistfully and sadly about her father when he was away from home on business trips, a sadness that Martha could parrot but did not really understand.

Just before the summer vacation, at 27 months of age, Janet began to masturbate and explore her genitals for the first time, at least eight to ten months later than the usual time of emergence of the early genital phase. We thought that the impending summer separation had hastened the pace of the separation–individuation process, which had been so distorted by her difficulty in establishing a stable, unified maternal mental representation.

In a fashion parallel to what was emerging during the joint mother and child sessions, an important breakthrough occurred in the mother's individual treatment sessions with therapist E. G. as the summer separation approached. She now recounted for the first time her severe reaction to the death of a dearly beloved male friend several years previously, memories that brought much sadness and weeping for the first time. Janet's conception had been consciously planned by her mother as a replacement for this man whose loss the mother had never really mourned. Even now she could barely tolerate the painful feelings these memories evoked. As she wept, she began to understand how these forbidden sad feelings over the loss of someone she loved were connected with her earlier fear of separation from her mother and her need to repress hostility toward her mother lest this lead to a rupture between them. She also remembered sadness and yearning for her father—feelings that had to be hidden from her mother for fear of being abandoned by her.

At the end of the summer, 29-month-old Janet was a pleasant, sociable child who was now capable of advanced semisymbolic play, interested in books, and able to use short sentences to express her wishes and needs. She often clung to her mother, however, and she had developed a rather severe sleep disturbance, which we ascribed to her advancing separation-individuation process. Janet now clearly experienced her anger and directed it toward the person whom she held responsible for her frustration—often, but not always, her mother. Her sense of herself as a feminine person was much more definite; she admired and wanted to wear shoes with high heels, and she loved earrings (both in identification with her mother and as possible phallic replacements). She explored her genitals and the genitals of dolls and animals during her joint sessions, and she was curious about her mother's genitals as well. Her human figure drawings now clearly demonstrated a knowledge of the sexual differences for the first time.

Martha reacted to Janet's increasing sense of separateness as well as her femininity with a paradoxical discouragement about her "lack of progress" and said she was afraid to return to full-time work because of its effect on Janet. It was only when Martha could begin to acknowledge her anger and anxiety about the summer separation that she began to wonder about her attitude toward her husband. It became clearer to her that he represented in part the father of her childhood, remote and unappreciative of her femininity as a child, a striking parallel to the long-delayed emergence of Janet's early genital phase.

Martha's professional life represented an identification with the father of her adolescence. But it was a situation fraught with potential danger because of the threat to the already highly ambivalent relationship with her mother. Martha began to understand why she had felt so threatened by the helplessness and dependency of her newborn infant: these traits had mobilized her fears of being drawn back into the early bondage to her mother, a bondage that had satisfied some needs but had so severely jeopardized her overall development. Small wonder that the birth of her baby had precipitated a major upheaval in Martha, interfering with the lifelong defenses by means of which she had maintained the split self-representation of a compliant, obedient little girl attached to her mother and a competent, self-reliant person identified with her father.

Martha's marriage remained unstable and eventually disintegrated. Janet's early genital phase and genital derivative behavior continued to emerge to a surprisingly full development, and her new exhibitionism and flirtatiousness was now enjoyed by her mother—and by her grandfather, in particular—but only halfheartedly appreciated by her father. Her language had become fluent and articulate, but her peer relationships were still unsatisfactory, since her need to remain in control so often interfered.

Janet's conjoint treatment continued for another year as she negotiated the separation and divorce of her parents. Her mother remarried when Janet was almost six years old, an event that caused an expected increase in Janet's oppositionalism, which continued until she slowly began to accept her stepfather as a more or less friendly addition to her family. Janet decided she wanted to stop treatment shortly after the marriage; her mother has continued in her individual psychotherapy and has come to realize the enormously crippling effect of her early symbiotic attachment to her infantile and angry mother. Yet she has not been able to free herself from this ambivalent relationship, and she continues to use pills in small amounts when under stress. Janet still needs to exercise control over her environment, obviously the remnants of her extremely traumatic and unsatisfactory early relationship with her caretakers.

CONCLUSION

We believe that this mother would not have been able to develop a relationship with her child if conjoint treatment had not been the vehicle for the unfolding of the mother's past maternal relationship through her direct exposure to her child's conflicts. There is a here-and-now quality, an aliveness that is provided by experiencing the child's reactions during the course of joint therapy and that cannot be conveyed through verbal channels. Young children utilize so many nonverbal channels for communicating, particularly in regard to affect, and can be adequately understood only if the adults, therapist and parent alike, join the child in the nonverbal areas of her life.

The task of basically revising the consequences of such a split maternal representation is extremely difficult and often not entirely successful. However, we hope this child will return for treatment at a later age for further individual therapy, therapy that we believe will be far more successful because of the early period of conjoint therapy in which she was joined by her mother.

REFERENCES

Bibring, G. L. (1959), Some consideration of the psychological processes in pregnancy. *The Psychoanalytic Study of the Child*, 14:113–121. New York: International Universities Press.
Blos, P., Jr. (1985), Intergenerational separation–individuation—Treating the mother–infant pair. *The Psychoanalytic Study of the Child*, 40:41–56.
Fraiberg, S., ed. (1980), *Clinical Studies in Infant Mental Health*. New York: Basic Books.
——— Adelson, E. & Shapiro, V. (1975), Ghosts in the nursery. *J. Amer. Acad. Child Psychiatry*, 14:387–421.
Galenson, E. (1984), Psychoanalytic approach to psychotic disturbances in very young children: A clinical report. *Hillside J. Clin. Psychiatry*, 6(2):221–244.
——— (1986), Some thoughts about infant psychopathology and aggressive development. *Internat. Rev. Psycho-Anal.*, 13:349–354.
——— & Roiphe, H. (1971), The impact of early sexual discovery on mood, defensive organization and symbolization. *The Psychoanalytic Study of the Child*, 26:195–216. New Haven, CT: Yale University Press.
——— & ——— (1976), Some suggested revisions concerning early female development. *J. Amer. Psychoanal. Assn.*, 24(5) Suppl.:29–57.
——— & ——— (1980), The pre-oedipal development of the boy. *J. Amer. Psychoanal. Assn.*, 28.805–827.
Mahler, M. S., Pine, F. & Bergman, A (1975), *The Psychological Birth of the Human Infant*. New York: Basic Books.
Roiphe, H. & Galenson, E. (1981), *Infantile Origins of Sexual Identity*. New York: International Universities Press.

17

Construction and Reconstruction, Semantics and Dynamics

Alvin Frank

History, Stephen said, is a nightmare from which I am trying to awake.
James Joyce, *Ulysses*

It is fitting that in recognition of Selma Kramer an author try to stretch beyond familiar and safe ground. Selma has offered us inspiration and incentive to break through the usual disciplinary boundaries and to view our subjects and ideas from broader vistas in more comprehensive ways. At the same time, her example imposes a constraint as well as grants us a freedom. She has taught us restraint and proportion as well as initiative and has shown us how to civilize ambition with the tempering application of reasonable self-examination and criticism.

I hope I do not exceed these limits in this exercise, whose aim several colleagues have criticized as foolhardy, however commendable. I advocate here changing our use of two words already firmly ensconced in analytic

---

*These ideas developed as part of my participation in the Study Group on Reconstruction of the Psychoanalytic Research and Development Fund, Inc. While the Group and Fund are not responsible for these particular formulations I am immensely grateful for the experiences they provided and ideas that were stimulated. In particular I thank Dr. Harold Blum, the Group's Chairperson, and Dr. Sidney Furst, the Fund's Medical Director.

usage: *construction* and *reconstruction*. Freud (1937) himself used them interchangeably in his writing, including his last essay on the subject (p. 259). Current practice generally follows his example. Moore and Fine (1990) include *construction* under *reconstruction* (pp. 46, 163–164), but their contributor favors *construction* because such formulations cannot exactly replicate the involved events. Laplanche and Pontalis (1973) formally define only *construction* while using *reconstruct* in their text (pp. 88–89). Current practice, as reflected in journal indices, at least in the English language analytic periodicals, seems to indicate a preference for the term *reconstruction*. The last available yearly indices (published in 1989) of the *Journal of the American Association,* the *International Journal of Psycho-Analysis, Psychoanalytic Quarterly,* and *The Psychoanalytic Study of the Child* contain, respectively, three, ten, two, and five citations under that heading. The only listing of *construction* was for a review in the *Psychoanalytic Quarterly* of a French article (Wilson, 1989). There has been only rare argument to distinguish between the terms. Greenacre (1981) proposed that an analyst's initial speculations and formulations on evaluating a patient, not to be communicated to him or her, be called *constructions*. In contrast, she would continue to use *reconstruction* in referring to shared hypotheses and conclusions as the result of extensive analytic work. But this suggestion is in the nature of an arbitrary convention, adding no semantic precision or enhanced dynamic meaning to these words in our technical vocabulary.

To change word usage is commonly acknowledged as a difficult task, and it is not difficult to hypothesize why. Freud imputed to words the capacity to transform the inchoate mental apparatus through the formation of the system pre-conscious, tempering primitive primary processes through logic and mentation. This is an idea confirmed by several generations of child observation. Language is thus a person's cornerstone of rationality and order. The so-called Whorfian hypothesis proposes that language imposes the ultimate shapes and dimensions of any culture. Its importance in groups of all sizes is readily confirmed, particularly in observations of usage, slang, and idiom. The concept of a connection between language acquisition and early object relations is hardly novel and is gaining renewed attention as a major thesis in the writings of the Soviet linguist Vygotsky (1988).[1] Further, words and their idiosyncratic usages

---

[1]For me this was demonstrated by my own past pedantic insistence on correcting anyone using "loan," rather than "lend," as a verb. (This distinction has been superseded in usage and dictionary status for some time.) This behavior was identified with a screen memory in which I was gently and constructively instructed in a halcyon time by a beloved aunt whom I later lost through her

can have narcissistic status as valued creations sometimes possessing actual utility.[2]

It is daunting, then, to propose an innovation that might be construed, however unconsciously, as constituting a danger to sanity and society, family and self. Yet language does irresistibly evolve, with its own momentum and obeying its own laws, as even a casual glance at most dictionary definitions will demonstrate; it is hardly immutable. I hope that the advantages of clarity and semantic and dynamic precision in refining the concepts of construction and reconstruction that I propose will make the effort to introduce an external rationale to their differentiation worthwhile. At the same time, learning a new language imposes its own problems (Stengel, 1939). *Construction* and *reconstruction* are words used in both everyday and scientific parlance that have contexts, connotations, and applications that are understood in both worlds according to explicit or implicit conventions. When the same word appears in vernacular and scientific use, a tension develops between the uses in the two spheres. My contentions here include an assertion that a reconciliation between the technical and the vernacular use of *construction* and *reconstruction* is possible and advantageous. The first such attempts may provoke judgments that I am guilty of carelessness with the words or concepts or that I have misunderstood or misapplied them. However, these representations were undertaken only after serious consideration and much reflection. I ask the reader to not give in to such initial skepticism until the involved reasoning, arguments, and examples are completed. I would not expect such forbearance for mere vocabulary instruction, but the issues presented here have at their center a reconsideration and integration of important principles involved in the recollections of childhood and in autobiography as well as of their relations to the analytic process.

When Freud (1937) wrote "Constructions in Analysis," he was balanced on the horns of a familiar personal dilemma: presenting new hypotheses without giving up the old. On one hand, he expressed his

---

marriage, geographical distance, and death. With understanding and acceptance of what the memory represented and concealed, and what my stubborn insistence on not changing meant, I found the matter had lost its importance.

[2]The following example was given by Dr. David Carlson (1989) in a discussion of these ideas: "A colleague presenting a case consultation said at one point, 'I presented a construction, no, I mean reconstruction.' As you can imagine, I asked the difference he saw between the terms and why he had corrected himself. 'Very simple,' he said. He'd felt a little tentative and perhaps speculative as he spoke to his patient, so what he had said seemed to him a construction. The material that followed amply confirmed the construction, so he had decided it was a reconstruction."

views as organized and related to an old topographical formulation, namely, that analysis cures through the removal of repressions and the recovery of lost memories for which symptoms and inhibitions are a substitute (p. 258). In this context he could consistently cite a feeling of conviction as equivalent to a recovered memory even in the absence of recall (p. 266). The idea was simply to fill a gap in the memory of one's childhood. In the same work, however, some propositions were relevant to later structural ideas of other theories of technique and cure. Both masters could be served in his proposed ambition for reconstruction: "What we are in search of is a picture of the patient's forgotten years that shall be alike trustworthy and in all essential respects complete" (p. 258). In the essay's example, however, Freud (1937) implied a much more complex scenario:

> Up to your nth year you regarded yourself as the sole and unlimited possessor of your mother; then came another baby and brought you grave disillusionment. Your mother left you for some time, and even after her reappearance she was never again devoted to you exclusively. Your feelings towards your mother became ambivalent, your father gained a new importance for you . . . and so on [p. 261].

It is difficult to believe that Freud considered the fact of the sibling's birth as initially repressed. What is new in this formulation is the recapturing of the patient's disillusionment and the explanation of his turning from the ambivalently experienced mother to the father. Or is it the correction of the isolations that had previously prevented a meaningful synthesis of these factors? Unfortunately, we cannot tell; Freud omitted an account of his hypothetical patient's original account with which to contrast the reconstruction. The "and so on" is evocative. It implies the possibility of an even more comprehensive understanding of the analysand's troubles and of a detailed point by point explanation of them in terms of the past.

To the degree that Freud (1937) used a model that limited the process of recovery to the removal of repressions, his personal enthusiasm for the comparison of analyst and archaeologist is understandable:

> His work of construction, or, if it is preferred, of reconstruction, resembles to a great extent an archaeologist's excavation of some dwelling-place that has been destroyed and buried or of some ancient edifice. The two processes are in fact identical, except that the analyst works under better conditions and has

more material at his command to assist him, since what he is dealing with is not something destroyed but something that is still alive—and perhaps for another reason as well. But just as the archaeologist builds up the walls of the building from the foundations that have remained standing, determines the number and position of the columns from depressions in the floor and reconstructs the mural decorations and paintings from the remains found in the débris, so does the analyst proceed when he draws his inferences from the fragments of memories, from the associations and from the behaviour of the subject of the analysis. Both of them have an undisputed right to reconstruct by means of supplementing and combining the surviving remains. Both of them, moreover, are subject to many of the same difficulties and sources of error [p. 259].

Why Freud used *construction* and *reconstruction* interchangeably here is unclear. In his analogy the original construction took place in the "ancient" past of the edifice (comparable to childhood) whereas the *re*construction, the construction anew or again, is the archeologist's (or analyst's) later work.

What is ignored in the archaeological metaphor is that the analysand presents himself or herself with a more or less extensive rendition of personal history. Freud's original interest was in what was not remembered, in what he called the "primally repressed." His early investigations concerned these amnesias and a few only latently revealing pseudomemories that "screened" the real stuff of childhood (e.g., 1899, 1900). But in his later work Freud required that the regained information, the reconstruction, be integrated and applied to an understanding of the patient's original story, and particularly to explaining and resolving the archaic transferences that represent the past (Freud, 1925).

Ernst Kris applied the term "personal myth" to the editing and shaping of initially presented historical narratives for defensive purposes in particular cases (1956). He described three patients with important investments in their autobiographical self-images, which were heir to important early fantasies of which they were partial reenactments. In one such instance, a second analysis, Kris attributed the limited success of the first to the fact that this "autobiographical screen" had not been "pierced" and that the patient's life continued under its spell (p. 656). Since Kris's publication the ubiquity of such compositions has been confirmed; we leave childhood having constructed an autobiography. From an infinite number of impressions, organizable in an infinite number of ways, a relative few have been selected and worked over. This history is, significantly, a product of much the same familiar unconscious processes responsible for dreams, myths, and fantasies. The history's basic features usually remain unchanged from the momentous years of childhood; it is an acquisition of the latency period with occasional, relatively minor modifications as one passes through the inevitable sequence of life's later inner and outer adventures. This history is what was constructed originally, the construction that is presented to the analyst.

Psychoanalytically directed and informed developmental studies have led to the proposition that the infant acquires the capacity for autobiographical self-contemplation and communication only with the advent of language and symbolic thinking. But inherent in those acquisitions are the seeds of self-estrangement, misperceptions, misrepresentations, and omissions—of the substitution of an edited, wishful, fanciful unreality for the direct impressions of personal experience (e.g., Stern, 1985, pp. 162–182). As such, these devices of self-deception cannot fail to influence the structures evolving *pari passu*.

To the degree that self-histories are viewed as the end products of something, that "something" must be the psychic organizations and functions that we label *structures*. This is to assert no more than that self-histories are the result of psychological work, and the site of the workplace in our epistemology is structure. These histories are much more than elements recalled after being passively subjected to shuffling and reshuffling within the mental apparatus's mnemonic systems. They are dynamically constructed in a sense actually coinciding with the vernacular *construction:* "the act or result of constructing, interpreting, or explaining" (*Webster's Ninth New Collegiate Dictionary,* 1987, p. 281). This fits our idea of the psychologic process more than adequately. The latency child creates a construct, "something constructed especially by mental synthesis" (ibid., p. 281). What is being discussed here cannot properly be called a reconstruction. *re*construction must come later; it invokes the circumstance of repetition: "again, anew" (ibid., p. 978). A construction is that composition with which one leaves childhood; a reconstruction, as in the lexicon, involves a revision of this construction.

Psychoanalysis began with Freud's naïveté, with his willingness to take seriously those neurotic patients his Viennese colleagues dismissed as unworthy of their interest. But it became a science through his benevolent skepticism and his refusal to take their symptoms and self-presentations at face value. He considered these phenomena the appropriate objects of his searching inquiries, rather than objects of his unquestioning acceptance. Histories derived from diagnostic anamneses are similarly invaluable psychological statements. However, to consider them as factual, comprehensive records is foolhardy. Almost inevitably, in time, the evolution of analytic process through the transference disaffirms these initial fables, as convincing as they might seem at first glance. At times there are grounds for suspicion from the beginning:[3]

A young woman sought help because of chronic intermittent anxiety and depression, which had been troublesome since adolescence. Having explained this, my notes state:

> She quickly interposes that this is the result of her outrageous parents' outrageous behavior—specifically her father, who is a "bastard." The father is a professional man, and according to the patient, she has wanted help since her teen years but the father has manipulated her in such a way that she didn't get it.

> The mother is described as a "masochist," beaten down by the father's cruelty. Actually, she spent little time with the patient during her childhood, worked for a number of years, and then went into . . . The father is interested only in his [profession] and social position; the parents are generous only with money. On the other hand, she says they also use money to maintain control over her life. A couple . . . joined the family household when the patient was six months old. She feels very close to both of them . . .

The interviewer noted the patient's focus on the father's mistreatment and her obvious pleasure as she "gleefully" detailed "many incidents where the father was cruel and (physically) hurt her." The summary states: "This young woman . . . has already formulated her case on the basis of her mistreatment by her parents."

This formulation was, of course, the patient's construction, her "authorized biography," the equivalent of her personal myth. *Webster's* would not tolerate calling it a reconstruction, that is, another or new construction. As far as could be then determined, and as confirmed by subsequent analytic data and process, this was the patient's original construction with which she left childhood.

------

[3]The first analytic account in this chapter is derived from notes dictated immediately after each hour. The extent of note taking varied from hour to hour, depending on the amount of time available to the analyst. The second is based on consistently extensive notes taken during and immediately following each analytic session. The third was put into writing about three months after termination and is a combination of identical, somewhat paraphrased, explicit, agreed-upon formulations verbalized by both patient and analyst during middle and termination phases. Each analysis was at a frequency of four sessions weekly and followed the usual technical procedures, including use of the couch and free association. There are no altered data in any example.

The corrected version of this narrative, the reconstruction ultimately synthesized through transferential evolution, understanding, and resolution, was quite different. The memories of childhood presented themselves as analytic experiences whose validity was unassailable. The father had indeed been the center of the young girl's life but in a warm, even adoring, caring mode. In part, father's behavior had compensated for the loss of attention from her mother in her first two years because of a chronic infectious disease diagnosed in the mother during the patient's infancy. The illness had mandated hospitalization and a prolonged invalidism. Moreover, the mother's recovery was heralded by the birth of a sibling. A couple, who had joined the family household actually in the last half of the patient's second year, were invaluable and loved caretakers; but the center of the child's universe, until something happened in the first half of latency, was her father. Indeed, her family *had* included an aggressive, sometimes abusive controlling presence—but it was the patient herself, as she eventually remembered and as substantiated by others' accounts and even home movies.

What had happened? In part it was the birth of still another sibling, one who immediately became the source of anxious preoccupation for both parents. In part it was an angry reaction to the disappointments of the young girl's oedipal strivings. Clearly, the original accounts of her father's mistreatments were, in part, thinly disguised masochistic sexual expressions. This was the reconstruction arrived at by the patient and analyst, a reconstruction intrinsic to the analytic curative process. Not only were the inner and outer childhood experiences recaptured but the original construction had been corrected, that is, reconstructed.

At times the original account given us is so compelling and convincing, and so consistent with prevailing theory, that we might be tempted to search no further. If nothing else this tendency can represent a inculcated bias in favor of Occam's razor, a preference for the simplest of competing theories and for explanation of the unknown first in terms of the known. But analytic experience repeatedly demonstrates the necessity to search out the complex hidden in the simple, just as we penetrate the complex to determine the unifying simple (Frank, 1991)

> A young woman began analysis because of enormous unhappiness as she lived a chaotic and seemingly uncontrolled life, particularly in the areas of sexuality and relations with men. She volunteered that she had understood her troubles from early on as products of the consequences of her childhood seduction by an adult family friend, with whose almost daily sexual fondling she cooperated from the ages of eight to eleven in return for candy and a few coins. A particularly painful and poignant memory was of being secreted away

by him. As he caressed her genitals she heard the voice of her father outside calling for her by name. Somehow she was frightened, as well as excited, that he was looking for her and couldn't find her. This vision of her past as it explained her present existence was her construction. Nothing that ensued in the analysis contradicted the fact of these childhood experiences or their destructive, disruptive, traumatic impacts. But, following the transference, the omitted central issue of the patient's childhood, which explained and, once recaptured, could lead to the resolution of the untoward effects of her seduction, emerged. It was of frustrated passive yearnings for the nurturing mother. In particular, she could not give up her driven, almost addictive, needs for chaotic excitement until she knew of the depressed, lonely inner void from which it was a desperate distraction. The presentation of the plaintive cry in the screen memory was a displacement and a reversal. In fact, it represented the patient's unfulfilled plea to her mother for sustenance and love. It was her deep hunger for such nurturance that explained her vulnerability to seduction and its perverse satisfactions. The neediness persisted as disguised and repressed, expressed through symptoms and acting out. This was the reconstruction as reenacted transferentially and understood, articulated, and accepted by analyst and analysand.

In both of the aforementioned cases the patient herself explicitly and consciously applied her constructed past's narrative to explaining the present. In most cases this is probably not the case, even in these times of psychological sensitivity and apparent sophistication, as in the following example.

An early-middle-aged man began his analysis with an account of his father as a successful businessman who was tyrannical and often sadistic and demeaning. He speculated at one point that his past commitment to the social causes of disadvantaged underdogs could be evidence of continuing rebellion to his unfair, arbitrary, intolerant, and authoritative parent. However, this narrow application was the only explicit reference to his history repeated as adult event, and was uttered with little emphasis or apparent conviction. In fact, the oppressed whom he sought to aid, persons unable to help themselves, reminded me at the time of his mother, as described by him, as well as of himself. Mother was characterized, by means of a number of remembered childhood manifest dream accounts that were cited as "proof," as ineffectual and suffering. The patient's memory of his childhood fantasy of parental intercourse reinforced this characterization of his mother: while both parents stood upright, the father penetrated the submitting mother from the rear, to her immense discomfort and perhaps pain. This thumbnail sketch was the essence of what I propose we term the patient's construction, dating from his emergence from childhood.

At the end of the analysis the narrative was significantly altered. There was an appreciation of the mother as extraordinarily seductive toward her son, frequently exposing her body to him as well as engaging him verbally in the most suggestive, endearing ways. In contrast, her conduct toward her husband had been noteworthy because of its provocativeness and vengefulness. The history that finally emerged, with requisite conviction, was of the mother's implacable daily search for her husband's vulnerabilities. Eventually, the calm of father's demeanor and that of the household were shattered by his explosion. Mother then assumed the posture of a martyr, protesting her helplessness in the face of father's unexplainable anger, unfairness, and brutality. The patient allied himself with his mother more and more as time passed, gaining at the same time a symbolic oedipal victory and an exclusive position, as well as a profound unrecognized identification with her that served his unconscious homosexual aims. This was the reconstruction; the process by which it was achieved was accompanied not only by a resolution of symptoms but also by dramatic and successful changes in the patient's self-concept, strivings, and life situation. That process was the consistent and careful understanding, analysis, and resolution of the evolving transference. At first the analyst was in the position of the father, with the patient's initial righteous rebelliousness gradually giving way to explicit, passive, masochistic homosexual wishes. The analyst then was reacted to as if he were the mother, in a manner inferable from the aforementioned reconstruction. The final working-through phase was noteworthy as a revival of the long-repressed and latent positive identification with the father and was particularly concerned with the problems of understanding, dealing with, and eventually renouncing difficult women.

The innovations in terminology that I propose can thus serve an important purpose in reinforcing, in the very processes of description and verbalization, the essential genetic-developmental status of a patient's constructed "authorized biography." Had the analyst swallowed the historical and psychological validity of any of the aforementioned case histories, the effect would have been deleterious on the course of the analysis. Even worse, suppose that on the basis of the original case history a diagnosis had been made and technical innovations implemented. For example, an approach instituting a pseudoempathic—actually sympathetic—analytic stance would have strengthened, through substantiation by reinforcement and collaboration, the pathologic structures represented by the construction. At best, only a supportive therapeutic result or one based on spurious transference cure would have been effected. To have tried, through benevolent gratification, to make up for the presented childhood deficiencies would have had the same consequences. A corrective emotional experience, with the analyst adopting a posture presumably contrary to that of the described childhood objects or energetically presenting himself as a rationally based "new object," could not eventuate in anything other than a more complicated scenario superimposing its own complexities on the original pathology. A truly empathic and therapeutic approach requires trial identifications based on feeling and respectful observations, communication based on patience and tact, and an awareness of the involved historical complexities. In this way analysand and analyst cooperate in the reediting, the reconstruction, of the original construction, which proceeds *pari passu* with the analytic process. What would have originally been an "unauthorized biography," unthinkable and intolerable, thus evolves.

What are the further specifications of a reconstruction? Kennedy (1971), observing from her work with children that with maturation and development new memory structures are continually evolving, proposed that even ordinary remembering is a reconstruction. She stated, "In the same way as every percept is a construction, every memory is intrinsically a reconstruction—an achievement of the mental apparatus of the child" (p. 396). But it is unlikely that her observational and clinical opportunities conveyed the profundity of the impact of the mental apparatus's major structuralization in latency. Most adult remembering involves the recall of a screen memory or construction. Occasionally, a remembrance presents itself as close to original experience, as with a traumatic neurosis, catastrophic trauma, or some of the bittersweet reminiscences experienced with nostalgia or mourning. But the extensive reorganization of one's vision of his or her past that merits being called a reconstruction is rarer. Sometimes it occurs naturally, but such instances deserve careful scrutiny and assessment.[4]

The therapeutic reconstruction to which this chapter is directed is our analytic privilege. The reconstruction refers to actual events in an analysis, something that was really said. Initially, most of the time it is the analyst's

---

[4]For example, the writer George Orwell extensively revised what had been a carefully nurtured personal myth of childhood poverty in a late essay called "Such, Such Were the Joys" (Frank, 1989). In the essay he replaced his thesis of childhood deprivation at home with one of persecution at prep school. But the circumstances and dynamics indicated that this "correction" was in fact a response to tragedy: a soon-to-be-fatal illness, sudden loss of his wife and older sister, the burden of a young child, and, paradoxically, a success that he had until that time been able to skillfully and energetically avoid. The contents and organization of the revised autobiography betrayed the misuse of such a reconstruction in the service of defense, regression, and psychopathology, which paralleled his downhill course.

voice articulating the reconstruction. As time passes, however, reconstruction often becomes much more a collaborative practice. Usually, elements of the reconstruction are enunciated at particular times and subsumed and combined in later propositions. The whole story may never be told in a single breath but may depend on serial explications. According to Freud, a reconstruction cites several, rather than a single, elements; the analysis of a single element is in the realm of interpretation (Freud, 1937, p. 261).

Further, the reconstruction hypothesizes deduced or demonstrated past circumstances and their original impacts. But it can also refer to a subtler, less circumscribed, more chronic trauma. To the extent that something is diagnosable, it is citable in a reconstruction. A reconstruction can include what happened externally or internally, acutely or over time. It also expands on the later sequelae of the childhood events, stresses, or strains. But it goes deeper than citation. The critical essence of reconstruction is the approximation of the child's inner experience and its meaning within the original context.

Ideally, a reconstruction should go beyond Freud's example cited earlier into his "and so on," continuing with an explanation of the patient's current symptomatology and syndromes in the previously elaborated contexts. The information should be supplemented by an understanding and explanation of the forces shaping and limiting their original choices of psychological dynamic strategy. All of these expositions must be based on observed phenomena and reasoned surmise in the psychoanalytic situation. The patient's external confirmation through investigation or serendipitious findings outside analytic hours may be useful in the editing of some details of the narrative, or in adding some further conviction to its truth, but is not a requirement or necessarily a useful factor in its creation (Frank, 1991).

The current generation of analysts works with a significant advantage. Freud's knowledge of infants and children was largely limited to prevalent 19th-century pediatrics, subservient to the culture and times. Only occasionally could he draw on fortuitous direct observations of children, such as his own grandchild, or on supervision of others directly involved with children, such as the junior colleague whose son had a fear of horses. Analytically informed studies of infants and children, as exemplified by those based on separation–individuation theory, bestow upon contemporary analysis a corpus of learning garnered from the vantage point of careful, systematic observations. Here we are back to the critical essence of reconstruction cited earlier: the approximation of the child's inner experience and its meaning within the original context.

Hence, analysis has moved apace with archaeology, preserving Freud's analogy. The contemporary archaeologist is no longer content with rebuilding walls and columns and repicturing murals and paintings; from the constructions that have been preserved he deduces the essentials of past cultures and lives, prior history and circumstances. From the stone is gleaned its age; its origins; the tools that quarried and shaped and erected it; the world and geography in which it was mined and transported; and the visions, needs, and capacities of the people who used it. From the painting's pigments are deduced the culture's mineralogy and agriculture; from its depictions, artist's imagery, and icons. The next step is the approximation of what befell the civilization and an attempt to explain why some elements of the culture were destroyed and buried while others survived in seemingly unmistakable or disguised form, ". . . and so on." These scholarly reconstructions are used to view and understand the "then" as integral to the "now." The result is a vision of man in the broadest sense.

I have gone much further than my opening paragraphs would have suggested, but the arguments and considerations that motivated me could not stop with dictionary definitions. If we carefully regard our choice of language, we cannot avoid a comparable examination of the ideas and experiences that they represent. Such consideration and the thoughts and theses so elicited can only be to the advantage of psychoanalytic science.

REFERENCES

Carlson, D. (1989), Discussion of "Constructions and Reconstructions, Thera-peutic and Inexact: George Orwell and 'Such, Such Were the Joys' " by Alvin Frank, M.D. Presented at annual meeting of the American Psychoanalytic Association, New York City.

Frank, A. (1989), Constructions and reconstructions, therapeutic and inexact: George Orwell and "Such, Such Were the Joys." Presented at the annual meeting of the American Psychoanalytic Association, New York City.

———— (1991), Psychic change and the analyst as biographer: Transference and reconstruction. *Internat. J. Psycho-Anal.*, 72:22–26.

Freud, S. (1899), Screen memories. *Standard Edition*, 3:303–322. London: Hogarth Press, 1962.

———— (1900), The interpretation of dreams. *Standard Edition*, 4 & 5. London: Hogarth Press, 1953.

———— (1925), An autobiographical study. *Standard Edition*, 20:7–74. London: Hogarth Press, 1959.

———— (1937), Constructions in analysis. *Standard Edition*, 23:255–269. London: Hogarth Press, 1964.

Greenacre, P. (1981), Reconstruction: Its nature and therapeutic value. *J. Amer. Psychoanal. Assn.*, 29:27–46.

Kennedy, H. (1971), Problems in reconstruction in child analysis. *The Psychoanalytic Study of the Child*, 26:386–402. New York: Quadrangle Books.

Kris, E. (1956), The personal myth. *J. Amer. Psychoanal. Assn.*, 4:653–681.

Laplanche, J. & Pontalis, J-B. (1973), *The Language of Psychoanalysis*. London: Hogarth Press.

Moore, B. & Fine, B., ed. (1990), *Psychoanalytic Terms and Concepts*. New Haven, CT: Yale University Press.

Stengel, E. (1939), On learning a new language. *Internat. J. Psycho-Anal.*, 20:471–479.

Stern, D. (1985), *The Interpersonal World of the Infant*. New York: Basic Books.

Vygotsky, L. (1988), *The Collected Papers of L.S. Vygotsky, Vol. 1.*, ed. R. W. Rieber & A. S. Carton. New York: Plenum.

Webster's Ninth New Collegiate Dictionary (1987), Springfield, MA: Merriam Webster.

Wilson, E. (1989), Abstract of Donnet, J-L: The stakes of interpretation. *Psychoanal. Quart.*, 58:324–325.

18   On the Treatment of Preoedipal Pathology

Calvin F. Settlage

One of the advances fostered in great measure by separation–individuation theory (Mahler, Pine, and Bergman, 1975; Mahler, 1979a, b) is a more complete understanding of preoedipal pathology and its resolution in treatment. This chapter focuses on pathogenesis and arrest in the separation–individuation process and the attendant impairment in the structuring of object and self constancy. The impairment is understood to be due to repressed anger and rage that interferes with structural integration. The presented clinical material is selected to illustrate therapeutic process in the resolution of such impairment.

OBJECT AND SELF-CONSTANCY

Preoedipal development is concerned with the early development of ego functions and the formation of primary regulatory structures in the area of object relationships and sense of self (Settlage, 1980a). Object and self-constancy are such regulatory structures and are outcomes of the separation–individuation process. As pivotal psychic structures, their adequate development and integration provide sound underpinnings for the oedipal and all subsequent stages of development (Settlage, 1980a).

351

On the other hand, their impairment contributes to the pathology of the more severe mental disorders (Settlage, 1964, 1977).

Object and self-constancy comprise integrated representations of good and bad experiences in the child–parent interaction. Mental representations of the mother and the self are initially closely intertwined. They are sorted out through the process of self-object differentiation (Jacobson, 1964). The thus differentiated representations are conceived to be organized by the child's subjective sense of emotionally charged, contrasting, pleasurable and unpleasurable, good and bad experiences in the mother–child interaction. At this early level of cognitive development the child is thus seen to have a disjunctive sense of unintegrated good and bad representations of the mother on one hand and of the self on the other.

It is the subsequent amalgamation and integration of these sets of good and bad representations that results in a unified representation of the mother and of the self as separate entities, each having good and bad features. With this integration, the possibility of dealing with angry and hostile feelings toward the love object through the defense of splitting yields to the defense of repression (Settlage, 1977, 1980b). Ambivalence is a consequence of this integration.

Effective structuring of object and self-constancy takes place under the aegis of a predominance of loving feelings over angry, hostile feelings in the child–parent relationship (McDevitt, 1975). The predominance of love is the glue of the unified representation. Object constancy as initially structured in the mother–child interaction is further structured in the interaction with the father and other significant love objects. Sometimes the structuring process is undermined by conflicting experiences with different love objects. For example, the structuring of object constancy can be seriously impaired by the inability to integrate disparate mother and father representations, such as those commonly associated with divorce.

The attainment of object constancy means that the parent is represented in a lasting way in the child's mental structure (Hartmann, 1952; A. Freud, 1965; Mahler and Furer, 1968). The parent now is always available to the child intrapsychically. At the close of the object constancy phase, at about 36 months of age, separation can thus take place without the former high degree of separation anxiety. The amalgamation of emotionally charged object images into object constancy means that the child has the expectation that the love relationship will survive hostile feelings and episodic angry confrontations. The internal "presence" of the parent tends further to diminish the child's need for the external presence of the parent in the support of developing regulatory functions. Object constancy serves the establishment, maintenance, and regulation of object relations.

Self-constancy is developed through entirely similar, codetermined processes. The loving and anger-evoking experiences in the relationship with the primary love objects contribute to both the object and the self-representation. The outcomes of self-constancy are analogous to those of object constancy. In addition to the sense of a single integrated self, there is the confidence that the self will survive separation from the love object. There also is the expectation that the integrated, predominantly good self will survive a temporary resurgence of the bad self. Self-constancy serves the regulation of self-esteem and the sense of self.

PREOEDIPAL PATHOGENESIS

In keeping with Freud's concept of the complemental series (Freud, 1917), both normal[1] and pathological structure formation hinge on the interaction between the child and the parent. Structural impairment stems from difficulty in the developmental interaction.

The dependency of the young child on the parent for survival makes maintenance of the child–parent relationship a necessity. Particularly during the rapprochement subphase of separation–individuation (Mahler, 1972a) intense separation anxiety and attendant feelings of helplessness stimulate angry, rageful feelings and fantasies toward the parent. Because these feelings and fantasies, and those associated with disciplinary interactions, jeopardize the relationship, they tend to evoke splitting and denial and the pathological use of repression in the interest of maintaining the relationship.

In the defense of splitting, the integrated good and bad representations of the object and the self are split apart. Splitting can serve to maintain a threatened object relationship or the good sense of self by getting rid of the bad aspect of the object or self. The bad aspect of the object is disavowed and displaced onto others, and the bad aspect of the self is projected onto an object in the outside world, as in the case of childhood phobias. Under extreme conditions, splitting can make the love object or the self all bad, sometimes with paranoid or severe depressive reactions. Repression has the aim of maintaining the relationship with the love object by removing hostile aggressive fantasies and feelings from conscious awareness.

---

[1]For example, separation-individuation oriented research on mother–child interaction during the second year of life led to the discovery and delineation of *the appeal cycle,* which is postulated to be an agent of developmental process and psychic structure formation (Settlage et al., 1988; Settlage et al., 1990; Settlage et al., in press).

The repressed angry feelings tend not to be experienced and processed in subsequent development and therefore remain outside of ego modulation. Because of their presence in the unconscious mind and the danger of their precipitous mobilization, they are felt by the individual to be a potentially explosive internal liability. The combination of intense longings for love and closeness paralleled by an equally intense fear of betrayal of trust creates merger–abandonment anxieties and problems with separation and closeness in childhood and adulthood.

In preoedipal pathogenesis, the developmental process leading to the structuring of object and self-constancy tends to be arrested. The consequent impairment of psychic structure formation causes a continuing dependence on the parent or on others for the regulation of urges and feelings and for the maintenance of structural integration and psychic organization.

CLINICAL MATERIAL

The clinical material is taken from the analytic treatment of a three-year-old girl and a 34-year-old woman. The child case is presented at greater length and in more detail than the adult case, which is more narrowly focused to demonstrate the progressive analysis of repressed anger and rage. The fact that both patients were female is not meant to suggest that the pathology under discussion is linked to gender.

The Child Case

Lisa was the intellectually precocious only child of psychologically sophisticated, professional parents. The presenting symptoms were an intense separation anxiety, a severe, chronic, stressfully conflicted constipation with sometimes painful bowel movements at intervals ranging from three to eight days, and fearful refusal to use the toilet. In addition, there was a fear of balloons popping and a sleep problem associated with fear that the darkness harbored monsters and snakes. These symptoms developed immediately after the family's move from Florida to California, when the patient was 30 months of age. Lisa's symptom formation thus took place during the object constancy subphase of separation–individuation theory and the overlapping beginning of the phallic-oedipal stage of psychosexual theory.

During the course of treatment Lisa developed a fear of being touched by anyone other than her parents. This symptom, which persisted despite relief of other symptoms and a return to generally normal functioning, was understood to represent unresolved anxieties impairing the formation of object and self-constancy.

The family's move took place in the context of circumstances posing threats and experiences of loss. Toilet training, begun at 23 months, and other disciplinary interactions involving anger-intensified feelings of loss were in process during the months preceding the family's move. The mother was depressed, withdrawn, and inconsistently available to Lisa. She attributed these affects and behaviors to concerns about serious marital difficulties and apprehensions about the move that she recognized as her own unresolved separation anxiety. The father was anxiously preoccupied by the grave illness of an older brother, a preoccupation that made him less available to Lisa than usual. The brother's illness and the preparations for the move to California required father to make frequent trips away from home.

The mother observed that Lisa was very anxious and distressed by the father's departures and by the move-related activities that caused changes in the physical home environment. Of specific interest is an event that occurred on the day the movers came. Lisa and a six-year-old girlfriend were playing upstairs by themselves. The patient became upset and cried. The mother found out that the children had been playing with a balloon and that the friend had tricked and surprised Lisa by letting air out of the balloon behind Lisa's back in a way that made a farting sound. The fear of popping balloons appeared a week later.

The meaning of the fear of popping balloons was first suggested by Lisa's statement to her mother that she and mother could pop like a balloon. She played out this fear with the analyst toward the end of the second year of treatment. She brought a girl doll that she had named "Pooby-Booby" to the sessions. The doll's name was a condensation employing the first letters of popping balloons and the slang terms *poop* and *boob* for *stool* and *breast*. Speaking for Pooby-Booby, Lisa informed me that girls could pop and shrivel up but boys could not. Although this fantasy expressed the fear of loss of the whole person, the fact that it contrasted girls and boys suggested that it also was a castration fantasy explaining the genital difference between girls and boys.

Concern about loss was expressed in another way during the third year of treatment when the family moved to a second home in California. In the same breath Lisa announced that she had for the first time moved her bowels on the toilet and that she had acquired an aluminum-foil balloon. She reported further that the (helium-filled) balloon had risen to the ceiling of her bedroom. She took pains to explain that the ceiling was peaked like an inverted V.

That Lisa imagined the balloon with respect to the ceiling to be in the position as the genital in the human crotch and that she was expressing castration concerns became evident from her associations. With anxious giggling she broke crayons and gave me the short ends while she kept the long ones. She crayoned with white crayons on white paper, renewing an earlier theme about invisible things; this theme had to do with her wish to have a penis and the denial of its absence.

I repeated to Lisa the interpretation that the idea of invisibility allowed her to believe she had a penis even though it could not be seen. Her response was to look for but not see a piece of crayon she had lost among the pieces she gave to me. She then touched the genital area of her jeans. When I asked whether she noticed what she had done when she couldn't find the lost piece of crayon, she again touched her genital area and then held a crayon to it. When I asked about this, Lisa readily indicated that the crayon was like a penis and that she was seeing whether it would fit.

Baby-making fantasies had been in the foreground of preceding sessions, and I knew that Lisa's parents had accurately answered her question about how babies were made. I said that I couldn't tell whether she was pretending that the crayon was her penis or that of someone else. Her response was to place the crayon inside her purse. This symbolic act suggested the beginning relinquishment of the wish to have a penis and the transformation of this wish into the wish to have a baby.

Lisa was now nearly six years old. Her psychic structure clearly was undergoing transition in the body-image and gender-identity aspects of the self. Through interpretation and working through, the treatment was enabling her to give up various loss-defending fantasies expressed in the treatment: the fantasy that she had a penis but that it was hidden or invisible; the fantasy that she had the genitals of both sexes; and the fantasy that she once had but later lost her penis. These reality-distorting fantasies were being replaced by her recently acquired factual knowledge about her internal sexual organs. She was accepting and embracing her identity as a girl, a person who could one day have a baby.

Although Lisa's presenting symptoms had disappeared and she generally was functioning very well, the symptomatic fear of being touched was still present. This was so despite its having been in some measure analyzed. It had been interpreted as a reversal of her wish—expressed in a grabbing gesture toward my crotch—to grab, pull off, and keep my penis as her own. In response to this interpretation, Lisa began to hand her drawings and written messages to me instead of tossing them to me from a distance. That she was less fearful of being touched was evident also in the fact that in handing me pieces of paper her hand inadvertently, or so she made it seem, brushed mine.

Another already analyzed determinant of Lisa's fear of being touched was her symbolically expressed concern about touching and damaging her genitals. There had been play involving placing checkers and pennies into various narrow slots, including the slot-like mouth of a Cookie Monster doll. In the context of other material expressing sexual curiosity, this had been interpreted as her wondering about how the tube-shaped penis could fit into the slot-like vagina without causing pain and injury. Lisa had experienced severe pain due to the stretching of the anus when she eventually passed the large, hard stools resulting from her constipation.[2]

Also pertaining to the fear of being touched was Lisa's fear-determined insistence that I open the sliding door to the toy cabinet even though she was capable of opening it by herself. The fear of opening the cabinet door was related to Lisa's anxiety about loss of control over sexual and aggressive feelings. The sexual anxiety stemmed prominently from conflict over her own masturbatory activity and sexual play with a girlfriend, which involved poking objects at each other's anal and genital openings. The anxiety about aggression was seen to derive from Lisa's anger and rage in response to the physical and libidinal experiences of loss of relationship with the parents and the fantasied threats of loss of body parts centering around the toilet training (Settlage, 1971).

Lisa gradually progressed from opening the door to a slit-like crack, to opening it more widely, to opening it fully and unfearfully. In the related fantasy play, the sliding door was gradually revealed to be a barrier closing off the dark insides of the cabinet which undoubtedly harbored a monster. It became possible to interpret Lisa's fear of the destructive potential of her own anger. In language suited to her vocabulary and level of understanding, I explained that the insides of the cabinet represented her own insides and that the slit-like crack represented her anal and genital openings, openings that threatened to allow both intrusion and the expression of the angry feelings that she feared might burst forth out of control.

Lisa's becoming able to open the cabinet door by herself meant that the treatment had dealt with a good deal of her anxiety about loss of control over her sexual and aggressive feelings. I felt that she had been particularly anxious about losing control over her repressively walled-off but unmodulated anal stage–rapprochement subphase aggression. As evidenced in the fear of monsters and snakes and popping balloons, the defensive mechanisms of phobia were evoked in the attempt to escape the danger in the inside world by projecting and transforming it into danger in the outside world.

The further analysis of the conflict underlying Lisa's fear of touching and

---

[2]The psychological determinants of Lisa's constipation were understood to be very much the same as those of a two-and-a-half-year-old girl (Settlage, 1971) and a three-year-old girl (Settlage, 1977) who had the same symptom.

being touched was initiated by new behavior in the beginning of the fourth year of treatment. Lisa would hide in the waiting room and inform her mother that she intended to have me believe she was not there. As the mother and I were so pretending, Lisa would suddenly and gleefully jump into view, enjoying both the surprise and the reunion. When this behavior was subsequently interpreted as playing at being lost, she responded, "I used to worry about that."

Lisa also revived earlier merry-go-round play involving the use of my swivel chair. She repeatedly went round and round in the chair, saying and waving good-bye and hello. She sometimes stopped the turning when she was out of sight, reappearing by resuming the turning or by popping up over the back of the chair in a jack-in-the-box variation of the peekaboo game (Kleeman, 1967). Her behavior was interpreted as a reenactment of the separation and loss experiences associated with the move to California.

It is noteworthy that Lisa also sought this activity at every opportunity on the real thing, both prior to and during the treatment. Her parents amusedly referred to her as a "merry-go-round addict." With Lisa on and her parents off the merry-go-round, their repeated disappearance and reappearance, along with the voiced and waved good-byes and hellos, can be seen to make the merry-go-round an excellent vehicle for reassurance against fears of loss and mastery of separation anxiety.

The developmental linkage between fear of object loss and fear of castration or loss of body parts (Settlage, 1971) was demonstrated when Lisa introduced into the sessions another game, which she played while engaged in the merry-go-round play. This was the disappearing and reappearing game of pretending she had lost her thumb while hiding it in the palm of her hand.

Lisa's nonverbal expression of concern about loss was also expressed at the verbal level. One night at bedtime she asked her mother, "Why is it that roads have an end?" Lisa answered her own question with the reflective observation: "I guess everything has to end—except merry-go-rounds." These thoughts followed, by some months, the death of the family's pet dog, a loss that had been addressed in the treatment. Because of the implied acceptance of endings, including the death of the pet dog, Lisa's question and answer were felt to indicate diminution of the interrelated fears of object loss and loss of control over her aggressive feelings and impulses.

The merry-go-round play now took a new twist. With each cycle of the chair, Lisa gleefully pretended the act of farting at me. She presented her buttocks to me while making farting sounds with her mouth. She thus appeared to express the fantasy that her angry, hostile feelings and impulses could drive me away or destroy me. In contrast to earlier transference enactments, this play was distinguished by the open and direct expression of aggression. Her behavior was a further sign that her repressed aggression was being brought under modulated ego control and that she was less afraid of object loss. The significance of Lisa's reaction of distress, at age 30 months, to the balloon-made sound of farting behind her back became apparent. Because the unexpected farting sound made it seem as though *she* had farted, it stimulated her fear of loss of control over her anal aggression.

In a commonly occurring, pathogenic reversal of cause and effect, Lisa likely fantasied that her anger was the cause rather than the consequence of her loss experiences: instead of becoming angry at her parents because they left or withdrew from her, it was her anger that caused them to leave or withdraw. This fantasy augmented her need to repress aggression in the maintenance of the all-important relationship with the parents.

Alongside the aggressive merry-go-round play, the balloon fantasy also appeared in a new form. Two large light globes hung suspended from the ceiling of the office like balloons on a string. Lisa now played a game with them. She stood on the couch and jumped from it, trying to touch one of the globes as she flew through the air. Repeated attempts demonstrated that it was beyond her reach. In the next session she stood provocatively on the desk where she could reach the other globe. With an anxious but also mischievous eye on me, she gently poked the globe several times.

Because of the primary context of object loss and the prior analysis of anxieties over loss of body parts, the globe play was viewed as reflecting mainly preoedipal pathology concerned with object loss, rather than oedipal pathology concerned with loss of love.[3] At the conscious level, the anxiety was over the possibility that the globe would break and disappear like a popping balloon. Unconsciously, it reflected Lisa's continuing concern that her anger could escape control and turn her poking finger into an instrument of destruction. She was given this interpretation. In addition, her anger was connected with her early loss experiences. Explanatory connections were made to her remark that she and her mother could pop like a balloon and to the experience with the girlfriend and the farting balloon.

---

[3]Preoedipal pathology and oedipal pathology often are closely interrelated (Arlow, 1963; Loewald, 1979). The threat of loss—object loss, loss of love, castration—is a factor in their pathogenesis (Settlage, 1971). In my experience, effective therapeutic process requires that transference representing preoedipal pathology be distinguished from transference representing oedipal pathology and that each be interpreted in its own terms. The same view is expressed and documented by Selma Kramer (1979).

These interpretations of the determinants of fears of object loss gained validation during the ensuing period of working through. Lisa, once again in the merry-go-round chair, hummed the melodies of "Pop Goes the Weasel" and "My Darling Clementine." When asked whether she knew the words to these songs, she demonstrated that she did, emphasizing the phrases, "pop goes the weasel" and "thou art lost and gone forever." Shortly thereafter the treatment was interrupted by the family's two-week vacation trip. The leave-taking session began with Lisa's reintroduction of the play of hiding in the waiting room. As the session proceeded, the initial affective tone of exuberance changed to one of subdued sadness. I commented that she must be having some sad feelings about our not seeing each other for a while. She made no response. At the close of the session, I suggested that a good-bye handshake would help us remember that we would be meeting again after her trip. Lisa contemplatively considered but rejected my suggestion. She did so with a knowing smile, suggesting her awareness that shaking my hand would indicate that her fear was mostly gone, and perhaps further that she no longer needed to continue to see me. As Lisa left the office, her own means of dealing with the separation was revealed. She wore a necklace made from my paper clips—a *tangible* keepsake that she had been assembling during the final minutes of the session.

The behaviors of hiding and being lost, pretending to destroy or drive me away with farting, and poking at the fragile light globe made possible the full analysis of the infantile anxieties about object and self loss, represented in the symptomatic fear of being touched. The emergence of the repressed aggression and the interpretation of the associated pathogenic fantasies served to ameliorate these anxieties and the bad representations of object and self. This amelioration permitted the further development and integration of the object and self-constancy structures. The developmental process involving these structures, arrested at 30 months of age, was thus resumed and carried forward.

The Adult Case

The patient was a 34-year-old school teacher, married to a lawyer and the mother of a five-year-old daughter. She was seriously depressed and anxiously concerned about whether she could make it on her own if she decided to leave her very troubled marriage. Symptomatically, she was intermittently phobic about crossing bridges and about certain foods that she feared would make her deathly sick.

The patient was an only child who grew up in a working-class Jewish family in Chicago. She felt that her parents were very close; they never expressed cross words or meanness to each other or to their daughter. She characterized her father as a loving, easygoing, mild-mannered man. She saw her mother as very nurturing but also as very controlling in ways that were not overtly aggressive.

The patient's memory began with her latency years. During childhood, she felt that she and her mother had a very close, good relationship. As an adult she came to see that mother interfered with her independence and autonomy. Mother was given to advising and nicely admonishing the patient "for her own good." She also would not tolerate disagreement or allow a give-and-take discussion. Disagreement was met by withdrawal into hurt silence; the patient would then feel "cut off" and guilty. She also became aware that mother created an aura of anxiety through her ever-present anticipation of something going wrong, particularly when the patient was doing well.

The patient's very involved relationship with mother was intensified after the death of father. Father died unexpectedly from a heart attack when the patient was 19, six months after she left for college. She felt guilty about his death and experienced it as the consequence of her leaving the family and striking out on her own.

At the time the treatment began, when the patient was 34, the patient and her mother, now separated by 2,000 miles, were in daily telephone contact, wherein the described relationship still prevailed. One of the patient's voiced concerns was that she might repeat in treatment her pattern of conformity and its "reward" of dependency.

About a year into the treatment, following my having been away for two weeks, the patient reported that she had had a very difficult time. During the first week of the interruption of treatment, she twice awakened screaming. She was unaware of having dreamed and had no idea why she screamed. She was angry that her husband made no effort to understand or console her. During the second week of the interruption of treatment she became afraid that her vitamin capsules were poisoned, even though she knew better because she had already taken half of them.

Noting that I brushed my cheek with my hand, she had the thought that something was wrong with me; maybe I had a skin cancer. Because her anger had been a focus of our work, I asked whether she might be angry at me. She said that she was not aware of any anger.

She then talked about people who close off their feelings. She used to do that with both her good and her bad feelings. Sometimes she felt that she was a totally unworthy, bad person. She spoke of the "craziness" of her fear of being poisoned. Such an idea did not fit with her image of herself as a healthy, good person, and it was mortifying to tell me about it.

I observed that the screaming in her sleep, the fear of being poisoned, and the idea that I had a skin cancer could be indirect expressions of suppressed anger. I wondered whether she had felt abandoned by me but had closed off her feelings for fear of hurting me, driving me away, or destroying and losing me. She intellectually agreed with my observations but had no emotional conviction about them because she still felt no anger.

I understood the patient's fear of being poisoned as a symptomatic expression of her unconscious anger and rage at me for "abandoning" her. The rage augmented the affective intensity of the bad object and self representations and disrupted the integration of the patient's constancy structures. The need to maintain the relationship with me as a good object evoked the defense of splitting. The rage and badness were projected onto the outside world in the form of the fantasy of being poisoned.

Four months later, the treatment was interrupted by the summer vacation period. The patient began the first postvacation session by sharing a thought that came to her as she approached the door to the waiting room. The thought was that she would find a note on the door stating, "Dr. Settlage cannot see you because he is dead." She recognized that the thought expressed her fear of losing me but again expressed no awareness of the anger that could be inferred from it.

Instead of focusing on her fear of losing me, she quickly shifted to telling me that she had suffered an asthmatic attack earlier that day. She felt the attack must have been triggered by a confrontation with her baby-sitter. Although enraged by the sitter's irresponsible behavior, the patient talked to her in a mild, controlled manner that did not vent the rageful feelings.

Later in the session I brought the patient back to her thought that I was dead. With great difficulty she told me that she did remember feeling angry about my leaving her. She then realized that her rage toward the sitter no doubt included rage toward me and that her thought that I was dead expressed both her anger with me and her fear of destroying and losing me.

Some months later, a few days before another planned interruption of the treatment, the patient felt sad and wondered whether she was depressed. At the same time, she felt and voiced her anger about my leaving. She noted that she did not feel the sense of panic that was associated with previous leave-takings; this time the emotions were different. She attributed the former sense of panic to having felt utterly dependent on me.

Further exploration made it apparent that her sadness was not a symptomatic expression of depression but the affect associated with mourning. The mourning was understood to reflect a long-delayed mourning of the loss of her father, engendered by the transference-related

SETTLAGE   363

pending loss of me. In addition to the effect of interpretation of the
transference, I felt that the mourning was made possible by the internalization of a representation of me as a reasonably constant object whom she
could trust and who could tolerate her expression of anger and rage. In
consequence, she could begin to relinquish the external relationship with
me in what can be thought of as resumption of an arrested separation–
individuation process.

Largely because the patient's problem with anger and rage was resolving,
she had begun to enjoy improved relations with her husband and daughter
and was experiencing a new sense of freedom and closeness in relationships
generally. She expressed gratitude to me for my role in these changes. In
the next session she reported a highly eroticized, frightening dream
involving a gray-haired man. She prefaced the dream by noting that there
were two gray-haired men in her life: her internist and her analyst. In the
dream, she is dancing with her internist in an abandoned, erotic manner.
She felt that they were losing control of their sexual feelings. The doctor
then whispers in her ear that he has "Ace." The dream stopped abruptly
and the patient awakened with the thought that *Ace* is a disguise for the
word *Aids*. She was at a loss to understand why she had the dream. Her
only thought was that its denouement fit with her usual anticipation (in
identification with her mother) that the consequence of enjoying something, as she was enjoying her new lease on life, is to be struck down.

I observed that the feelings of gratitude she expressed to me in the
previous session must have made her feel close to me. I wondered whether
these loving feelings had frightened her, as was suggested by the way she
slammed the brakes on her sexual feelings in the dream by invoking the
specter of Aids. She said that she had always found it difficult to express
loving feelings for fear of being rejected as unworthy of love. She realized
that she tended to use her sexuality, as in the dream, to defend against the
hurt of rejection simply as a person: it was her sexual behavior and not
herself that ran the risk of rejection. In the postulated reversal of cause and
effect noted in Lisa's case, it became clear that a major determinant of the
patient's fear of being rejected was the repressed rage that made her feel she
was a destructive, bad person.

The presented excerpts from the treatment were selected to give a sense
of the progressive analysis of the patient's repressed anger and rage. As for
the question of pathogenesis, the patient's difficulty in feeling and
expressing anger was seen to result mainly from the childhood interaction
with her mother. As remembered by the patient, her mother's intolerance
for anger was such that angry confrontations were avoided if at all possible.
The patient's anger in response to mother's intrusive instructions and
control was labeled unacceptable and irrational because mother's actions

were always in the best interest of the patient. The patient's angry feelings were not accepted, not validated as normal feelings, not sufficiently expressed, and not managed and mastered in the developmental interaction. Therefore, the patient had not developed internal models for the modulated regulation of aggressive feelings or for straightening out a relationship disrupted by hurt and anger.[4]

The mother's attitudes appeared to foster dependency at the expense of independence and autonomy. The dependency was then frustrated by the mother's withdrawal into emotional unavailability in the face of disagreement. The patient's angry reaction at mother's intrusions was augmented by mother's unavailability in the face of the fostered dependency. Because the angry feelings threatened the all-important relationship with the mother, they were defended against by splitting and by suppression and repression.

The cited interpretation that the patient felt abandoned by me and had closed off her angry feelings for fear of hurting me, driving me away, or destroying and losing me was aimed at her preoedipal experience. A similar, earlier interpretation had been made in terms of her late adolescent transference. This transference was understood to express the fear that her going away to college and striking out on her own had caused the death of her father. The patient felt that this was a correct interpretation.

But the persistence of her anxieties and symptoms, as well as the defensive operations and transference manifestations involving splitting, suggested earlier origins as well. These are reflected in the patient's seeing herself or me at times as mostly good and at other times as mostly bad. The anxiety and splitting associated with the resurgence of repressed anger and rage is a phenomenon of inadequate structuring of object and self-constancy. The guilt that was a prominent feature of her remembered latency and adolescent years, and which incorporated oedipal guilt, is a product of intrapsychic conflict involving structuralization at the oedipal level, including a structured superego (Arlow, 1963).

In keeping with preoedipal pathology, the cited clinical material indicates the tenuousness of the patient's close object relationships, the instability of the underlying constancy structures, and the strong transference resistance to experiencing the affects and anxieties associated with both loving and angry feelings. Therapeutic process involving the affective reenactment and interpretation of preoedipal transferences in this adult

---

[4]In this regard, the aforementioned research (footnote 1) suggests that such regulatory models derive from preoedipal development in the context of the *appeal cycle* (Settlage et al., in press).

patient was essential to the further development and integration of object and self-constancy embodying a predominance of loving over angry feelings.[5]

CONCLUSION

The presented cases demonstrate the pathogenic role of untoward loss or threats of loss of relationship in preoedipal development. Such loss generates anger and rage and evokes defensive splitting and repression in the service of preserving the child–parent relationship. The thus defended, now unconscious anger is not subject to the usual processing in the child–parent interaction that leads to its ego-modulated control and socially appropriate expression. The possibility of its escape from defensive control constitutes a threatening internal liability. Further defensive operations can lead to symptom formation, as illustrated by the phobic attitudes in both of the presented cases.

The ongoing preoccupation with maintenance of the threatened relationship tends to preclude feelings of safety and security in the relationship, as does the readily triggered rage that tends to block or negate the experiencing of loving feelings. This interferes with the relinquishment and mourning of the incremental losses of relationship that occur in the normal separation–individuation process. Mahler (1972b) observed that "inherent in every new step of independent functioning is a minimal threat of object loss" (p. 333). Failure to confront and mourn such developmental loss interferes with internalization and the formation and integration of object and self-constancy.

The presented cases also demonstrate the evocative power of interruptions of the therapeutic relationship. Given that the pathology under consideration stems from pathogenesis in the separation individuation process, this is no surprise. The presented material is focused mainly on physical interruptions of the therapeutic relationship, but libidinal interruptions, such as are caused by failure of therapeutic empathy and attunement, are equally evocative.

Finally, the clinical material illustrates the importance of mobilizing, tolerating and accepting, and analyzing the transferences and defenses

---

[5]In my view, developmental process as well as therapeutic process takes place in the therapist–patient interaction and contributes to the further development and integration of object and self constancy (Settlage et al., 1988; Settlage, 1989). The focus here, though, is on the undoing of the pathology.

interfering with the appropriate expression of both loving and angry feelings. Such is essential to the further development and structural integration of object and self constancy.

REFERENCES

Arlow, J. A. (1963), Conflict, regression, and symptom formation. *Internat. J. Psycho-Anal.*, 44:12–22.

Freud, A. (1965), *Normality and Pathology in Childhood: Assessments of Development.* New York: International Universities Press.

Freud, S. (1917), Introductory lectures on psychoanalysis: Part 3. General theory of neuroses. *Standard Edition*, 16. London: Hogarth Press, 1963.

Hartmann, H. (1952), Mutual influences in the development of the ego and the id. *The Psychoanalytic Study of the Child*, 7:9–30. New York: International Universities Press.

Jacobson, E. (1964), *The Self and the Object World.* New York: International Universities Press.

Kleeman, J. A. (1967), The peek-a-boo game: 1. Its origins, meanings and related phenomena in the first year. *The Psychoanalytic Study of the Child*, 22:239–273. New York: International Universities Press.

Kramer, S. (1979), The technical significance and application of separation–individuation theory. *J. Amer. Psychoanal. Assn.*, 27(Suppl.):241–262.

Loewald, H. W. (1979), The waning of the Oedipus complex. *J. Amer. Psychoanal. Assn.*, 27:751–775.

Mahler, M. S. (1972a), Rapprochement subphase of the separation–individuation process. *Psychoanal. Quart.*, 41:487–506.

———— (1972b), On the first three phases of the separation–individuation process. *Internat. J. Psycho-Anal.*, 53:333–338.

———— (1979a), *Infantile Psychosis and Early Contributions: Selected Papers 1.* New York: Aronson.

———— (1979b), *Separation–Individuation: Selected Papers 2.* New York: Aronson.

———— & Furer, M. (1968), *On Human Symbiosis and the Vicissitudes of Individuation: Infantile Psychosis.* New York: International Universities Press.

————, Pine, F. & Bergman, A. (1975), *The Psychological Birth of the Human Infant: Symbiosis and Individuation.* New York: Basic Books.

McDevitt, J. B. (1975), Separation–individuation and object constancy. *J. Amer. Psychoanal. Assn.*, 23:713–742.

Settlage, C. F. (1964), Psychoanalytic theory in relation to the nosology of childhood psychic disorders. *J. Amer. Psychoanal. Assn.*, 12:776–789.

———— (1971), On the libidinal aspect of early psychic development and the genesis of the infantile neurosis. In: *Separation–Individuation: Essays in Honor of Margaret S. Mahler*, ed. J. B. McDevitt & C. F. Settlage. New York: International Universities Press, pp. 131–154.

_____ (1977), The psychoanalytic understanding of narcissistic and borderline disorders: Advances in developmental theory. *J. Amer. Psychoanal. Assn.*, 25:805–833.

_____ (1980a), Psychoanalytic developmental thinking in current and historical perspective. *Psychoanal. Contemp. Thought,* 3:139–170.

_____ (1980b), The psychoanalytic theory and understanding of psychic development during the second and third years of life. In: *The Course of Life: Vol. 2. Early Childhood,* ed. S. I. Greenspan & G. H. Pollock. New York: International Universities Press, pp. 365–386.

_____ (1989), The interplay of therapeutic and developmental process in the treatment of children: An application of contemporary object relations theory. *Psychoanal. Inq.,* 9:375–396.

_____ , Bemesderfer, S., Rosenthal, J., Afterman, J. & Spielman, P. M. (in press), The appeal cycle in early mother–child interaction: The nature and implications of a finding from developmental research. *J. Amer. Psychoanal. Assn.*

_____ , Curtis, J., Lozoff, M., Lozoff, M., Silberschatz, G. & Simburg, E. J. (1988), Conceptualizing adult development. *J. Amer. Psychoanal. Assn.,* 36:347–369.

_____ , Rosenthal, J., Spielman, P. M., Gassner, S., Afterman, J., Bemesderfer, S. & Kolodny, S. (1990), An exploratory study of mother–child interaction during the second year of life. *J. Amer. Psychoanal. Assn.,* 38:705–731.

19

Treatment Implications of Separation–Individuation Theory in the Analysis of Young Adults

Philip J. Escoll

The consolidation of psychic structure in the context of mastering difficulties associated with earlier developmental phases is, as Blos (1977) has observed, a hallmark of young adulthood. Yet, such consolidation does not proceed as rapidly as previously thought, frequently extending into the period of adulthood proper (Escoll, 1987). Among young adult analysands, then, it is often a central clinical issue. Recent contributions have highlighted the special nature of this consolidating activity in patients with borderline and narcissistic disorders (Settlage, 1977) and anorexia and bulimia (Schwartz, 1988; Fischer, 1989); Kluft (1990) and Levine (1990) have written about the difficulties of consolidation in patients subjected to physical and sexual traumatization. In this chapter I offer a further contribution to our understanding of the consolidation of psychic structure in young adulthood, an understanding framed in terms of Mahler and colleagues' (1975) theory of symbiosis and separation–individuation.

Although Mahler's theory of symbiosis and separation–individuation enriches analytic work with patients of all ages, it is especially important in the analysis of young adults (see Panel, 1973). In young adulthood problems associated with the separation–individuation phase are especially likely to be revived, for such problems bear directly on the consolidation of identity and the achievement of autonomy and independence, which are central goals of this stage of life.

In what follows I discuss how sensitivity to separation–individuation issues influences analytic work with young adults. I am concerned with the impact of the Mahlerian paradigm on both the understanding of clinical issues and the elaboration of technique (Kramer, 1979; Edward, Ruskin, and Turrini, 1981). Before illustrating these claims with clinical examples, let me briefly consider the situational and psychological factors that suggest why the separation–individuation process is essential to the struggles of young adulthood. In this context I will comment on the question of analyzability and also address some preliminary technical issues that are relevant to forming a therapeutic alliance with young adults.

YOUNG ADULTHOOD:
SEPARATION–INDIVIDUATION REVIVED

Young adulthood bridges and overlaps both adolescence and adulthood. As such, it is a major transitional stage on the route to full adulthood. Like the middle child, the young adult is very much in-between, looking back with some regret over recently departed adolescence and childhood yet looking ahead to adult years not yet fully reached. Erikson (1950, 1968), a pioneer in his studies of youth, described in his epigenetic outline the stages of identity versus identity confusion and of intimacy versus isolation, both stages applicable to young adults. Identity versus identity diffusion correlates most closely with individuation. Intimacy, and its counterpart "distantiation," correlates with separation, particularly rapprochement. The moratorium for youth, described by Erikson (1968), has been stretched with periods of "dropping out," longer and longer periods of education in the middle class, and delays into the work force with a longer period of economic and related emotional dependence on parents. Today, some young adults return to live for a time with their parents; others, with drug dependence and other serious personality problems, congregate in college towns. These chronically ill young adults constitute one of the major mental health problems of this era.

While it is difficult to assign an age range to the young adult group, one can roughly consider the ages of those in college and graduate school. Rather than defining young adulthood by age or by the external tasks that are demanded at this time, such as choosing a career and finding a mate, it is more significant to delineate young adulthood by the central developmental tasks of consolidation and integration of psychic structures.

For the young adult population, the vicissitudes of the rapprochement subphase of the separation–individuation process have special significance.

The reason is obvious: rapprochement issues are implicated in the various external separations and the intrapsychic ramifications accompanying the developmental unfolding of this phase that the young adult must undergo. There are, for example, physical and emotional separations from parents, friends, and home, as the young adult leaves for college. Romantic ties, frequently culminating in engagement and marriage, signify a further separation from family and home. Career choice, graduation from college—which often means overcoming ambivalent ties to teachers—and entrance into the work force are separations that follow in fairly rapid sequence. Pine (1979) states that separation refers to a sense of one's separateness, not to physical separations; physical separations are different from one's sense of separateness. In young adults major physical separations and their many ramifications tend to rekindle separation and individuation experiences of the earlier years together with whatever psychic vicissitudes are associated with negotiating aspects of this phase.

To be sure, the revival of separation–individuation issues with respect to these various separations has a normal and desirable component. As analysts, however, we are necessarily concerned with young adults for whom the normative revival of the separation–individuation phase is compounded by significant failures to work through the separation–individuation process of early life. For these individuals, the aforementioned events all reverberate with underlying conflicts involving basic issues of dependence and autonomy (Kramer and Akhtar, 1988). These young adults present to the analyst with feelings of depression, loss, and confusion. Eating disorders, frequently kept secret, are common. In certain cases, there are accompanying narcissistic and borderline disturbances.

The importance of separation–individuation, and especially rapprochement, issues in the analysis of young adults has treatment implications. A basic issue that frequently crystallizes during the initial interviews concerns the optimal distance between analyst and young adult analysand in the analytic relationship. Failure to reach an acceptable balance between intimacy and aloofness may sabotage the treatment at the outset, since the analyst will be perceived as either intrusive and engulfing or cold and distant. The key is immediately to engage the prospective analysand in a manner that is both neutral and sufficiently direct and responsive to establish a therapeutic alliance.

The matter of treatment "rules" also has special importance with this population. Young adults frequently take trips abroad, study at institutions other than their own, and undertake work experiences outside their immediate area. Such events, along with issues like missed hours, responsibility for continuing the analysis during a vacation period, and the prerogatives of parents (frequently paying the bills) to speak with the analyst, necessarily involve separation–individuation issues. If the analyst handles such matters by fiat rather than by discussion and exploration in which realities, developmental issues, and conflicts, together with resistance and transference, are recognized, he risks disrupting the treatment at a later date. These contingencies should not only be anticipated at the beginning of treatment; they should be discussed in a spirit of accommodation appropriate to the life circumstances of the young adult. Solutions should be acceptable to patient and analyst alike.

My own clinical experience and supervision of candidates suggests that analysis with young adults can weather phase-appropriate interruptions such as a semester of study at another university. To insist that the young adult remain in one area for the sake of the analysis invites the interpretation that the analyst is thwarting the patient's strivings for autonomy— the very strivings that analysis purportedly seeks to strengthen! Of course, one has to always be alert to whatever resistances may also be involved. Likewise, it may be ill-advised to insist that the young adult remain on campus over the summer vacation to continue analysis: the patient may end up lonely and depressed in the vacated dormitory (Ritvo, 1971).

The very issue of the young adult's analyzability involves issues of separation–individuation. Given the young adult's transitional stage of life, it is appropriate to question whether he or she will be in one place, psychically and geographically, long enough for analysis to take place. One must, as Abend (1987) says, accept the situation as one finds it. If the analyst knows that a prospective patient will only be in the area for two years, he may rule out analysis on this basis alone. On the other hand, if analysis is otherwise indicated, offering the short-term patient psychotherapy may be a disservice: the patient will likely relocate and continue with therapy, never again considering the analysis that was originally deemed appropriate. If one begins analysis with a young adult whose future plans are uncertain, an analytic process is at least engaged and the patient can be referred to a colleague on leaving the area. Very commonly, be it noted, a young adult engaged in and benefiting from analysis will manage to remain in one location long enough to terminate.

Other aspects of analyzability concern the young adult's commitment to analysis. The analyst needs to consider the strength of the young adult's outside interests typical of this age. Is the patient so preoccupied with the opposite sex or so avid in pursuing a career as to be unable to become adequately invested in the analysis at this point? Will he or she resist fleeing from the strong transference feelings bound to arise? Will he or she be able to cope with termination? An example is that of a college junior with long-standing depressive symptoms who was deeply involved in a romantic relationship with a boyfriend from abroad. She was also involved in a research project in molecular biology and was applying to medical schools in this country and abroad. She was completely preoccupied with these issues and would talk about nothing else. She fled when a previous therapist insisted on analysis. She was not able to make a commitment to analysis at this time, and psychotherapy was recommended. It proved to be useful especially for ventilation, clarification of her difficulties, and symptom relief. The student was most amenable to undertaking analysis at an appropriate point in the future.

None of the aforementioned factors, of course, rule out analysis. Rather, they must be weighed in the evaluating process to determine whether or not they might interfere with the ability of the young adult to engage in the analysis at this time and sustain it. They could be manifestations of the conflicts themselves that could respond to analysis or represent resistances that could be dealt with through interpretations. It is in the context of determining analyzability that the analyst must likewise consider the impact of revived separation–individuation conflicts on issues specific to other developmental stages.

CLINICAL EXAMPLES

Mr. R

Mr. R, a 25-year-old salesman, began analysis depressed and confused about an affair he had begun a year earlier. This young married adult had initially found his involvement with another woman tremendously pleasurable owing to the way he could talk to and be understood by her. This gratification remained primary even as the relationship became sexualized. Complications ensued when his lover became periodically reinvolved with her own husband, from whom she had separated. During these junctures, Mr. R began pondering his future with his own wife, alternating between an inclination to leave her and a resolve to strengthen their relationship.

As tension entered into the extramarital affair and Mr. R began to withdraw from his lover, the latter gave mixed signals of her own: she alternated between pleading her devotion and asking Mr. R to wait for her and announcing that the affair was over and that she was contemplating returning to her husband. Mr. R responded to these contradictory messages with confusion and unhappiness, periodically lapsing into depression. He would wait by the phone for his girlfriend to call, feeling enormously relieved when she did but depressed to the point of tears and hopelessness about his future when she did not.

As we tried to understand these disturbing episodes, Mr. R's relationship to his mother during the separation–individuation process assumed major importance. Specifically, Mr. R associated back to what was probably a rapprochement crisis when he was between two and three. He recollected his mother's own on-again, off-again behavior during this time: she could be loving one moment but cold and withdrawn the next. Her sudden recourse to angry silence followed some small act on Mr. R's part that gave her displeasure. The misdemeanors that got Mr. R "into trouble" with his mother were nothing more than phase-appropriate claims for autonomy and the associated use of his budding motor skills to do things around the house. The patient poignantly recalled his sadness and despair when, following some minor mishap, his otherwise attentive mother subjected him to the "silent treatment."

The mother's alternating pattern of engagement and withdrawal persisted into Mr. R's young adulthood. He was aware of periods when she was tender and solicitous, but he was equally aware of periods when, displeased with her son, she would withdraw and maintain a stubborn silence, refusing any communication with him. In the present, as in early childhood, it took very little to occasion such maternal displeasure; often it was simply a matter of Mr. R's not calling or visiting his mother frequently enough.

What were the derivatives in Mr. R of his separation–individuation (especially rapprochement) experiences in the light of his mother's own difficulties in handling this phase? We see many by-products, such as great ambivalence, splitting, identification with his mother, and the recapitulation of the rapprochement pattern in his young adult years. Mr. R yearned for closeness, intimacy, and sexuality with his wife but could not sustain it; he periodically withdrew from her, culminating in his engaging in an affair. Related to his mother's withdrawal and silent treatment, he was exceedingly sensitive to slights and hurts; he tried to avoid them, and when he encountered them he was terribly injured and withdrew. He also experienced great anger, with wishes to destroy the person whom he saw as hurting him or rejecting him. He was afraid of his own aggression at these times, his murderous fantasies representing a derivative of the devouring fantasies of his childhood. This pattern was seen in his young adult life and also in the analysis.

Mr. R had difficulty in sustaining emotional ties with friends, wife, and girlfriends. Yet he remained in the relationship with his lover despite all the vicissitudes and rejections, unable to break away yet unable to come to a resolution involving further intimacy with her. In a recapitulation of his reactions to his rapprochement experiences with his mother when she would withdraw from him, he remained glued to the telephone for hours and would not leave it waiting for his lover to call. He clung to her. He told her not to call him but would feel rejected when she did not. He came to realize that he saw her calls as indications that he was still loved, that lover/mother was not shunning him with the terrible silent treatment and withdrawal. In the face of the withdrawal and silent treatment and scolding, Mr. R became filled with guilt, feeling he had done something terribly wrong to lover/mother, and suffered anxiety and remorse that he had hurt her. He experienced a great need to undo this, manifested by his urgency to return a telephone call in which he had become angry or reproachful.

Mr. R felt that he was not truly loved by his mother and, as a result, was filled with hurt and rage. He reenacted his own rapprochement by pushing away his lover/mother; however, he did not do this completely, sending her mixed signals so as to invite a return. Revenge was also a motive. The mixed invitation to return led to an overture on his lover's part—one that he then spurned in retaliation. He assumed his mother's part, enacting it with his lover, whom he identified as himself. In his fantasies his lover became a larger-than-life figure, the very powerful and idealized mother. Mr. R was very much admired and praised; he experienced his mother as engulfing him with her intense wishes for him to be the "golden boy" in the family. He felt that his mother's expectations of him to be the golden boy were to fulfill her own unfulfilled ambitions. These expectations were intensified by a severe illness sustained by his father, which led father to use a wheelchair some of the time and to be much handicapped in his own work. Mr. R was the chosen one and was triumphal yet anxious and guilty in the role of the oedipal victor. He resisted the role of the golden boy yet had to achieve it to maintain love; he resented very much being in this position, one that left him feeling inferior and anxious about abandonment on one hand if he didn't measure up, and grandiose and guilty on the other.

These same feelings were reexperienced with his lover. Mr. R felt that he had to measure up to her expectations; at the same time, he resented this and felt a tremendous burden to be powerfully successful in his business. With his lover he would feel terribly rejected and angry, with a sense of loss of his prowess and masculinity if she would hint in periods of withdrawal from him that she might become involved with another man or return to her husband. Mr. R would also berate himself for having done something wrong to elicit this, thus recapitulating the pattern in his childhood when he would alternate between feeling that he had done nothing wrong to lead to mother's rebukes and withdrawal and feeling that he had done everything wrong. He resented, yet felt that he warranted mother's scathing rebukes and periods of emotional withdrawal and silence. This pattern was relived with his lover. In his identification with his mother, the aggressor, Mr. R treated his lover in this hostile way, and she treated him similarly; to a lesser degree he treated his wife this way as well. Interestingly, Mr. R's younger brother was described as a clinging person, ambivalently attached to his parents. His brief marriage, which ended in divorce, was fraught with arguments and punctuated by separations and reunions.

It is obvious that many other dynamic issues are involved in Mr. R's problems, character, identifications, and relationships with mother, wife, and lover. The multifaceted oedipal conflicts have not been elaborated on here, since the focus of this volume is on separation–individuation conflicts.

Mr. R gradually realized that his lover's conflicting signals about their relationship paralleled his mother's erratic behavior. He also came to recognize that the despair and hopelessness that followed his mother's withdrawal were the same feelings that followed his girlfriend's intermittent resolve to leave him and return to her husband. Predictably, this pattern, as well as the rapprochement issues inherent in it, was replayed in the transference. To Mr. R, I was attentive and responsive at certain times and coldly withdrawn at others. The latter perception was typically associated with analytic silence; it tended to supervene when Mr. R felt he had said or done something (e.g., cancel a session) for which I might be angry. Transference interpretations were central to Mr. R's understanding of his conflicts in this area.

Reconstruction was likewise critical. As we arrived at an understanding of Mr. R's interaction with his mother during the separation–individuation process and of the intrapsychic derivatives of this interaction, Mr. R came to see his lover in a new light. This woman, like Mr. R's mother, had difficulties with intimacy, probably associated with her own separation–individuation experiences. Mr. R saw that she yearned to be intimate with him but withdrew uneasily when such intimacy was realized, urging him to "cool it" until she could be sure about her future plans.

The separation–individuation process also provided a handle for understanding Mr. R's use of splitting. He tended to see his wife as the cold, asexual mother and his lover as the warm, sexual mother with whom he could have intimate discussions. In addition to the images of the "good" and "bad" mother as residues of the rapprochement subphase, an additional source of the split related to the "Madonna" and "whore" split. Mr. R's wife was seen as the asexual Madonna and the lover as the fun-loving whore. During periods when he and his lover were estranged,

Mr. R saw himself stuck in the house with the bland, dull, asexual wife–mother, and he was filled with envy of the other "kids" who were outside with the daredevil, fun-loving group engaged in sexual exploits with available girls. The preoedipal (Madonna) and oedipal (whore) split reinforces the earlier split and contributes to its tenacity.

Mr. R's lover functioned as a vehicle by which he could separate from the wife–mother on whom he was still quite dependent, even though the lover herself represented another, more favorable side of his mother. Mr. R himself was prone to take on his mother's role, especially toward his wife: he would periodically become deeply engaged with her, emotionally and sexually, only to withdraw abruptly at a later date. This pattern was played out on the periodic vacations Mr. R and his wife took. Vowing to leave his lover, Mr. R would schedule an extended trip, such as a cruise, during which he and his wife would get along wonderfully. While on the trip, however, he would find himself preoccupied with his lover, and immediately on his return, he would call her and become reinvolved.

As the foregoing pattern was worked through genetically, transferentially, and in the context of Mr. R's current relational triangle, his view of both his wife and his lover changed dramatically: the former was seen as warmer and more affectionate, the latter—toward whom he continued to have tender feelings—as more troubled and manipulative. These reassessments corresponded to a diminished need to recapitulate with these two women the different aspects of his rapprochement experiences with his mother, that is, a diminished need to split the women, albeit interchangeably, into contemporary versions of the "bad mother" and the "good mother" of the rapprochement subphase. To that extent, Mr. R's changed feelings toward them betokened structural personality change.

Mr. B

Mr. B, a 24-year-old psychology graduate student, came for analysis because of long-standing anxiety that intensified during his graduate studies. He had considered therapy earlier in his life but had postponed it until his graduate school years, when, in addition to increasing anxiety, he experienced depression and psychosomatic symptoms. He believed his symptoms had to do with his troubled relationship with his father, a professor of architecture who was strong and successful and who placed great demands on his son.

A middle child with an older and younger sister, Mr. B saw himself as the family favorite. Much was expected of him, and he invariably achieved enough to satisfy parental expectations. He had always been close to his mother, who was professionally less successful than his father but quieter and more reflective; she had returned to school when her children were in high school, earning a graduate degree in art. Mr. B shared her aesthetic sensibility, and mother and son formed a special bond on the basis of their mutual appreciation of art, music, and reading. Acutely aware of his mother's refinement and artistic leanings, Mr. B grew up believing that his father did not treat her with adequate sensitivity; during childhood and later during adolescence he felt he could do better. When father was out of town lecturing, which was quite often, Mr. B would enact his oedipal fantasy, being caringly sensitive to his mother in the manner she deserved. At such times he enjoyed oedipal triumphs that were unsettling: he felt responsible for his mother in a way that was simultaneously exhilarating and burdensome.

Despite being close to his mother and receiving attention within the family, Mr. B felt like an outsider in grade school, rejected by the boys despite his academic success and athletic prowess. He regarded himself as an "alien" whose functioning depended on the security of mother and home. As an adolescent, he enjoyed greater acceptance, became more confident, and developed social skills. In his early teens he began to date and by sixteen was going steady with a girl in a higher grade who was particularly interested in music. This powerful attachment, which lasted many years, helped Mr. B separate from his mother at the same time that it mimicked the nature of his bond with his mother. During this time as well, Mr. B's father became more important both as an object against whom to rebel and an object with whom to identify. It was as an adolescent that Mr. B contemplated following in his father's footsteps by pursuing an academic career in architecture or engineering.

Mr. B's mother, an obese woman, had a family history of cardiovascular disease. While still a child, Mr. B took it upon himself to educate her about her condition, admonishing her to exercise and be more careful with her diet, but he was unable to persuade her to change her lifestyle and felt himself a failure on this count. He emerged from childhood deeply resentful of a mother whose disregard of her health was self-destructive. When Mr. B entered college his mother, who continued to ignore the warnings of friends and doctors as well as her son, suffered a major heart attack. Several months later she suffered a second myocardial infarction and died. Mr. B's worst fears for her—and worst fears about the consequences of his own failure as a son—were thereby confirmed.

Although at the time of his mother's death Mr. B assumed a supportive role toward his devastated father, he was otherwise numb. At the funeral and during the family's period of mourning, he shed not a tear. Over the years he intermittently experienced feelings of loss, sadness, guilt, and resentment but, until the analysis, was unable to express or integrate these feelings. Only in treatment, where mourning proper began, did he discover the connection between his mother's death and earlier maternal losses experienced during the separation–individuation process.

As with Mr. R, reconstruction and transference analysis, both occurring in the context of the analytic regression, were essential ingredients of internal change. Mr. B associated frequently to an early feeling of being disconnected from his mother, a feeling that seemed to refer to the rapprochement subphase and birth of his younger sister when he was two. Memories from adolescence dealt with imagery of quiet intimacy—his playing the violin while his mother listened or painted—that abruptly ended when his mother made some mundane demand of him, like asking him to take out the garbage or go to the store to pick up groceries. Associations to this imagery underscored both the preoedipal and oedipal dimensions of Mr. B's anger; that is, at different times and in different contexts, he understood the mother who ended these meaningful interludes with unfeeling banality to be severing both a symbiotic tie and an oedipal tie. The former was reactivated at the time of the patient's rapprochement crisis; the latter was especially salient during his father's lecture trips, when Mr. B became the man of the house.

Such memories pointed to the admixture of rage and guilt that typified Mr. B's delayed mourning process. He wrestled with the feeling that he had never done enough for his ailing mother, had never adequately satisfied her needs, even as he acknowledged that she used his solicitous concern manipulatively, inducing him in a tone of whiny martyrdom to run errands and perform household chores. When his mother made these indirect demands, implying that he was remiss in easing her burdens, Mr. B perceived her as both engulfing and degrading. Her oblique way of requesting that he take out the garbage had the effect of making him feel like garbage. By ignoring his pleas that she exercise and change her dietary habits, she ultimately—and, so it seemed, spitefully—foiled his attempt to rescue her from self-destruction.

In the transference Mr. B's need for consistent maternal engagement, thwarted throughout childhood, was revived and worked through. Unlike his mother, who brusquely ended interludes of intimacy, I was to give him all the time he needed. At one session in treatment he reported that he had forgotten his watch, expressed the feeling that he was in the midst of a "timeless session," and asked if the session could in fact be extended.

There was, throughout the analysis, a vigilance on Mr. B's part, as if he were skeptical of my ability to be any more available and engaged than his mother had been. But there was also the correlative fear that the analyst, no less than his mother, might suffocate him through engulfment.

Sometime after Mr. B's experience of the timeless session he reported the following dream: Mr. B and I are both asleep in the office; he is startled awake and observes me sleeping. After several minutes I too awake, and we both walk to the window and look outside. I take Mr. B's hand, as if to make up for having fallen asleep. Mr. B is not reassured.

Associations to the dream involved childhood memories of piling into bed with his parents on weekends and experiencing disappointment when such desired closeness proved uncomfortable; being in bed with his parents literally proved too close for comfort. The latent message was the patient's simultaneous yearning for closeness and fear of engulfment.

Weekend separations were difficult for Mr. B because they recapitulated the abrupt manner in which his mother had put an end to the gratifying interludes when they read, painted, listened to music, and confided in one another. Vacations were even more difficult, since they recapitulated not only Mr. B's feeling of outright maternal abandonment but his sense of futility at being unable to do anything to prevent such abandonment. Just as he felt deserted by his mother, so he felt deserted by his analyst. And just as he had failed to persuade his mother to change her lifestyle in a way that might well have prolonged her life, so he now failed to induce me to forgo vacations in order to remain available to him. My refusal to grasp the full extent of his neediness, no less than his mother's disregard of his heartfelt advice, was a rupture of a rapprochement bond.

Predictably, derivatives of Mr. B's separation–individuation experiences played an important role in his current life. In the counseling work that was part of his graduate training, he saw himself as the rescuer of sick women. Yet he felt burdened by the task and was prone to guilt when his clients could not be rescued. With his wife, who herself had medical problems, he was chronically anxious that her illnesses would worsen and that she, like his mother, would die. These anxieties were reexperienced, and ultimately mastered, in the transference, especially in the transference analysis of two episodes of minor but manifest illness on the analyst's part. Termination provided an obvious opportunity for working through separation–individuation themes and consolidating new insights, since the ending of treatment, equated with desertion, abandonment, and the analyst's death, recapitulated Mr. B's abandonment by the mother who would not be saved.

DISCUSSION

As noted earlier, consolidation and integration of psychic structures are seen as the hallmark of young adult development (Blos, 1977); yet consolidation is not readily achieved by many young adults (Escoll, 1987). There are many factors involved in this, including the individual's constitutional makeup and cultural influences. The manner in which developmental phases are negotiated is a key factor. Obviously, the oedipal phase is supremely important in this connection, as is the separation–individuation phase and all its derivatives.

In the two cases presented in this chapter consolidation is interfered with by derivatives of problems in the separation–individuation process, especially in the rapprochement subphase (Edward, Ruskin, and Turrini, 1981). Within this frame many authors have emphasized different aspects of consolidation, all of which are significant in these two cases.

For example, Laufer (1976) and Isay (1980) stress the importance of the consolidation of the final sexual orientation and a reasonably consistent self-image. Settlage (1977) focuses on superego and ego-ideal development; he also considers the stabilization of self and object representations as most significant. Ritvo (1971) emphasizes the resolution of the negative oedipal conflict and its derivatives in the ego-ideal and the reworking of the superego. Blos (1977) and others, such as Isay (1980), refer to late adolescence as the second separation stage. Separation–individuation issues in all of the subphases exert a significant influence on the integration and consolidation of all of the aforementioned psychic structures, which are so important in young adult development.

To illustrate these points I now focus on some of the major similarities and differences in the two clinical cases presented in this chapter. Mr. R's case illustrates the difficulty in sustaining a close tie with a woman involving intimacy and sexuality. He is drawn into a pattern of on-again, off-again relationships similar to the pattern experienced with his mother, as ascertained in the analysis in reconstructing his rapprochement experiences with her. This was also demonstrated in the transference. Mr. R yearned for closeness and desperately tried to please to obtain it. His obsessive worries, including fear of his own wishes to hurt (devour), were all derivatives of his separation–individuation, and especially rapprochement, issues. In the case of Mr. B, a recovery, as we reconstructed his rapprochement experiences, of his perceptions of his mother as someone exceedingly close to him yet capable of readily breaking the tie led to important understanding of his personality and behavior. Some of his responses included periods of depression and loss and a certain level of suspicion and uncertainty in relationships. Also, related to his reactions to his mother's obesity, cardiac history, and eventual death, Mr. B experienced a wish/need to help and rescue others. This was accompanied by feelings of being burdened, resentful, often futile, and impotent. In both cases the patients experienced the weight of great responsibility, particularly in connection with women, with concomitant resentment and rage. They experienced fears and guilt related to the strength of their own aggressive wishes. Incomplete consolidation of self and ambivalent object representations, especially with Mr. R, were also involved; Mr. R's questions about his masculinity readily arose if he thought of his girlfriend with someone else. There were important negative oedipal features (Ritvo, 1971) with both Mr. R and Mr. B.

In both clinical cases there was a replay of elements of the rapprochement subphase in the young adult years with love objects. Also, in both cases, the mother (especially Mr. R's mother) had difficulties with her own rapprochement issues, which were played out in the handling of her son's rapprochement period. There were important difficulties related to father in both cases. Mr. R's father was chronically ill, incapacitated to an important degree, and not fully available emotionally to mother; in Mr. B's situation, father was very successful and occupied with his career and mother turned to the patient, reinforcing the rapprochement bond, with the complications previously noted. Father was not sufficiently available to these patients to help them attenuate the ambivalent attachment to mother (Mahler, Pine, and Bergman, 1975). Unresolved oedipal issues were prominent with both patients, including oedipal victories with related anxiety and guilt; disillusionment, rage, and depression accompanied oedipal defeats.

There are differences. Mr. B was better able to sustain object ties, and he did considerably less splitting. Oedipal issues were heavily colored by rapprochement difficulties with Mr. R; his splitting of the maternal imago, good and bad, sexual/asexual, was not resolved in the oedipal period but reinforced because of rapprochement issues. There was some of this splitting also in the case of Mr. B but considerably less so.

These cases demonstrate that considerations of incomplete consolidation and integration are significant and important to recognize in the analysis of young adults. Young adults may seem to be functional, healthy, typical college or graduate students yet show considerable vulnerability related to incomplete integration and consolidation underneath. Here the question of analysis as a developmental phase and the controversial issue of the analyst as a new object (Loewald, 1960) may be raised. Robbins (see Panel, 1977) refers to analysis as a developmental process. Settlage (1989) describes the interplay of therapeutic and developmental processes and sees these as separate but related aspects of the analysis. My view, as reflected in these cases, is that there are elements of a developmental process in the analysis of the young adult. However, the analysis, with significant elements of transference interpretation and reconstruction, embodies more than the developmental experience. Regarding the issue of analyst as a new object, the consistency and impartial yet ongoing neutral concern of the analyst is most important. Loewald (1960) wrote of the importance of the encounter with a new object in the analysis, with such an encounter leading to a new discovery of objects (rediscovery) and a new way of relating to objects. In the analysis the analyst is the old object, a rediscovered object, but he also needs to be a new object for the transference to be understood and analyzed, allowing and aiding the developmental process to proceed.

In the cases presented here issues around separation–individuation, especially rapprochement, became apparent and subject to interpretation in the transference. Often these came to the fore with the stimulus of actual separations such as canceled hours and vacations. There were important reactions and significant questions in the here and now experience regarding the analyst's emotional availability. Both patients were sensitive to my manner and mood if they saw me as less available. Both Mr. R and Mr. B were also especially sensitive to any physical illness or related changes in me; this was important in both the maternal and paternal transferences. Mr. B was particularly concerned with illness, fearing that I might develop a serious ailment and die; not only would he be bereft (of mother) but he would have failed to save me. Issues regarding parental availability were triggered by Mr. B's perception of me as tired or not exhibiting sufficient energy in a session. If I was ill, Mr. R saw his father in me and also himself in me as the golden boy now knocked from his pedestal.

There are interesting differences in regard to reactions to my silence in an analytic session. Mr. B often seemed to welcome silence; quiet times with his mother were very precious for him. For Mr. R silence awakened painful memories and anxieties related to mother's withdrawal and silent treatment. It also reminded him of his own silent withdrawal from both wife and lover.

In both cases the other side of feelings about closeness—that is, anxiety and resentment rather than comfort—appeared. Both young men had feelings of being restricted, held onto, possessed or unduly influenced or controlled by the analyst; if, for example, I raised a question about a vacation of theirs or about lateness or a missed hour, this was sometimes seen as possessiveness or control. Mr. R was very reactive if he experienced himself as being rebuked by me along these or related lines. Mr. B was very sensitive and reactive if he felt I was breaking the mood of a session by raising a question about an unpaid balance; this was seen as my accusing him of not giving me enough. It also reminded him of a prosaic request, such as those issued by his mother, breaking the bond of intimacy.

Countertransference was stimulated in me at times by many of these

Treatment Implications of Separation–Individuation Theory

responses, especially a feeling of frustration in attempting to deal with these patients' ultrasensitivity. The balance easily swung from my being seen as available to being seen as unavailable, from intimate to withdrawn, from hot to cold. There were also derivatives of the Madonna/whore construction in the transference. However, each patient was able to sustain a sufficiently strong therapeutic alliance to analyze these strong transference reactions and, therefore, to weather the vicissitudes in the analytic process. This helped balance my countertransference wariness.

Reconstruction (Blum, 1977; Friedman, 1983) was helpful. Data came from derivatives of rapprochement experiences that appeared in current life, childhood recollections, and dreams, as well as from what was expressed in and inferred from transference material. We were able to piece together early experiences, and the patients gained a firmer sense of their own history (Erikson, 1968). There was a greater appreciation of their childhood experiences and a development of compassionate identifications (Arlow, 1989) with their parents. As Arlow pointed out in his discussion of his cases, these patients begin to experience, as the analysis progresses, empathy for their parents' difficulties as well as for their own.

Ticho (1976), Gilligan (1982), and many others point to the special complexities in the female developmental process and the implications for consolidation in the young woman. Ticho stresses the need for the girl to disengage from her infantile anaclitic claims on her mother and to establish a positive oedipal attachment to father. This has significant implications, which will not be elaborated on here, for female development in all phases, including the young adult experience. Gilligan points to the importance of relationships and connectedness in the female as opposed to the stress on individuation and independence in the male, which can mean more separateness. A fuller explication of these important gender differences is beyond the scope of the present chapter.

Treatment implications in work with young adults in regard to separation–individuation matters relate to all phases of the analysis, from the evaluation phase to termination. In the evaluation phase it is essential to balance the need to be involved with an avoidance of intrusiveness. In assessing analyzability, the analyst needs to consider the overall situation, including the ability of the young adult to make a commitment to analysis at the time; nevertheless, it is vital to always respect the need for analysis and deal with the situation as one finds it. Many young adults can begin analysis right away; for those who enter psychotherapy, conversion to psychoanalysis is often feasible (Bernstein, 1983, 1990). In the analysis it is important to recognize the young adult's particular circumstances and needs related to reverberations of the separation–individuation process. For college students it may be very important to take an independent trip abroad during vacation time or to be involved in some job or research experience that may take them out of town for a while. These opportunities may have substantial implications for self-fulfillment and for furthering autonomy; as such, they could be undermined by a rigid insistence on a continuation of the analysis rather than allowing for the temporary interruption. These factors are obvious in the analysis of the young adult, they may be less obvious but equally important to consider with adult patients. Naturally, resistance and transference need to be considered and analyzed along with these factors.

SUMMARY

Young adults, who have yet to consolidate psychic structure out of earlier developmental struggles and whose life situation entails a series of expectable separations, characteristically experience a revival of separation–individuation issues. It is the analyst's task, of course, to distinguish between the normal and the problematic recrudescence of these issues. I have presented two cases in which separation–individuation issues, especially in relation to the rapprochement subphase, were centrally implicated in the presenting psychopathology. For both Mr. R and Mr. B, rapprochement material was essential to understanding underlying conflicts and adult character structure. In both analyses, reconstruction of childhood perceptions of maternal availability during the rapprochement subphase fueled the analytic process. Therapeutic change tantamount to internal personality change followed not only from such reconstruction but from interpretation and working through of the patients' rage, guilt, depression, and anxiety over perceived strong maternal intimacy and subsequent abandonment as they gained expression in the transference. Both genetic and transference interpretations were subtended by the regression mobilized by the analytic process.

The technical implications of this case material point to the need to be alert to unresolved separation–individuation issues, especially those of the rapprochement subphase, in analytic work with young adults. Equally important, the analyst is enjoined to be cognizant of the way in which separation–individuation problems can become intertwined with the conflictual issues of later stages of development. In both of the case examples, for example, oedipal conflicts were embedded in a matrix of separation–individuation issues and could only be dealt with interpretively in the context of these preoedipal issues.

REFERENCES

Abend, S. (1987), Evaluating young adults for analysis. *Psychoanal. Inq.*, 7:31–38.

Arlow, J. (1989), Psychoanalysis and the quest for morality. In: *The Psychoanalytic Core: Essays in Honor of Leo Rangell, M.D.*, ed. H. Blum, E. Weinshel, & F. Rodman. Madison, CT: International Universities Press, pp. 147–166.

Bernstein, S. (1983), Treatment preparatory to psychoanalysis. *J. Amer. Psychoanal. Assn.*, 31:363–390.

———— (1990), Motivation for psychoanalysis and transition from psychotherapy. *Psychoanal. Inq.*, 10:21–42.

Blos, P. (1977), When and how does adolescence end: Structural criteria for adolescent closure. In: *Adolescent Psychiatry, Vol. 5*, ed. S. Feinstein & P. Giovacchini. New York: Aronson, pp. 5–17.

Blum, H. (1977), The prototype of preoedipal reconstruction. *J. Amer. Psychoanal. Assn.*, 25:757–785.

Edward, J., Ruskin, N. & Turrini, P. (1981). *Separation–Individuation Theory and Application*. New York: Gardner Press.

Erikson, E. H. (1950), *Childhood and Society*. New York: Norton.

———— (1968), *Identity: Youth and Crisis*. New York: Norton.

Escoll, P. (1987), Psychoanalysis of young adults: An overview. *Psychoanal. Inq.*, 7:5–30.

Fischer, N. (1989), Anorexia nervosa and unresolved rapprochement conflicts: A case study. *Internat. J. Psycho-Anal.*, 70:41–54.

Friedman, L. (1983), Reconstruction and the like. *Psychoanal. Inq.*, 3:189–222.

Gilligan, C. (1982), *In a Different Voice: Psychological Theory and Woman's Development*. Cambridge, MA: Harvard University Press.

Isay, R. (1980), Late adolescence: The second separation stage of adolescence. In: *The Course of Life: Psychoanalytic Contributions Toward Understanding Personality Development, Vol. 2*, ed. S. Greenspan & G. Pollock. Washington, DC: U.S. Dept. of Health & Human Services, pp. 511–522.

Kluft, R., ed. (1990), *Incest-Related Syndromes of Adult Psychopathology*. Washington, DC: American Psychiatric Press.

Kramer, S. (1979), The technical significance and application of Mahler's separation–individuation theory. *J. Amer. Psychoanal. Assn.*, 27:241–262.

Kramer, S. & Akhtar, S. (1988), The developmental context of internalized pre-oedipal object relations. *Psychoanal. Quart.*, 57:547–576.

Laufer, M. (1976), The central masturbation fantasy, the final sexual organization, and adolescence. *The Psychoanalytic Study of the Child*, 31:297–316. New Haven, CT: Yale University Press.

Levine, H., ed. (1990), *Adult Analysis and Childhood Sexual Abuse*. Hillsdale, NJ: The Analytic Press.

Loewald, H. (1960), On the therapeutic action of psychoanalysis. *Internat. J. Psycho-Anal.*, 41:16–33.

Mahler, M., Pine, F. & Bergman, A. (1975), *The Psychological Birth of the Human Infant*. New York: Basic Books.

Panel (1973), The experience of separation–individuation in infancy and its reverberations through the course of life: 2. Adolescence and maturity, reporter, I. Marcus. *J. Amer. Psychoanal. Assn.*, 21:155–167.

Panel (1977), The contribution of psychoanalytic developmental concepts to adult analysis, reporter P. Escoll. *J. Amer. Psychoanal. Assn.*, 25:219–234.

Pine, F. (1979), On the pathology of the separation–individuation process as manifested in later clinical work: An attempt at delineation. *Internat. J. Psycho-Anal.*, 60:225–242.

Ritvo, S. (1971), Cultural values and the superego in late adolescence. *The Psychoanalytic Study of the Child*, 26:241–263. New York: Quadrangle Books.

Schwartz, H. (1988), *Bulimia: Psychoanalytic Treatment and Theory*. Madison, CT: International Universities Press.

Settlage, C. (1977), The psychoanalytic understanding of narcissistic and borderline personality disorders: Advances in developmental theory. *J. Amer. Psychoanal. Assn.*, 23:805–883.

——— (1989), The interplay of therapeutic and developmental process in the treatment of children: An application of contemporary object relations theory. *Psychoanal. Inq.*, 9:375–396.

Ticho, G. (1976), Female autonomy and young adult women: Supplement on female psychology. *J. Amer. Psychoanal. Assn.*, 24:139–155.

20

Termination and Separation–Individuation

Sydney E. Pulver

Psychoanalytic understanding of the dynamics of termination of treatment (Firestein, 1978; Shane and Shane, 1984; Loewald, 1988) and of the dynamics of the separation–individuation phase of childhood development have increased dramatically in the last two decades, yet the two areas of understanding seem to have had little influence on each other. In spite of the many similarities between individuating and separating from mother and leaving one's psychotherapist, there is relatively little mention of separation–individuation in papers on termination, except for a few exceptions that deal with the topic in a general way (Ablon, 1988; Blanck and Blanck, 1988; Kupers, 1988). Nor do papers on separation–individuation deal at any length with termination. In this chapter I try to connect these two topics by describing some of the clinical issues of termination that have links to separation–individuation. By now, separation–individuation issues have become so integrated into our general clinical work that their manifestations in termination may at times seem obvious. Nevertheless, an explicit description of the connections may be helpful.

I use the phrase "have links to separation–individuation" rather than "derive from" or "are manifestations of" separation–individuation advisedly. As is now well understood, there is no direct, linear correlation between the here-and-now of the relationship that occurs in therapy and specific early phases of childhood development. Making such a correlation is called the "genetic fallacy," the problems of which have been described by many. Garza-Guerrero (1988) gives a general discussion of the genetic fallacy, and Pine (1979) discusses the problem from the standpoint of separation–individuation, pointing out that not everything related to separation is related to separation–individuation. The concept of separation in separation–individuation involves the growth of awareness of separateness, *not* actual physical separations. Individuation refers to "the taking on of those characteristics that mark the person as a person in his own right" (Pine, 1979, p. 226), not to simple independent or autonomous behavior or feelings. Pine makes a powerful argument for limiting the application of the term separation–individuation to phenomena that clearly reflect psychic events occuring during the actual separation–individuation period. He would not, for instance, consider pathological anxiety about separation a direct manifestation of separation–individuation pathology unless there was evidence that the patient had an actual impairment of his sense of separateness from his objects (in older terms, an "impairment of ego boundaries").

Pine's caution is a good one. In discussions of the clinical impact of separation–individuation, the genetic fallacy is encountered all too often. For the purposes of this chapter, however, such a strict definition is too limiting. As Pine points out, termination itself does not usually stir up actual separation–individuation phenomena as he defines them. In my own practice, expression of this more narrowly defined kind of separation–individuation phenomena in termination is quite rare, probably because I do not work with the sicker patients in whom it tends to occur. However, Pine also describes in some detail material "suggestive of *post-differentiation* pathology that is, nonetheless, *tied to* the early separation–individuation process" (p. 233). This broader use of the term is the one most frequently encountered, both in this book and elsewhere (Panels 1973a, 1973b, 1973c). It holds that certain behaviors are *linked* to similar behaviors and dynamics occurring during separation–individuation. While these behaviors have undergone developmental changes during later developmental stages, and always have meanings unrelated to separation–individuation, the link to separation–individuation is strong enough to be an aid in understanding them when they appear clinically. It is this broad definition of separation–individuation phenomena that I use here.

There is one area in which Pine's narrow definition must be taken into account. Recognizing the broader manifestations of separation–individuation in patients helps us to understand them and thus optimizes our interpretive efforts, but it does not change our basic therapeutic stance. When, however, we encounter pathology that is *directly due to* separation–

individuation trauma, the situation is different. Such patients have either
a developmental arrest or a regression to some aspect of the separation–
individuation phase and show specific problems in maintaining a sense of
separateness or a feeling of individuality. In such cases, purely interpretive
efforts are usually not enough. These patients do not have an ego intact
enough to maintain a continued therapeutic alliance and establish a joint
participation in the analytic process. In addition to interpretation, they
need the experience of a real relationship. By this, I do not mean
gratification of infantile needs. I mean, instead, neutral but participatory
behavior on the part of the analyst—such as the careful avoidance of
artificial distancing, greater verbal activity, use of the sitting position, more
frequent acknowledgment by the analyst of the part he is playing in the
relationship, increased affective response by the analyst, and so forth. For
this reason, as well as for better understanding, it is important for the
analyst to recognize phenomena that are direct manifestations of separation–individuation pathology.

The need for more active involvement on the part of the analyst is
apparent in the therapy of Mrs. A, a young lawyer[1] who entered analysis
with me complaining of intense shyness and difficulty in speaking in
groups. The patient had struggled with this problem all of her life. Law
school had been agony, but she had been able to overcome her inhibitions
and participate successfully enough to graduate and get a job. Her family
had always denied that she had problems, and she had thus been unable to
obtain their support for therapy. However, after law school she began
earning her own money and was determined to do something to get some
relief.

Mrs. A, in analysis for several years, made considerable progress. She was
now going to have a baby, and the question of termination arose. The
combination of the new baby and certain inescapable professional obliga-
tions made the continuation of the analysis very difficult. Though it was
clear to both of us that there was considerable work left to be done, we
decided that termination seemed the best course, at least for the moment.
We planned it for shortly before the baby was due. A few sessions after
making that decision, Mrs. A casually mentioned that she would not be in
the next day, since she had scheduled a preceptor session with a junior
clerk during our appointment time. I was startled by the uncharacteristic
abruptness of this announcement, and attempting (unwisely, I now
believe) to suppress my reaction, I asked her to tell me a little more about
that. She immediately became defensive, explaining that things *can* happen

---

[1]All case descriptions in this paper have been heavily disguised and at times
distorted. They are for illustrative use only, and should not be used for research.

rapidly in the practice of law and that this appointment was dictated entirely by the needs of reality. By now, however, she was far enough along in her treatment to become suspicious of her own defensiveness and, with a little exploration, soon realized that she felt that she had hurt my feelings. She not only felt it; she believed it. Why else would I have disguised my reaction?

My response at this point illustrates the manner in which an understanding of separation–individuation can lead to a more active than usual technical approach. With many patients, I might have simply explored their feeling of having hurt me and interpreted its genetic origins. During this analysis, however, we had come to understand that her mother, in order to feel happy, had needed the patient to be physically present as well as cute and sweet. When the patient did something autonomous, something that threatened to take her away from mother, mother felt both frightened and sad. The struggle between her need to be autonomous and her need to keep mother happy had begun as early as the practicing subphase of separation–individuation, as evidenced by home movies taken of her and her mother during her infancy. It had influenced the oedipal constellation, had been worked through to a good extent in the transference, and now, under the stress of termination, was reappearing. She was planning to leave me before, she felt, I was 100% satisfied, and I was hurt.

As one would expect, the aforementioned scheduling incident had determinants on a number of levels. It was Mrs. A's way of retaliating against me as father for not keeping her in analysis forever as my special favorite. It was a defiant leaving of mother and turning to father (the clerk was a young man in whom she had some sexual interest). But a powerful part of the interaction was her positive assertion of autonomy from the separation–individuation mother, with the immediate feeling that she had hurt her. Because of the early roots of her pathology, this patient at that moment was unable to stay distant enough from her intense guilt to be able to utilize a purely interpretive intervention. Instead, it was necessary for me to describe the interaction as I saw it, including some aspects of my own feelings. When it became clear that she felt she had hurt me, I examined my own reactions; I realized and then told her that I definitely *had* been surprised and thought that, in fact, I *had* felt a little hurt by her apparent lack of caring about our work together. But, I continued, I didn't feel it very strongly and she seemed to be reacting as if she had demolished me. Could she say any more about the intensity of her feeling or perhaps just describe what it felt like in more detail? With this feedback about what I was really feeling, the patient was able to realize that she had been defensive about the cancellation even before she mentioned it in the session. She could then connect it with her feelings about terminating and with her feelings about her mother.

It should be emphasized that this shift in technique is a matter of emphasis. All good analysts are sufficiently involved in the relationship with their patients to permit themselves to be seen as a potential transference object. The analyst who silently sits and makes one or two interpretations in every session is a thing of the past. But we do tend to be more interpretive in patients without severe early pathology, and more interactive in patients with it. This tendency, incidentally, is based on our intuitive assessment of the patient's needs. We do not merely think, "Aha! That's a manifestation of separation–individuation pathology; I'll have to be more active." Our intuitive judgment of the proper approach to use at any single moment is based on many factors. Among them is the ability to recognize separation–individuation pathology (in the present discussion, in termination), which helps us make those automatic assessments that lead to variations in technique.

As Kramer (1978) has pointed out, a major advantage of knowing about separation–individuation is that it makes it easier for us to recognize and feel comfortable with separation–individuation manifestations that appear in our clinical work, just as knowing about the psychosexual stages helps us recognize and feel comfortable with psychosexual derivatives. Who, for instance, would recognize the anal aspects of fastidiousness, were they not familiar with the anal stage of development? Who would recognize the full meaning of the need for verbal feedback that some patients show, were they not familiar with 'checking back' in the differentiation subphase? Knowing about separation–individuation in theory, however, is not as helpful as knowing about the characteristic ways that separation–individuation phenomena appear in certain clinical situations. It is this that I wish to describe for termination. Almost invariably, separation–individuation manifestations that arise at that time will have manifested themselves earlier in the analysis, usually around other separations. Termination, of course, is the greatest separation of all and is thus likely to stir up manifestations of separation–individuation to a greater degree than elsewhere in therapy. Let us now look at some of the forms these manifestations are liable to take.

THE ASSERTION OF INDEPENDENCE AND AUTONOMY

An understanding of separation–individuation highlights the fact that togetherness is not all good and leaving is not all bad. One's drive toward autonomy and independence is a crucial part of one's development and often involves leaving one's objects, either temporarily or permanently. This, of course, includes one's analyst. Unfortunately, most analysts have been conditioned to view all movement away from the analytic situation physically and the analytic process emotionally as resistance, and we have a strong tendency to interpret it as such. This tendency is enhanced by the importance of analytic patients to analytic candidates for training purposes and the difficulties currently being encountered in getting analytic patients. It is multiplied tenfold if the analyst has personal problems with separation. True, lateness, absence, cancellations, and other varieties of "early termination" often *are* resistance. The analyst must realize, however, that they frequently are expressions of independence and autonomy, which are an essential and desirable part of the analytic process and which, if encouraging were part of good analytic technique, we would encourage in our patients. The drive toward autonomy is of profound importance not only in separation–individuation but in many phases of later development. Recognizing this can have a marked impact on the analyst's technique. It might be likened to the impact on parenting style that comes about when a previously naive parent realizes that the negativism of his two-year-old is a manifestation of something very important and positive, a drive to independence, and not the mark of a bad seed.

Awareness of the positive aspects of leaving is especially important in termination, particularly in the handling of what seems to be premature termination. It is centrally important that the analyst not want the patient to stay in treatment for personal reasons. He *will*, of course, want the patient to stay if he feels that their work is not done, but this will be balanced by his knowledge that the patient's wishes must be respected and that, in any case, the analyst is not such an infallible predictor, even professionally, of what is good for other people. The analyst must be conscious of any intense desire on his part for the patient to stay in analysis, and he must set it aside as best he can. He must be aware of and interpret the positive aspects of the patient's desire to leave, as well as the avoidant and defensive aspects. This stance, incidentally, is akin to the adoption of what Schafer (1983) calls the "appreciative analytic attitude." Many years ago, I saw my patients' wishes to leave analysis as pure resistance; I so interpreted them, usually with little success. Today, I am deeply aware of the constructive aspects of leaving and point them out, as well as the resistance aspects, and many fewer patients leave prematurely. Undoubtedly, my technique has improved with experience in other ways, and that improvement may be responsible for my patients' tendency not to leave prematurely. My impression, however, is that it is the diminution in my efforts, however subtle, to pressure patients to stay that is the key factor.

Mr. B was a master's degree student who had a year in analysis and was going to finish his degree in another year. He had entered analysis with the firm plan of continuing his education in Philadelphia. He had a social inhibition and complained movingly and accurately of his inability to get close to anybody. After a brief initial intense ambivalent transference to me, he settled down into a rather distant relationship. His feelings about me, he said, had "disappeared," and we spent most of our time clarifying his ambivalent relationship to his mother, to whom he was deeply attached, although she irritated him considerably. He felt that she would be distraught if he did not call her every day, and they often talked for hours. Gradually, during the first year of analysis, Mr. B became somewhat more independent of her. During the same period, I began to detect evidence of a gradually developing attachment to me that seemed to be maternal in nature.

On a more manifest level, the patient began thinking of moving to San Francisco to continue his education. He had received a tentative offer from an internationally known scientist there, and he would be away from his mother. When he began talking about this, I felt a bit of alarm. I saw the move as a threat to the analysis and explored the resistance inherent in it: was he not beginning to feel trapped by me as he had felt trapped by his mother? Fortunately, I soon regained my more neutral perspective and was able to keep the positive aspects of the move in mind as well as the negative ones. Not only were the reasons he cited valid but, on a deeper level, this appeared to be an appropriate, if somewhat late, way to separate from his family in reality as a counterpoint to the intrapsychic separation that was in the process of taking place. My maintenance of a more balanced stance seemed useful to the patient. He felt less trapped by me, and the resistance aspects of the move emerged almost on their own. Though he ultimately decided to go, I believe that the remaining year of analysis was much more productive than it would have been if my focus had been solely on the resistance aspects of his leaving.

PROBLEMS WITH OBJECT CONSTANCY

A major task of development during the separation–individuation stage is the achievement of object constancy, which I use here in the sense that Mahler used it: "By object constancy we mean that the maternal image has become intrapsychically available to the child in the same way as the actual mother had been libidinally available—for sustenance, comfort, and love" (Mahler, 1968, p. 222). Note that Mahler named the last stage of separation–individuation "*on the way* to object constancy" [my emphasis]. Object constancy is never completely attained: it remains a developmental task throughout life.

Problems in developing object constancy often manifest themselves in difficulties with separation in later life. They often can be noticed as an aspect of the psychopathology of everyday life. Many years ago, for example, a patient and her husband built a new house. One of the design features the husband insisted upon was what seemed to my patient an inordinate number of windows between rooms, ostensibly for the purpose of providing a sense of spaciousness. It gradually became clear to her that the openings were designed to permit her husband to maintain visual contact with her as she moved from room to room. This interpretation was supported by the way he followed her around the house when he couldn't see her. He did this in such a casual manner that it took her several years to recognize that he became anxious when he could not maintain contact with her. As manifest behavior, this kind of clinging may in fact have nothing to do with a defect in object constancy; one may need visual contact with wife and mother for a variety of reasons. In this situation, however, my patient's mother-in-law had a clinging neediness for her children of a type that often produces problems in separation–individuation, a neediness that was similar to the more subtle clinging of her son.

Patients who have inordinate difficulty in terminating may have problems in the development of object constancy. Other issues, however, may be present, and it is important to distinguish them. Miss C, for example, had intense reactions to such separations as weekends and vacations. Each time the analyst left, it was additional proof to her of her own unlovableness, a terrible feeling that was compounded by her inability to even hint at it. Expressing loss, loneliness, or grief was utterly humiliating, and she had no choice but to lapse into silence. Fortunately, she was able to endure the long, painful silent intervals, and the analysis continued. Her silence was at times so intense that, as we began to relate it to the separations, I began to wonder whether problems of object constancy were involved. However, Miss C's sense of separateness from me was unimpaired, and she had no difficulty maintaining a sense of my being there, even though she felt, at times, that I was cold and indifferent to her. It quickly became clear that the patient had no difficulties maintaining object constancy. Rather, her intense feelings about separation seemed to be due to several important traumas involving physical separation (including the death of her father) during her early years, combined with her mother's inability to face these with her in a way that would have helped her master them. One result of this experience was that the patient developed a deep sense of responsibility for her father's death and a conviction that she was unworthy of abiding love. My vacations were to her proof of that fantasy: I was leaving because I could not stand her.

Another patient had great difficulty with termination owing to a sense of finality about "the end," a fatalistic feeling that proved to be identical to the way he felt when his parents divorced when he was four years old. He felt that once the analysis was over and he left me, he would never see me again. This feeling was a reflection of what had actually happened with his father. Neither Miss C nor this patient had any difficulty maintaining an intrapsychic image of me that was available for sustenance, love, and comfort. Miss C, for example, was able to affectively picture me as a warm (though at other times rejecting) person even when I was away. Her anxiety arose from the feeling that she was unworthy of my love. The specific manifestation of a failure in object constancy, on the other hand, is an inability to maintain a concrete pictorial image of the analyst or to maintain a sense of affective connection, either loving or hating. It is as if the analyst drops out of the patient's life.

A failure in object constancy is always accompanied by anxiety or some dysphoric state, in contrast to the narcissistic defenses in which the disconnection from the analyst is used defensively and is frequently comforting. John's mother was an anxious, wheedling person with such a poor picture of herself that she never could feel satisfied with him. This feeling was summed up in Mr. D's description of an incident he told me about early in his analysis. He had telephoned his mother after a not unusual length of time, and she answered the phone with, "John! I was just wondering why you haven't called"—a statement that left the patient both enraged and guilty. He entered analysis with depression, a sense of doom, deep guilt (based on mother's imparting to him that he was somehow responsible for her suffering and, of course, on his own rage at her lack of closeness), self-esteem problems, and a fierce determination not to be in analysis long. His prediction (he was psychoanalytically sophisticated) was that his analysis would last about a year. This was a defense against his dependent needs, which manifested themselves in a peculiar constellation linked to object constancy. He was basically comfortable as long as he had an appointment in a day or two. He used the knowledge of the coming appointment as a support for the idea that I was there and on his side. At vacations and even weekends, however, he tended to get panicky. Manifestly, this anxiety was about some concrete aspect of his future: his livelihood was going to disappear, he would not be a good father to his children, and so on. During that time, he could not picture me or derive any comfort from the idea that he would be seeing me soon. During termination this pattern was particularly severe, since he felt he would never have any further contact with me. He knew that we would be seeing each other professionally, and he did not feel that in reality I would cease to exist. But it became clear that underneath I did not exist for him. He was unable to keep within him any of our interactions; he felt that once I stopped seeing him I would lose any sense of emotional connection with him, any warm feeling for him, and he would be utterly alone. Termination in the presence of this kind of feeling took three years, during which we came to understand the nuances of the anxiety that arose each time he set a termination date. Many factors, as always, entered into this: termination meant oedipal triumph, and it meant hostile desertion of me as mother. However, its main meaning was that I would disappear. It was only by keeping my knowledge of separation–individuation at hand that Mr. D and I were able to gain deep insight into the experience itself and the rage, guilt, and need for mother that drove it. As one might expect, Mr. D was not able to overcome these feelings completely, but he functioned better and was relatively comfortable when he ultimately was able to terminate.

CONTROL AND COERCION

If one had to pick one aspect of the first two years of life that is the most upsetting to parents, it would probably be the struggles that take place around control. The toddler attempts valiantly, angrily, persistently, and forcefully to do things himself (whether or not he is capable of so doing) and to maintain complete control over mother. This is important to him for several understandable reasons. He has begun to discover that he is a separate person, that he can act alone, and he is constructively developing that ability and the sense of autonomy that goes with it. At the same time, his autonomy carries with it the twin dangers of loss of mother and loss of omnipotence. Both of these can be averted if only he can maintain the illusion of mother being under his complete control. Knowledge of separation–individuation makes it clear that these control issues are not only derivatives of the anal stage; they arise from much broader issues of separateness and autonomy. For the analytic patient under the stress of termination, previously resolved control issues are likely to reappear. Appointments may be changed, fees not paid on time, interpretations resisted; the specific manifestations are legion.

OTHER TERMINATION PHENOMENA LINKED
TO SEPARATION–INDIVIDUATION

Problems with Maintaining Closeness

The ability to maintain an optimal emotional distance from the people we relate to is of crucial importance in interpersonal relations. We do not acquire it easily. It is one of the most important outcomes of the process of separating from mother. The separation–individuation child is struggling not only to be separate from mother and to attain an identity of his own but to manage the optimal interpersonal distance, first between himself and his libidinal objects and later between himself and everyone he relates to. "Interpersonal distance" refers, of course, to emotional distance, the proper degree of intimacy versus detachment. Furthermore, the process is not simply the development of a conflict-free skill. The child is struggling between powerful impulses: the wish to maintain the symbiotic state, to merge with mother, and the wish to be independent, self-sufficient, and thus to give up mother entirely. Closeness and intimacy can carry with it the threat of complete engulfment by mother and loss of a sense of independence or even of a sense of being a separate person whereas independence can lead to a sense of distance and ultimately utter isolation and aloneness. Major problems in this area are the borderline patient's central dilemma, but lesser problems related to it are seen frequently in less ill patients and may lead to premature termination.

Miss E, after a number of years of psychotherapy and analysis with another therapist, began treatment with me. Her central problems were a sense of not belonging, regardless of the group she was with, and an inability to form a satisfying long-term relationship with a man. An attractive and warm woman, Miss E had had many relationships, but they were either short-term or not satisfying enough for her to desire marriage. She began therapy twice-weekly (although I had recommended analysis), increased her visits to three times a week after a few months, and several months later decided to increase to four times a week. There were no specific changes in her outside circumstance that led to this; she simply felt that she wanted to work more intensely on her problems. As the frequency of her sessions increased, Miss E's positive feelings toward me increased also, although these never developed into an overt erotic transference. I felt that the increasing positive feeling led to the increased frequency of sessions, rather than vice versa. As her closeness, both sexual and affectionate, became more overt, Miss E became anxious and more distant. At the same time, she encountered financial difficulties, which, she felt, required her to decrease her visits to three times per week. We came to understand, during these alternating movements toward and away from me (movements that were repeated on a smaller scale within each session and from session to session), that while an important dynamic of them was oedipal anxiety, a significant contributor was the terrible struggle she had had in her earlier years achieving a workable type of intimacy with both mother and father. Closeness to father was difficult: although he was sometimes involved with her, he was sick and always emotionally distant. However, the patient's difficulties with mother were even more important in the development of her problems with intimacy. Mother was a demanding and critical woman who felt entitled to unflagging love and devotion from her daughter. Her imperious nature and her need to control her daughter's behavior were deeply disturbing to the little girl. This, plus her innate desire for autonomy, led Miss E as a little girl to try to escape from her mother's demands and, indeed, from her very presence. These attempts, however, were invariably met by accusations of ungratefulness. Mother was often depressed, and there was little doubt in anyone's mind that this was at least partly due to her 'ungrateful' daughter. Miss E was caught in a dilemma. Her needs for affection and her guilt drew her to mother, but the closeness always carried with it the threat of control and guilt-provoking criticism. As a result, the patient oscillated between closeness and distance with mother, in the transference, and in many other relationships. Although we were never able to be certain, it seemed that this difficulty with optimal closeness arose during separation–individuation.

The Changing Sense of Self

Both a sense of separateness and a sense of becoming an individual are basic to the development of the sense of self, a crucial part of our psychic integrity. Though we may wish for change, change means being different from before and thus not the same self that we have become familiar with and love. In some patients, therapeutic changes develop gradually but come to fruition in a kind of climactic movement, and the accompanying sense of change can be disruptive. Mrs. F, after a lifetime of docile and guilt-laden submission to her parents and her husband, gradually became less guilty and more assertive. As she considered termination, these changes consolidated. Although she valued her new assertiveness highly, she was plagued for several months by the feeling that this trait was not really her own. At first she wondered whether she felt this way because her improvement was indeed false, something she had done merely for the sake of pleasing me. When she examined her feelings, however, she realized that she no longer had her crying, her sense of self-pity, her feeling of being the victim of injustice. She felt a loss of her old self and, just as important, a loss of a destructive but very effective way of maintaining a relationship to her mother.

The Termination Triad: Separation Anxiety, Mourning, and Narcissistic Rage

Anyone who has worked with patients through termination recognizes that certain phenomena are almost universal at that time. Inasmuch as therapy has taken place in a meaningful relationship, the end of that relationship means separating from a valued object; inasmuch as that separation represents a danger, anxiety will be present; inasmuch as it represents a loss, mourning will take place. And if the patient feels that the therapist is permitting the separation because he (the patient) is not valued, his self-esteem will be hurt and he will be angry. As always, these reactions may originate at any developmental level, since losses occur at any time. I mention them here to call attention to the importance of pinpointing those losses that involve separation–individuation. The most common indicators of such involvement are the dyadic nature of the transference in which they are manifested, the intensity of the reactions (greater intensity being suggestive of separation–individuation), a history of trauma or early maternal failure, and specific manifestations of problems with the sense of separateness or identity. When self-esteem is a major issue, for example, struggles around omnipotence will occur, with the patient desperately trying to first prove and then disprove his own and the analyst's omnipotence. Anxiety about separation that arises in separation–individuation is particularly likely to lead to action rather than cognitive mastery. One patient in psychotherapy, for example, announced on the last day of treatment that he and his wife had decided to go into marital therapy; the search for a replacement for me was quite clear. Another patient made a variety of attempts during termination to handle the rather intense anxiety he felt about the coming loss. He first tried to get me to help him develop a comprehensive cognitive overview of just what had happened in therapy, why he felt better, and how he could use this information to help himself feel better in the future. As we came to understand the purposes of this project, the patient began to verbalize a fantasy about termination (an extremely common fantasy, incidentally), which had been present for some time but which we had not previously identified. He fantasied that after our last session he would never be permitted to contact me again in any way or for any reason. As we came to understand that this represented his wish to come back and his superego reaction against it, this fantasy subsided and was replaced by a compulsion to contact his old girlfriends, not for the purpose of reestablishing a relationship but "just to be sure they are there." All of these behaviors were characterized by a desperate pressure that arose from a deep sense at a very early age that he could not rely on the steady affection of his distant and critical mother.

SEPARATION–INDIVIDUATION AND THE ANALYST'S FEELINGS DURING TERMINATION

Criteria for termination are usually described in cognitive terms. Has symptomatic improvement occurred? Have character changes taken place? Has an analytic process evolved, and has the transference neurosis that developed now been resolved? Can changes be observed in the various psychic structures, and have the resultant modifications of compromise formations become less pathological? These and similar questions might suggest that deciding on termination is an intellectual process. Yet as any experienced practitioner knows, the analyst's feelings about the situation play an important role in the position he takes. As Glover's 1938 survey showed (Glover, 1955), "a majority admitted that their criteria are essentially intuitive. Their summated experience of the patient gives rise to a feeling, or impression, that the 'end' is approaching" (p. 327). This intuition is thought by many analysts to be based on a preconscious assessment of all the changes that have taken place during the analysis. They hold that the intuition, a feeling, is the result of a cognitive process—although, to be sure, at least one author (Held, 1955) has wondered whether telepathy was involved!

I would agree with Akhtar (1990, personal communication) however, that more than cognition is operative. One of the determinants of the analyst's intuition that termination is near seems to be an awakening of feelings analogous to those that a parent feels during separation–individuation. These feelings are twofold in nature. The parent feels a lessening of the demand for attention and libidinal gratification from the child who has successfully negotiated rapprochement; the analyst of the termination-ready patient feels a decrease in the transference demands. The analyst is less likely to be drawn into transference–countertransference enactments and feels less pressure to behave in ways foreign to himself. In addition to this direct response, the parent, by identification, senses the child's readiness to do more on his own; he can, for example, envision the child's spending the afternoon with a friend with the excitement that he himself feels about such activities rather than anxiety. Similarly, the analyst can picture the autonomous activities the patient describes with pleasure rather than with the feeling that this is a defensive retreat from the relationship. Of course, these feelings are not pure. Defense always operates, and true independence is always intermixed with defensive independence. But in the patient ready for termination, like the child ready for separation, the balance has shifted, and the analyst feels it.

SUMMARY

Phenomena linked to the separation–individuation phase of development often occur during the termination of psychotherapy and psychoanalysis. Understanding these manifestations is important in understanding the patient and has specific effects on technique. Examples of these effects are the greater need for activity and a focus on some of the real aspects of the therapist's experience in patients with early pathology. Among the phenomena having separation–individuation links is the use of assertions of autonomy and independence as a developmentally appropriate way of separating from the therapist. Problems with object constancy also occur, as do attempts at control and coercion of the therapist. In handling these and similar behaviors, a deep familiarity with separation–individuation theory and its actual manifestations in childhood is invaluable.

REFERENCES

Ablon, S. (1988), Developmental forces and termination in child analysis. *Internat. J. Psycho-Anal.,* 69:97–104.
Blanck, G. & Blanck, R. (1988), The contributions of ego psychology to understanding the process of termination in psychoanalysis and psychother- apy. *J. Amer. Psychoanal. Assn.,* 36:961–984.
Firestein, S. (1978), *Termination in Psychoanalysis.* New York: International Universities Press.
Garza-Guerrero, C. (1988), Ego and superego alterations in borderline structures: Their effect on the process and outcome of treatment. *Internat. J. Psycho- Anal.,* 69:205–219.
Glover, E. (1955), *The Technique of Psycho-analysis.* New York: International Universities Press.

Held, R. (1955), Les criteres de la fin du traitement psychanalytique. *Rev. Fran. Psychanal.*, 19:603–614.

Kramer, S. (1978), The technical significance and application of Mahler's separation–individuation theory. *J. Amer. Psychoanal. Assn.*, 27(Suppl.):241–262.

Kupers, T. (1988), *Ending Therapy*. New York: New York University Press.

Loewald, H. (1988), Termination analyzable and unanalyzable. *The Psychoanalytic Study of the Child*, 43:155–166. New Haven, CT: Yale University Press.

Mahler, M. (1968), *On Human Symbiosis and the Vicissitudes of Individuation*. New York: International Universities Press.

Panel (1973a), The experience of separation–individuation in infancy and its reverberations through the course of life: 1. Infancy and childhood. *J. Amer. Psychoanal. Assn.*, 21:135–154.

Panel (1973b), The experience of separation–individuation in infancy and its reverberations through the course of life: 2. Adolescence and maturity. *J. Amer. Psychoanal. Assn.*, 21:155–167.

Panel (1973c), The experience of separation–individuation in infancy and its reverberations through the course of life: 3. Maturity, senescence, and sociological implications. *J. Amer. Psychoanal. Assn.*, 21:633–645.

Pine, F. (1979), On the pathology of the separation–individuation process as manifested in later clinical work: An attempt at delineation. *Internat. J. Psycho-Anal.*, 60:225–242.

Schafer, R. (1983), *The Analytic Attitude*. New York: Basic Books.

Shane, M. & Shane, E. (1984), The end phase of analysis: Indicators, functions, and tasks of termination. *J. Amer. Psychoanal. Assn.*, 32:739–772.

Author Index

Subject Index